CEREMONIES

of the

LIBERAL CATHOLIC RITE

✠

By

✠ IRVING S. COOPER
Regionary Bishop of
The Liberal Catholic
Church for the United States

Footnotes added by
✠ **Dean E. Bekken,**
Editor

The St. Alban Press
741 Cerro Gordo Avenue
San Diego, California 92102 USA

First Edition 1934/35

Retypeset Ascension 2010

ISBN 978-0-935461-28-2

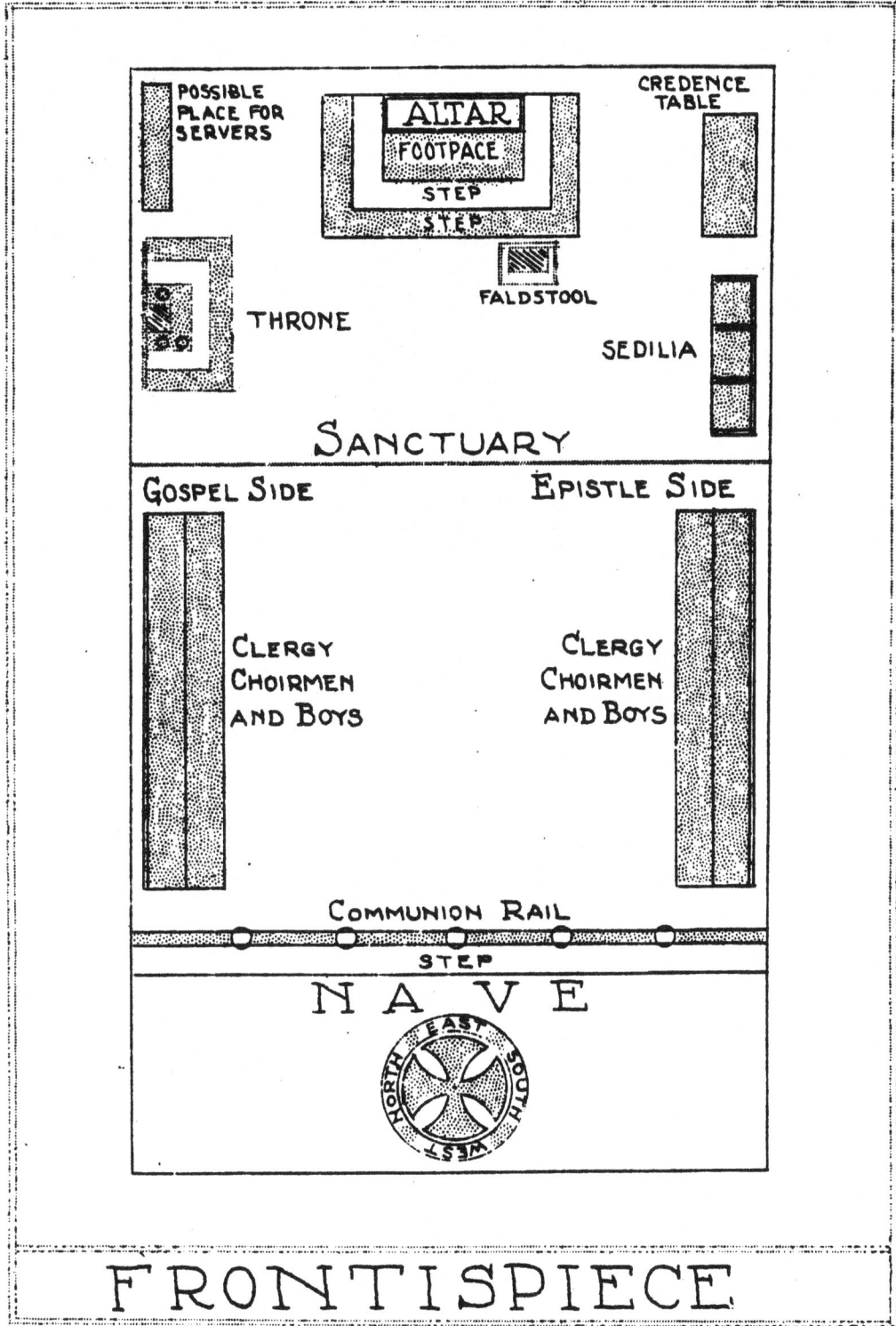

B

POSSIBLE PLACE FOR SERVERS

CREDENCE TABLE

ALTAR
FOOTPACE
STEP
STEP

FALDSTOOL

THRONE

SEDILIA

SANCTUARY

GOSPEL SIDE

EPISTLE SIDE

CLERGY CHOIRMEN AND BOYS

CLERGY CHOIRMEN AND BOYS

COMMUNION RAIL

STEP

NAVE

NORTH EAST SOUTH WEST

FRONTISPIECE

C

AUTHORIZATION

This book is authorized for use
in the
LIBERAL CATHOLIC CHURCH

✠ Frank Waters Pigott
PRESIDING BISHOP

ALL SAINTS, 1935.

PREFACE TO THE FIRST EDITION

This book is intended to be a complete and detailed description of the ceremonies prescribed in the Liberal Catholic Rite. The ceremonial directions given are based largely upon those of the Roman Catholic Latin Rite, although in many cases we have preferred to follow Anglican usage. We have not hesitated, however, to depart from both when required by the needs of the Liberal Catholic Liturgy, or when instructions given in the older rites were thought to be unnecessary. In short, we have sought to retain the essential and valuable and to drop the nonessential and merely customary. This has led to a much-desired simplification of the ceremonies.

All the rulings and all the corrections and additions to the Liturgy which were authorized by the First, Second and Third General Episcopal Synods have been incorporated in the text, although the third revised edition of The Liturgy has not as yet been printed. Its contents have been checked carefully with "The Ceremonies of the Holy Eucharist" by the late Julian Adrian Mazel, published in Sydney in 1924 after the first draft of this book had been prepared. Bishop J.I. Wedgwood has carefully revised the manuscript, a labour for which the author cannot too strongly express his gratitude. Bishop Charles Hampton assisted by suggesting numerous minor changes and additions to the manuscript. Various comments by Bishop F.W. Pigott were also extremely helpful in the final revision of the book. The Rev. G.N. Drinkwater of England and the Rev. William H. Pitkin of the United States of America have been of the greatest help in checking the manuscript and in drawing attention to various matters in a series of voluminous notes. The latter has also undertaken, largely at his own expense, the arduous labour of duplicating the manuscript so that copies may be sent to all of the clergy. It is difficult to express adequately one's appreciation of such an invaluable gift to the Church.

Every effort has been made to insure accuracy and clearness, but the subject matter is so complicated and interlocked that complete success cannot be expected. Should inaccuracies, contradictions, omissions, or obscure statements be found, the author will greatly appreciate having them brought to his attention. This book has been in preparation over a period of many years, its publication being delayed by a breakdown in health and other causes. Its writing has been arduous and wearisome, but if the book proves of real assistance to the clergy of the Liberal Catholic Church, the author will feel well repaid for all that it has cost him.

1934   ✠ IRVING S. COOPER

St. Alban's Pro-Cathedral
2041 Argyle Avenue
Los Angeles, California.

E

CEREMONIES OF THE LIBERAL CATHOLIC RITE *Change No. 1*

[On October 1, 1935 a set of changes to the Book was issued preceded by the following explanation. Ed.:]

"The author of this book having passed into the Peace before its completion, the work is under the supervision of the Presiding Bishop; consequently all errors noted should be reported to the Presiding Bishop's office.

"Errors and changes noted in this change sheet are located by page, paragraph and line. Any portion of a paragraph appearing at the top of a page is considered Par.I of that page. Any indented subdivision is considered as a paragraph.

"Changes and corrections should be made in coloured ink (red or green preferred) so as to contrast with the original. Please make changes immediately upon receipt of a Change Sheet, so that your ceremonial will be up to date.

"These change sheets will be issued from time to time, as errors may be discovered, or in the case ritual modifications are promulgated."

[Changes to the Episcopal Services were made by hand at a later date and these changes have also been incorporated. Father (later Bishop) W.H. Pitkin took over the publication after Bp. Cooper's death. Ed.]

———

PREFACE TO THE RETYPESETTING

This reprinting of the Book of Ceremonies of the Liberal Catholic Rite follows the exact wording of the First Edition of the book as issued in 1934 with the changes inserted in the appropriate places. The First Edition and the Change were distributed in black, two-ring binders in Mimeograph™ format. ["The mimeograph machine (commonly abbreviated to mimeo) or stencil duplicator, along with spirit duplicators was used to print short-run office work, classroom materials, and church bulletins before Xerox™ became feasible." Wikipedia] The Book of Ceremonies as distributed to some parishes did not include the various ordination services and other services reserved to bishops, but these are included in what follows. This printing has been completely reset and uses photo-offset printing for the entire contents. Where Bp Cooper was limited to a plus sign "+" for crosses it is now possible to substitute Greek ✠ and open ✚ crosses as used in The Liturgy. Some of the illustrations were lithographs and these have been retained in the best photo-offset reproduction available.

Because it was composed on a typewriter, Bishop Cooper used underling both for Latin and Greek words and for quotations from The Liturgy. He reserved normal quotation marks for other quotes. This reissue uses italics wherever Bp. Cooper used underlining. He did not adopt American spellings for various words, such as "colour" and his spellings have been retained.

A Table of Contents and Bp Pitkin's original Index have been added.

2010   DEAN BEKKEN, Editor

St. Francis Cathedral Chapel
741 Cerro Gordo Avenue
San Diego, California 92102

DRAWINGS REFERENCED IN THE TEXT

HANDS JOINED — THUMBS SIDE BY SIDE — Fig. 1

HANDS JOINED — THUMBS CROSSED — Fig. 2

HANDS JOINED — FOREFINGER & THUMB of EACH HAND TOUCHING — Fig. 3

HANDS EXTENDED or OUTSPREAD — Fig. 4

HANDS EXTENDED or OUTSPREAD — FOREFINGER & THUMB of EACH HAND TOUCHING — Fig. 5

BLESSING BY a PRIEST — Fig. 6

PLATE 1

BLESSING OBJECTS WITH THE HAND   Fig.1.

BLESSING OBJECTS FOREFINGER & THUMB JOINED   Fig.2.

OFFERING HOST AT OFFERTORIUM   Fig.3.

HOLDING HOST WHILE SAYING WORDS of CONSECRATION   Fig.4.

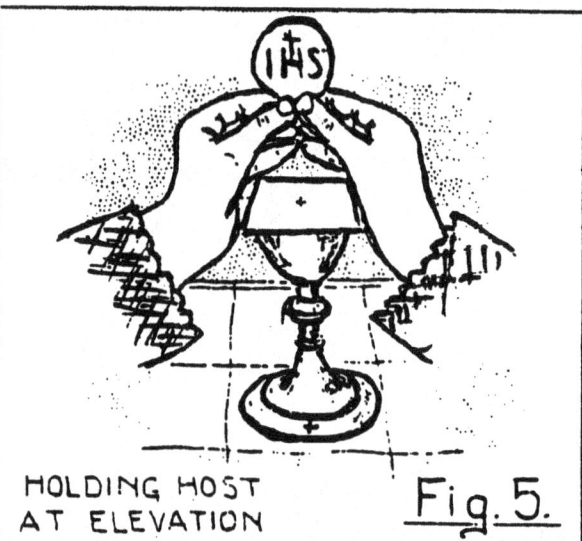

HOLDING HOST AT ELEVATION   Fig.5.

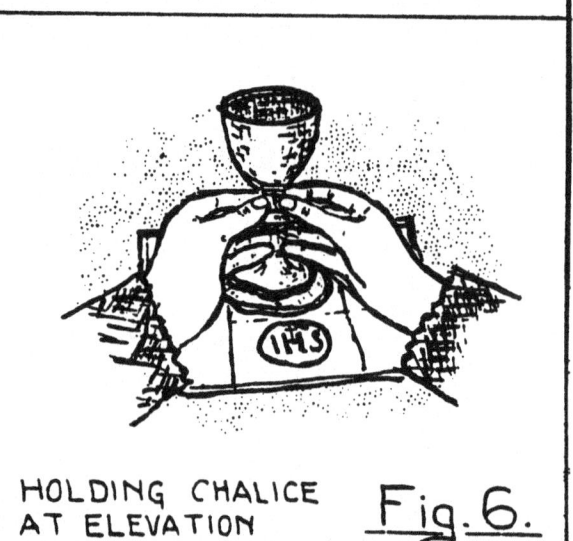

HOLDING CHALICE AT ELEVATION   Fig.6.

PLATE 2

HOLDING HOST WHILE MAKING ✠ OVER CHALICE & BETWEEN CHALICE & SELF — Fig. 1.

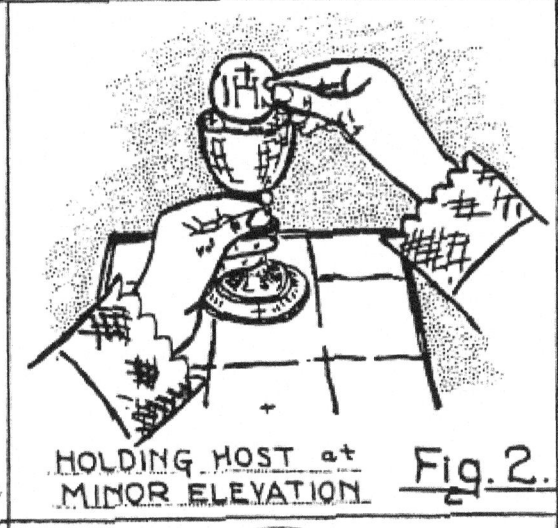

HOLDING HOST at MINOR ELEVATION — Fig. 2.

PICKING UP PATEN BEFORE MAKING ✠ WITH IT OVER SELF — Fig. 3.

SLIDING HOST ONTO PATEN — Fig. 4.

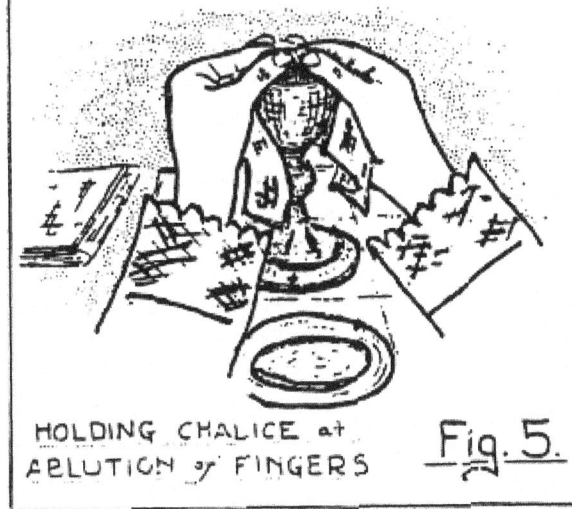

HOLDING CHALICE at ABLUTION of FINGERS — Fig. 5.

BLESSING by a BISHOP — Fig. 6.

PLATE 3

SYMBOLS: † = CELEBRANT   ✶ = MASTER of CEREMONIES
          ♎ = DEACON   ◊ = CLERGY
          ♏ = SUBDEACON   ⊙ = THURIFER   O = SERVER

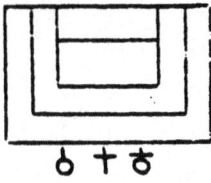

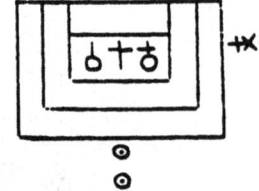

ASPERGES Fig. 1.	INVOCATION Fig. 2.	CONFITEOR Fig. 3.
ABSOLUTION Fig. 4.	BLESS INCENSE Fig. 5.	CENSE ALTAR Fig. 6.
CELEBRANT CENSED Fig. 7.	INTROIT Fig. 8A.	INTROIT (1ST ALTERNATIVE) Fig. 8B.
INTROIT (2ND ALTERNATIVE) Fig. 8C.	GLORIA Fig. 9.	GLORIA (WITH 2 CENSERS) Fig. 10.
COLLECTS Fig. 11.	EPISTLE Fig. 12.	COMMENCE GRADUAL Fig. 13.

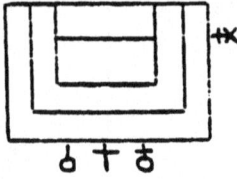

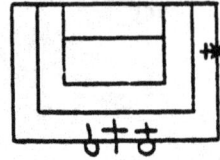

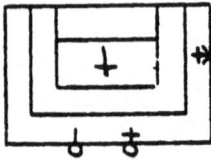

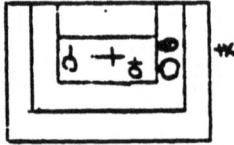

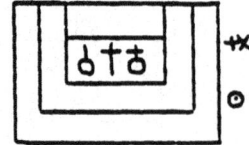

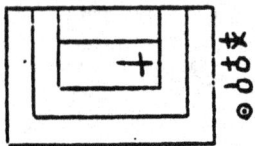

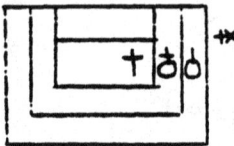

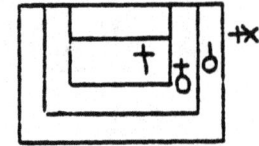

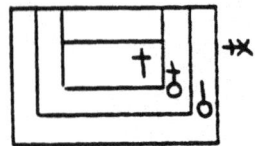

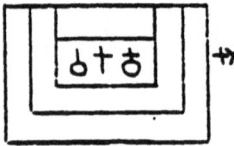

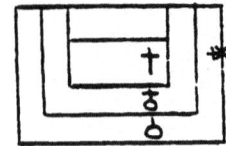

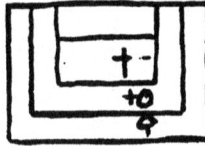

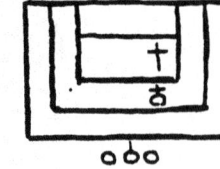

PLATE 4

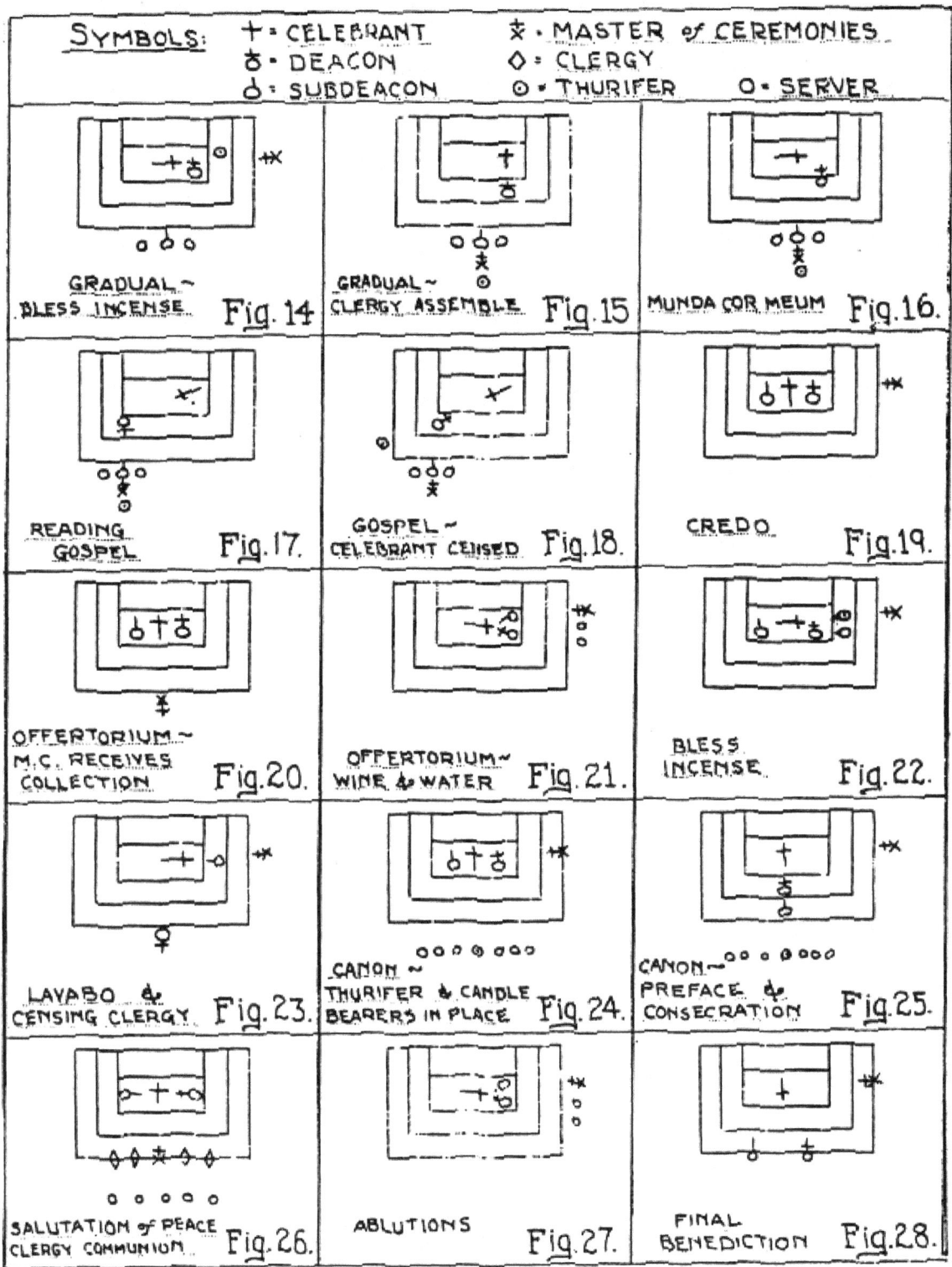

SYMBOLS: + = CELEBRANT   ✗ = MASTER of CEREMONIES
          ♂ = DEACON   ◇ = CLERGY
          ♀ = SUBDEACON   ☉ = THURIFER   O = SERVER

GRADUAL ~
BLESS INCENSE   Fig. 14

GRADUAL ~
CLERGY ASSEMBLE   Fig. 15

MUNDA COR MEUM   Fig. 16

READING
GOSPEL   Fig. 17

GOSPEL ~
CELEBRANT CENSED   Fig. 18

CREDO   Fig. 19

OFFERTORIUM ~
M.C. RECEIVES
COLLECTION   Fig. 20

OFFERTORIUM ~
WINE & WATER   Fig. 21

BLESS
INCENSE   Fig. 22

LAVABO &
CENSING CLERGY   Fig. 23

CANON ~
THURIFER & CANDLE
BEARERS IN PLACE   Fig. 24

CANON ~
PREFACE &
CONSECRATION   Fig. 25

SALUTATION of PEACE
CLERGY COMMUNION   Fig. 26

ABLUTIONS   Fig. 27

FINAL
BENEDICTION   Fig. 28

PLATE 5

·1· (S. of S. Pl. 16)

THE IMPOSITION OF HANDS AT THE CONSECRATION OF A BISHOP.

Church of St. Alban, Sydney, at Consecration of Bishop I. S. Cooper by Bp. Wedgwood, assisted by Bp. Leadbeater (right) and Bp. Mazel (left).

Showing High Altar and Side Altar.

Mitre
Crozier
Morse
Fanon of Mitre
Rochet
Pectoral Cross
Ring
Gloves
Cape of Cope
Stole
Orphreys
Cope

Pectoral Cross
Cinture Ring

2. (S. of S. Pl. 25-1) **3.** (S. of S. Pl. 25-2)   **4.** (S. of S. Pl. 20-2)

FULL PONTIFICAL VESTMENTS OF A BISHOP.
(C. W. LEADBEATER)

BISHOP IN CASSOCK.
(IRVING S. COOPER)

Biretta
Hood of Mozetta
Pectoral Cross
Mozetta
Ring
Rochet
Ring
Mantelletta

Cape
Biretta
Cassock

5. (S. of S. Pl. 24-1) **6.** (S. of S. Pl. 24-2) **7.** (S. of S. Pl. 20-1)

BISHOP IN MOZETTA
(I. S. COOPER)

BISHOP IN MANTELLETTA

PRIEST IN CASSOCK

PLATE 6.

1. (S.of S. Pl. 19-2)   **2.** (S.of S. Pl. 22-1)

PRIEST VESTING FOR EUCHARIST.

3. (S. of S. Pl. 22-2)

DEACON VESTED FOR EUCHARIST.

Apparel of Amice — Amice — Cassock

Amice — Stole — Girdle — Maniple — Alb

Amice — Stole — Maniple — Dalmatic — Alb

Amice — Stole — Orphreys — Central Disc — Maniple — Chasuble — Orphreys — Alb

Surplice — Stole

4. (S. of S. Pl. 23-1)   **5.** (S. of S. Pl. 23-2)

PRIEST VESTED IN CHASUBLE.

6. (S. of S. Pl. 21-1)

PRIEST IN SURPLICE & STOLE.

Burse — Cross (front) — Veil — Corporal

Burse — Corporal — Purificator — Chalice — Paten — Ciborium — Pall — Veil

a- Monstrance
b- Glass enclosed centre
c- Lunette for holding the Host.

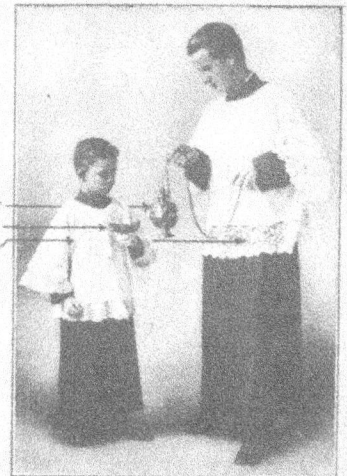

Censer — Boat — Cotta

7. (S. of S. Pl. 18, 1-2)

ALTAR EQUIPMENT.

8. (S. of S. Pl. 19-1)

MONSTRANCE.

9. (S. of S. Pl. 21-2)

VESTMENTS OF SERVERS.

PLATE 7.

A- Tabernacle
B- Tabernacle (Second Ray) Cross
C- Altar Cross
D- Six Large Candlesticks
E- Small Candlesticks
F- Missal Stand
G- Sanctuary Lamp
H- Chalice Veil
I- Gradine or Shelf
J- Altar Frontal
K- Superfrontal
L- Orphreys
M- Footpace

1. (S. of S. Pl. 17) THE HIGH ALTAR, ST. ALBAN'S PRO-CATHEDRAL, SYDNEY.

2. ST. WILLEBRORD'S PRO-CATHEDRAL, BATAVIA, JAVA.

A- High Altar
B- Credence Table
C- Sedilia
D- Censer Rack
E- Hanging Sanctuary Lamp
F- Suspended First Ray Cross

G- Seat for Clergy
H- Bishop's Throne (*)
I- Sanctuary Rail
J- Altar Cross
K- Ray Cross (Third)

* Note that this Throne is triple, seating the Bishop with his Deacon and Subdeacon.

PLATE 8.

TABLE OF CONTENTS

PART I

GENERAL INSTRUCTIONS REGARDING CEREMONIES

CHAPTER I

The Altar and its Appointments

Whenever a church or oratory in which an altar is placed is used for no other purpose than the work and services of the Church, it should be consecrated by a bishop according to the Form in The Liturgy. Because of the value of such consecration to the worshippers, the church need not be entirely free of debt before the consecration, but the debt must not be large. When it is necessary to use a church or oratory before a bishop can attend to consecrate it, or when an oratory is used for meetings other than those of the Church, a priest may bless it by using the prescribed portion of the service of "The Consecration of a Church," namely, first, saying the Collect of Purification; second, sprinkling the altar and church with holy water; third, saying the Collect of Consecration. Private or semi-private oratories should, unless permanent, be blessed not consecrated. That they should be blessed by a bishop is preferable. A duly consecrated church shall not be used for any service or meeting other than those prescribed in our Liturgy, except with the written permission of the Bishop of the Diocese.

In preparing for the consecration of a church six brass crosses, called *Ray Crosses*, may be provided in addition to the tabernacle cross and the altar cross. These crosses need not be of any specified size or design, but it should be borne in mind that they are intended not only to act as channels for the influence of the Rays, but also to serve as ornaments. Hence pleasing proportions and careful workmanship are essential. Those crosses placed round the walls may either be attached to wooden panels or medallions or, if the architecture of the church permits, placed in small shrines or niches. On the face of each cross, where the two arms intersect, should be engraved the symbol of one of the Rays. (Diagram 1) An inconspicuous hole is drilled in each of the crosses which are to be placed round the walls, either on the reverse side opposite the symbol, or from above downwards into the metal of the cross. This hole should be about one-eighth to one-quarter of an inch in diameter, depending upon the size of the consecrated jewel to be placed therein. The hole should not be drilled to such a depth that an opening appears on the front of the cross. The hole in the First Ray cross, which need be only about one-eighth of an inch in diameter, should be drilled downwards from the upper edge of the cross, because both sides of this cross are visible to the people.

RAY	SYMBOL	JEWEL FAMILY
FIRST	⊙	Diamond
SECOND	+	Sapphire
THIRD	△	Emerald
FOURTH	⚭	Jasper
FIFTH	☆	Topaz
SIXTH	⚘	Ruby
SEVENTH	⌐⌐	Amethyst

DIAGRAM 1

The set of *consecrated jewels* which has been obtained from the bishop for the purpose should be opened carefully over a white plate or tray, and the tiny spicules sorted out and dropped into their respective holes. If, on account of the minute size of the spicule (the diamond is usually not larger than a grain of sand) it is necessary to use a pair of tweezers extreme care should be exercised to prevent the particle suddenly being snapped into space by undue pressure on the tweezers. One jewel is placed in each of the six Ray Crosses leaving the Sapphire to be inserted in the tabernacle cross. The jewel associated with each Ray is given in Diagram I. (Page 1) The holes are now filled either with plaster of Paris, pure beeswax, vegetable glue or dental cement, which should be smoothed over and allowed to harden. The crosses of the Fourth, Fifth, Seventh, Sixth and Third Rays (to enumerate them clockwise in the order in which they are placed round the church) are then bolted to the wall panels or placed in the wall shrines. The First-Ray cross is usually suspended from the ceiling, but, if the seating arrangements permit, it may be supported by a standard fastened to the floor. (This was done at St Alban's Pro-Cathedral, Los Angeles, where there were two wide side aisles but no central aisle.) Obviously the cross should be suspended at a sufficient height so that the processional cross when carried may pass beneath.

It is not advisable or possible, owing to widely varying architectural arrangements, to lay down rigid rules as to the exact position in which each Ray Cross should be placed. The Second-Ray cross is always fastened to the door of the tabernacle, but those situated outside the sanctuary may be placed in the alternative positions indicated hereafter. Assuming that the altar is in the east, the *positions of the Ray Crosses* are as follows:

First-Ray Cross: In line with the middle of the altar, near the centre of the church.
Fourth-Ray Cross: Either (a) in the south-east corner, (b) on the south wall between this corner and the centre of the church, or (c) on the south wall opposite the First-Ray cross.
Fifth-Ray Cross: Either (a) in the south-west corner, or (b) on the south wall midway between this corner and the centre of the church.
Seventh-Ray Cross: On the west wall in line with the middle of the altar and therefore opposite the First-Ray cross.
Sixth-Ray Cross: Either (a) in the north-west corner, or (b) on the north wall midway between this corner and the centre of the church.
Third-Ray Cross: Either (a) in the north-east corner, (b) on the north wall midway between this corner and the centre of the church, or (c) on the north wall opposite the First-Ray cross.

The Second General Episcopal Synod granted permission to consecrate *movable Ray crosses* to be placed in oratories used temporarily for the services of the Church. Such temporary oratories may be blessed but not consecrated.

The *tabernacle cross* is different in certain respects from the other six Ray crosses. It is the cross of the Second Ray, and should be a plain Latin cross with square ends. There is no necessity of engraving upon it the symbol of the Second Ray, inasmuch as the cross itself is the symbol of that Ray. Before being fastened to the door of the tabernacle a hole should be drilled on the reverse side, and the sapphire cemented into place. The reason the tabernacle cross is chosen to represent the Second Ray instead of the altar cross is that the former is directly in front of the Host reserved in the tabernacle, and therefore transmits without difficulty the force flowing from the Host. If the altar cross were used the force would have to rush upwards to the cross and then turn at right angles to pour out over the people. Another reason is that in some churches it is necessary to move the altar cross in order to make room for the monstrance at Benediction.

Whenever possible the *altar* should be placed in the east end of the church so that the people and priest may face eastwards during the services. In describing ceremonies hereafter, reference will be made from time to time to the "east" and "turning to the east." By this is meant the direction of the altar, quite irrespective of its geographical position. "Eastwards" in a church always means the direction taken by a celebrant when he faces the altar. Hence also "south" means to his right, and "north" to his left. In describing ceremonies it is customary to speak of the gospel and epistle sides of the altar. The gospel side is that portion to the left of the priest as he stands in the middle facing the altar; the epistle side is that portion to his right. (See Frontispiece.) The gospel end of the altar, or of the footpace, is that end to his left; the epistle end is that end to his right. The middle of the altar is that central position which the priest takes during the greater part of the service of the Holy Eucharist.

The *size of the altar* varies according to the dimensions of the church, and whether it is to be used as the principal or high altar, or as a side altar. The usual height is thirty-nine inches, but it may range from thirty-seven to forty inches. The length may be anything from five feet to ten feet or more. In width the altar should be between three and four feet, the exact measurement depending on how much space is needed for the gradines carrying flowers and candlesticks. A *tabernacle*, which is a strongly constructed box of wood or metal to hold the consecrated Host, should be firmly fastened in the middle line of the altar. To allow the proper room for the incensing of the oblations, the distance from the front edge of the altar to the tabernacle should be about twenty-seven inches. It is convenient to have a tabernacle with two narrow doors instead of one wide one, but the difficulty is that a draw bolt is needed for the door that shuts first, otherwise the tabernacle cannot be locked safely. (There is a patent metal tabernacle with two curved doors which part and swing back into the tabernacle itself sold in Catholic supply shops in America, but it is very expensive.) If the tabernacle has a single door, it is advisable to have the hinges on the left side, so that the right hand may be used for access. If the left hand is used, there is a risk of dragging the maniple across the corporal. Also at a High Celebration it is much more convenient for the Deacon to take the Host from the tabernacle if the hinges are on the left. The door (or doors) should be high enough to clear the altar cloths when opened. The tabernacle should be equipped with a secure lock, the key to which must be kept in a safe place by the priest. The hinges must not have removable pins. The interior of the tabernacle should be lined with white silk, but there is no need to have curtains in front of the door within or without the tabernacle. A linen corporal should be spread on the bottom of the tabernacle. Holy oils should not be kept in the tabernacle. On either side of the tabernacle, to the rear of the altar, may be built one, two, or three shelves or steps, called *gradines*, upon which are placed candlesticks and vases of flowers.

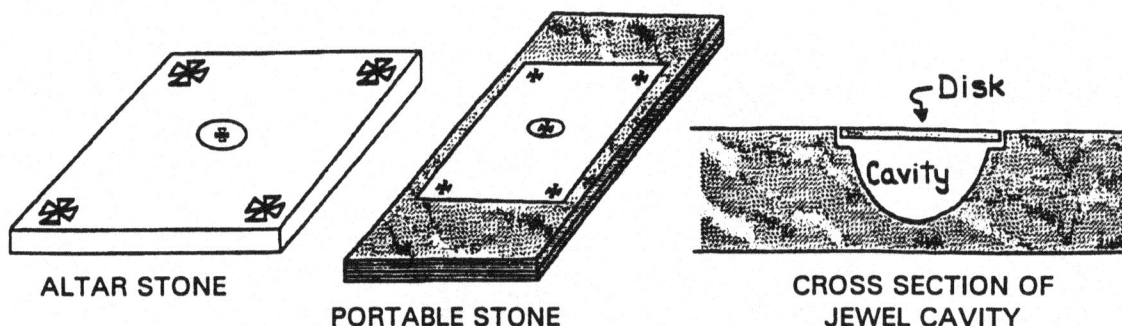

ALTAR STONE   PORTABLE STONE   CROSS SECTION OF JEWEL CAVITY

DIAGRAM 2

The *altar may be built* either of natural stone, of tiles or marble slabs over a base of brick or concrete, or of wood. It is well to avoid black or dark colours in selecting materials out of which an altar is to be built. If the altar is built of other than of natural stone, a slab of natural stone, usually marble, must be inserted in the top of the altar in the middle about midway between the tabernacle and the front edge of the altar. The usual size of this slab, called the *altar stone*, is twelve inches square by one inch or one and one-half inches thick. (Diagram 2) It should be set in the altar nearly flush with the top, leaving just enough stone above the altar level so that its position may be determined when the altar is covered with the linen cloths. Such altar stones are kept in stock by some Catholic church good shops. If it is necessary to order one from a marble cutter, it should be understood by him that a small maltese cross (set square with the stone) is to be carved at each of the four corners on the upper surface of the marble, and that a cavity for the reception of the consecrated jewels is to be chiseled exactly in the centre of the stone and from the upper side. (Diagram 2) The size of this cavity is determined as follows: Lay a silver coin, either a quarter of a dollar or a shilling piece on the marble in the centre and draw around it a line. The marble is then cut away until a shallow circular cavity is formed into which the coin fits exactly. The coin is now removed and the central part of the cavity made deeper. In this part of the cavity the consecrated jewels are embedded, a disk of silver the size of the coin being used as a cover. (Diagram 2) One side of the silver disk should be polished and a maltese cross engraved thereon. This disk may be gilded. It has been suggested that the silver cover is not essential; that the cavity can be filled flush with plaster of Paris or beeswax; that a cross can be incised on the plaster or wax with a pen knife. I doubt the advisability of this, especially in a portable altar stone. There is too much danger of fragments of the plaster breaking away, or of the wax being gouged out, leading to loss of one or more of the jewels. The altar stones sold in Catholic shops are usually prepared with a cross chiseled in the exact centre and the cavity about an inch or so from the centre. The cover for the cavity in such stones is usually a circular disk of marble. It is permissible to use an altar stone of this description as the slight difference in the position of the consecrated jewels will not materially affect the inner side of the eucharistic celebration.

To *prepare the altar stone* for consecration another set of jewels obtained from the bishop is opened with the same care as before over a white plate. A small amount of plaster of Paris (or beeswax) is now prepared and enough dropped into the cavity to fill it half way. Using a pair of tweezers if necessary, the spicules are placed on the plaster in the following hexagonal order, it being understood that the stone is lying in the same position relative to the priest as it will be when placed on the altar:[2]

Sapphire

Emerald   Jasper

Diamond

Ruby   Topaz

Amethyst

The jewels should be carefully embedded and then covered with enough moist plaster (or beeswax) nearly to fill the cavity. The metal disk is now pressed down into the cavity (the polished side bearing the maltese cross being uppermost) until it is flush with the surface of the marble. The surplus plaster is wiped away and the remaining plaster allowed to set and harden. Before the stone is moved it is well to label the edge (not the upper surface) nearest the amethyst with the phrase: *Towards the Celebrant* or the edge nearest the sapphire with the phrase: *Towards the Tabernacle*. A still better way is to chisel a tiny arrow on the under surface of the stone pointing to the edge which should be placed nearest the tabernacle. This of course should be done before the jewels are placed in the cavity. Whatever the method of marking the stone, it is essential to make clear the correct placing of the stone upon the altar.

If the whole altar is built of natural stone, a maltese cross is carved on the upper surface of each corner and in the centre, and, at about the place where the celebrant will stand the chalice, a cavity is chiseled and filled with a set of jewels as in the case of the altar stone.

Before being used, if possible, *an altar stone should be consecrated* by a bishop. If circumstances prevent this, the priest himself should *bless* the stone using the Form in the Liturgy for "The Blessing of Objects in General."

As the Holy Eucharist must not be celebrated without an altar stone, it is necessary for the priest who travels on behalf of the Church to carry with him a *portable altar stone*. (Diagram 2, Page 4) The best stone for this purpose is a thin slab of marble, measuring about five by seven inches, which is held by means of its beveled or splayed edge in a frame of polished wood (made of two slabs screwed together, in one of which is set the marble slab) the outside dimensions of which are about seven by eleven inches. (Inasmuch as the portable type of stone is not flush with the top of the altar, it must be of adequate size to receive the Host and the major part of the base of the chalice. The greater part of the marble slab need be only about one-quarter of an inch in thickness but in the centre, where the cavity is chiseled, it should be at least a half-inch thick. This additional thickness in the centre may be obtained by cementing a small block of marble to the under surface of the larger slab, the whole being concealed and strengthened by the wooden frame.

The altar should be raised above the floor of the sanctuary by at least one and preferably three steps, particularly if it be the principal altar of the church. (See Frontispiece.) The sanctuary floor should be higher than the floor of the church so that the people may be able to see the ceremonies. There should not be more than seven steps between the level of the church floor and the level of the altar base. The broad top step on which the priest stands while celebrating the Holy Eucharist is called the *footpace*. Its length should be at least eighteen inches longer than the altar at each end in order to give room for the ministers at censing, and its width about three feet six inches, so that when the priest genuflects there may be no danger of the foot suddenly slipping over the edge. The other two steps extend not only round the footpace but also across the ends of the altar. They ought to be at least from twenty-one to twenty-four inches wide at the front, as the deacon and subdeacon stand or kneel on them during High Celebration. At the sides these two steps may be narrower, say twelve to fifteen inches. The first step up from the sanctuary floor is called the subdeacon's step, the second the deacon's step. To stand on the sanctuary floor is to be *in plano*.

The *altar is covered* with three layers of white linen cloth. The two lower layers are usually quite plain and may be either separate cloths each the size of the top of the altar or one cloth twice the size of the top folded once. The upper cloth should be long enough to extend the full length of the altar and to reach nearly to the base of the altar at either end. It should be as wide as the altar top and the ends which project beyond the altar top may be worked in *white* linen embroidery. Under these three cloths there may be a cere-cloth of waxed linen.

In front of the altar may be placed an ornate, *embroidered* frontal, with two orphreys, the principal colour of which is the colour of the Day or of the Festival celebrated. If only a white frontal is available, it is permissible to change the colour of the orphreys to agree with the colour of the Day or Festival. In case of need, the white frontal and orphreys may be used on every occasion, except Good Friday and Holy Saturday. It should be understood that by "white" is not meant that the entire frontal should be white but only that the background shall be white or light in colour. Many colours may be embroidered on a "white" frontal. The "colour" of any frontal, or of an orphrey, is determined, not by the colour or colours which may be embroidered upon it but by the predominating colour of the background. A frontal of cloth of gold may be used at any service, except on Good Friday or Holy Saturday. Frontals of silver cloth are not used in our rite. Frontals may either be hung from the under side of the front edge of the altar, or stretched upon a frame which may be attached to the altar by hooks. If the altar is made of costly stone, of tile, or is beautifully ornamented or carved, there is no need to use a frontal. When a frontal is not used, a superfrontal of heavy lace about six to ten inches in width, which is attached to one of the under linen altar cloths, should be hung from the front edge of the altar. Under this superfrontal may be placed a broad band of ribbon of the colour of the Day or Festival. A superfrontal of suitable material is often used above a frontal.

The *altar cross* stands in the middle either upon the tabernacle or upon a shelf immediately behind and above the tabernacle. It should be of such size and placed sufficiently high so that it can be seen easily by the worshippers. In the Liberal Catholic Church the crucifix is avoided, a cross without a suffering human figure attached thereto being used. There is no objection, however, to using a cross with the figure of Christ "reigning from the tree of glory," with a golden crown, joyous and in the attitude of benediction.

On the altar of every church or oratory there should be six metal *candlesticks* with candles, arranged so that three stand in line on either side of the altar cross. At all celebrations of the Holy Eucharist, private, low, sung or high, the rule is that these six candles are lighted. In case of necessity the Eucharist may be celebrated using only two candles. At all other services of the Church, which take place before an altar, with the exceptions of Baptism and "A Form of Admission," these six candles are always lighted. There may be and often are many other candles on the altar, but the six candles must always be there. A seventh candle may be placed before the altar cross whenever a bishop celebrates, but it should not be so large as to hide the cross. At Baptism, or when admitting a member using "A Form of Admission," when separate from other services, and at Prime and Complin when these services are conducted, especially by a layman, in a home or school, it is permissible to use two candles. The six candlesticks should be of the same material, shape, height and size, preferably gold coloured. On each of the six candlesticks, either on a detachable metal shield or on the candlestick itself, may be engraved the symbol of one of the Rays (with the exception of the Second Ray) and, when possible, in each shield or a candlestick is embedded a tiny jewel associated with the Ray. These jewels are cemented in place exactly as in the case of the Ray Crosses.

It will be noted that three sets of consecrated jewels are necessary fully to equip a church: one set of seven jewels for the Ray Crosses, one set of seven jewels for the altar stone and one set of six jewels for the altar candlesticks. The purpose for which each set is desired should be specified when writing the bishop. It is not always possible at present to supply every church with three sets of jewels, especially the set for the candlesticks, but ultimately of course every church will be supplied. These sets of consecrated jewels, which have little intrinsic value, but must be guarded because of the consecration, are the property of the Liberal Catholic Church and not of any priest or congregation. They are loaned to the priest to be used in the services of the Church. The First Episcopal Synod ruled that "in order to safeguard the specially consecrated altar jewels which are entrusted to priests to use in their respective altar stones and churches, it is asked of all bishops that they obtain from each priest receiving such jewels a pledge similar to the following:

> "I hereby pledge myself that I will return to the Regionary Bishop of the Liberal Catholic Church in the Province of .... upon his request in writing, the set(s) of seven consecrated jewels entrusted to my care, and I further pledge myself that I will insert in my will instructions to return said set(s) of jewels in case of my death to said Regionary Bishop."

_____   _____
Witness   Priest

_____
Witness

When the six candlesticks are placed on their shelf at the altar they should be arranged in the following order on either side of the altar cross:

☩

Sixth	Third	Seventh	Altar	First	Fourth	Fifth
Ray	Ray	Ray	Cross	Ray	Ray	Ray

The *number of extra candles* to be placed upon the altar is of importance, but must be left largely to the discretion of the priest because of the different conditions prevailing in different churches. Some help may be given, however, in guiding the judgment of the priest if the Festivals, Holy Days, and Sundays are divided into four classes according to the number of extra candles used. (This division is not the same as that appearing in The Liturgy where the different Days are classified as Class A, B, C and D.)

In the first class are the two greatest Festivals of the Christian Year: Easter and Christmas. On these two occasions as many extra candles should be placed on the altar as the church can afford.

In the second class the Festivals and Days are: New Year's Day (the Octave of Christmas), The Epiphany, Baptism of Our Lord, Transfiguration, Maundy Thursday, Low Sunday (the Octave of Easter), Ascension Day, Whitsunday, Trinity Sunday, Corpus Christi, Assumption of Our Lady, St. Michael and All Angels, and All Saints' Day. On these festivals many candles should blaze upon the altar, though perhaps not quite so many as on the two greater Festivals. In this class come also the Festival in honour of the Patron Saint of a Church or of a Country, and the Dedication Festival or the anniversary of the Consecration of a Church. If National Holidays are observed they may be placed either in this class or in the one which follows.

In the third class are placed the following: Third Sunday in Advent, Presentation of Our Lord in the Temple, Annunciation of Our Lady, Septuagesima, Sexagesima, Quinquagesima, Fourth Sunday in Lent, St. John Baptist, St. Peter and the Holy Apostles, Nativity of Our Lady, All Souls' Day, Third Sunday after Trinity, Seventh Sunday after Trinity, Fifteenth Sunday after Trinity, and the Sunday next before Advent. On these days there may be fewer candles on the altar.

In the fourth class are all the rest of the Days and Sundays on which only the usual six candles are lighted.

Certain Festivals have an octave; that is, they are celebrated for eight days. When the "Octave," or eighth day, is celebrated, the number of candles may be slightly less than the number used on the Festival itself. On the intermediate days, or "within the octave," the number of candles may be still smaller. An exception is made on the Sunday within the octave of a Festival. At such times the number of candles used should be the same as on the Festival itself. It is the custom in some churches to light the candles of a side altar when the Festival of the Patron Saint of that side altar is being celebrated at the High Altar.

The *extra candles may be placed* in candelabra of various designs and sizes or in single candlesticks. They may stand on the altar, the gradines, or the tabernacle. If desired, branching candlesticks on tall standards may stand on the sanctuary floor, or on one of the steps at both ends of the altar. With the possible exception of the bishop's candle none of the extra candles should stand higher than the six altar candles. The six candles may be made to look longer by using simple tubes or stocks painted the colour of the candles. One end of the tube is inserted in the candlestick, while in the other end the candle is inserted. The junction between tube and candle may be hidden by a metal shield.

The *candles* used on the altar may be made of beeswax, of paraffin, or a mixture of mineral and vegetable fats. The use of candles containing animal fats should be avoided. The candles used by the Roman Catholic Church, which are manufactured of beeswax and other fats, are allowable. It has been found that pure paraffin candles cannot be used in very hot weather because they bend so easily.

Trouble is sometimes experienced by *draughts* causing the candles to burn unevenly and to be consumed rapidly. This difficulty may be eliminated by obtaining glass caps, sold for the purpose, which fit over the top of the Candle. They are practically invisible and as the candle is consumed, they descend the flame. Another way to overcome the difficulty, so far as the six altar candles are concerned, is to use special long tubes or stocks, sometimes called *sauches* which are painted white on the outside to resemble candles. The candle, when placed in the tube, is forced against the upper orifice by a plunger, actuated by a spring, which presses against the base of the candle. When such stocks are used just enough wax is melted to keep the candle burning, even though draughts may cause the flame to flicker. This arrangement has two great advantages: the candle flames remain always at the same height; paraffin candles may be used inside the tubes even in very warm weather. Such stocks, of course, are not suited for use with extra candles.

Care should be taken to see that all candles placed on the altar are plumb. Sometimes when a candle is slightly bent it is possible to make it appear vertical from the front by turning the candlestick on its base. Care should also be exercised to place the six altar candles an even distance apart, and that the extra candles are placed symmetrically.

If a candle is a little too small for the candlestick, a strip of paper wound round the base will rectify matters. If it is too large, it may be made smaller by paring with a knife, or, better still by using a candle parer sold for the purpose, which works on the same principle as a pencil sharpener. Some churches save the candle ends, bits of wax, etc., and make their own candles out of the residue, although this requires some skill and patience. It is possible to buy candle molds and wicks. It is not worth while trying to repair a broken candle. The best thing to do is to cut through the wick at the break and to use the two halves when opportunity offers.

The *candles on the altar are lighted* in the following manner and order: The server goes to the middle, genuflects *in plano* (that is, on the sanctuary floor) if the Blessed Sacrament is reserved, otherwise he bows, walks round to the epistle side and ascends the side steps at that side. The altar candle on the epistle side nearest the cross is lighted first, then the central one on that side, and then the outermost one. If there are extra candles those on the epistle side they are now lighted. Descending by the side steps on the epistle side, he passes round to the middle, either genuflects *in plano* or bows, goes to the gospel side and ascends the side steps to the footpace. The server now lights the altar candle nearest the cross on the gospel side, then the centre one of these three, and then the outermost one. If there are extra candles these are now lighted. He descends the side steps, passes round to the middle, genuflects or bows, and departs. If there are many extra candles, two servers should light them, one ascending to the epistle side, one to the gospel side. When they approach the altar for this purpose they should walk side by side, or one behind the other (depending upon the arrangements of the church) genuflect or bow together in the middle, ascend to the footpace by the end steps, light the candles, descend the same way, genuflect or bow in the middle, and depart. The two servers should so time their movements that the candles placed in the same relative positions on either side of the altar are lighted at the same moment. The candles should be lighted five minutes before the service. They are extinguished in reverse order to that in which they were lit. Candles should not be blown out but extinguished with an extinguisher made for the purpose.

Priests are warned not to permit drapery of inflammable material to be hung behind the altar near the candles. If drapery is used it should be secured in some way so that it cannot become loose or blown about by a sudden gust of wind.

Flowers add to the beauty of the services, and may be placed upon the gradines and even upon the altar in such abundance as the church can afford. The exclusive use of white flowers ought to be avoided, even on those days when the colour of the vestments is white. Carefully blended colours enhance the beauty of the altar and remove the rather chill effect of pure white. It is a pleasing custom to place flowers upon the altar which match the colour of the vestments used, but there is no reason why flowers of other colours should not appear at the same time. Green foliage may be mingled with the flowers so as to obtain a more pleasing effect. Potted plants may not be placed on the altar or its gradines but they may stand elsewhere in the sanctuary.

A *missal stand* usually of brass or wood is placed on the epistle side of the altar not far from the middle. It need not be covered. A cushion covered with a veil of the colour of the Day may be used instead of the stand.

The *credence* is a small table or shelf placed in the sanctuary near the epistle end of the altar. The credence should be covered with a white cloth, except on Good Friday and Holy Saturday. Upon it are placed the cruets and tray, lavabo basin and towels, book or books of Epistles and Gospels and any other things needed during a service. The sacring bell, chimes or gong is sometimes placed on the credence table, but more often elsewhere in the sanctuary.

During the hours when the altar is not in use it is well to keep it covered with a light-coloured *dust-cloth*. This cloth may be made of any pleasing and suitable material. It is, of course removed when the preparations for a service begin. It is not usual to keep extra candlesticks upon an altar unless they are required for use. The missal stand may remain upon the altar after a service is over, but in many churches it is removed when the people have departed. If extra candlesticks and missal stand are removed the placing of the dust-cloth is of course made easy.

A *sanctuary lamp* of ruby-coloured glass should be placed near the altar. (In the Liberal Catholic Church white glass is not used in the sanctuary lamp even at the high altar.) This lamp is kept burning whenever the Host is reserved in the tabernacle. Preferably it is suspended by long chains from the ceiling in the middle before the altar, placed at such a height as to be well above the heads of the officiating clergy; it may rest on a brass pedestal or standard at one end of the altar; it may be placed on or in front of the tabernacle; it may hang from a bracket near one end of the altar. The oil used in such lamps ought to be pure olive oil, although mixtures of vegetable oils are permitted. Animal fats and oils must not be used. Large eight-day candles manufactured especially for sanctuary lamps, and equipped with special fittings and a ruby glass, may be obtained from Catholic Church Goods shops. They are very much more convenient than lamps using olive oil. If an oil lamp is used, care must be taken when filling the lamp not to put in too much oil that the flame from the floating wick extends above the top. It is better to fill the bowl in the sacristy, or some other convenient place, than to run the danger of spilling some of the oil on the sanctuary carpet. Obviously the lamp should be replenished or lighted when there is no congregation present. The Second Episcopal Synod ruled that "the use of an electric lamp as a sanctuary light is permissible, but not recommended, inasmuch as a naked flame is more suitable for the purpose in view."

Except in cathedral churches where there is a throne, a bishop should be provided with a *faldstool*. A faldstool is built either with or without a back and is shaped like the letter X, so far as the frame is concerned. If a cushion is used it may have four covers, one in each of the four liturgical colours. Whenever a faldstool is not available a suitable chair with a low back will suffice.

The chancel, referred to in Roman Catholic books as the Choir, is in front of, or west of, the sanctuary. It is usually raised from the church floor by one or more steps, and separated from the sanctuary by a step, a railing, or both. In the chancel are seated the singers and the clergy in choir dress.

On the epistle side of the sanctuary is the seat or sedilia for the celebrant and his ministers. It may be a bench with room for three persons, or three separate chairs. It may be covered with a cloth varying in colour according to the season.

Because of the convenience and the much-to-be-desired elimination of announcements before and during the services, each church ought to obtain a suitable *hymn board* to be fastened securely in some position where it may be seen by all the congregation. Such boards are not very difficult to make by a worker in wood, and they may also be bought in Church Goods shops. Usually they are ornamented at the top with a wooden cross, or other ecclesiastical design, and are fitted with several horizontal slots into which cards bearing the name of the Festival or Sunday, and numerals giving the numbers of the hymns, may be slipped. It is advisable to obtain a board of sufficient width and with at least five or still better seven of these horizontal slots, because not only should there be a card inserted bearing the name of the Festival or Sunday, but on occasion (as at Palm Sunday) there are more than the usual three hymns during the morning service. Also when there is a Proper Gradual this should be brought to the attention of the congregation by use of a special card. In the evening indication should be given whether the service is that of Solemn Benediction only, or Vespers and Benediction. The numerals, each printed on a separate oblong of cardboard in heavy black type, may be bought in sets, but the names of the Festivals, Sundays, etc., and cards bearing the words: Proper Gradual, Vespers, Benediction, Prime, Complin, etc., will have to be drawn each on separate cards in bold, black lettering, by some talented member.

CHAPTER II

The Vestments

The dress of those taking part in Church services, either in the sanctuary or the choir consists always of a *cassock* over which other vestments are worn. [For illustrations of vestments references are made to plates in the front of this book. [Ed.]]??? As prescribed by the First General Episcopal Synod, cassocks vary in colour and style according to the work, age and rank of the wearer. They are usually fastened by a single row of buttons down the middle. Cassocks should be long enough to look dignified and to conceal the trousers as much as possible, yet they must not be of such length as to interfere with walking.

Youths serving at the altar or otherwise employed in the sanctuary wear plain scarlet cassocks. Tall youths or adults performing the same functions wear plain scarlet or dark blue cassocks. All such cassocks are worn without cuffs, cincture, cape or biretta.

Ordained subdeacons, deacons and priests wear deep purple cassocks. Such cassock may be plain or may possess cape and false oversleeves, ornamented with buttons, which project slightly below the cape. (Plate 6, Figures 4 & 7) A cincture is worn, consisting of a band of cloth or silk of the colour of the cassock, ornamented with fringe at the ends, which is passed round the waist, knotted on the left side in front, the loose ends falling to the knee or a little lower. The material of which the cassocks are made is not specified; it may be cotton, wool, or silk, or a mixture of any of the three. It may have silk cuffs. What in England is called "Russell Cord" makes very durable cassocks. White cassocks may be worn by priests (and presumably by deacons and subdeacons) in hot weather or in the tropics, according to a ruling of the Second General Episcopal Synod.

A bishop wears a plain rose-purple cassock of silk or merino with or without a train. The train is hooked up at the back so that it does not drag on the floor. It is let down on solemn occasions. The cassock is edged with red and has buttons of the same lighter colour. It should have red cuffs. A cincture of the colour of the cassock is worn, the fringe of which is green and gold. The fringe of the cincture used on greater occasions may be quite elaborate. In the tropics or in hot weather a bishop may wear a white cassock.

It is seemly to avoid entering the sanctuary unless in cassock. This is especially true when preparing for a service. The cassock, with biretta if the wearer is entitled to one, may be worn on any suitable non-liturgical occasions, but other vestments should not be worn except on the occasions for which they are specified.

Subdeacons, deacons and priests are entitled to wear a dark purple biretta, and bishops a rose-purple biretta. A *biretta* is a square cap with three peaks or ridges, which may be folded. Attached to the top in the centre is a pompon of the colour of the biretta.

It is worn so that the corner without a peak is over the left ear. In putting on or taking off the biretta the right hand grasps the middle peak. (Plate 6, Fig. 7)

A *clerical collar* must of course be worn at church services by all those of the rank of subdeacon and higher. In some churches all of the choir and adult altar servers wear clerical collars, while the youth are dressed in special collars, not unlike Eton collars.

Boots and shoes worn in the sanctuary should not be brown in colour. The custom of removing the shoes worn in the street and wearing in the church shoes used exclusively for that purpose is highly desirable. Sanctuary shoes may be of purple or red [or black [Ed.]] to match the cassock.

The *vestment of boys* serving at the altar or in the choir is a white cotta, (Plate 7, Fig. 9) The *cotta* hangs only part way down the thigh and has short sleeves extending a little below the elbows. The bottom of the cotta and the ends of the sleeves are edged with lace. The cotta is never worn by men.

The *vestment of men* serving at the altar or in the choir is a white surplice without lace. (Plate 7, Fig. 6) The *surplice* should fall to the knees and have ample sleeves, called angel sleeves, which so widen down to the hands that the tips of the sleeves nearly touch the sides of the body when the arms are held out horizontally from the shoulders. There should be an opening nearly circular, sometimes oval, just large enough to permit the surplice to be drawn over the head, and all folds and gathers at the neck band should be avoided as much as possible.

The server carrying the crozier or mitre of a bishop should wear a scarf of thin white silk, sometimes edged at the ends with gilt fringe, which is called a *vimpa*. The vimpa is worn round the neck and tied or joined in front with the ends hanging down. The server covers the palms of his hands with the ends of the vimpa while carrying the crozier or mitre.

The *vestment of a subdeacon* is a white *linen* surplice.

The *vestments of a deacon* are a white linen surplice and a stole, which is worn over the left shoulder and crossed under the right arm. The *deacon's stole* is usually made with fasteners or tapes so that it may be fastened in this crossed position. Both the deacon and the subdeacon wear other vestments, to be described hereafter, when they assist a celebrant at a High Celebration or at Benediction of the Most Blessed Sacrament.

The *vestments of priests*, except on occasions specified hereafter, are a white linen surplice and stole. The stole (Plate 7, Fig. 6) is a narrow piece of silk brocade or other material, bordered with braid and its ends edged with fringe, which is worn over the shoulders, the two ends hanging down in front to about the knees of the wearer. When celebrating the Holy Eucharist a priest is vested in amice, alb, girdle, stole (crossed in front, right over left, and secured in position by the girdle) maniple and chasuble. (Plate 7, Fig. 2) The general rule is that whenever a priest is vested in alb and girdle he wears the stole crossed in front as at the Eucharist. This does not hold, of course, when a priest is serving as deacon at the altar. The *amice* is a cape of white linen, which is placed over the shoulders and round the neck, and held in place by means of two tapes which are wrapped about the body and under the arms and tied in front. (Plate 7, Fig. 1) The important part of the amice is the band of stiffened silk shaped to fit the shoulders, which is attached to the upper edge of the linen cape where it comes into contact with the neck. This silk band, known as the *apparel*, is either made of gold brocade, or brocaded silk covered with gold metal lace. (It is permissible to use the apparel alone without the linen cape.) In vesting, the amice is put on first of all immediately over the cassock. The linen part is therefore worn under the alb, but the apparel should be outside the alb. The *alb* (Plate 7, Fig. 2) is a long linen gown which reaches nearly to the bottom of the cassock. It has close fitting sleeves the ends of which are edged with lace. An oblong panel of lace is inserted in the front and in the rear near the bottom hem of the alb. The Third Episcopal Synod ruled that in extremely hot weather it was permissible to use an alb without a cassock, but it was recommended that the openings, if present, be backed up with silk of the colour of the cassock. The *girdle* is a quarter-inch cord, twelve feet long, with tassels at either end. The girdle of a priest, deacon or subdeacon has both cord and tassels of linen, usually white, but sometimes of the colour of the Day. The girdle of a bishop is a metallic gilded cord with metallic tassels. The *maniple* (Plate 72, Fig. 21) is a band of silk brocade, or other material, not unlike a short stole, which is worn over the left fore-arm. The maniple is worn only while celebrating the Holy Eucharist, never at any other service. The *chasuble* is worn over all the other vestments and should be of the gothic form with a small oval neck hole. (Plate 7, Figures 4 & 5) The Y-placed orphreys are of metal braid, metal cloth, or silk braid. The chasuble, stole and maniple are of the colour of the Festival or Day. The chasuble is worn only at celebrations of the Holy Eucharist, and usually only in the sanctuary. At Low Celebrations and at ordinary week-day services, even though sung, it is permissible to wear the chasuble in procession to and from the sanctuary. On Sundays and at Festivals, especially if processional and recessional hymns are sung, the cope should be worn in procession, the chasuble being used exclusively in the sanctuary. The *cope* (Plate 6, Figures 2 and 3) is a large semi-circular cloak worn over the shoulders and fastened across the breast by a broad strip of braid or metal called a *morse*.

The *subdeacon at a High Celebration* is vested in amice, alb, girdle, maniple and tunicle. The *tunicle* (Similar to Plate 7, Figure 3) is a short-sleeved, loose-fitting garment which is slit up the sides. It shuld be of the colour of the Festival or Day. The subdeacon at the Eucharist, even though an ordained priest, does not wear a stole. By ruling of the First General Episcopal Synod the subdeacon at Vespers or Benediction of the Most Holy Sacrament is vested in a similar manner, but does not wear the maniple. The

Third General Episcopal Synod ruled that the subdeacon at Vespers or Benediction may vest in cope instead of the tunicle. If the acting subdeacon at a High Celebration has not been ordained to that rank, he may not wear the maniple.

The *deacon at a High Celebration* is vested in amice, alb, girdle, stole, maniple and dalmatic. (Plate 7, Fig. 3) The *dalmatic* is of the colour of the Festival or Day. The deacon, even though he be an ordained priest, wears the stole over the left shoulder and crossed under the right arm, the point of junction being about over the right hip. The stole is held in this crossed position either by passing it under the girdle, or leaving it outside the girdle and tying it in position with the ends of the girdle. If a deacon's stole is used it is held in its crossed position either by metal fasteners, by cords, or by tapes, fastened to the stole itself. By ruling of the First General Episcopal Synod the deacon at Vespers or Benediction of the Most Holy Sacrament is vested in a similar manner but does not wear the maniple. The Third General Episcopal Synod ruled that the deacon at Vespers or Benediction may vest in cope instead of dalmatic.

The maniple is not worn outside the sanctuary and is used only at Celebrations of the Holy Eucharist. At the Eucharist the chasuble is worn only by the Celebrant. In some churches it is customary, however, at the ordination of a priest for all the priests present, but not the bishops, to wear the chasuble, not only during the celebration itself, but also in the procession to and from the sanctuary.[15]

The *cope is worn* by the celebrant in formal processions, during the *Asperges* in the Longer Form, at Vespers and Solemn Benediction, at Solemn Marriages and Solemn Funerals in the church, and at Solemn Blessings. On the greater Festivals, at Vespers and Solemn Benediction all the priests may wear copes if they have them. On such occasions copes may also be worn by the Cantor and Master of Ceremonies. The colour of the cope is usually that of the Festival or Day. A stole of the same colour is worn under the cope, if the wearer is entitled to use the stole.

When *preaching*, a priest, unless he is acting as celebrant, wears a linen surplice and stole of the colour of the Festival or Day. He may wear the biretta. On greater occasions he may wear a cope. If the celebrant himself preaches standing in the sanctuary near the altar, he takes off only the maniple. He does not wear the biretta. But if he preaches in a pulpit some distance from the altar he should take off the chasuble as well. In this case he may wear the biretta. If the biretta is worn while preaching, it should be removed during the Invocation preceding the sermon, and the Ascription following the sermon. While uncovered, the preacher holds the biretta by the right hand against the breast, grasping it by the middle peak.

The occasions *when the biretta should be used* have not been finally determined in our rite. It is worn in processions except in processions in which the Blessed Sacrament is carried. It is removed before the first genuflection upon arriving in the sanctuary, and is replaced after the genuflection before leaving the sanctuary at the end of the service. It is also worn by priests, deacons and subdeacons in the sanctuary (with the possible exception of the preacher) during the sermon. It is worn during the greater part of Vespers. It way be worn on non-liturgical occasions when the cassock is used. A bishop wears a biretta when he does not require a mitre. It is never worn by anyone when the Blessed Sacrament is exposed, nor while standing, kneeling or making an act of reverence. There is no question of the use or non-use of the biretta at these points. The complications arise when the use of the biretta during the service of the Eucharist is studied. The general rule in the Roman Catholic Church is "*that when the clergy sit they cover the head, except when the Blessed Sacrament is exposed. They never stand or kneel with covered head. Before standing they take off the biretta; they put it on again after they have sat down.*" If this rule is applied in our rite, the clergy in the sanctuary, with the exception of the celebrant and his ministers, will use the biretta during the First Censing, Epistle, Sermon, Offertorium, Second Censing (but not while being censed), and from the consumption of the first ablution to the Communio. To do this unnecessarily complicates the ceremonial actions and prevents the clergy from concentrating on the one essential thing, the service itself. Until a ruling has been received from the General Episcopal Synod, it is recommended to the clergy that during the celebration of the Holy Eucharist birettas be not worn except at the sermon. The only exception to this is a ruling by the Third General Episcopal Synod that a bishop in choir dress should wear his biretta while being censed.

In *administering other Sacraments* and when giving blessings a priest usually wears a surplice and a stole of the colour prescribed in the rubrics.

The First Episcopal Synod limited the size of *crosses worn ceremonially by priests* to two inches in length, and requested that they be worn under the vestments except when the priest is celebrating the Holy Eucharist. When celebrating they may be worn outside provided they are of the prescribed length.

The *choir dress of a bishop*, in addition to the rose-purple cassock, consists of a white linen rochet, stole, mozetta, rose-purple biretta, pectoral cross, ring and crozier. The *rochet* is a shorter vestment than a surplice, is deeply edged with lace, and has close fitting sleeves with flame-coloured cuffs covered with lace. The lace of the rochet should not extend below the lower edge of the mantelletta. The *mantelletta* is a rose-purple cloak-like garment, with broad lapels folded back, which has slits at the sides through which the arms pass. It is worn by a bishop outside his own province or diocese. The *pectoral cross* is usually suspended from the neck by a green and gold cord. The *mozetta* is a short, cape-like vestment worn over the shoulders. It has an ornamental hood and is rose-purple in colour. The mozetta is a sign of jurisdiction and is worn by the bishop only in his own province or diocese. It is worn by the Regionary Bishop in the presence of his Diocesan Bishops, and by the Presiding Bishop in the presence of his Regionary Bishops. The *crozier* (Plate 6, Figures 2 and 3) may be carried by a bishop, or by a server who walks immediately in front of the bishop. Bishop Wedgwood holds that the crozier should be carried by a chaplain or server when the bishop is in choir dress. The Third Episcopal Synod ruled that this was optional with the bishop.

On greater Festivals a bishop vests in rochet, stole, cope, mitre, pectoral cross, ring and crozier. He may wear gloves. *Mitres* (Plate 6, Figures 2 and 3) are of two kinds: Gold, when made of cloth of *gold; Precious,* when heavy with embroidery and ornaments of gold and jewels.

When *celebrating the Holy Eucharist* a bishop vests exactly as does a priest, except that instead of a biretta he wears a mitre, and instead of crossing the stole in front he wears it with the two ends hanging straight down. He also wears the ring, the pectoral cross suspended by a green-gold cord, and either carries the crozier in his left hand or has it carried before him by a server wearing a vimpa. For greater Festivals or for High Mass, the bishop may wear gloves. In processions the pectoral cross is worn over the alb under the cope, but after the chasuble has been put on at the altar the cross is worn outside the chasuble.

Vestments made with silk braid instead of metal braid are permissible for convenience in traveling or because of economy, but those with gold-covered metal braid are preferable. It is recommended, however, that the colour of gold shall predominate in the silk braid.

The colours used in the Liberal Catholic Rite are white, red, violet or purple, green, and rose. The "colour" of any given vestment material is determined by the predominating colour of the background.

White is used for all Feasts of Our Lord, for all Festivals in honour of Our Lady and in honour of saints who are not martyrs, for Trinity Sunday, for St. Michael and All Angels, for the Anniversaries of the Consecration of a Church, for National Holidays, the second part of Baptism, Confirmation, Ordination to Major Orders, the Marriage Service and Nuptial Eucharist.

Red is used for the season of Septuagesima, Sexagesima and Quinquagesima, for Whitsunday and six days thereafter, during the weeks of the seventh and fifteenth Sundays after Trinity, the week of the Sunday next before Advent, for Martyrs, at the Service of Healing, and Ordaining to Major Orders when the colour of the Day is red.

Violet or Purple is used during the season of Advent and Lent (except when rose coloured vestments may be used) on All Souls' Day, at Requiem Eucharists, Funerals, Exorcisms, at Holy Unction, the first part of Baptism, and at Confession and Absolution.

Green is used from the end of the octave of the Epiphany until Septuagesima (except when superseded, as is frequently the case, by a Festival of a different colour), and from the Second Sunday after Trinity until the Sunday next before Advent, with the exception of those days for which another colour is designated.

Rose is used only on the Third Sunday in Advent and the Fourth Sunday in Lent. If rose-coloured vestments are not available, violet should be used.

Black is not used in the Liberal Catholic Rite.

Cloth of Gold may always take the place of white, red or green, but not of violet. In a small church, white may take the place of all colours, except that there should be a violet stole for use in baptisms and blessings.

It is desirable that a bishop should bless the vestments, except those of linen.

The proper *care of vestments* should not be overlooked. Vestments, especially copes and chasubles, should be hung on hangers in a wardrobe kept for the purpose. If possible a separate wardrobe should be provided for cassocks. The use of dust-bags to cover copes and chasubles is advisable.

Some churches provide a chest of drawers or a vestment press for the storage of vestments. Drawers are especially useful for the safe keeping of stoles, maniples, burses, veils, humeral veils, dalmatics and tunicles. Even copes and chasubles may be placed therein if care is used in folding them. The detachable cape or shield should be removed from the cope *before* folding. The cope is then folded by holding it in the middle of the neck-band bringing (lining outside) the two ends (that hang down at the feet when the cope is worn) together. It is then folded lengthwise in half. It may be folded once more lengthwise, and then across once or twice. In order to fold a chasuble, first turn it inside out and place it flat on a table. Then fold it lengthwise in three, that is, parallel to the central orphrey. This prevents the ornamentation at the junction of the orphreys from being cracked or wrinkled. The chasuble may then be folded at right angles to the original folds, either in half, or in three, depending upon the position of the ornamentation.

CHAPTER III

Liturgical Vessels, Instruments and Accessories

The chief eucharistic vessels are the *chalice* and *paten*. (Plate 7, Fig. 7) The cup of the chalice is the most important part as it holds the consecrated wine, and, while the stem and base may be made of any electroplated metal, the cup of the chalice and the paten should if possible be made of silver or gold. If this is prohibited on account of cost, electroplate is permissible. When either electroplate or silver is the material used for the cup of the chalice and the paten, the interior of the cup and the upper surface of the paten must be plated with gold. Chalices should not be selected which are less than six inches, or more than eleven inches, in height, or whose cups are so narrow or so long that the fingers cannot touch the bottom of the interior of the cup. If the stem of the chalice has a node or knob midway between the top of the base and the bottom of the cup it is much easier and safer to handle. A cross is engraved on the base of the chalice to indicate the side which faces the celebrant. The upper surface of the paten should be plain so that no particles of the consecrated Host may adhere to it. There is a difference of opinion as to whether a slightly concave paten, or one with a depression to fit the cup, is the best to use. The former is easier to purify just before the Ablutions; the latter is less likely to slide to one side when it is placed on the chalice and at the same time it holds the host more securely. The chalice and paten ought to be consecrated by a bishop before being used, but if this is not possible, a priest may bless them.

The *ciborium* (Plate 7, Fig. 7) which is used to hold the consecrated Hosts while they are being administered at Communion, or while reserved in the tabernacle, resembles a chalice in form, but it is usually wider and shallower in the cup and is supplied with a lid. The base and stem may be of any metal, but the cup if possible should be of silver. If the cup is made of any metal other than gold, its interior must be gold plated.

When possible a *pyx* or *custodia* should be kept in the tabernacle to hold the large consecrated Host used at Benediction of the Most Holy Sacrament. (In some churches, where the tabernacle is large, the entire monstrance is kept within the tabernacle. It has been claimed that this practice is inadvisable because at times an offensive odour is emitted by the brass. This has not been noticed at all in those churches where this arrangement has prevailed for several years.) The pyx is usually a small silver box, gold plated inside, large enough to contain the Host and the lunette which holds the Host while it is exposed in the monstrance. There is a smaller pyx made, not unlike an empty watch-case, which is used to carry the reserved Host to the sick. This also should be made of silver, gold plated inside. Every church should possess such a pyx to use in sick calls.

The general rule regarding the consecrated Host is that it should touch only gold or linen, hence the requirement that those portions of the chalice, paten, ciborium, pyx or lunette which come into contact with the Host or Wine should be gold plated.

When a ciborium which has contained consecrated Hosts is emptied, it should be carefully cleansed at, or immediately after, the Communion at which it was emptied, and must be so cleansed before unconsecrated wafers are put therein. This is done by pouring water (which has been blessed as at the offertorium) into the ciborium and then consuming the water. This should be repeated until all small Particles have been consumed. The ciborium is then wiped dry with a purificator.

When a chalice, paten, ciborium or pyx becomes so worn that the inner metal begins to show through the gold plating, it must be replated. After replating, it must again be consecrated, or at least blessed by a priest, before being used.

The *Monstrance* (Plate 7, Fig. 8) is simply a large pyx of metal, usually gold-plated brass, surmounting a metal stem and base and surrounded by an aureole of radiating rays of metal. The sides of the monstrance are of glass so that the Host can be seen. The monstrance is used whenever a large consecrated Host is exposed on the altar or throne for the adoration of the people, or carried in procession as at Benediction of the Most Holy Sacrament. The Host within the monstrance should not touch the glass, but should be held in place by the lunette, which is so constructed that only gold surfaces touch the Host. When not in use the monstrance is covered with a white veil.

The *cruets* are two small jugs usually of glass or crystal for holding wine and water. They usually stand on a dish or tray of glass or metal. A separate bowl is often placed on the credence to use at the Lavabo. If the celebrant prefers to have water from the cruet poured over his fingers at the Lavabo the bowl is empty. If on the other hand the celebrant prefers the more convenient method at the Lavabo of dipping his fingers in water, the bowl should be filled with water. The *lavabo towel* is a small coarse linen cloth used in drying the fingers at the Lavabo. It is often ornamented with a small embroidered cross at one end, or one corner.

At the Service of Healing and at the Administration of the Holy Communion with the Reserved Sacrament it is permissible to place a small glass bowl of water, with cover, on the altar near the tabernacle. After the administration of Communion the officiant should dip his fingers carefully in this water, drying them on a lavabo towel placed nearby, or on the edge of the corporal. This water may be drunk by celebrant or poured on clean grass after the service.

Certain cloths are used at the Eucharist. The *corporal* is a white linen cloth which is spread on the altar in the middle during a Celebration. Its size, usually about twenty inches square, depends upon the distance between the front of the tabernacle and the front edge of the altar. Its upper surface is often marked with a *small* embroidered cross on the portion of the corporal which is nearest the celebrant when the corporal is spread out on the altar. The corporal should always be ironed on the wrong side and then turned right side up and folded as follows, using the iron to smooth the folds: Fold 3

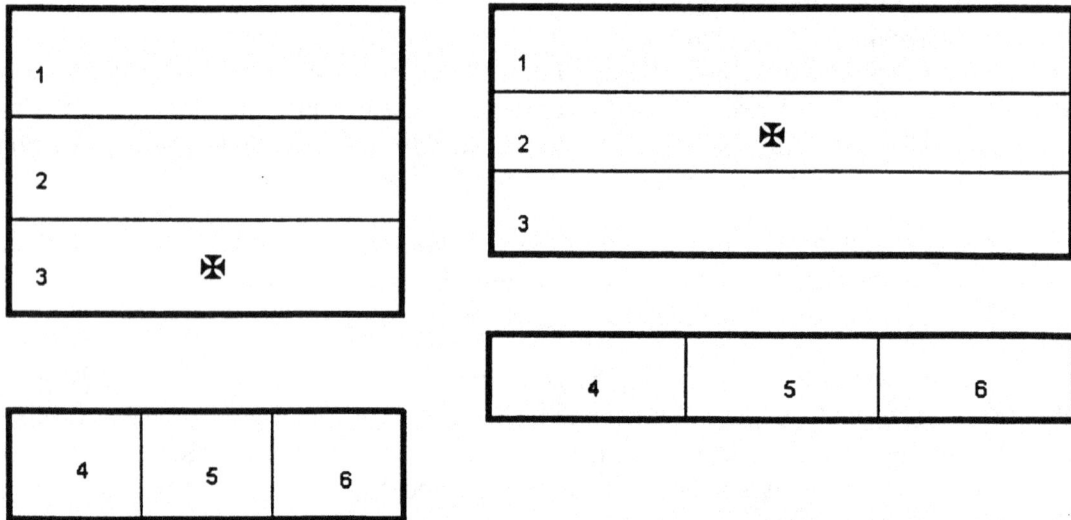

DIAGRAM 3

over 2 and 1 over 3. (Diagram 3, Left Top) Then fold 6 over 5 and 4 over 6. (Diagram 3, Left Bottom) Each time after being used, the corporal should be folded by the priest exactly in this way, in order to retain any Particles of the consecrated Host which may still be clinging to its upper surface. After being folded, it is placed in the burse. The *burse* (Plate 7, Fig. 7) is a pocket stiffened with cardboard or strawboard and covered with the same materials as in the vestments used. A convenient size for the burse is nine by ten inches, although it may be somewhat smaller. It is used to hold only the corporal. The *purificator* is a white linen cloth about ten by sixteen inches in size. It is used by the celebrant to wipe the chalice just before the wine is poured into it at the offertorium, and to dry his fingers, his lips and the chalice after the Ablutions. It should be marked in the centre by a tiny cross embroidered in red. It is ironed on the wrong side, and, without turning it right side up, is folded as follows, the iron being used to smooth the folds: Fold 3 over 2 and 1 over 3. (Diagram 3, Right Top) Fold 6 over 5 and 4 over 6. (Diagram 3, Right Bottom) The *pall* (Plate 7, Fig. 7) is a thin piece of cardboard covered on both sides with white linen and marked in the centre of the upper side with an embroidered cross. It is usually about six inches square, but must in all cases be large enough to cover the paten. The upper surface of the pall may be embroidered. The *veil*, (Plate 7, Fig. 7) which is of the same material as the vestments, covers the sacred vessels on the altar during the time they are not in use. It is square in outline and its width should be equal to twice the height of the chalice added to the width of the pall. The veil is ornamented with a cross or some other device on the side which is seen by the people when it is draped over the sacred vessels.

During the Asperges and whenever sprinkling objects with holy water a special *stoup* or bucket may be used to hold the holy water. It is advisable to buy one lined with white enamel so as to prevent the formation of verdigris. The sprinkler or *aspergill* may be either in the form of a brush or of a hollow, perforated ball which may contain a sponge. If the latter form of aspergill is used, it is well to have the inside and the outside of the ball gold plated in order to keep the salt from attacking the metal. There is a style of aspergill sold which is quite convenient. It consists of a glass bottle, to hold the holy water, the stopper of which is the aspergill. The stopper, which is of glass, has a long extension reaching down into the water, at the end of which is a hollow ball containing a piece of sponge. Hollow metal aspergills are also made which hold the water, the perforated head of which can be opened by turning the head round slightly. With the sprinkler type of aspergill a stoup is not required, unless the church itself is being aspersed as at the Consecration of a Church.

The *censer* or thurible (Plate 7, Fig. 9) for burning incense should be of sufficient size to contain two or even three blocks of charcoal placed side by side. There are various styles of censers sold. The globular form with three chains to support the base and a fourth chain to raise the lid is the most satisfactory. The spherical shaped censer is much more easily managed than the elongated or Gothic form. If the base is of sufficiently heavy metal to give a musical ring when the censer is swung, so much the better. Care should be taken to see that the chains are of such a character, and that they are attached to the censer in such a way, that they do not easily kink or become twisted and thereby shortened. The chains should, if possible, be of fine smooth mesh in order to lessen the noise when the censer is opened or closed. This must be taken into consideration, especially in small oratories, because it is sometimes necessary to replenish the censer during a part of the service when there should be quiet. It is difficult to use the censer in a dignified way if the chains are too short. The best length seems to be about three feet. Care should be taken that the lid is properly closed when the censer is being used as there is danger of fragments of burning charcoal falling out. When at those times during a service the censer is not needed it is well to raise the lid which otherwise becomes uncomfortably hot. At private Celebrations a small censer may be used. The *incense boat* is a small receptacle in which the incense used during a service is kept. With it goes a *spoon* which is used to sprinkle the incense on the glowing charcoal. A spoon and boat are usually supplied with every censer. Sometimes the spoon and boat come chained together. It has been found more convenient to remove the chain, so that the spoon may be used more freely. The charcoal used, which usually comes in blocks, is specially prepared for use in a censer by the addition of nitre which causes it to remain glowing after being heated in a candle or gas flame. It is important to use the best grade of incense, which is not always easy to obtain. Many of the incense mixtures sold are not suitable for our use. A mixture of one part of benzoin to about five or six parts of olibanum is satisfactory. Tears of olibanum should be used in preference to cheaper grades. The mixture should be coarsely ground, not reduced to powder. It has been found that if incense is sprinkled on charcoal which is not properly glowing, a choking, acrid smoke is emitted.

Processional candlesticks are of various sizes and are usually of brass or wood. They should have wide flanges to catch the dripping wax. Note that the two candlesticks which are carried in procession on either side of the cross are placed, when the procession reaches the sanctuary, either on the credence table, if the candlesticks are not too large, or on the floor at either end of the credence. Should there be insufficient servers to carry these candlesticks in procession, the usual practice is to light them as they stand on the credence table immediately after the candles on the altar are lighted. The *processional cross* is a cross, not a crucifix, attached to the end of a wooden shaft and carried at the head of all processions. When not in use during the service it is placed in the chancel or sanctuary, usually on the epistle side, and held upright by a special holder or stand. *Processional banners* may be of any pleasing size and design: The Patron Saint of the Church, Our Lady, the Arms of the Church, and so on. The banner is carried suspended from the top of a wooden shaft, which is usually surmounted by a small wooden cross.

Whenever the Blessed Sacrament is carried in procession in a monstrance it is customary to hold a *canopy* over it. Such canopies are usually oblong in form, made of cloth of gold and often richly embroidered, supported by two, four or six poles carried by as many men. In small churches or when sufficient men to carry the canopy are not available, a procession with the Blessed Sacrament without a canopy is permissible.

The *sacring bell* is a small hand-bell made of silver or brass, which is rung at the Sanctus, and when the Blessing is given with the Blessed Sacrament at Solemn Benediction. A sweet-toned ecclesiastical *gong*, or a cluster of little bells called chimes may be substituted for the sacring bell. Whatever is used, the sound should be sweet, musical and not too loud and distracting.

The *gremial* is a white linen cloth, sometimes embroidered in colours, which is placed on the knees of the bishop at Confirmation and at ordinations to protect the vestments at the time he is using holy oils. A convenient size for the gremial is twenty by thirty inches.

The *humeral veil* is a scarf of silk, of silk and metallic gold thread, or of cloth of gold, which is worn by the celebrant round the neck and over the shoulders whenever he carries, or blesses the people with, the monstrance containing the Blessed Sacrament. It is sometimes equipped with ribbons, cords, or a clasp so that the veil may be fastened across the breast. The veil is used to cover the hands of the celebrant when the monstrance is carried, or held while blessing. The humeral veil should be about eighteen to twenty-four inches wide and from eight to ten feet long.

Inasmuch as the *Book of Gospels* with use becomes an object of spiritual influence, it is advisable not to use a casual copy of The Liturgy, but to have a special book prepared for the purpose. Furthermore the use of such a book of large size, suitably adorned with a cover of gold brocade or other pleasing material, is much more in keeping with the dignity and beauty of the Holy Eucharist. To prepare such a book, a large loose-leaf binder should be bought, together with a sufficient number of sheets of heavy durable paper punched to fit the rings in the binder. Only one Gospel should be typed on a sheet of paper. If a typewriter equipped with Large Roman or Magna Primer type can be found, it is recommended that the Gospels be typewritten in this type as it is very much easier to read. (Teachers in primary schools sometimes use the Magna Primer type because the letters are of the same large size as those used in books for children beginning to read.) If in the typing, space is left at the beginning of each Gospel for drawing a large Maltese Cross, the book will be ideal for liturgical purposes.

The *wine* used in the Liberal Catholic Rite is pure, unfermented grape juice. It may be either red or white, preferably red. In cases of necessity fermented wine may be used. Under no circumstances is any substitute for the juice of the grape permitted, although concentrated grape juice is allowable. Care should be taken to see that the "Grape Juice" bought really is the juice of the grape. Pasteurized grape juice and that to which a small amount of sugar has been added are satisfactory, but it is well to avoid if possible that to which preservative has been added, although this may be used in emergency.

The *altar breads* must be made of pure wheaten flour. They are unleavened and are prepared in the form of thin wafers, upon which are often pressed a cross or other ecclesiastical design. They come in two forms: large, for the use of the priest at the altar; small, for administration to the clergy and people. The most convenient size for the latter is a circular wafer one inch and a quarter or more in diameter. Wafers smaller than this in size are difficult to administer without touching the tongue of the communicant. In case of necessity, ordinary wheaten bread may be used.

There are two styles of *Oil Stocks*. The first style, which is intended for the storage of Holy Oils at a church, consists of three thick-walled metal bottles (each fitted with a tight screw cap) contained in a leather-covered, plush-lined wooden box which may be locked. Such stocks are sold in Catholic Church Goods shops and each church should possess one. Each bottle is plainly marked with a distinctive label, usually as follows: *S.CHR* is intended for the Sacred Chrism; *O.CAT.* is intended for the Oil of Catechumens or Baptismal Oil; *O.INF.* is intended for the Oil for the Sick. Each year the old oil in the bottles should be poured onto a quantity of absorbent cotton and reverently burned. The bottles themselves should then be cleansed with hot water and with water and soap, the water afterwards being poured on clean soil in a garden. This should be done just before Easter, inasmuch as the bishop blesses the Holy Oils on Maundy Thursday. The Oil Stock is then sent to the bishop, *with sufficient money to pay return carriage charges*, for a new supply of the oils for the coming year.

The other style of oil stock is that used by the clergy in their various ministrations. It consists of a metal cylinder, usually of silver, sometimes gold-plated, about one inch in diameter and two and a half inches long. When this cylinder is unscrewed, it resolves itself into three circular compartments and a lid. Each compartment is labeled, usually with a distinctive letter: *C* for Holy Chrism; *B* for Baptismal Oil; *I* for Oil for the Sick. When preparing this style of stock for use, each compartment should first be stuffed with cotton wool, or absorbent cotton, and then saturated with its respective oil.

Each year the old cotton should be removed from the stock, reverently burned, the compartments thoroughly cleaned and refilled.

The *Baptismal Shell*, which is used in Baptism to pour Holy Water over the head of the candidate, is usually made of silver, sometimes gold-plated. It is shaped not unlike an open shell. The most convenient type of shell is that in which half of the open part is covered with a septum which retains the water in the shell when it is tipped. At the pouring end is a small hole through which the water can be easily directed on to the head and forehead of the candidate, instead of pouring out generally as is the case when the open type of shell is used. At the other end of the shell is a handle, either a projecting strip of metal, or a metal ring placed vertically to the horizontal plane of the shell. Care should be taken to rinse the shell in ordinary water and dry it thoroughly, after it has been used in order to prevent corroding of the metal by the salt.

In a carefully conducted church the *care of brassware* should be given constant attention. Articles of brass used in the church are usually lacquered. If metal polish is used this lacquer is removed and the brass quickly tarnishes. It is well then on most occasions to wipe lightly with a soft cloth such things as offertory plates, processional and altar crosses, croziers, etc. Candle grease can often be removed from metal candlesticks by pressure with the thumb. Grease may be removed from wooden candlesticks by holding them over a current of hot air rising from a gas burner. Lacquer should always be removed from brasses before applying metal polish. An effective solvent for this purpose is methyl ethyl ketone. It will be necessary to polish the thurible frequently, because the incense smoke leaves a gummy deposit upon the metal, but care should be taken to see that the chains are free from traces of polish, otherwise the fingers of the celebrant are soiled when censing the altar. If the church can afford it, an excellent plan is to buy a small electric motor equipped with a polishing brush and buffer. The use of this device reduces the labour of polishing brasses to the minimum, especially if the metal is re-lacquered immediately after a thorough polishing. Such lacquer is easy to apply with a brush, and maintains the lustre of the brass for many weeks.

If *candle grease* is spilled *on vestments*, it is easily removed by placing a piece of blotting paper above and below the grease spot and then pressing with a hot iron on the top piece of paper.

The proper care of *purificators and corporals* must not be overlooked. The general rule is that the first washing of purificators and corporals should be done either by a priest or deacon. No soap is used at this first washing. The water is not allowed to run down the drain, but is carefully poured on clean grass, on soil in the garden or around some plant.

Servers in the sanctuary should be taught the need for scrupulous cleanliness, both of person and clothing. Well scrubbed hands, clean finger nails and polished shoes free from the dust of the street are essentials in liturgical service.

CHAPTER IV

Ceremonial Actions and Rules

What the Priest Should Memorize

It is conducive to a smoothly flowing service for the priest to memorize the following portions of the eucharistic liturgy so that he may not be dependent upon his missal:

1. The *Asperges* in the Shorter Form, part of which must be said while aspersing oneself and the altar, and part while facing the people.

2. The *Absolution* which is said facing the people.

3. The Third General Episcopal Synod ruled that the taking of the Missal from the epistle side to the gospel side during the Gradual was optional. If this change is made, and if the celebrant does not himself make the transfer, the Gradual of the regular Eucharist, of the Nuptial Eucharist and Requiem Eucharist should be memorized.

4. The *Munda Cor Meum*, which must be recited while kneeling on the edge of the footpace whenever a priest acts as deacon at a High Celebration. Deacons should memorize this also.

5. The verses of the *Lavabo* in the Full Form, which are said facing away from the altar while engaged in cleansing the fingers.

6. The *Orate Fratres*, which is said facing the people. Note that the wording in the Shorter Form is different from that in the Longer.

7. The *Minor Benediction,* the *Sursum Corda* and the *Salutation of Peace*, all of which are said or sung while facing the people.

8. The verse, *Thee we adore....* following the Consecration, which is said or sung while kneeling on the footpace.

9. The words inviting the people to come forward to Communion: *Ye that desire....*

10. The words said while administering Communion to each person: *The Body of Our Lord Christ keep thee unto life eternal.*

11. If the missal has been changed to the gospel side at the Gradual and is moved back either just before or while saying: *Under the veil....* these words must be memorized.

12. The *Benediction* at the end, which is said facing the people.

13. The words used whenever incense is blessed: *Mayest thou be blessed by Him in Whose honour thou shalt be burned.*

All other portions of the Eucharistic service, and indeed all the services throughout the Liturgy, should be read from the book and not recited from memory, because the priest's recitation must be word perfect.

Tones of Voice

Three tones of voice are used in reciting the Eucharist:

1. *Silent*: The following portions are said either mentally or inaudibly upon the lips:

    A. The words: *Mayest thou be blessed....* used when the incense is blessed.

    B. Any private prayer before receiving Communion.

    C. The words just before receiving the Bread and Wine: *The Body of our Lord Christ keep me unto life eternal.*

2. *Moderate*: The following portions are said so that they may be heard in the sanctuary, but not necessarily over the whole church:

    A.The two prayers at the end of the second censing: *As this incense rises....* and *May the Lord enkindle....* on those occasions when the offertory hymn is sung during the censing.

    B. The verses said at the Lavabo.

    C. The hymn, Thee we adore.... when said at Low Celebration should be recited softly, but with sufficient strength so that the people may hear and follow.

    D. The words of administration at the Communion.

3. *Clear*: All other portions of the service should be said or intoned in a clearly articulated, well modulated voice, which can be heard by the people throughout the church. The Words of Consecration should be said slowly, in a reverently lowered voice, yet clear enough so that the people can hear. Clearness of pronunciation and freedom from slurring are essential. The priest should be careful that, while putting feeling into his tones, he does not become too dramatic, unctuous, pompous, or indulge in unusual fluctuations of the voice. Simplicity of utterance backed by real feeling will produce the best effects. Pay full attention to the meaning of the words; do not utter them mechanically. Care should also be taken to regulate the flow of speech; excessive speed painfully suggests the gabbling not infrequently heard in some churches, while excessive slowness is wearying. There is a pleasant medium between these two extremes, which is reverent and at the same time does not delay the progress of the Celebration. A speed which is brisk may be counterbalanced by suitable pauses, as at the end of sentences.

Whenever priest and people take part in versicle and response, the priest should commence his versicle the instant the people have finished theirs. There should be no unnecessary pauses between different parts of the service, but the whole should move smoothly to its close. Thorough knowledge of the ceremonial actions will eliminate those pauses sometimes noticed when a priest stops to read the rubrics in the Missal to see what he is to do next. He ought to know what to do at a glance without stopping to read the rubrics.

At a Sung Celebration, either a *Missa Cantata* or High, the celebrant need not actually intone those words which are not set to music. They may be said or intoned. If the service is intoned, it is customary to say reverently, not intone, the Words of Consecration.

Inclinations

Three degrees of bows are prescribed in the Liturgy:

1. The *simple bow* is made by bowing the head slightly and inclining the shoulders just enough to avoid any suggestion of stiffness. This bow is made on the following occasions:

A. While being aspersed at the Asperges.

B. During the words: *Glory be to the Father, and to the Son, and to the Holy Ghost*, whenever they may occur.

C. Before each Minor Benediction. The bow is made to the altar cross.

D. In the Canticle of the Full Form at the words in the seventh verse: *for the Lord our God is holy*.

E. In passing the middle of the altar while censing it, provided the Blessed Sacrament is *not* reserved in the tabernacle.

F. In the *Gloria in Excelsis* at the words: *we worship Thee, we give thanks to Thee*, and *receive our prayer*.

G. In the Creed at the words: *Jesus* and *is worshipped*.

H. Whenever the name *Jesus* is said.

I. Before and after being censed by a deacon or server, and before and after censing any person or persons.

J. When accepting or returning any liturgical object, such as a censer, cruet, ciborium with *un*-consecrated altar breads, the Book of Gospels, and so on.

K. When saluting or acknowledging the salute of a bishop, priest, or other minister.

L. When entering or leaving the sanctuary, provided the Blessed Sacrament is not reserved in the tabernacle.

M. When entering of leaving the sanctuary, provided the Blessed Sacrament is not reserved in the tabernacle.

N. In general, at such times as a genuflection would be made if the Blessed Sacrament were reserved in the tabernacle.

2. The *medium bow* is made not only by bending the head, but by bending the body slightly from the waist. This bow is made on the following occasions:

A. On arriving at the lowest step before the altar at the beginning of a service, provided that the Blessed Sacrament is not reserved in the tabernacle.

B. During the saying or singing of the *Kyrie*.

C. At the opening words of the *Gloria in Excelsis*. Note that the celebrant and his ministers bow after the opening gesture.

D. At the opening words of the Creed or Act of Faith. Note that the celebrant and his ministers bow after the opening gesture.

E. After the *Sursum Corda* while saying or singing: *Let us give thanks unto our Lord God*.

F. During the saying or singing of the *Sanctus*.

G. While uttering the Words of Consecration over the Bread and Wine.

H. During the whole of the prayer: This do we present ... eternal Sacrifice, and the corresponding prayer in the Shorter Form: *and we pray that Thou wouldst ... eternal Sacrifice*.

I. On leaving the altar at the end of the service, provided the Blessed Sacrament is not reserved in the tabernacle.

J. Before and after censing the Exposed Host at Solemn Benediction, while kneeling.

3. The *low bow* is prescribed only once in the Liturgy. It occurs during the singing of the *Tantum Ergo* in Solemn Benediction when a profound bow while kneeling, is made at the words: *This great Sacrament revere*.

In general it should be noted that in bowing, the hands are held joined before the breast, unless they are holding something. Whenever the head is bowed at a word or phrase it is done in the direction one is facing without turning to the cross. Do not bow while making the sign of the cross. Care should be taken not to bow too deeply or with great speed, as such inclinations look to the congregation either highly affected or jerky and therefore unpleasing. The biretta, if worn, should be removed while a bow is being made. At such times it is held by the right hand with its opening against the breast. If the hands are holding some object, bows may be made without removing the biretta.

Genuflections

To genuflect, first stand upright facing the altar, and join the hands before the breast, unless they are holding some object. Then, still keeping the body and head erect, bend the right knee and touch the floor with it exactly where the right foot was. Except in a few cases, to be noted hereafter, one rises at once, hence, in this manual where a genuflection is mentioned, the act includes the kneeling on one knee for an instant and the rising again immediately afterward. In cases where kneeling on the right knee is difficult or impossible because of some physical handicap, it is permissible to kneel on the left knee. The biretta, if worn, should be removed and held against the breast during the genuflection. Genuflections should be made facing the Blessed Sacrament, oblique genuflections being avoided. *It is not necessary either to bow or genuflect just after rising from a kneeling position before the altar.*

It is unnecessary to specify all of the occasions on .which a genuflection is made, because all special instances will be explicitly mentioned hereafter, but there are general rules which should be followed whether mentioned hereafter or not.

1. When the Blessed Sacrament is reserved at an altar; genuflection is always made upon reaching the sanctuary and leaving the altar. The only exception is that the cross bearer an his two attendant candle bearers do not genuflect when the former is carrying the processional cross.

2. In passing the middle line, either on the footpace or the sanctuary floor, a genuflection is always made if the Host is reserved. The exceptions to this rule are (a) when a priest is carrying the Host either in a monstrance or ciborium, (b) when the subdeacon of the Eucharist goes at certain times during the service to take his place on the epistle side

3. On entering or leaving a church in which the Host is reserved it is customary for all to genuflect either at the door of the church or in the aisle before going to one's seat.

The genuflection is prolonged on the following occasions:

1. At the Creed while saying: *and was incarnate of the Holy Ghost and the Virgin Mary and was made man.*

2. At the Consecration, before and after the Elevation of the Host, and before and after the Elevation of the Chalice, the genuflections are prolonged slightly so that the Consecration may be done reverently and the people given an opportunity to receive the holy influence of the Sacrament. On no account should there be that quick "bobbing up and down" which so disfigures the act of Consecration in some Churches.

3. At the Communion immediately after receiving the Host and after receiving the Wine, the time of genuflection should be somewhat prolonged. Some feel that it is more reverent to kneel on both knees at this time.

Care should be taken when genuflecting on the footpace that the right foot does not project over the edge and mar the beauty of the movement. A bishop does not remove his mitre while genuflecting, but he does remove his biretta.

Kneeling

At *Missa Cantata* in the Full Form the celebrant kneels, and at High Celebration the celebrant and his ministers kneel, during the singing of the antiphon and the first few verses of the Asperges Psalm. After he has aspersed himself and the altar, the celebrant rises and asperses the ministers, who thereupon rise together.

At Low Celebration and *Missa Cantata* the celebrant kneels, and at High Celebration the celebrant and his ministers kneel, during the saying of the Confiteor, and during the saying or singing of the hymn: *Thee we adore....* which follows the Consecration. The celebrant should take the kneeling position immediately after the Elevation of the Chalice and keep it until the beginning of the hymn: *O Come, all ye faithful....*

At High Celebration the deacon kneels on the edge of the footpace on the epistle side while saying the *Munda Cor Meum*.

Both the deacon and subdeacon at High Celebration kneel from the words: *Who the day before He suffered....* which precede the Consecration, until the beginning of the hymn: *O come, all ye faithful.* In the Full Form the deacon and subdeacon kneel during the prayer: *O Lord Jesu Christ, Who didst....* and remain kneeling to the time (except when giving the Salutation of Peace to another) when they receive Communion from the celebrant, whereupon they rise together. In the Shorter Form they kneel at the end of the prayer: *O Thou Who in this adorable Sacrament....* and remain kneeling until they receive Communion, whereupon they rise together. They kneel during the final Benediction.

In Benediction of the Most Holy Sacrament the celebrant and his assistants kneel during the singing of the *O Salutaris Hostia*, the *Tantum Ergo*, and the Versicles which follow. The celebrant then rises and begins the prayer: *O God, Who in the wonderful....* but the assistants remain kneeling.

In general when changing from a sitting position to that of kneeling, first stand and then kneel. It is not pleasing ceremonially to slide off the seat onto one's knees. Unless otherwise stated in this manual, the servers, choir and clergy follow the rubrics set forth in the Liturgy for the people in regard to standing, sitting, or kneeling.

Prostrations

In prostrating, the candidate for ordination lies stretched out upon the sanctuary floor, face downward or turned a little to one side, head towards the altar, with the arms bent and hands under the forehead. This position is taken by the ordinands during the singing of the Litany in the ordination of subdeacons, deacons and priests, and in the consecration of a bishop. A cushion is supplied to place under the elbows and head.

General Deportment and Other Movements

While standing at the altar or taking part in any ceremonial do not stoop or bend the body or head to one side. Be careful also not to acquire the irritating habit of swaying backwards and forwards on the feet. Do not lean against the altar or rest the hands, forearms, or elbows upon it. It is best during a service to refrain as much as possible from touching the altar. Hymn books should not be laid upon the altar, but only those objects expressly required by the rubrics. Do not kiss the altar, book, or any object connected with the ceremonial. The ceremonial kiss has been entirely eliminated from the Liberal Catholic Rite. Some of the clergy in putting on a stole, kiss the small cross in the middle in token of their allegiance to Christ, but this is optional.

While moving to and fro in the sanctuary it is well to avoid decided mannerisms, such as swaying of the shoulders, undue slowness or unseemly haste. Do not step sidewise, nor backwards for more than one short step, but turn and walk in the direction one is to go.

If a mistake is made in a ceremonial action that is unimportant, it is better left unrectified. If it must be corrected, do so in a manner as little noticeable as possible. If a correction is made without any appearance of haste or embarrassment and as if it were part of the service, it will usually pass unnoticed. Dignity and easy composure should mark all movements and gestures.

Unless actually ministering at the altar, avoid going up and down the altar steps. If it is necessary to pass from one side of the sanctuary to the other, do so on the sanctuary floor, not by making a short cut across the steps. When using the steps, go up and down them at right angles, not diagonally. Whenever anything has to be presented to, or received from, the celebrant or his ministers while at the altar, servers should approach them by the side steps, not those in front. On such occasions it is best that the server advance only to the second step and not to the footpace, provided the giving or receiving of the object can take place conveniently there. The altar steps should not be used as a place to deposit birettas and books during the service.

Ceremonial action in which a number of servers or clergy take part simultaneously, such as making the sign of the cross over oneself at certain parts of the service, facing the east together, kneeling together, and so on, should be practised until they synchronize accurately. To achieve this precision it is best to take the lead from the celebrant, the Master of Ceremonies, or one appointed for the purpose. Irregular timing of action in kneeling and rising is especially noticeable to the congregation, and mars greatly the beauty of ceremonial action.

There are four principles underlying successful ceremonial action:

1. Never make an unnecessary movement.
2. Learn to think and act as a group instead of as separate individuals.
3. Always know what action is coming next so as to be prepared.
4. Never cause unnecessary delays.

In turning to the people always turn to the right, that is, by the epistle side. In turning back to the altar, do so by the left, which is the exact reverse of the previous turn. Only on two occasions during the Holy Eucharist is a complete circle made by the celebrant—that is, turning to the people by the right and turning back to the altar by the right—at the *Orate Fratres* and at the end of the Benediction at the close of the service.

Whenever in a Canticle, Introit, Gradual or Psalm, the *Gloria Patri*: *Glory be to the Father, and to the Son. and to the Holy Ghost*, is said or sung, all, unless seated as a Vespers, should turn and face the east. At the same time a simple bow is made by all. The head is raised when the words *Holy Ghost* have been said or sung, but not until the words: *as it was ... world without end. Amen.* have been said or sung do all turn back to the normal position. All should face the east while saying any Creed or Act of Faith.

The Eyes

The dignity of ceremonial action can easily be marred by careless or thoughtless use of the eyes. It is not required in our rite that a priest should walk in procession with down-cast eyes and that he should look downward when turning to the people as, for example, at a Minor Benediction, but it is eminently desirable that he should not on any occasion let his gaze wander from side to side. When he turns during any ceremonial action to the people he should glance at the congregation firmly, steadily yet kindly, try-ing to remember that for the time he is acting as the representative of the Christ. Some celebrants prefer when turning to the people to direct their eyes at a point slightly above their heads. In processions particularly it is better to keep the gaze fixed quietly ahead instead of glancing at the people. While carrying the Host in procession the eyes of the

priest should be fixed on the Host (but not to the exclusion of seeing where he is going). This is also true of the assistants when in such a procession they hold the cope of the celebrant. Acolytes and choirmen should be instructed that when in procession or serv-ing at the altar, they should pay strict attention to the work they have in hand and not let their eyes wander over the congregation. Care should be taken especially not to stare thoughtlessly at the people who come forward to receive Communion. The altar should be the absorbing centre of attraction in every church.

Positions of the Hands

The position of the celebrant's hands, especially during the celebration of the Holy Eucharist, is important.

DIAGRAM 4

Joined before the breast. (Diagram 4) This is the normal position of the hands throughout the service, whether standing, walking, bowing or kneeling, unless the hands be otherwise engaged. In this position the hands are joined palm to palm, finger to finger. The thumbs may either be straight and touching one another or crossed, the right thumb over the left. (The Third General Episcopal Synod ruled that this was optional. Bishop Leadbeater, because of the flow of certain forces, preferred the position where the thumbs are placed side by side. The Roman Rite prescribes the thumbs in the crossed position.) The joined hands are turned forwards and very slightly upwards from the horizontal. (Plate 1, Figs. 1 and 2)

In the Eucharist from the time of the Consecration of the Host until the Ablutions the thumb and forefinger are according to Roman usage kept together (Plate 1, Figs. 3 and 5) except when it is necessary to pick up the Host. This is to ensure that any small Particles of the Host that may be clinging to the skin be not brushed off if some other object is contacted. Hence it is that when the hands are joined between the Consecration and the Ablutions, the thumb and forefinger of each hand are still kept together, leaving only the palms and the remaining three fingers in actual contact, (Plate 1, Fig. 3) The Liberal Catholic Church enjoins the utmost caution in everything that concerns the handling of the Host, and prefers that this custom be observed. It leaves the strict observance of this rule when elevating the Chalice to the discretion of the priest. It asks that its priests exhibit care, unfailing reverence and self-recollection in all that pertains to the handling of the Host.

The hands are always joined before the breast for *Let us Pray*, but outspread at the level of the shoulders for the prayer itself.

Outspread, or Extended at the level of the shoulders. (Plate 1, Fig. 4) This position is prescribed during the recitation of the Collects and during most of the Canon of the Eucharist. The hands are held apart before the breast, the palms facing one another, the fingers extended but held together, at about the height, and in front of, the shoulders. The elbows are kept at the sides of the body.

Between the Consecration and the Ablutions, on account of the thumb and forefinger of each hand being joined, only the remaining three fingers of each hand should be extended when the hands are outspread at the level of the shoulders. (Plate 1, Fig. 5)

This position when the hands are outspread is prescribed either (1) when the priest desires to spread force out over a congregation as at a Minor Benediction, at the *Orate Fratres*; or at the Salutation of Peace in the Shorter Form, or (2) when he receives force flowing from the Sacred Elements, the Angels or the Christ and desires to pass it on to the people. In the case of a Minor Benediction, the *Orate Fratres*, and the Salutation of Peace in the Shorter Form, the priest does not disjoin his hands until he has faced the people. He holds them in this position until the people have commenced the response, then joins his hands and, as the response begins, turns back to the altar.

Extended and raised. At the beginning of the Gloria and of the Creed or Act of Faith, the hands are first joined together before the breast, then lifted together until they are above the head. Immediately they are separated and, as they are brought down to the breast again, the lines of movement are those which would trace a heart-shaped form. This action should be completed by the time the word "God" is reached, whereupon the celebrant (with deacon and subdeacon) bows. The movement should be done slowly and gracefully so as to make one continuous and harmonious whole. The gesture is one of exultation and rejoicing.

While facing the people and saying or singing: *Lift up your hearts*, the hands, which are already extended in the Minor Benediction, are raised upwards and then joined before the breast. On this occasion, however, the palms are turned upwards so as to suggest the lifting up of the heart to God.

Right hand extended towards the people. (Plate 1, Fig. 6) At the Absolution and whenever blessing the people as at the final Benediction in the Eucharistic service, the priest holds up his right hand with the palm towards the people. The elbow is bent somewhat so that the forearm slopes upwards, the fingers are all extended and also point upwards. A bishop in giving Absolution or blessing the people or any object extends only the thumb, first and second fingers, the third and little fingers being bent. (Plate 3, Fig. 6) When giving a blessing, the palm of the hand, not the edge, should be turned towards the person or object blessed. (Plate 2, Fig. 1 and 2)

In general, whenever the hands are unoccupied, they should be joined before the breast. When the right hand alone is occupied, as in the case when the sign of the cross is being made, or a blessing is being given, the left hand should be held at or near the breast. (Plate 1, Fig. 6) In standing with the biretta in the right hand, the left should hang at the side. In sitting both hands are usually placed on the knees, and if the biretta is held for a time while being seated it should be held on the right knee.

Sign of the Cross

In making the sign of the cross over himself the priest should first join the hands before the breast. Immediately the right hand is raised (the left being dropped a little and held over the breast) and, with fingers extended and united, palm towards himself, he touches his forehead, solar plexus, left shoulder, right shoulder. After the Consecration and until the Ablutions, because the thumb and forefinger of each hand are joined, he touches himself with the remaining three fingers of the right hand, taking care that the thumb and forefinger do not brush the chasuble.

When the priest blesses any object he turns the palm of his hand towards it. If he is celebrating the Eucharist, it is well while making the sign of the cross over the altar to hold back slightly with the left hand the edge of the chasuble which falls over the right arm, so that it may not brush the altar or the corporal.

The sign of the cross is not made by a sweeping circular motion in the direction of the object, nor by the fingers only, but by an even movement of the hand and arm in two intersecting straight lines over the object. These lines should be on the same level or plane and of about the same length, the equal-armed Greek cross being used as the sign, not the Latin cross. In making the sign of the cross the hand moves as follows: 1 to 3; 3 to 2; 2 to L; L to R. The underscored movements are made with intention; the others are merely connecting movements.

$$1$$

$$L \quad 2 \quad R$$

$$3$$

In general the length of the lines of the cross should not exceed the width of the object blessed. When made over the Host and Chalice together, the first line should be traced in the air from about the far edge of the Chalice to the near edge of the Host, passing over the centre of each. The second line should come between the Host and Chalice and be the same length as the first. When making the sign over the Host or Chalice care should be taken not to strike the Chalice. In making the sign over the mouth of the Chalice, either with the entire Host or with a Particle, the whole hand and not merely the fingers should move, but the limits of the cross should not extend much beyond the rim of the cup.

The pugnal cross, traced by the extended thumb (the other fingers being clenched) is prescribed several times in the Liturgy. As the priest or deacon announces the Gospel he makes the sign of the cross with the right thumb over the book where the Gospel begins. Immediately after the announcement, he and all present cross themselves thrice with the thumb, once over the forehead, the lips, the breast. These crosses are quite small but should be made clearly and with definite intent.

A cross is made with the thumb when anointing with oil at Baptism, Confirmation, Unction and the Service of Healing.

Salutation of Peace

The Salutation of Peace is given in two ways. At Low Celebration of both Forms of the Holy Eucharist and at a Missa Cantata of the Shorter Form, the celebrant turns towards the people and with extended hands says (or sings): *The Peace of the Lord be always with you.* He joins his hands as the people respond, and turns back to the altar. (The Second General Episcopal Synod ruled that this way of giving the Salutation of Peace might be used at a *Missa Cantata* or High Celebration of the Full Form at the discretion of the celebrant.)

At High Celebration in the Full Form the celebrant may give the Salutation of Peace to the deacon and subdeacon in the following manner: He places his hands one on either shoulder of the kneeling deacon and says in a low tone of voice: *The Peace of the Lord be always with you.* The deacon, who in the meanwhile has touched with the tips of his fingers the elbows of the priest, responds in a low voice: *And with thy spirit.* The celebrant immediately turns to the subdeacon, by way of the altar, and gives him the Salutation in the same way. The deacon and subdeacon rise together. The deacon goes to the first in the line of kneeling priests (if any) and gives him the Salutation. (The one giving the Salutation always stands, the one receiving it always kneels.) This priest rises and gives it to the one next to him, and so on until all in the line have received the Salutation. In the meantime the subdeacon has gone to the first acolyte at the epistle end of the line of acolytes and given him the Salutation. The acolytes pass it on from one to another, the last acolyte rising, facing the people, extending his or her hands and singing or saying the words of the Salutation. (It is advisable to see that the acolytes are so arranged that the last one in the line can sing!)

In those churches where there are many acolytes the celebrant may give the Salutation to the first of the clergy (having of course first given it to the deacon and subdeacon), the deacon to the first of the acolytes at the epistle end, and the subdeacon to an acolyte about the middle of the line. This acolyte in the middle thereupon rises and gives the Salutation to the person on his left and so on. Either the last acolyte on the gospel end of the line, or some one appointed for the purpose, such as the Master of Ceremonies, rises, faces the people with extended hands, and sings or says the words of Salutation.

When a bishop is present, the celebrant gives the Salutation as usual first to the deacon and subdeacon, then to the bishop. It is customary in some churches for the bishop to go forward and kneel at the footpace at the time the other clergy kneel before the altar just before the Salutation. When this is done, matters are simplified, because the celebrant need not give the Salutation to the Master of Ceremonies to convey to the bishop, but can turn and give the Salutation to him direct When the bishop comes forward in this way to the footpace, he remains kneeling there until he has received Communion. Non-communicating bishops receive the Salutation either from the Master of Ceremonies or the Deacon. The celebrant does not leave the altar for this purpose.

When a priest gives the Salutation to a bishop he touches the elbows of the bishop, while the bishop places his fingers on the shoulders of the priest. When bishops exchange the Salutation, each touches the left shoulder and right elbow of the other.

Other arrangements may be made in passing the Salutation from one to another in the sanctuary. The general rule is that it should be given first to those of highest rank and then passed on one by one to the youngest or lowest in rank. The Salutation may be given while the clergy and servers kneel in their places at the sides of the sanctuary. This is frequently the best way in order to avoid movement and confusion.

At High Celebration in both forms, when using the first way of Salutation, the celebrant gives the Salutation first to the deacon, then to the subdeacon and lastly to the people. It may be given to the people by the deacon, but preferably by the celebrant.

Using the Censer

Incense should be used at all Celebrations of the Holy Eucharist including Low Celebration, whether in church or private. It should be used at other services as prescribed in the Liturgy. When using incense, it is well to employ two servers when they are available, one to swing the censer and the other to carry the boat. One server can perform both functions, but it is more difficult. On the greater Festivals and at Vespers and Solemn Benediction there may be two thurifers.

Incense should be blessed immediately after it is sprinkled on the glowing charcoal and not while it is in the boat. If a bishop celebrates he invariably blesses the incense. If a priest celebrates he blesses the incense unless a bishop be present. If there be more than one bishop present in the sanctuary when a priest is celebrating, the bishop of highest rank in that diocese blesses the incense. (The thurifer may add incense to the censer at any time that the rubrics do not require the celebrant or bishop to do so. Normally he will need to do this only at the Prayer of Consecration.) The only occasions on which incense is not blessed is when it is placed in the censer during the time the Blessed Sacrament is exposed on the altar as at Solemn Benediction, or while the Host is being carried in procession through the church.

Charcoal for the censer is prepared by holding one or two squares or pieces in a flame suitable for the purpose until one surface of the charcoal is glowing, The squares of charcoal may be held in the flame, either with the aid of steel tongs or forceps, or still better, in a coarse wire basket supplied with a handle, which is sold for the purpose. In placing the charcoal in the censer the glowing side is of course turned uppermost. Care should be taken to see that the boat contains enough incense for the service. When "self-light" charcoal is used, it is necessary only to light several places on the edge from whence the glowing will spread on its own over the entire surface.

While waiting for the censer to be used, the thurifer usually holds it by the chains in his left hand, swinging it gently with his right hand to keep the charcoal red.

To hasten this he may slightly lift the cover of the censer.

When the incense is to be blessed, the thurifer accompanied by the boat bearer, goes to the celebrant, who (if at the altar) faces southward towards the epistle end of the footpace. The thurifer carries the censer in his left hand by grasping the chains just below the disk to which they are attached, or by putting his thumb through the disk ring. On reaching the priest he bows slightly, lifts the cover of the censer about five or six inches by pulling up the chain connected with the cover. He grips this chain between the thumb and forefinger of the left hand to prevent the cover from sliding down again. With his right hand he grasps the chains about midway and lifts the censer to a convenient height.

Meanwhile the boat bearer presents the opened boat with spoon to the celebrant. (Some celebrants prefer that the boat be presented at High Celebration to the deacon who in turn holds it open conveniently before the celebrant. Either way is permissible.) The celebrant with spoon sprinkles incense on the charcoal and blesses it while saying silently: *Mayest thou be* ✠ *blessed by Him in whose honour thou shalt be burned.* (The boat is now returned by the deacon if he has been holding it.) The boat bearer retires to the sanctuary floor. The thurifer lowers the cover, pushes down the ring surrounding the chains until it encircles the top of the cover, and hands the censer to the celebrant (at High Celebration to the deacon, who gives it to the celebrant). The priest with the left hand grasps the chains just below the disk, while with the right hand he takes hold of the chains either about four inches above the shut cover if it be the globular type of censer, or nearly at the level of the top of the cover if it be an elongated or Gothic type of censer. The most convenient way to hold the censer is to pass all the chains between the first and second fingers of the right hand, the second, third and fourth fingers, held together, being under the chains.

To cense any person or object, the left hand is lowered until it is against the lower part of the breast. The censer is then lifted with the right hand until it is about the level of the throat or face. Now by a slight movement of the wrist of the right hand, assisted by an outward pressure of the fingers, a decided swing is given to the censer, which, upon its backward sweep should strike with an audible click or ring against the taut chains. One forward and backward movement with its accompanying click constitutes what is called a swing.

One swing is given towards each of the six large candles on the altar. After each such swing the arms are slightly lowered until the next swing is made.

Three short single swings with a slight pause between each, are given when any of the clergy of lower rank than deacon, or when any of the servers, are censed.

Three short double swings, that is, six swings arranged in three groups of two each, are given to a deacon or a priest when present in the sanctuary, to the officiating subdeacon (even when a cleric), and to the Book of Gospels at the reading of the Gospel.

Three short triple swings, that is, nine swings arranged in three groups of three each, are given to the Most Holy Sacrament at Solemn Benediction, to the altar cross at the time the altar is censed, and to a bishop when present in the sanctuary.

When there are several priests present in the sanctuary it is permissible to cense them collectively with three short double swings. The censing of groups of deacons and subdeacons may be handled similarly. The bishops, if more than one are present in the sanctuary, are always censed individually.

At the time of being censed, stand erect, with hands joined before the breast in the usual manner. Simple bows are exchanged before and after being censed. A bishop, while being censed, wears his biretta or mitre, but does not hold his crozier. A priest does not wear his biretta while being censed. Whenever a group as such is censed, the members thereof should be on the alert to rise together, bow together, sit together. Do not hold any book or other object in the hands while being censed.

When the thurifer censes the people he should go to the middle to stand either behind the communion rail or at the entrance to the chancel. He bows slightly to the people, takes the censer with one or both hands at the disk and makes three long sweeping swings towards the people, the first down the middle of the church, the second to the left and the third to the right. (If space does not permit the long swings, he may use three short ones instead.) After censing the people, he again bows to them and returns to his place.

Cross Bearer

The bearer of the processional cross should be a senior server, preferably in Orders. In procession he should be careful to hold the cross above his head, to carry it facing straight forward and sloping a little in that direction. The cross bearer (and his attendant candle bearers) never genuflects when carrying the cross. Thus, on entering or leaving the sanctuary, he only bows slightly to the altar, even though the Blessed Sacrament may be reserved in the tabernacle. It is customary during the service to stand the cross on the epistle side, held by clips or some other device, so that it faces due east and west. The arrangements in the church may make this position of the cross impossible, but it should always be placed so that it may be seen by the congregation.

Candle Bearers

Whenever possible, candle bearers in procession should walk in pairs and not singly, but not unless the two are nearly of the same height. It looks better if a uniform method of holding the candlesticks is adopted. Thus the bearer on the right of a pair of servers should hold the base of his candlestick with his left hand and grasp the candlestick half-way up with his right. His partner should hold the candlestick in a similar manner, but with the hands reversed.

The Crozier Bearer

The crozier bearer to a bishop should cover the palms of his hands with the loose ends of the vimpa before taking hold of the crozier. The practical reason for this is to prevent the shaft of the crozier becoming contaminated with perspiration. The crozier is carried in procession with its head above the head of the server, and its volute curving forward, in the direction the bearer is walking. The crozier bearer always walks in front of the bishop except during a procession with the Blessed Sacrament at which the bishop carries the monstrance. In this case the crozier bearer walks in front of the thurifer, or thurifers. Care should be taken in handing the crozier to the bishop, that he need not turn it after receiving it in order that the curve of the volute may face towards the people. During a service, if the bishop is celebrating, his crozier is placed between clips, or held in some other way, either at the gospel end of the altar or on the east wall near the gospel end. If the bishop is seated at his throne during the service the crozier should be placed in a holder to the left of his throne.

Master of Ceremonies

The Master of Ceremonies should, if possible, be a priest. He must be thoroughly conversant with every detail of the ceremony which he directs, and be fully acquainted with the rules of ecclesiastical rank and etiquette.

The Procession

At Low Celebration, when a hymn is not sung, it is not customary to go round the church in procession, but to go either direct from the vestry to the sanctuary if there be a communicating door, or from the vestry door to the sanctuary gates by the shortest way. On other occasions, the shorter way from the vestry to the sanctuary may be chosen if the congregation is very small.

When a procession moves round a church, it is not necessary that it actually skirt the walls of the building, unless that is the most convenient route. It may move down a side aisle to the west end and return to the sanctuary by the central aisle. Or, if the vestry is at the west end of the church, it may move through the midst of the people along the central aisle only from the west end to the sanctuary. Whenever the route of a procession is in the form of a loop, that loop must be made by a clockwise movement, not the reverse.

Processions vary widely according to the size of the Church and the solemnity of the Festival. In a small church where there is one priest and a few acolytes to assist, the procession to the sanctuary on an ordinary Sunday might be as follows:

Thurifer
Cross bearer
Two candle bearers
Celebrant

On greater occasions in the same church the procession might be expanded to something like the following:

Thurifer

Boat bearer

Candle bearer - Cross bearer - Candle bearer

Choir

(In pairs)

Candle bearer - Candle bearer

Celebrant

Banner bearer

In a somewhat larger church where on greater Festivals it is possible to have a High Celebration, the procession would be more elaborate.

Thurifer

Boat bearer

Candle bearer - Cross bearer - Candle bearer Banner bearer

Choir

(In pairs)

Candle bearer - Candle bearer

Subdeacon

Deacon

Candle bearer - Candle bearer

Celebrant

Banner bearer

It is impossible to indicate all the possible variations; but it will be helpful to describe in detail an extremely elaborate procession such as would take place only on rare occasions even in a cathedral church, because from such a description sufficient information can be drawn to organize any kind of procession.

There are a few general principles to keep in mind which will make simple the organization of even a very long procession.

1. Those who have a function to perform in the procession take their place without reference to their ecclesiastical rank. Such special functions include those of Master of Ceremonies (M.C.), thurifer, boat bearer, cross bearer, candle bearer, crozier bearer, mitre bearer, banner bearer, officiating subdeacon, officiating deacon, celebrant, and, when there is a procession of the Blessed Sacrament, canopy bearers. Thus a crozier bearer, whether cleric or priest, takes the same relative position in the procession.

2. Those who have no special function take their place in order of rank, those of lower rank preceding those of higher.

3. Those of the same rank, servers, choir, lesser clergy, arrange themselves in pairs according to size, those of nearly the same height walking together, pairs of lesser height in front of those of greater height.

4. The Master of Ceremonies may take any position in the procession ahead of the celebrant and his ministers. He may even lead the procession, which is sometimes advisable at the Consecration of a Church, when there are several halts to be made for the consecration of Ray Crosses.

The following points should be noted. There may be two *thurifers*. In such case they walk side by side, swinging the censers alternately, so that first one censer swings forward, then the other, an even rhythm being maintained. The thurifer always leads the procession, unless the Master of Ceremonies elects to do so. It is therefore essential that the thurifer should know the number of verses in the processional hymn and so gauge the pace at which the procession moves that the celebrant arrives at the altar just before the end of the last verse. It is advisable for the thurifer to observe from time to time whether the procession is following with the proper distance between groups. On such occasions he should look round in as little noticeable a manner as possible. (The habit of others looking round in the procession should be checked.) Immediately after, sometimes with the thurifer(s) comes the *boat bearer*. Following him walks the *cross bearer* with the processional cross, flanked on either side by a candle bearer. The cross bearer and his two attendant candle bearers never genuflect while he is carrying the cross, but only give reverence to the altar with a simple bow. The two best-trained and attentive servers should be selected for the function of candle bearers to the cross, and, whenever in the service, two candle bearers are required, they should be the ones to assist. The other candle bearers in the procession should take part in the service only when more than two acolytes with candles are required. During the service, the candlesticks which were carried on either side of the processional cross are placed, either on the credence table, or one at either end of it. These candles remain lighted during the service. If the aisles are inconveniently narrow for three persons to walk abreast the two candle bearers to the processional cross may walk behind the cross bearer. Any additional candle bearers are paired off according to height and placed in the procession as follows: (a) immediately preceding the celebrant, if a priest, or his crozier bearer, if a bishop; (b) preceding the crozier bearer of any other bishop present; (c) preceding any groups which may form part of the procession, such as a group of priests, choir, etc. The *crozier bearer* walks immediately in front of the bishop whose crozier he is carrying. The *mitre bearer*, if any, walks beside the crozier bearer. *Banners* may be carried either by servers or choirmen. If there be only one banner it is usually carried at the end of the procession. The *Subdeacon and Deacon* of the Eucharist or the two assistants at Vespers and Benediction may walk one behind the other, the Subdeacon preceding the Deacon; or side by side, the deacon on the right. When there is a long procession it is advisable for the Master of Ceremonies to supervise its formation. Those taking part in the procession should be on the alert to keep about three feet from the individual or pair immediately in front. Unequal distances between the units in a procession are unsightly and mar the beauty of the service. No book is ever carried in procession by a server who has some other object to carry, such as a candlestick, crozier or banner. Those with their hands free may carry hymn books, but liturgies and service books should be placed beforehand on the seats in the chancel and sanctuary. Services should begin *punctually* at the appointed time, the procession starting when the singing of the first line of the hymn begins.

Bishops in procession bless the people from time to time as they move through the church. This is not done on any occasion by priests in procession.

The chart which follows indicates the order of a very elaborate procession. Only that part of the chart which applies to the conditions of any given church at a given festival need be taken into consideration. Thus if no bishop be present, that portion of the chart referring to bishops may be disregarded, the rest of the chart indicating the relative order in procession of the different servers and groups.

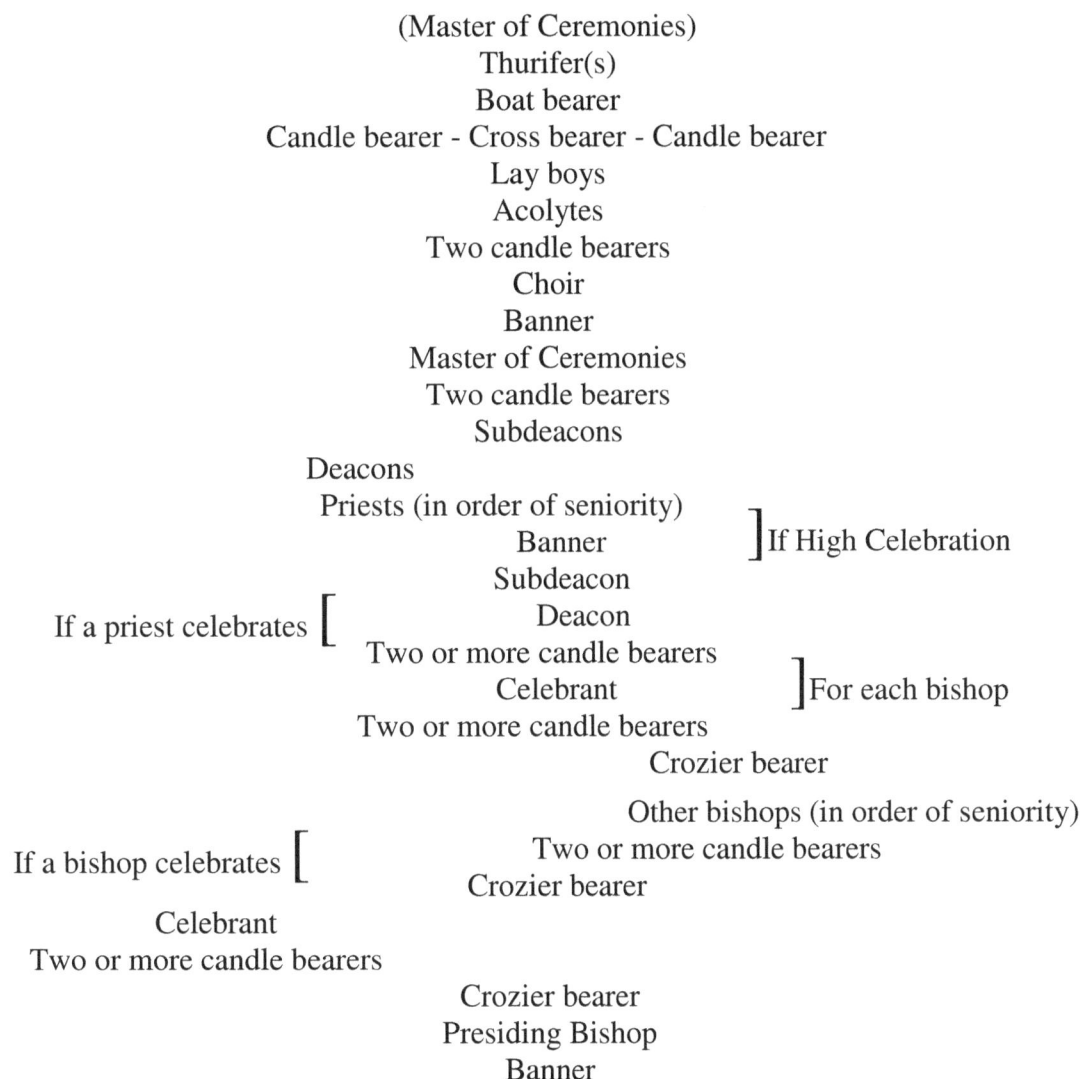

(Master of Ceremonies)
Thurifer(s)
Boat bearer
Candle bearer - Cross bearer - Candle bearer
Lay boys
Acolytes
Two candle bearers
Choir
Banner
Master of Ceremonies
Two candle bearers
Subdeacons
Deacons
Priests (in order of seniority)
Banner] If High Celebration
Subdeacon
If a priest celebrates [Deacon
Two or more candle bearers
Celebrant] For each bishop
Two or more candle bearers
Crozier bearer

Other bishops (in order of seniority)
Two or more candle bearers
If a bishop celebrates [Crozier bearer

Celebrant
Two or more candle bearers

Crozier bearer
Presiding Bishop
Banner

In the following description of what takes place when the procession reaches the sanctuary, it should be understood that if the Host be not reserved in the tabernacle a medium bow is made by all instead of the usual genuflection. It should further be understood that there are two possible arrangements in connection with the actions of the various servers after they genuflect upon entering the sanctuary gates: either (1) they go immediately two by two as they enter to put away their candles, extinguish them and return in file as a group to their assigned places in the sanctuary, or (2) they go with their candles to stand at assigned places until the celebrant has reached the altar, at which time they genuflect with the celebrant and go to put their candles away, extinguish them, and return to the places assigned them during the service itself. Which plan is adopted will depend upon local conditions, the size and arrangements of the sanctuary, and the number of servers.

When the gates of the chancel or sanctuary (as the case may be) are reached, they are opened by the thurifer. Entering therein, he (and the boat bearer) genuflect and go either to put the censer in the place where it hangs during the service, and stand at his assigned place, or he stands at some convenient place on the epistle side holding the censer until the celebrant genuflects.

The cross bearer and his two attendant candle bearers bow to the cross upon entering the sanctuary. In some churches he stands on one side (usually the epistle side) until the Processional hymn is finished and everyone has entered the gates. He then places the cross in its holder. In other churches, where the choir is seated outside the sanctuary in the chancel, the cross bearer, on reaching the sanctuary gates, turns and faces the oncoming procession, still holding the cross upright. The moment the last of the choir has genuflected and turned to go to their seats and the oncoming clergy are near at hand, the cross bearer goes to put the cross in its accustomed place, thereby allowing the clergy to enter the sanctuary. In either case, the attendant candle bearers either go to put their candles on the credence and stand in their assigned places for the service, or go with the candles to the places where they are to stand with the other candle bearers until the time of genuflecting as a group with the celebrant.

The servers and acolytes without candles go to their assigned places.

The members of the choir genuflect two by two, turn one to the epistle side, one to the gospel side, and go to their seats.

The Banners are taken to the places where they stand during the service.

The other members of the clergy, including the Master of Ceremonies, genuflect and go to their seats.

The Deacon and Subdeacon of the Eucharist do not genuflect, but take their stations before the lowest altar step, leaving a space between them for the celebrant. They genuflect with him, after removing their birettas, then hand their birettas either to the Master of Ceremonies or to a server. The celebrant genuflects as soon as he arrives in the middle before the lowest altar step, unless a bishop follows, in which case he pauses until all are in the sanctuary before genuflecting.

Bishops who have followed or preceded the celebrant, genuflect upon entering the gates and their crozier bearers with them. The latter should stand to the left of the bishop, a little to the rear. If the celebrant is a bishop the crozier bearer places the crozier in its place at the gospel end of the altar, unless the Shorter or Brief Form of the Asperges is being used in which case he waits until after the Invocation before putting the crozier away. The croziers of any other bishops are taken to their thrones and placed in the holders there.

If the second arrangement in regard to the candle bearers has been followed, by the time the last of the procession has entered the sanctuary, there will be a row of servers carrying lighted candles standing facing the altar. This row may be arranged in front of the sanctuary rail, an equal number of acolytes being stationed on either side of the gates. When the celebrant genuflects, all of the candle bearers as a group genuflect with him, go out in file, deposit their candlesticks, extinguish the candles, return in file, genuflect together when they reach their assigned places. If there are but few servers, they may remain in the sanctuary and extinguish their candles there.

The procession leaves the sanctuary at the end of the service in the same order that it entered. If the procession is a short one and there is room for it to form between the lowest altar step and the gates, all arrange themselves in processional order facing the altar, with the thurifer at the gates. All genuflect with the celebrant, except the cross bearer and attendant candle bearers, turn by the right and proceed out of the sanctuary, sometimes round the church, but more often by the short way to the vestry. When the procession is too long to form in this way, the thurifer and cross bearer take their positions at the gates, the candle bearers go in pairs to those parts of the sanctuary and chancel where they can most easily join the procession, all others remaining in their places, except the clergy who group themselves in the middle before the altar. Again, when the signal to start is given by the genuflecting of the celebrant, all genuflect with him (they are of course facing the altar) turn and join the procession as it forms and pass out the gates. If the procession is very long, it is sometimes necessary to start it before the celebrant genuflects. This is usually done by signal from the Master of Ceremonies or the thurifer.

The *Order of a Procession with the Most Blessed Sacrament* is somewhat different, although the general rules governing the organization of processions still prevail. There may be two thurifers (there usually are two on greater Festivals celebrated in large churches) but they walk backwards immediately in front of the monstrance censing the Blessed Sacrament, instead of walking at the head of the procession. The celebrant carrying the monstrance walks under a canopy, flanked by two assistants or the Deacon and Subdeacon, who hold up the corners of the cope. The order of the usual procession is much as follows: Cross bearer, flanked by two acolytes bearing candles; choir; banner bearer; two candle bearers; clergy, if any are present, arranged in order of rank; two candle bearers; thurifer or thurifers; celebrant walking under a canopy, flanked by deacon and subdeacon or two assistants; banner bearer. If there be a Master of Ceremonies, he usually walks immediately behind the cross bearer. The Cantor walks in that part of the procession in accordance with his status, and, if in Orders, according to his rank. The canopy, according to its style and size, is carried by two, four or six servers, who should be vested in cassock and surplice. It is advisable for the cross bearer, who controls the rate at which the procession moves, to walk forward moderately as he leaves the sanctuary until the procession is extended in proper order and the celebrant is under the canopy. He should then slacken his pace so that the procession moves very slowly among the people. The procession should of course go round the church clockwise, that is, down the church on the epistle side to the west end and back to the sanctuary either by the gospel side or the centre aisle. During the procession the cantor sings all the odd-numbered verses of the Litany and the people the even-numbered. As the thurifer walks backwards facing the Host, he should cense It with long sweeping swings. If there are two thurifers, they walk side by side and swing alternately. It may be necessary by the time the west end of the church is reached to replenish the charcoal with incense. This may be done by the boat bearer or one of the servers. The incense is not blessed. During the procession the celebrant should keep his eyes fixed on the Host. The cross bearer periodically must notice whether the procession is moving too fast, thereby causing gaps between its various units, or too slowly. The rate of movement should be so timed that the celebrant can reach the altar during the singing of the verse next before the last in the Litany. As the canopy bearers reach the sanctuary gates, they stop, and each man in his place turns to face the altar. As soon as the celebrant has moved from beneath the canopy and stepped within the gates, the canopy is folded, carried to its place by one person, the bearers genuflecting and returning to their seats where they kneel.

If the procession with the Blessed Sacrament take place during a celebration of the Holy Eucharist, the Second General Episcopal Synod recommended that the procession start after the singing of the *Adeste Fideles*.

Ecclesiastical Rank and Etiquette

No one may celebrate the Holy Eucharist who has not been ordained priest, and it is desirable, when possible, that priests should serve at High Celebrations as Deacon and Subdeacon. In any case the one serving as Deacon must have been ordained to that Order. In case of necessity it is permissible for one of lower rank than an ordained subdeacon to serve as Subdeacon at High Celebration, but no one must serve in that capacity who has not been ordained cleric.

None lower in rank than a priest shall officiate at the following offices and services, with the exceptions noted hereafter: Administration of Holy Communion with the Reserved Sacrament, Vespers, Benediction of the Most Holy Sacrament, Confession and Absolution, The Service of Healing, Holy Unction and Communion of the Sick, The Burial of the Dead, Admission to the Liberal Catholic Church, The Admission of a Singer, and The Admission of a Server. None lower in rank than a priest may use the Forms of The Blessing of Holy Water, The Blessing of Objects in General and The Blessing of a House. Under certain restrictions to be noted hereafter a Deacon may officiate at Vespers, The Marriage Service, administer Communion using the Form for the Administration of Holy Communion with the Reserved Sacrament, and may use the Form In Extremis. He also, if requested by the priest, may administer Communion at the Holy Eucharist and carry Communion to the sick. In the absence of the priest, he may administer baptism using the full service as printed in the Liturgy. In case of grave necessity a cleric of any rank or a layman, may baptize, using the formula given in the chapter on baptisms. It is preferred that a priest conduct the services of Prime and Complin, but it is permissible for a cleric of any rank, or even a layman, to act as ministrant.

Whenever possible, especially in large churches, the Master of Ceremonies should be a priest. Certain functions may then be delegated to him by the celebrant. When questions of procedure arise before a service, they should be addressed to the M. C. and not to the celebrant. The general rule is that no one should speak to the celebrant before the service, especially while he is vesting, unless it is really necessary.

Experience has shown that it is inadvisable to ordain boys and men to Minor Orders unless there is some possibility that they are fitted by character and may be prepared by training to advance to higher Orders. Therefore it is best, until the possible candidate can be tested and studied, not to present him to a bishop for ordination to Minors, but for the priest to admit him using the Form for The Admission of a Server. His work in the sanctuary will not be affected by the lack of ordination to Minors and his hopes for the future, oftentimes impossible of fulfillment, will not be raised.

The following services, blessings and consecrations are performed only by bishops: Confirmation, Conferring of Holy Orders, Blessing of Holy Oils, Consecration of a Chalice and Paten, Consecration of an Altar Stone, Laying the Foundation Stone of a Church, Consecration of a Church, Consecration of Altar Jewels, Blessing of a Church Bell.

The following are the ranks of the clergy in ascending order according to the spiritual powers conferred at ordination: clerics, doorkeepers, readers, exorcists, acolytes, subdeacons, deacons, priests and bishops. The general rule is that those of higher rank take precedence over all clergy of lower rank, and, where two of the clergy are of equal rank, the one ordained first takes precedence over the other. The exceptions to this rule are:

1. A priest in charge of a parish takes precedence over all visiting priests, and all priests who may assist him for the time being.

2. A priest representing his bishop as vicar-general takes precedence over all other priests in the diocese of that bishop, but not elsewhere except by courtesy of the priest whose parish he may visit.

3. The rank of a bishop varies according to his jurisdiction. In ascending order of precedence the different ranks are as follows: bishop acting as assistant to a diocesan bishop; bishop in charge of a diocese; bishop acting as assistant to a provincial bishop; bishop in charge of a province; the Presiding Bishop of the Liberal Catholic Church. (The titles used to designate these various offices may change from time to time as the Church grows, but the functions will remain the same.) All bishops are equal so far as their spiritual powers are concerned and so the various titles indicate only jurisdiction. Hence outside his own diocese a diocesan bishop does not take precedence over the bishop in charge of the diocese in which he may be, even though the date of his consecration is earlier. In the same way a Regionary Bishop outside his own province does not take precedence over the bishop of any territory he may visit, even though he may have been much longer in the episcopate. The Presiding Bishop, by virtue of his international office, takes precedence over all other bishops of the Liberal Catholic Church throughout the world.

If the Ordinary be present in a church of his province or diocese, or an Auxiliary Bishop charged with a mission, he has the right to officiate. A bishop *outside his own jurisdiction* does not possess any inherent right to officiate in any Liberal Catholic Church. If he is invited to officiate, it is a matter of courtesy, not of right. As a matter of courtesy and correct procedure, a priest would not invite a priest or bishop of another diocese or province to officiate and exercise the functions of his office without first consulting his own bishop. The same rule applies to the invitation of clergy or laymen from other denominations to officiate or preach. Although visiting clergy and servers do not take a place by right in the church they are visiting, yet on most occasions the priest in charge will invite them to assist.

Subdeacons, deacons and priests are entitled to use the title of "Reverend," Vicars-General use the title "Very Reverend," bishops "Right Reverend." The Presiding Bishop may use the title of "Most Reverend."

Seating Arrangements

The priests, other clergy and servers may sit on either side of the sanctuary according to the provisions of the church. It will be found most convenient to seat the cross bearer, candle bearers, altar servers, thurifer and boat bearer on the epistle side. In cathedral churches the bishop has a fixed throne on the gospel side of the sanctuary (see Frontispiece), raised by two or three steps from the sanctuary floor. The level of the platform for the throne should not be higher than the footpace of the altar. When a deacon and subdeacon assist a bishop, their seats are placed usually one on either side of the throne at a lower level, but their seats may be at the sedilia on the epistle side. The personal servers of a bishop are usually seated to the east of his throne. In churches visited by a bishop a seat of honour is placed for him on the gospel side.

Women in Chancel and Sanctuary

Women in choirs may be seated, if desired, in the chancel, provided there is a rail separating the sanctuary from the chancel. Women are not given seats in the sanctuary during the course of a service. Women preachers should preach from a point outside the sanctuary.

Communion

It is helpful to the priest if all recipients of Communion are instructed how to receive the Sacrament. They should hold the head with chin slightly raised, the mouth open, the tongue slightly extended. The sign of the cross is made by the communicant over himself immediately before receiving the Blessed Sacrament. As the priest stands before a communicant he takes a Wafer between the thumb and forefinger of the right hand, meanwhile holding the chalice, or ciborium or paten in the left, and with the Host makes the sign of the cross vertically over the ciborium or chalice, saying: "The Body of our Lord Christ keep thee unto life eternal. " The sign of the cross is made quite small, so that the Host at all times is held over the cup of the chalice or ciborium. If Communion be in both Kinds, the priest then dips the Host into the Chalice. The priest now places the Host on the outstretched tongue of the communicant, taking care not to touch the lips or tongue with his fingers, and goes on to the next person, repeating the sign and words of administration. In giving Communion it is customary to begin at the epistle end of the line of communicants and move towards the gospel end. A deacon may assist in the administration of Holy Communion.

During the giving of Communion to the people it is practically necessary, if the congregation is of any size, to assign one or two laymen or servers to direct the people and see that they come forward promptly to kneel at the rail. Generally it is more convenient if the people approach the communion rail by the side aisles and return to their seats by the central aisle. In small churches they should come forward by one aisle and return to their seats by the other. The laymen or servers who direct the people should count the communicants so as to make it unnecessary for anyone in the sanctuary to keep looking in the direction of the communicants. Communicants should be instructed in the etiquette of not kneeling, or rising, during the time the person adjoining is receiving Communion. The General Episcopal Synod is of the opinion that it is not usually advisable to administer Communion to children under seven years of age. A server may assist at any number of services on any one day, but he should communicate only once each day.

Safeguarding the Host

Permission may be granted by the Ordinary, at his discretion, for the reservation of the Host in private oratories, where there is no priest in charge, provided, (1) that the oratory must be used for spiritual purposes only; (2) that the Host be reserved in a locked tabernacle; (3) that there must be some trust-worthy person in charge; (4) that some provision be made in the event of the death of the person in charge.

The General Episcopal Synod considers it inadvisable to carry the Sacred Host for the purposes of administering Communion to a congregation in a distant city, especially if the journey includes a night on the train.

Use of Other Liturgies

The General Episcopal Synod has ruled that in case of emergency and in services not held in Liberal Catholic Churches, it is permissible for clergy to use the Anglican Prayer Book or the Roman Catholic Missal.

Use of a Cantor

The Second Episcopal Synod ruled that if handicapped or prevented from singing himself it is permissible for a celebrant to employ the services of a cantor in singing any or all parts of any service, provided that in the case of the Holy Eucharist the celebrant should also accompany the cantor by singing or saying softly the words of the *Sursum Corda* and Preface.

Parts of the Eucharist Which are Variable

The following parts of the Liturgy of the Holy Eucharist vary according to the season and the Eucharist celebrated:

Canticle. Special Canticles are said or sung when celebrating a Nuptial or Requiem Eucharist.

Introit. A special Introit is said or sung when celebrating a Requiem Eucharist. (Note that the sign of the cross should be made by all over themselves at the beginning of this special Introit exactly as is done at the regular Introit.)

Collects. In addition to the two Collects always said in the Full Form and the one Collect always said in the Shorter Form, there is a Collect for:

(1) Every Sunday in the year, except those Sundays which invariably fall within the Octave of a Festival of a higher rank, such as the first and second Sundays after Christmas, the first Sunday after the Epiphany, the Sunday after Ascension Day, and the first Sunday after Trinity.
(2) All Festivals and Holy-Days observed by the Liberal Catholic Church.
(3) The Requiem Eucharist and the Nuptial Eucharist.
(4) The Ordination of a Subdeacon, Deacon, or Priest, and the Consecration of a Bishop.
(5) The Consecration of a Church.
(6) In some churches a custom is made of reciting the Collect of the Patron Saint of the Church at every service after the Collect of the Day.

Epistle. An Epistle is prescribed for each of the five classes of eucharistic celebrations appearing under the heading of "Collects, " with the exception of the Ordination of a Subdeacon. The Epistle may be omitted, but in this case the Gospel also is omitted.

Gradual. A special or proper Gradual is prescribed for Christmas Day and seven days after; for Easter Day and until Ascension; for Ascension Day and nine days after; for Whitsunday and six days after; for Trinity Sunday; for Festivals of Our Lady; for Festivals of the Angels; for the Requiem Eucharist and for the Nuptial Eucharist. The Gradual is omitted if the Epistle and Gospel are omitted.

Gospel. A Gospel is prescribed for each of the five classes of eucharistic celebrations appearing under the heading of "Collects, " with the exceptions of the Ordination of a Subdeacon. The Gospel may be omitted, but in this case the Epistle also is omitted.

Preface. A special or proper Preface is inserted between the first and second paragraphs of the regular Preface on the following occasions: Christmas Day and seven days after; on Easter Day and seven days after; on Ascension Day and nine days after; on Whitsunday and six days after; on Trinity Sunday; on Festivals of Our Lady; and on Festivals of the Angels.

Communio. A special Communio is used when celebrating a Nuptial or Requiem Eucharist.

Postcommunio. A special Postcommunio is used when celebrating a Nuptial or Requiem Eucharist.

Benediction. A special final Benediction is used when celebrating a Requiem Eucharist.

The Calendar

In general the Collect, Epistle and Gospel assigned to a Sunday, as well as the colour of the vestments worn on that Sunday, are used throughout the remaining six week-day services, unless as is frequently the case some Festival intervenes which takes precedence. It should be noted that:

The Collect for Advent Sunday is said after the Collect of the Day at every service during the Advent season until Christmas Eve.

The Collect for Easter Sunday is said up to and including the first Sunday after Easter, while the Epistle and Gospel are said until that Sunday.

In general the Collect, Epistle and Gospel assigned to a Festival or Holy Day, as well as the colour of the vestments worn, are used on that one day only, unless some greater Festival takes precedence, when the Collect alone of the lesser Festival is said after that of the greater Festival. It should be noted that:

The Collect, Epistle and Gospel for Christmas Day are said every day until New Year's Eve. On New Year's Day alone the Collect for Christmas is said after that of the Day.

The Collect, Epistle and Gospel for New Year's Day are said every day until the Epiphany.

The Collect, Epistle and Gospel for the Epiphany are said every day until the Baptism of Our Lord, or until the Second Sunday after the Epiphany, if that should fall earlier than the Baptism.

The Collect, Epistle and Gospel for the Baptism of Our Lord are said for seven days after.

The Collect Epistle and Gospel for the Transfiguration are said for seven days after.

The Collect for the First Day of Lent is said at every Eucharist during the Lenten season after the Collect for the Day, but the Epistle and Gospel are said only until the first Sunday in Lent.

The Collect Epistle and Gospel for Ascension Day are said for nine days after or until Whitsunday.

The Collect, Epistle and Gospel for Corpus Christi are said until the second Sunday after Trinity.

The Collect, Epistle and Gospel for the Assumption of Our Lady are said for seven days after.

The Collect, Epistle and Gospel of St. Michael and All Angels are said for six days after, while on the seventh day are said the Collect, Epistle and Gospel of the Third Sunday after Trinity.

The Collect, Epistle and Gospel of All Saints' Day are said for seven days after, except that on All Souls' Day the Collect alone is said after the Collect for the Day.

The Collect, Epistle and Gospel of the Patron Saint of a Church or Country are said in that Church or Country on the Festival of the Saint and seven days after.

The Collect or Collects and the colour of vestments used at any service in the late afternoon or evening may be of the Day following. Should Complin be conducted in the evening the Epistle and Gospel of the Day following should be read as Lessons.

Substitute Collects[1]

The following Collects, prepared at the request of the General Episcopal Synod, may be substituted for those appearing in the Liturgy:

Collect for Advent Sunday

Almighty God, Who didst wonderfully create man in Thine own Image, we pray for strength to cast away the works of darkness and put upon us the armour of light; that we, being ever mindful of our spiritual heritage, may hasten the coming of The kingdom upon earth; through Christ our Lord, ℟. Amen.

Collect for the Third Sunday in Advent

O Christ our Lord, we pray for strength to increase and multiply within our hearts Thy heavenly grace; that we, loving Thee above all things, may faithfully serve Thee in all good works; Thou Who livest and reignest in the unity of the Father and of the Holy Spirit, one God throughout all ages of ages. ℟. Amen.

Collect for St. Alban's Day

We praise Thee O Lord for the example and assistance given to us by The Holy Martyr, St, Alban, the Patron of our Church; and we pray that under his guidance and protection Thy Church may continually serve Thee in all good works; through Christ our Lord. ℟. Amen.

Collect for the Second Sunday after Easter

O Lord Christ, the Sun of Righteousness, Who as at holy Eastertide didst rise

---

[1]. These Collects are included in later editions of *The Liturgy.*

from the darkness of death to shine with exceeding glory upon The people, grant unto Thy Church so to prepare and make ready Thy Way that the earth may be filled with Thy glory even as the waters cover the sea; Thou Who livest and reignest ever in the unity of the Father and of the Holy Spirit, God throughout all ages or ages. ℟. Amen.

Precedence of Feasts and Holy Days

The Sundays, Festivals and Holy-Days have been classified into four groups according to their importance. Those of highest rank are indicated in the Liturgy by the letter A, of next rank by B, of next rank by C, and of lowest rank by D. A Day of rank A takes precedence over B, C and D; a Day of rank B over C and D; a Day of rank C over D.

When the Collect, Epistle and Gospel of any Day are prescribed for seven or more days after, that Day is said to have an octave, and the celebration of any other Festival or Holy Day falling within the prescribed number of days must follow the rule given in the Liturgy. The saying of only a Collect beyond the usual number of days does not constitute an octave nor affect in any way the colour of the vestments used. It is a safe rule to follow, that the colour of the vestments to be used on any Day must be in agreement with the Epistle and Gospel said, but not necessarily with the Collect.

Use of Certain Terms in This Manual

Throughout this manual, except where indicated otherwise by the context, the terms "acolyte" and "server" have been used as synonyms; thus boys may be spoken of as acolytes even though they are not in Minor Orders. Similarly, in order to avoid constant repetition of one word, the terms "priest" and "celebrant" have been used interchangeably. Also when it is said that the "people" or "congregation" respond, it is to understood that all in the sanctuary and chancel, except the celebrant, join in with the people in singing or saying the response.

PART II

THE HOLY EUCHARIST

Important Note

The Holy Eucharist may be celebrated only in the morning. The Consecration of the Bread and Wine must take place not earlier than the hour of midnight and preferably not later than thirty minutes after the hour of noon, *sun time*, not daylight saving time. It is therefore advisable to begin the Eucharist so that the consecration falls within the prescribed time limits. Eucharists beginning at twelve noon are permissible, but not after that hour.

A priest is supposed to celebrate and to receive Communion only once a day. On occasion it may be necessary, with the consent of the bishop, to break this rule. Too frequent communion is a strain upon the physical body and should be avoided. If possible each priest should celebrate once a day, though it is only to say private Mass. Every priest, if he so desires, may celebrate three times on All Souls' Day and on Christmas Day: at the Midnight Eucharist at an early morning Christmas Eucharist, and at the regular Celebration later on Christmas Day. The Liberal Catholic Rite does not require a condition of fasting before celebrating the Holy Eucharist or receiving Communion, but practical experience has shown that to eat too soon before celebrating is inadvisable from the standpoint of health.

The three chapters which follow describe the various ways in which the ceremony of the Holy Eucharist may be performed. It should be noted that the instructions given under *The Longer Form by a Priest* in Chapter V form the basis of all that is said thereafter. Thus the directions given in Chapter VI for the Missa Cantata take for granted all that has been said about Low Celebration in Chapter V, and similarly the directions in Chapter VII for High Celebration take for granted all that has been given in the *two* preceding chapters. In other words, always read each new division of the subject in the light of what has been written before.

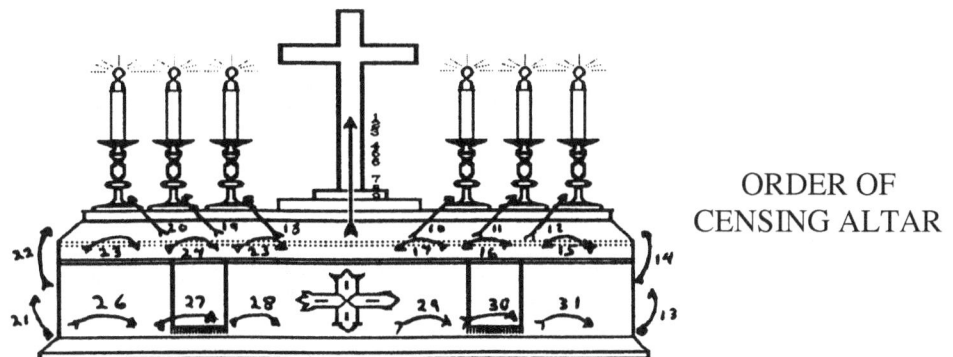

ORDER OF
CENSING ALTAR

DIAGRAM 5

CHAPTER V

Low Celebration of the Holy Eucharist

The Longer Form when Said by a Priest

Preparations

Before celebrating the Holy Eucharist the following preparations are made:

The Altar. The dust cloth is removed from the altar leaving the three altar-cloths of white linen. Care should be taken to see that the six altar candlesticks are arranged in their proper order on either side of the altar cross (Page 8, also Diagram 5, Page 55). These six candlesticks should be regarded as fixtures in their assigned places and not to be shifted about to suit the whim of those arranging the flowers. Vases of flowers may be grouped upon the altar and gradines, but it is desirable that flowers and additional candlesticks should be placed as far as possible on the gradines rather than on the altar itself. In any case the front portion of the altar table should be unencumbered. The frontal, orphreys, or the strip of ribbon behind the superfrontal should be of the colour of the Day. The missal stand is placed on the epistle side of the altar at a convenient reading distance from the centre and on it placed the missal (unless carried by the celebrant) marked at the beginning of the service and at any other points to which it may be necessary to turn during the service. The missal if closed, should be placed with its edge towards the epistle end of the altar. The missal is often adorned with a silken cover of the colour of the Day.

(It is useful to have the services of the Church, including at least the Collects and if possible the Epistles and Gospels, printed or typewritten on loose leaves. These may be assembled, before each service, in a binder, which serves as a missal. The use of loose leaves makes it unnecessary to turn backwards and forwards as is required when using a bound book.)

On the *credence table* are placed the cruets containing wine and water, the tray on which the cruets stand, a bowl either empty or filled with water as desired, a towel for the lavabo, the aspergill, the Book of Gospels (unless the priest uses his missal), collection plates, or collection bags of the colour of the Day, and the sacring bell. If desired, the bell, gong, or chimes may be placed near the place where the server will kneel who rings the bell at the Sanctus and the Consecration.

If the Host is reserved in the tabernacle the *sanctuary lamp* should of course be burning.

At private Low Celebration there need be only one *server*, or even none, but if said before a congregation there may be two or more servers, at the discretion of the priest. Five servers are acceptable if obtainable: the thurifer, boat bearer, cross bearer, and two candle bearers who act as altar assistants. The two altar assistants should be .specially reliable.

In the *vestry* the vestments to be used by the celebrant are laid out on the vesting table. If the cope is to be worn during the procession to the altar, then the chasuble and maniple are placed on the priest's seat in the sanctuary, while the cope is laid out and the cape fastened thereon. If, as is frequently the case at Low Celebration when there is no procession, the chasuble is worn by the priest who takes the short way to the altar, then the following preparations are made: The chasuble is first laid on the table, so folded that it can be put over the head with the least difficulty. Upon the chasuble are placed the maniple, stole, linen girdle, linen alb, and amice in the order named.

If prayers for any persons have been asked, their names should be written on a piece of paper, which is laid upon the altar at the foot of the missal stand or upon the ledge of the latter.

All of these preparations heretofore mentioned may be made by a server.

Meanwhile the priest puts on his cassock and washes his hands. He then prepares the sacred vessels. The purificator, folded lengthwise, is laid across the top of the empty chalice, so that the two ends hang down equally on each side. Upon the purificator is placed the paten on which a large host has been laid. The paten is now covered with the square linen pall, and over the whole is draped the veil, so arranged that when the chalice is put upon the altar, the lower edge of the veil will touch the altar cloths and hide the foot of the chalice. The burse, containing nothing but the folded corporal is placed on top, resting on the veil. (Plate 7, Fig. 7) The priest should be careful to see that the large host is unbroken and that it is free as possible from little clinging particles.

It cannot be too strongly emphasized that immediately before the Eucharist the celebrant should keep silent and that all others present in the vestry should respect his silence. The casual conversation not infrequently heard in vestries before the service is not a fitting preparation for the Holy Sacrifice which is to follow. In order that the thought of the celebrant may be steadied and brought into harmony with the eucharistic offering, prayers to be said silently while vesting are recommended. The following, prepared by Rev. Kenneth Hurgon (*The Liberal Catholic*, December 1932) are excellent for the purpose. The priest says while

Washing his hands: Cleanse my hands, O Lord, in Thy strength that I may render unto Thee a pure offering and a perfect work.

Taking the amice: Place, O Lord, upon my head the helmet of salvation, that Thy servant may be freed from evil.

Donning the alb: Endue me with the garment of innocence and the vesture of light, that I may worthily receive Thy gifts and worthily dispense them.

Tying the girdle: Bind me to thee, O Christ, with the cords of love and the girdle of purity, that Thy power may dwell in me.

Taking the maniple: May this sign of the ministry be unto me as a guerdon of Thy promises.

Placing the stole round his neck: O Thou Who hast said, "My yoke is sweet and my burden light," grant that I may bear Thy blessing to all the world.

Donning the chasuble: May the vesture of grace which I put on and the offering I go to make, crown in me a labour of righteousness and a holy work, to the glory of God and of the Angel Hosts, the joy of Saints and the salvation of mankind; through Christ our Lord. Amen.

The priest now puts on the eucharistic vestments. He first puts on the amice, placing it over his shoulders and round his neck so that the apparel is centred and smooth, and then crossing the strings over his breast and passing them round his body under the arms so that they may be brought round to the front and tied. (Plate 7, Fig. 1) If the apparel alone is used, it is merely fastened round the neck. He puts on the alb and ties the girdle round his waist. This is done by doubling the girdle, passing it round the waist, slipping the free ends through the loop of the doubled end, and knotting them so that the two ends hang down in front to be used in fastening the stole. He puts the stole over his shoulders and round his neck, crosses the two ends over the breast, right over left, and fastens them in place with the ends of the girdle. (Plate 7, Fig. 2) The crossed ends of the stole may be placed under the girdle, if this arrangement is preferred, the ends of the girdle in this case hanging down at the left side.

At this point in his vesting the celebrant, carrying the tabernacle key, takes the stem of the covered chalice in his left hand, and with the right hand laid upon the burse to steady it, goes to the altar. Upon reaching the altar footpace, the priest places the chalice on the gospel side of the altar. Taking the corporal from the burse, he lays it on the altar immediately over the altar stone, and unfolds it so that the centre of the corporal is just over the centre of the stone. The edge of the corporal bearing the embroidered cross should be nearest the front edge of the altar. He stands the empty burse on the gospel side of the altar if it is the kind which forms an inverted V when opened, but if it is of the pocket type he leans it against a candlestick or vase standing on the gospel side, or against the gradine. Unless he has previously ascertained the number of reserved Hosts available for the Communion of the people, he now opens the tabernacle door, genuflects, removes the ciborium and places it on the corporal. His inspection made, he replaces the ciborium in the tabernacle, again genuflects, and closes the door, leaving the key in the lock. He now lifts the covered chalice and stands it upon the centre of the corporal, so that the cross or ornament on the veil is towards the people. Care should be taken to arrange the veil symmetrically and to see that the front edge, which touches the altar cloths, is parallel to the front edge of the altar.

If additional hosts for the use of the people are required, the priest may bring them in at the same time as the chalice and paten. Alternatively, he may return to the vestry for them, or a server may bring a supply up to him. The peoples' wafers to be consecrated are placed preferably in an empty ciborium, which has been cleansed as hereinbefore described; failing this, they may be piled upon an extra paten or heaped upon the corporal near the foot of the chalice. If a ciborium is used, it is stood upon the corporal between the chalice and the tabernacle, where it remains until needed at the Consecration.

(The celebrant may delegate to another of the clergy the duty of carrying the sacred vessels to the altar and arranging them thereon, but no one lower in rank than a subdeacon may do this. If a subdeacon arranges the vessels, he may not open the tabernacle. At private or semi-private Masses, the celebrant may carry the vessels in with him when he goes to commence the Mass, and likewise carry them out with him at its conclusion.)

Genuflecting in the middle before the altar, the priest returns to the vestry to complete his vesting. If the cope is to be used, he puts it on, otherwise he places the maniple on his left forearm between the wrist and the elbow, securing it in place either by means of a pin, a pressbutton, or an elastic band sewed to the lining of the maniple, and lastly puts on the chasuble, taking care that the central orphrey falls straight and not twisted to one side. If desired, a pocket handkerchief may be drawn under and suspended over the girdle in some place hidden by the cope or chasuble, or it may be thrust up a sleeve.

Meanwhile the candles on the altar have been lighted and the censer prepared and taken into the sanctuary. Some incense may have been sprinkled on the charcoal and blessed, if there be a congregation of some size. Care should be taken to see that the boat contains enough incense for the service.

When the time arrives to begin the Celebration, the priest puts on the biretta and walks to the sanctuary, preceded by the server or servers.

(The ceremonial at a Low Mass should be simple and restrained. The use of the cope, of several servers (as outlined on Page 56), of the processional cross and candles, and of incense on the same scale as at *Missa Cantata*, is not in keeping with tradition. Part of the charm of Low Mass rests in its simplicity of rite. Where a Low Mass is the principal service on any or a Feast Day, especially if, as sometimes happens, hymns are sung, the censer may be carried in procession during the opening hymn and more attendants employed than at other said Masses.)

Upon reaching the sanctuary, the server (or servers) goes to his position. (See subsequent articles on "The Server at Mass," where detailed instructions will be found).

Arriving in the middle before the lowest altar step the celebrant, facing the altar, removes his biretta and, holding it before the breast in his right hand, genuflects (or bows) without, however, making any other inclination, the server(s) genuflecting with him, he gives his biretta to the server. If a hymn is being sung the server waits in his place until its conclusion; otherwise he at once places the biretta on or near the priest's seat, and returns with the aspergill to his appointed place.

Asperges

It is permissible at Low Celebration to say without abbreviation the *Asperges* as given in the Longer Form, and, if used, reference should be made here to the instructions given in Chapter VI. But it is advisable usually to shorten the *Asperges* at Low Celebration, so we shall here describe that given in the Shorter Form. If the cope should have been worn, it will be exchanged for the chasuble as described in Chapter VI.

To begin the service the priest makes the sign of the cross over himself with the right hand in the usual manner saying: *In the Name of the Father,* ✠ *and of the Son and of the Holy Ghost.* Taking now the aspergill (which has been dipped into or filled with holy water), he crosses himself with it, saying: *May the Lord... service.* The priest then asperses the altar in the middle, the sanctuary to his left and to his right, and says: *In the strength... sanctuary.* Now turning towards the people, the priest asperses them with the same triple motion—down the centre of the church, to his left, to his right—saying as he does so: *and from ... Him.* The movement made with the aspergill should not be aimed low, but well above the heads of the people. Turning back to the altar, he gives the aspergill to the server (who places it on the credence) and, unless he is holding the missal, joins his hands before his breast while saying: *I pray ... Christ our Lord.*

When he turns to the people from the altar, and to the altar from the people, he should do so by facing the epistle side as he turns. Except on two occasions, to be noted hereafter, he always turns in this manner to the people and back to the altar again.

The response, *Amen,* having been made by the people, the priest gives his book to the server, turns to the congregation and, with hands extended (Plate 1, Fig. 4) says: *Brethren ... Temple.* He joins his hands, turns back to the altar, and receives his book again.

To the Gospel

Without a pause he then says in a clear voice the antiphon and canticle in the Longer Form, the servers and people saying the words with him. All bow the head in the seventh verse at the words: *for the Lord our God is holy*. During the canticle and antiphon the hands of the priest remain joined before the breast, unless he is holding the missal.

During the recitation of *Glory be to the Father, and to the Son and to the Holy Ghost* the priest bows his head. All present in the sanctuary turn to the east and bow their head. All stand erect while saying: *As it was in the beginning, is now, and ever shall be, world without end. Amen.* These words ended, all who have faced eastwards turn to their normal position. (No further reference will be made to this procedure, which is always followed whenever in any service the *Gloria Patri* is said or sung. The only exception is at Vespers when all are seated.)

The versicles which follow the second antiphon are repeated alternately by priest and people, all crossing themselves at the beginning of the first versicle: *Our help ... Lord.* All now kneel and say the Confiteor with the priest who speaks in a clear tone and takes care to give no impression of hurrying. The celebrant's hands remain joined before the breast, unless he is holding the missal. At the close of the Confiteor, the priest rises, ascends to the footpace, bows to the cross and, standing in the middle, turns to face the people. Placing his left hand on his breast and extending his right arm towards them (Plate 1, Fig. 6) with palm to the front and all fingers extended, he pronounces the Absolution. At the words: *God the Son* and *absolve* he makes the sign of the cross over the people.

The priest now turns back towards the altar, moves to the south end and, facing south, awaits the thurifer. Placing incense upon the charcoal in the censer, he blesses it in the usual manner and takes the censer. (For details under various conditions, see "The Server at Mass.") The thurifer retires to the sanctuary floor, taking the missal stand if this is desired by the celebrant.

The celebrant genuflects in the middle while holding the censer, and, still standing in the middle, censes the altar cross with nine short swings arranged in groups of three (Diagram 5, Page 55). He genuflects as before and, facing slightly towards the epistle end of the altar, takes three regular steps each with the right foot (bringing the left foot forward after each step) while with each step he swings the censer once towards one of the three candles on the epistle side, beginning with the candle nearest the altar cross, then the middle one, then the outermost one. (If there are only two altar candles instead of the usual six, as may happen at a private celebration, the censer is swung thrice toward the one candle). Reaching the epistle corner, he swings the censer twice along the end, first near the bottom and then near the top. He then returns to the middle of the altar, making as he does so three circular swings along the upper edge. These swings should be made carefully, somewhat deliberately, pausing slightly between swings. Genuflecting, he turns slightly towards the gospel end and takes three steps as before, but with the left foot leading, censing each candle on the gospel side with a single swing in the same order as that previously mentioned. Censing now the gospel end of the altar with two swings, he turns and standing still at the gospel corner makes three circular swings along the upper edge of the altar. Then, lowering the censer somewhat by means of the chains (so as to avoid bending the body which does not look well) he walks slowly towards the middle, making as he does so three circular swings along the frontal about two-thirds of the way down from the top of the altar. Reaching the middle he genuflects and makes three similar swings along the lower part of the frontal on the epistle side of the altar. (All swings of the censer should be made in the directions indicated in Diagram 5, Page 55.) Arriving at the epistle end, the celebrant hands the censer to the thurifer, (who replaces the missal stand on the altar, if he removed it from the altar at the beginning of the censing, before taking the censer) and remains at the end of the footpace, facing south. He is now censed by the thurifer with six swings, arranged in three groups of two swings each, the server standing at the foot of the steps facing north. He bows slightly before and after being censed, standing meanwhile with hands joined before the breast. After the censing the thurifer hangs the censer in its place and goes to his normal position.

The priest returns to the middle, bows slightly to the altar cross, turns to the people and with outspread hands says the Minor Benediction. As the people respond, he turns back to the altar, walks to the epistle corner at a point about opposite the middle altar candlestick (or about midway between this point and the corner of the altar), faces east, crosses himself, and begins to read the *Introit* in a clear voice accompanied by the people. Throughout the reading the celebrant's hands are joined before the breast. The Introit ended, the priest returns to the middle. (He should turn and walk in that direction. Not taking steps sidewise.) With bowed head and joined hands he says the *Kyrie* with the people. He remains standing, facing the altar.

As soon as the last *Kyrie Eleison* has been said, he stands erect, and while the first words of the Gloria are being said by all together, he raises, separates and lowers his hands as described on p. 35. At the word *God* he joins them before his breast and bows. All bow the head at the phrases: *we worship Thee, we give thanks to Thee* and *receive our prayer.* (At Low Celebration, the thurifer does not swing the censer to and fro while standing in the middle, as is done when the Eucharist is sung.) The priest turns to the people when the Gloria is ended and says the Minor Benediction.

Going to the epistle side of the altar at the Introit, the celebrant, still with joined hands, says: *Let us pray*. The people and servers kneel. With hands outspread at the level of the shoulders (Plate 1, Fig. 4) the priest reads first the Collect of the Eucharist, then the Collect of the Day which is being celebrated, then the Collects of any other Festivals or Days to be commemorated, and finally the Peace Collect. At the end of each Collect he should await the *Amen* coming in response, before beginning the next. He does not say, *Let us pray*, before any Collect except the first one read. The number of Collects may be either odd or even. They should be arranged carefully in the order of the precedence of the Days, that of the Day celebrated coming immediately after the Eucharistic Collect.

At any Celebration, either Low, *Missa Cantata*, or High, the Epistle, Gradual, *Munda Cor Meum* and Gospel may be omitted. When omitted, the celebrant proceeds at once to the recitation of the Creed, provided there is not to be a sermon. If they are not omitted, and no one has been appointed to read the Epistle, the procedure is as follows:

Taking a copy of the Liturgy (or missal) in which the Epistle of the Day has been marked beforehand, the priest still at the epistle side, turns to the people in the usual way and reads the announcement appearing at the beginning of the Epistle: *The Epistle is taken from....* He then reads the Epistle while standing on the footpace. At the end he must be sure to say: *Here endeth the Epistle*, so that the people may know when to rise and respond: *Thanks be to God*. The priest turns back to the altar and remains at the epistle side. He joins his hands and all say the *Gradual*.

Some of our clergy, following the custom of the Roman Rite, prefer that the missal stand be transferred at this point from the epistle side to the gospel side of the altar. The Third Episcopal Synod ruled that this was optional. If the transfer is made a server ascends to the footpace by the epistle end, takes the missal stand, descends by the epistle end, walks round *in plano* to the gospel end of the altar (genuflecting in the middle) ascends to the footpace and places the stand on the gospel side of the altar. He then returns to his station. The transfer is made most conveniently at the end of the Gradual. If the celebrant is alone, or if there be only one server, the priest may change the position of the missal stand, but in doing so he does not leave the footpace. If the Epistle, Gradual and Gospel are to be omitted, the stand should be transferred immediately after the last Collect. It is returned to the epistle side just after the Ablutions.

At the end of the Gradual at Low Celebration (but during the Gradual when the Eucharist is sung), provided the Gospel is to be read, the thurifer goes to the priest by way of the epistle end of the footpace and the incense is blessed as usual. If the Gospel is to be read, the priest, at the end of the Gradual, and after blessing incense, goes to the middle and standing with bowed head and joined hands says the *Munda Cor Meum*: *Cleanse my heart ... our Lord*. He also says the prayer which follows: *May the Lord ... manifest*, substituting *my* for *thy* and making the signs of the cross over himself. Standing erect, he turns to the people and gives the Minor Benediction in the usual manner, turns back to the altar after the response, genuflects, and proceeds to the gospel side of the altar.

From the Gospel to the Canon

If the missal stand has been transferred to the gospel side of the altar, as has just been described, and there is but one server to assist, the priest places his missal (or the book which contains the Gospel of the Day) on the missal stand. He then reads the announcement appearing at the beginning of the Gospel: *The Holy Gospel is taken from......* As he says these words, he stretches out the right hand, palm downward, fingers closed and makes the sign of the cross with the extended thumb at the beginning of the text of the Gospel he is about to read. The server and people say: *Glory be to Thee, O Lord*. Immediately he makes the sign of the cross, quite small and still with the right thumb, upon his forehead, lips and breast successively, the left hand resting upon the breast a little below the place where he is to make the sign of the cross. Now taking the censer from the server (who ascends the steps at the gospel end), the priest censes the book with six short swings, two towards the centre of the book, two towards the left and two towards the right. The priest hands the censer back to the server (who steps down to the sanctuary floor) and reads the Gospel. If there be a congregation, it is usual for him to take the book and turn to face the people while reading the Gospel. But if there is no congregation, he may read the Gospel facing east, the missal resting on the stand. In either case the thurifer swings the censer to and fro while standing *in plano*, either in front of the altar on the gospel side facing the priest, or at the gospel end of the altar facing south, whichever is most convenient. If there be no server, the priest fetches the censer himself and censes the book on the stand, returning it afterward; or, he may omit the censing.

If the missal stand is not transferred, and the Gospel is read, two servers are desirable. The book containing the Gospel is given to a server to hold. He takes his place on the first or second step (whichever brings the book to the most convenient height) on the gospel side before the altar. He faces east and holds up the open book in such a position that the celebrant may easily announce, cense and read the Gospel. After the priest has announced the Gospel, he makes the sign of the cross over the book and himself, takes the censer from the thurifer (who is standing behind the bookbearer) and censes the book exactly as described above. While doing so he, of course, faces the book and therefore the congregation. The thurifer, during the reading of the Gospel, stands in plano behind the server holding the book, faces east, and swings the censer to and fro. Should the sanctuary be too small to allow this, he may stand at the gospel side facing south. If there be but one server, he allows the censer to hang from his right hand, if holding the book, otherwise he swings the censer.

Whenever possible the Gospel should be read from a special Book of Gospels or Liturgy kept for the purpose and presented to the celebrant after the *Munda Cor Meum*.

At the end of the Gospel, after the people have responded: *Praise be to Thee, O Christ*, the celebrant takes the book from the server (unless a separate Book of Gospels has been used) turns back to the altar, walks to the middle and genuflects. When the celebrant himself reads the Gospel he is not censed afterward by the thurifer.

The servers return the Book of Gospels (if one has been used) and the censer to their places and go to their usual positions.

If there is to be a *sermon* it follows here, preceded by any notices (which should be terse) which the priest may have to give to the congregation. (In order to maintain a complete record of the activities of a Church, it is helpful to enter all notices in a neatly bound notebook under the name and date of the Sundays and Festivals. It looks better to read the notices from such a book than from miscellaneous pieces of paper.)

When the celebrant himself preaches, he may do so from the pulpit or lectern, or standing at the gospel side on the sanctuary floor, on one of the steps below the foot-pace, or on the footpace itself. Unless he goes to the pulpit, he need take off only the maniple, which he should hand to a server or place upon the altar. If the celebrant does not preach, he goes to his seat vested in maniple and chasuble and sits there during the sermon wearing his biretta. If he goes to the pulpit, he removes the chasuble and maniple at the sedalia.

If the preacher is not the celebrant, he vests, if ordained priest, in surplice and stole of the colour of the Day. If ordained deacon, he wears a surplice and a stole crossed deacon-fashion. If of lesser rank he vests only in surplice. He wears a biretta, if entitled to one. Clergy seated in the sanctuary or chancel wear their birettas during the sermon. They stand, with birettas off, during the opening invocation and the concluding ascription.

After he has reached the place where he is to preach and before he begins the sermon, the preacher faces east, removes his biretta and crosses himself as he says: *In the Name of the Father and of the ✠ Son, and of the Holy Ghost.* The people and servers respond, *Amen.* At the conclusion of the sermon he again turns to the east removes his biretta and without crossing himself, says the following ascription: *And now to God the Father, God the Son, and God the Holy Ghost, Three persons in one God, be ascribed, as is most justly due all honour, might, majesty, power, dominion and praise, now henceforth and for evermore.* All respond: *Amen.*

The sermon is not a necessary part of the Eucharist, and its delivery or omission is left to the discretion of the priest. It is wise to limit the length of the sermon to fifteen minutes, in order that the service may not be unduly long.

Vested in chasuble and maniple, the celebrant returns to the altar, genuflecting on the sanctuary floor in the middle before the lowest altar step and ascending to the footpace. He begins the recitation of the *Creed* accompanied by the congregation. At the opening words: *We believe in one God*, he raises, separates and lowers his hands as described on p. 36, joining them and bowing as he says the word *God*. He also bows at the words *Jesus* and *is worshipped*. At the words *and was incarnate*, he genuflects, remaining on one knee until the words: *and was made man*, which are recited slowly. Great reverence and devotion should mark all that is said during this genuflection. After a slight pause, he rises again and continues the Creed. All join in this prolonged genuflection. At the end of the Creed he crosses himself.

It is permissible for any of the forms given in the Liturgy under the heading: CREEDS AND ACTS OF FAITH, to be used instead of the Creed appearing in the Longer Form. In all cases the priest raises his hands at the opening words and crosses himself during the saying of the last sentence. Everyone in the chancel and sanctuary, during the recitation of the Creeds, should turn to face the east.

The Creed ended, the celebrant gives the Minor Benediction and turns back to the altar.

If there is to be a collection the server takes the collection bag or plate from the credence table, genuflects before the altar and passes down the nave among the people. If two servers are available and are needed for this work, they genuflect together. If it meets better the needs of the occasion, or if no server be available, one or two members of the congregation are asked beforehand to take the collection and are supplied with bags. The bags are finally presented to the server (or, failing a server, to the priest) at the entrance to the sanctuary. (Instructions for taking the collection on a larger scale are given under the heading of *Missa Cantata*.)

The celebrant turns to face the server who comes to him with the collection, he may walk to the epistle end of the footpace, takes the bag, turns back to the middle, holds up the bag at about the level of his breast, and with it makes the sign of the cross vertically above the altar saying, "All things come of Thee, O Lord, and of Thine own have we given Thee." He then returns the bag to the server to be placed on the credence, or in a safe place.

Standing in the middle facing the altar and with joined hands the celebrant now says the *offertorium*: *From the rising ... house of the Lord*. He removes the veil from the chalice by lifting the corners farthest from him. He folds the veil and places it within reach, but beyond the corporal, either to his left if the missal stand has not been transferred, or to his right if it has. He stands the chalice to his right, but still on the corporal and, by ruling of the General Episcopal Synod, leans the pall against the gradine or the edge of the tabernacle with the bottom edge resting on the corporal if possible, or places it on the back right corner of the corporal. (The veil is folded so that the colour and not the lining is outermost.)

It should be noted that if wafers for the people are to be consecrated, they should at this time (if not already present on the corporal) be placed there, either in a ciborium (which must now be *uncovered*), or on an extra paten, or heaped on the corporal itself, but not of course on the place where the chalice is to stand, or there the large host is to be laid.

Taking now the paten, upon which rests the large host, he holds it with both hands over the centre of the corporal and at about the level of his breast. (Plate 2, Fig. 3) The thumb and forefinger of each hand should touch the edge of the paten, the other fingers being curved beneath it. He now says: *We adore Thee...giver of all*. When he finishes this prayer he lowers the paten until it is close to the corporal and with it makes the sign of the cross horizontally over the centre of the corporal. The first line of the cross is traced towards himself, the second from left to right. He slides the host onto the corporal, placing it in the middle and a little to the front (so as to allow space for the foot of the chalice exactly in the centre of the corporal), and then slips the empty paten, right side up, about half way under the right-hand edge of the corporal.

He now picks up the chalice by its knob with the left hand and, using the right hand, wipes it thoroughly inside with the purificator. The folded purificator is then laid over the exposed portion of the paten or, better, it is carried by the celebrant when he goes to obtain wine and water. Meanwhile a server has come forward with the cruets of wine and water and stands holding them, on the upper step to the south of the footpace. When the celebrant moves south, after wiping the chalice, this server hands the cruet of wine to the celebrant. (The server should present the cruets with the handles towards the celebrant and not hold the handles himself.) The priest pours a sufficient quantity into the chalice, usually a little more than half the contents of the cruet, if the latter be small. Returning the cruet, he makes the sign of the cross with the right hand over the cruet of water, which is held by the server, takes it and pours a *few* drops of water into the chalice, saying: *According to immemorial custom, we now mix water with this wine, praying Thee, O Lord that we may evermore abide in Him and He in us.* (Note that the words: *O Lord,* have been transposed, by ruling of the Episcopal Synod, from the way the prayer is printed in the [Second Edition Ed.] of the Liturgy.) He returns the water cruet to the server who places it and the wine cruet on the credence.

The priest turns to the altar and partly by gentle movement of the chalice and partly by wiping with the purificator, removes any drops of wine or water which may be clinging to the inside of the chalice. It is suggested that this action take place with the chalice resting on the altar, to the right of the corporal. Replacing the folded purificator over the exposed portion of the paten, he walks to the centre, faces the altar cross, holds up the chalice by the knob with the right hand to the level of the eyes and steadies its foot with the left hand. With it in this position he says: *We offer ... Christ our Lord.* He lowers the chalice, makes the sign of the cross with it horizontally over the centre of the corporal in the same manner as was done with the paten and stands the chalice in the centre of the corporal. He covers the chalice with the pall. This is essential to prevent any dust or particles from the swinging censer from contaminating the wine, and in hot countries to exclude flies. (It is advisable whenever the chalice is being covered or uncovered to steady it by touching the base with the left hand, thus eliminating the possibility of upsetting it.)

Facing south towards the thurifer who has approached with the censer, the priest blesses incense as usual. If he desires the missal stand removed during the censing, this is now done as before explained, except that if there is only one server and the stand is on the gospel side, he must go around to that side, returning the missal stand to its place and himself returning to the epistle side while the priest is saying the words: *As this incense ... blessing.* The celebrant, taking the censer, turns to the altar and, without bowing or genuflecting traces the sign of the cross three times with the censer over the oblations. (Diagram 6) (The thurifer meanwhile retires to the sanctuary floor at the end of the footpace.) Then without pause he traces three circles in the air around them, the censer moving clockwise from left to right. (Diagram 6) The priest now genuflects and censes the altar exactly as before. (Diagram 5, p.55) When the censing of the altar is finished, the priest returns to the middle, faces the altar, holds up the censer with the right hand and says: *As this incense ...Thy blessing.* Lowering the censer, he goes to the epistle end of the footpace and gives it to the thurifer, (who steps up to take it), saying as he does so. *May the Lord ... charity.* Joining his hands, he bows slightly to the thurifer (who has returned to the sanctuary floor) and is censed by him as on the previous occasion.

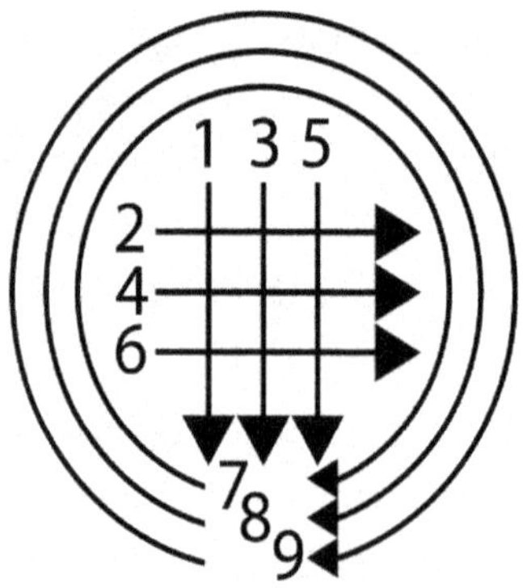

DIAGRAM 6

The thurifer, standing in the middle on the sanctuary floor, censes all the clergy present in order of rank, then the servers in the sanctuary, and finally the people. Those about to be censed rise when the thurifer turns to them, return his bow before and after censing, and at the end remain standing.

Meanwhile a server goes to the priest with a small bowl or tray with a cruet filled with water, together with a small lavabo towel laid over his left forearm. The server pours a little water over the priest's fingers as he holds them over the bowl or tray. It is permissible to have the server bring forward a small bowl filled with water into which the priest dips his fingers. In either case the priest says the first four verses of the *Lavabo* while he washes and dries his fingers, and returns to the middle to face the altar for the *Gloria Patri*. (This seems to be a better custom than saying the *Gloria Patri* while standing at the epistle end of the footpace, because in either case one should face the altar cross and bow.) The first four verses are always said in a low tone, but he may raise his voice, if desired, while saying: *Glory be to.... world without end.*

If only one server is available the lavabo takes place after the people have been censed. Alternately, the priest may go to the credence table and dip his own fingers, drying them on a lavabo towel left there.

Standing in the middle and bowing slightly to the altar cross, the celebrant turns to the people and, with extended hands, says: *Brethren, pray ... Almighty.* He then joins his hands and turns back to the altar by the gospel side (that is, to his right), this being one of the two occasions when the celebrant makes a complete circle in turning to and from the people.

Standing in the middle and still with joined hands he continues: *We lay before Thee...ages of ages.* At the word, *token* he makes the sign of the cross over the host and chalice collectively. This sign and all others over the oblations, except where noted, are made with the fingers extended and the palm turned towards the oblations (Plate 2, Fig. 1). The left hand is carried to the heart as the cross is made with the right. At the conclusion of the words, *Sacrifice unto Thee*, he extends his hands and keeps them extended for the remainder of the prayer.

The Canon to the Communion

Turning to the people and extending his hands as usual the celebrant says: *The Lord be with you.* After the response and still facing the people with hands extended, he lifts his hands in a gesture of aspiration (see p. 35) saying: *Lift up your hearts*; and then joins his hands. As the people respond the priest turns back to the altar, and with hands still joined, bows and says: *Let us give thanks unto our Lord God.* The people respond: *It is meet and right so to do.* With hands outspread, as at the Collects, the priest now says the Preface. The celebrant should be careful on the prescribed Festivals and on the prescribed number of days after each Festival, to add the Proper Preface found in the Liturgy, he should also note that on Trinity Sunday the words "Holy Father" are omitted from the Preface, which on this day is addressed to the Holy Trinity.

The celebrant joins his hands and bowing, says: *Holy ... most High.* Meanwhile a server rings the sacring bell once each time the word *Holy* is said, and the thurifer, if available, should give one swing to the censer so that a cloud of incense rises up before the altar. When such incensing is done the thurifer should be kneeling on the floor of the sanctuary before the lowest altar step.

The priest stands erect and, with hands still joined, says: *Blessed ... Lord.* At the words: *Hosanna in the highest* all make the sign of the cross over themselves.

If a ciborium containing wafers to be consecrated for the people, it has been covered during the second censing. It must now be uncovered until after the Consecration.

With hands outspread, the normal position during the Canon, (Plate 1, Fig. 4) the celebrant begins the prayer: *Wherefore, O most....* He makes the sign of the cross three times over the host and chalice collectively. The words: *N. our King, N. Our Presiding Bishop, N. our Bishop*, vary according to the country in which the priest is celebrating, the name of the Bishop who for the time is holding the office of Presiding Bishop, and the name of the Regionary Bishop of the country. (In the United States of America, the words: The President of the United States, are used, without mentioning any name.) The first name only of the Bishop is mentioned, thus: *Frank, our Presiding Bishop.* Where there are Diocesan Bishops, the name of the Bishop in whose diocese the priest is celebrating should be mentioned following the name of the Regionary Bishop. The names of Auxiliary Bishops (who are without special jurisdiction) are not mentioned.

If the prayers of the Church have been asked on behalf of any one *in trouble, sorrow, need, sickness, or any other adversity*, or if the priest has any such in mind, he should mention their names in full following the word, *especially*, as indicated in the Liturgy. He may pronounce these names silently or aloud. Silently is preferred in most cases—but either way he should think intently of the person, if known to him. In the same way the names of those who have died should be mentioned after the words *especially for*, as indicated in the Liturgy. The hands are joined while the special names are being commemorated.

The prayer: enclosed in brackets, which begins: *In this joyful Sacrifice...* and ends: *nourished and sustained...*, may be omitted at any celebration when it is necessary to shorten the service. It is said with hands outspread.

As he begins the prayer: *Wherefore, O Holy Lord....* he spreads his hands over the oblations in the following manner: he separates the lower part of the hands, until the hands are spread out in the same horizontal plane, palm downward. Depending upon whether it is the custom of the celebrant to keep the thumbs side by side or crossed when the hands are joined, will be the position of the thumbs when the hands are thus outspread. If the former custom is followed, then the thumbs continue to touch one another side by side; if the latter is the custom, then the thumbs are interlocked, the right thumb being joined over the left. The tips of the fingers should extend over to about the middle of the pall, which, however, is not touched. At this point it is customary for the server to sound the sacring bell or chime one time.

During the recitation of the next paragraph, five crosses are made, the first three over the host and chalice collectively, the fourth over the host alone and the fifth over the chalice alone. Note, however, that if there are wafers to be consecrated for the people, the cross over them should be made immediately after the cross is made over the large host and before being made over the chalice, thus making six crosses in all. If there is an extra host to be consecrated for use in the monstrance or for any other purpose, it too must be crossed. In short, crosses must be made at the word, *Body*, over each large host to be consecrated and over wafers for the people which are to be consecrated. The intention to consecrate is the essential thing, and this is met if the cross over all the hosts to be consecrated insures that the intention to consecrate all of them is indicated. (See * below.)

It is a wise precaution at this point, if thought necessary, to rub lightly for an instant the thumb and forefinger of each hand on the forecorners of the corporal in order to remove any particles of dust which may be clinging to the skin.

The priest now says: *Who the day before He suffered....* and picks up the host with the thumb and forefinger of each hand. (Plate 2, Fig. 4) To do this most easily, touch the edge of the host nearest the chalice with the forefinger of the left hand. The opposite edge immediately tips up and may be picked up by the right hand. Lifting the host an inch or two off the corporal with both hands he continues without pause: *took bread into His Holy and Venerable hands....* The priest looks up for a moment at the altar cross or picture of Christ above the altar, as he says: *and with His eyes lifted up to heaven unto Thee, God, His Almighty Father, giving thanks to Thee, He blessed....*

He makes the sign of the cross over the host with the right hand—holding the host meanwhile with the left—and once more over any other hosts to be consecrated. It should be remembered that whatever hosts are consecrated are determined by the intention of the celebrant. He should therefore think not only of the large host he is holding but also of the people's wafers when he makes the sign of the cross and a moment later when he utters the words of consecration.* One way to insure this is to hold the large host over the ciborium, or heap of wafers, so that all are in line of sight. If this is done he need make only one sign of the cross over the large host and wafers collectively, and may direct his attention to both at the words of consecration.

Holding the host between thumb and forefinger of each hand the priest continues: *brake, and gave it to His disciples, saying....* He bows as he says the next words: *Take and eat ye all of this, for....* Neither his hands, nor his arms, nor the host at this moment should touch the corporal. He does not touch any of the other hosts or wafers to be consecrated. The celebrant includes in his thought all of the bread to be consecrated and says: *THIS IS MY BODY.* These words should be said in a clear but subdued tone of voice, rather slowly and with the utmost reverence.

Immediately the priest stands erect, places the consecrated Host reverently upon the corporal, and genuflects slowly and reverently, (At this point a server should now sound the sacring bell, the most pleasing way being three short tinkles or strokes. If a gong is used, it should be sounded thrice. The thurifer, if there be one, should as he

---

* Note that the words: *Take and eat ye all of this*, and those which follow later: *Take and drink ye all of this*, imply that all present are to partake, not that they are to partake of all. A slight pause after the word *all* will convey this meaning in each case.

kneels on the sanctuary floor, cense the Host with three short swings.) The priest, as soon as he has risen, takes the Host between the thumb and fore-finger of each hand (Plate 2, Fig. 5) elevates it above the level of his head immediately over the corporal. Again the sacring bell is sounded thrice, the censer swung thrice. The celebrant should keep his eyes fixed upon the Host. The priest lowers the Host and places It reverently upon the corporal, genuflects slowly while the bell sounds and the censer is swung thrice. (If the server is taught to ring the bell at equal intervals and for the same length of time, the priest can make his two genuflections and the elevation in equal rhythm with the sound of the bell, thereby greatly improving the ceremony.)

It has been the immemorial custom of Holy Church that from this time forward until the ablutions at the end of the Eucharist the thumb and forefinger of each hand are held together (Plate 1, Figs. 3 and 5) except when the celebrant touches the consecrated Host. It is an act of reverence in all that appertains to the handling of the consecrated Host, and is based on the thought that those fingers which have held the Host should not come into contact with anything else. Therefore, in all manual and other actions hereafter until the ablutions the forefinger and thumb of each hand are not disjoined (except when picking up the Host) either in turning the pages of the missal, lifting the chalice, or when turning to the people. (See p. 34.) The strict observance of this rule when elevating the chalice is left to the discretion of the priest.

The priest rises, uncovers the chalice (picking up the pall between the forefinger and second finger) and places the pall upon the folded veil, or upon the right side of the corporal. Standing erect, he says: *In like manner after he had supped....* The chalice is now grasped with both hands as follows: the tips of the joined thumb and forefinger of each hand are pressed against the stem above the knob; the tips of the ring finger and little finger of each hand touch one another in front of the stem below the knob; the tips of the middle finger of each hand touch one another behind the knob or stem. (Plate 2, Fig, 6) In this way the chalice can be held firmly and safely without separating the thumb and forefingers. It is necessary to practice lifting the chalice until it can be done without danger of spilling the wine. Some prefer to lift the chalice with the right hand, steadying it meanwhile by holding the base with the left. (Diagram 7) Others prefer to place the left hand under the knob and the right hand above the chalice. The method used depends upon the size and shape of the chalice. Use whichever way gives the greatest sense of security. If through age or physical disability, the chalice cannot be lifted in one of the ways just described, the celebrant may grasp the chalice in the usual way, but he must be careful that Particles of the Host are not adhering to his fingers when he does so.

DIAGRAM 7.

(Note: This custom of maintaining the thumb and forefinger of each hand joined is strongly recommended, but not rigidly enjoined, in the Liberal Catholic Rite. The utmost care, reverence and neatness in the handling of the Blessed Sacrament are enjoined. Throughout the instructions given in this book, however, it is supposed that thumb and forefinger of each hand are kept joined from the Consecration to the ablutions.)

The chalice is held a few inches above the corporal as the celebrant says: *taking also this noble chalice into His Holy and venerable hands...* but it is replaced on the corporal when he begins to say: *again giving thanks to Thee....* As he says: *He blessed it....* the priest, makes the sign of the cross over the chalice with the right hand, steadying it meanwhile by placing his left hand upon its base. He continues: *and gave it to His disciples saying....* He picks up the chalice again (Plate Fig. 6 or Diagram 7, Page 74) bowing slightly over it says: *Take and drink ye all of this for....* He says clearly, but in a subdued tone, and with intention to consecrate: *THIS IS MY BLOOD.* These words should be said with the utmost reverence and rather slowly. While saying: *As oft as ... remembrance of me,* he replaces the Chalice on the corporal, in the centre, just behind the large consecrated Host. He stands erect, genuflects slowly in rhythm with the sacring bell which is rung thrice. The thurifer swings the censer thrice. The priest rises, lifts the Chalice with both hands (Plate 2, Fig. 6 or Diagram 7) and carefully elevates it above the level of his head immediately above the corporal. He should keep his eyes fixed on the Chalice. The bell is sounded and the censer rung thrice. He replaces the Chalice on the corporal, picks up the pall with the right hand between first and second fingers, covers the Chalice, kneels on both knees while the bell sounds and incense arises.

During the consecration of the Bread and Wine there is no better way for the celebrant to enter into the exaltation of the moment and bring into his soul genuine reverence, than to go back in thought to the first Eucharist when Our Lord broke bread and drank wine with the disciples the night before His death. Picture the love and reverence felt by them for Him, and then reverently try to merge the consciousness with that of the Christ as the narrative proceeds and the words of consecration are said, endeavoring to feel the tenderness and affection which He felt for His disciples as he spoke to them, knowing that in a few hours time His body would be slain. If the celebrant can do this while consecrating the Elements, he will find that the Sacred Mystery takes on new loveliness, depth and meaning.

Care should be taken when replacing the Chalice upon the corporal after the elevation, that the maniple hanging from the left arm does not brush the consecrated Host lying on the corporal onto the footpace.

After a moment of silent adoration the priest, still kneeling and with hands joined before his breast, repeats softly in company with the congregation the verse: *Thee we adore....* This ended, he remains kneeling for a moment and than rises. If a ciborium has been used to hold the wafers consecrated for the people, it should now be covered and placed out of the way on the far side of the corporal between the chalice and the tabernacle or to one side, but still on the corporal. It has been the custom in some churches to remove at this time from the tabernacle the ciborium (if any) containing consecrated Hosts which will be needed later on during the Communion of the people. This has been done during the saying of the hymn: *O come, all Ye faithful....* in accordance with directions given in Bishop Mazel's book, *The Ceremonies of the Holy Eucharist.* It is recommended that the ciborium be removed after the Communion of the priest, which is the usage of the Roman Church. It is desirable that the celebrant should not divert his attention from the hymn, the more so when the congregation is small. It is permissible at all services the second and third verses of the *Adeste Fideles* although this should not be done on occasion at the whim of the celebrant, but by mutual agreement between the priest and people, or when necessary to shorten the service.

Standing erect, with hands extended as is usual during the Canon, but with thumb and forefinger joined (Plate 1, Fig. 5) the priest begins the prayer: *Wherefore, O Lord....* At the words: *we do offer unto Thee*, he should join his hands in token of the offering made by himself and the congregation. The first three crosses which follow are made over the Host and Chalice together, the fourth cross over the Host alone and the fifth cross over the Chalice alone. (Plate 2, Fig. 2)

With a medium bow and still with joined hands, the celebrant lays this offering at the feet of our Lord with the prayer: *This do we present....* When he begins the prayer: *And as He hath ordained...* he stands erect and extends his hands (Plate 1, Fig. 5) At the word, *Body*, he makes the sign of the cross over the Host; at the word, *Blood*, he makes the same sign over the Chalice; at the word, *filled*, he makes with the right hand the sign of the cross over himself. During the prayer: *Likewise we pray Thee...* his hands are extended as usual at shoulder level, until the time comes to make the sign of the cross. At such times the left hand is lowered and held at the breast, while the right hand makes the sign of the cross, in this case over the Host and Chalice together. (Plate 2, Fig. 2)

He now uncovers the Chalice—lifting the pall between the fore and middle fingers of the right hand and laying it on the folded veil, or to the right side of the corporal, and steadying the base of the Chalice with his left hand as he does so—and picks up the Host between the thumb and forefinger of the right hand as he says: *All these things....* Holding the Chalice by the knob with the left hand (grasping the stem between the fore and middle fingers) (Plate 3, Fig. 1) he makes during the prayer the sign of the cross with the Host three times over the mouth of the Chalice, taking care neither to touch the metal of the Chalice with the Host nor to extend the sign much beyond the rim of the cup. While making the sign, the Host is held horizontally over the Chalice.

In the prayer which follows: *To Whom with Thee...* he makes two crosses horizontally with the Host--still in the horizontal position—between the Chalice and his breast. (Plate 3, Fig. 1) At the conclusion of the prayer he holds the Host upright over the Chalice, steadying it by resting the ring finger of the right hand upon the rim of the Chalice. (Plate 3, Fig. 2) With the Host in this position he elevates the Chalice to about the level of his shoulders. This Minor Elevation, as it is called, takes place as he says the words: *be ascribed all honour and glory throughout the ages of ages*. He replaces the Chalice on the corporal, puts the Host in its usual place on the corporal, rubs the thumb and forefinger of the right hand momentarily over the mouth of the Chalice in order to dislodge any clinging particles, covers the Chalice with the pall and genuflects.

If the Lord's Prayer is said the priest joins his hands before the breast at the words: *Let us pray*. At the words: *Our Father*, he extends them and keeps them in this position (Plate 1, Fig. 5) until the end of the prayer. The saying of the Lord's Prayer is optional.

The celebrant now moves the purificator to the right, uncovering the right edge of the paten. Gripping the paten between the fore and middle fingers of the right hand (Plate 3, Fig. 3), he draws it from beneath the corporal and holds it vertically, its lower edge resting on the purificator, just outside the corporal. The upper, or concave, side of the paten should face towards the middle. As he does this he says: *Here do we give.... generations. (*Note that in the Commemoration of the Saints the Third General Episcopal Synod ruled that the words: *the ever-virgin Mother*, should be changed to *Mother of our Lord*.) At the words: *And we join...* he crosses himself with the paten, holding it vertically while doing so. Immediately he lowers the paten and while continuing the prayer, slips it under the Host with the aid of the left forefinger, (Plate 3, Fig. 4) He then places the paten on the corporal in the middle, just in front of the Chalice.

The celebrant uncovers the Chalice. Pushing the Host with the left forefinger over the right edge of the paten so that it can be readily picked up, he takes the Host between the thumb and forefinger of each hand and holds It over the mouth of the Chalice, saying: *O Son of God....* Upon reaching the words: *we break This Thy Body*, he breaks the Host, using both hands, straight down the middle. Care should be taken to hold the Host horizontally quite close to the mouth of the Chalice while breaking It, and to break It by pressing downward with the thumbs, so that any Particles which may fly off will fall into the Chalice. The Portion of the Host held in the right hand is immediately deposited on the paten. Again, using the right hand, he breaks off a small particle from the left half of the Host remaining in the left hand, which in the meantime he has continued to hold over the mouth of the Chalice. Holding this Particle over the Chalice, he deposits the Portion remaining in his left hand on the paten in the position it held before the fraction. Steadying the Chalice by holding the knob with the left hand, he makes the sign of the cross with the Particle thrice over the Chalice from rim to rim, saying as he does so: *praying that by ... Thy blessing*. At the words: *to be one in Thee*, the celebrant drops the Particle into the Wine, rubs the right thumb and forefinger momentarily over the Chalice, and covers it with the pall. If the Particle is dropped into the Chalice near its front edge, there is less likelihood of It adhering to the sides of the Chalice at the Communion.

The prayer: *O Lord Jesu Christ...* is said with the hands extended and while facing the altar. This ended, the priest joins his hands, genuflects, steps one pace to his left (this is done so that he may not turn his back directly on the consecrated Host) and turns to face the people. He extends his hands as at a Minor Benediction (Plate 1, Fig. 5) and says: *The peace of the Lord be always with you.* At the response he turns back to the altar and returns to the middle. With hands extended he now says: *O Thou Who in this adorable Sacrament....*

The Communion to the Benediction

The priest may now say silently the prayer: *Unto Thee, O Perfect....* Genuflecting, the celebrant rises and communicates. He may either place the two Portions of the Host (resting on the paten) one upon the other, or he may break each of these two Portions in half, thus making four. (This latter practice is best, because four smaller pieces are easier to consume than two large ones, and also, at High Celebration, two of the Portions may be administered to the deacon and subdeacon.) With the left hand he lifts the paten, and then with the right hand picks up the Portions of the Host, making with them the sign of the cross over himself, saying silently as he does so: *The Body of our Lord Christ keep me unto life eternal.* He should be careful to hold the paten under the Portions of the Host while making the sign and not to go much beyond the edge of the paten in signing himself. These precautions are taken to catch any Particles of the Host which may fall. The celebrant reverently receives the Host, inclining himself over the altar, but not touching it. In consuming the Host it is best to break It against the roof of his mouth and not between the teeth. Not only may this latter be considered irreverent, but also parts of the Host may lodge between the teeth. While consuming the Host the hands are joined. As soon as it is consumed, he kneels on the right knee or both knees, and remains for a few moments in meditation.

Rising, he uncovers the Chalice. He inspects the paten to see if any Particles are there. If so, he pushes them into the Chalice with the right forefinger. He also examines the corporal for Particles. If any are seen he gathers them on to the paten in some seemly manner and transfers them to the Chalice. Lifting the Chalice by the knob with the right hand, while steadying it with the left (Diagram 7, Page 71) he makes with it the sign of the cross over himself, saying silently: *The Blood of our Lord Christ keep me unto life eternal.* Raising the Chalice to his lips he drinks all the Wine, taking care to receive the Particle floating in It. To prevent the Particle from adhering to the sides of the Chalice at the time the Wine is consumed, some gentle motion may be imparted to the Chalice. The Wine should be consumed in one or two draughts, touching the lips as little as possible. The celebrant should not throw back the head any more than is absolutely necessary. Placing the chalice on the corporal, but not covering it with the pall, he joins his hands, and kneels on one knee, or both knees, saying silently: *Thanks be to God for His unspeakable Gift.* After a moment of meditation he rises. At this point it is customary for the celebrant to take from the tabernacle the ciborium containing the reserved Hosts, provided enough have not been consecrated at the Eucharist to communicate the people.

For the reception of Communion it is necessary for the servers and clergy present in the sanctuary to arrange themselves in some convenient order, either upon the steps and sanctuary floor before the altar, or at the sides, depending upon local conditions. The exact grouping must be left flexible as it depends upon the arrangements in the sanctuary and the number of clergy and servers present. The servers usually kneel in one or more rows on the sanctuary floor in front of the altar steps, but leaving room for any clergy present to kneel on the lowest step, and for the celebrant to pass between the rows of communicants. The clergy kneel on the lowest altar step.

All should take their places and kneel together. If there be no clergy present and only one or two servers, they kneel for Communion at the epistle end of the footpace. All who have received Communion at a previous Celebration should of course remain at their seats.

The celebrant now administers Communion to any of the clergy and the servers present; the general rule is that Communion is administered from left to right; that is, the celebrant begins with the one at the epistle end of the line and continues to the gospel end. This is not possible, of course, when, because of greater convenience, those in the sanctuary receive Communion kneeling at their seats.

If the Hosts for the people were consecrated in a ciborium, the priest of course administers from the ciborium. If the Hosts were consecrated while lying on the corporal, he may place a sufficient number upon the paten and administer therefrom, but it is more convenient and safer to administer from a ciborium, if one is available.

When all the clergy and servers have been communicated, the priest ascends to the footpace, and, standing in the middle facing the people, makes the sign of the cross vertically in the air with one of the Hosts, holding the ciborium or paten beneath it as he does so. He says at the same time in a clear voice: ✠ *Ye that desire ... holy Sacrament.* The cross should not be much larger than the diameter of the ciborium.

If clergy and servers have been kneeling before the altar for the reception of Communion they should at this time rise *together* and, *without* genuflecting, go to their seats in the sanctuary where they immediately kneel and remain kneeling until the priest has gone to the communion rail, thereupon they are seated. As soon as all have retired from before the altar the priest walks to the communion rail and administers to the first person at the epistle end with the usual sign and words. Passing on to the next person, and to the next, he communicates all who are kneeling at the rail. By this time others may have come forward for Communion. If so, he returns to the epistle end and begins to administer. When all have received Communion, he returns to the altar and places the ciborium or paten or chalice on the corporal. It should be remembered that no one ever genuflects while *carrying* the Host.

If there are any consecrated Hosts left over which are not to be put in the tabernacle, the priest consumes them now, doing so reverently and while inclining over the altar. If the ciborium with the reserved Sacrament is to be put in the tabernacle, the celebrant places the lid and the ciborium veil (if any) on the ciborium, opens the tabernacle door, puts the ciborium therein, genuflects, closes and locks the door. All in the sanctuary genuflect while the door is open. If any ciboria have been emptied they should be purified at this time. Gathering any remaining Particles of the Host from the corporal or paten into the chalice, he takes it by the knob between fore and middle fingers of the right hand, holds it slightly to the epistle side, but still over the corporal, and allows the server who has come to the footpace with the cruets to pour a little wine into the chalice. The server retires to the upper step at the epistle end of the footpace. The priest, facing the altar, gently swirls the wine in the chalice so that it may gather up any Particles of the sacred Host and any drops of consecrated Wine. He should see that the wine which has just been poured into the chalice moistens all that portion of the interior of the cup where the consecrated Wine has touched. He now drinks the wine, touching his lips to the same part of the rim contacted while receiving the Wine during Communion. (That side of the chalice to be touched by the lips is marked with a small cross engraved or chased on the base of the chalice.) During these ablutions, no words are said nor is the sign of the cross made.

Taking the purificator he wraps it once round the bowl of the chalice and at the same time so grasps the bowl that while the thumb and forefinger of each hand are held together over the mouth of the chalice, the other fingers hold the bowl itself (Plate 3, Fig. 5). Going now to the server who is standing at the epistle end on the step below the footpace, a very little wine and then a considerably larger quantity of water are poured over his thumbs and forefingers. This is done to wash off any tiny Particles of Host which may adhere to the skin. It is well to rub the fingers together slightly as the water is being poured over them. The priest returns to the middle, places the chalice on the corporal, and dries his fingers on the purificator. *From this time onward the thumb and forefinger of each hand may be separated.* Lifting the chalice with the right hand he drinks the ablutions. Wiping his lips with the purificator, he places it on the altar to the right of the corporal. Taking the chalice, but not the purificator, he goes again to the server who pours some water directly into the chalice. The server bows, returns the cruets to the credence, and goes to his place. The priest returns to the middle, cleanses further the chalice and its rim, drinks the water, takes the purificator in the right hand and thoroughly wipes the interior of the chalice as well as the outside edge where his lips have touched.[*]

_____

[*] When the priest is celebrating alone, without the aid of an assistant, the following modification of the usual procedure is recommended at the Ablutions. The tray with the cruets is either placed before the service begins on the altar at the extreme epistle end, to the rear, or brought there from the credence by the celebrant when ready for the ablutions. At the ablutions the priest goes to that end, taking the purificator and carrying the chalice by his left hand. Picking up the wine cruet between the fore and middle fingers of

The priest places the chalice on the altar just off the corporal, folds the purificator lengthwise and lays it over the mouth of the chalice, puts the paten on the purificator and the pall on the paten. He folds the corporal and places it in the burse. Lifting the chalice he stands it in the centre over the altar stone and covers it with the veil. Upon the veil he lays the burse. The ablutions and the arrangement of the chalice should not take more than a minute and a half, or two minutes at the most.

If earlier in the Eucharist the missal stand has been transferred to the gospel side, it is now brought back to the epistle side.

Standing in the middle with hands joined and facing the altar the celebrant now says: *Under the veil ... Father's glory*. Still with joined hands, the priest walks to the epistle end of the altar, turns to face east and reads in unison with the people the Communio: *Amen... ever and ever. Amen*. Walking to the middle, he turns to give the Minor Benediction. At the response he turns back to the altar, walks again to the epistle end, faces east and says: *Let us pray*. The servers and people kneel and remain kneeling until the end of the Benediction. The priest, extending his hands, continues: *We who have ... Christ our Lord*. At the end of the Postcommunio the priest returns to the middle, turns to the people and says the Minor Benediction. Turning back to the altar, opening and then joining his hands, he says the words of dismissal to the Angels: *Ite, missa est*. The people respond: *Deo gratias*.

He again faces the people, standing in the middle with the right hand upraised in blessing (Plate 1, Fig. 6), the left hand being held lightly over the heart. He now pronounces the Benediction: *The peace... with you always*, making the sign of the cross with his opened hand over the people at the word, *Son*. After the people have responded *Amen*, the priest joins his hands and turns back to the altar by the gospel side, thus completing the circle. This is the second time in the Eucharistic service that such a complete turn is made.

---

* [Cont.]

the right hand, he pours sufficient wine into the chalice, replaces the cruet, returns to the middle and consumes the wine. Again going to the epistle end, he stands the chalice on the altar, and, grasping the wine cruet as before between the fore and middle fingers of the right hand, pours a little wine over the thumb and forefinger of the left, which he holds over the chalice. Then he pours a little water in the same way. Drying the fingers of the left hand on the purificator, he picks up first the wine and then the water cruet with the left hand in the ordinary way and pours wine and water over the fingers of the right hand. Drying the fingers of this hand, he consumes the contents of the chalice, pours water into the chalice, consumes this and returns to the middle to dry and cover the chalice as usual. Or, if preferred, the cruets may be left on the credence in the usual way, the priest going to the credence for the Ablutions instead of to the epistle end of the altar.

(Note that the second, or First Ray, Benediction appearing in the Liturgy [Second edition. Ed.] has been deleted from the Eucharist and placed among the Occasional Prayers. It is recommended that this Benediction be used rather at private gatherings than at public services.)

Closing the missal, he descends the front steps and, standing on the sanctuary floor in the middle before the lowest step, turns to face the altar. Genuflecting, (if the Host is reserved in the tabernacle, otherwise bowing) he puts on the biretta and returns to the vestry, usually by the most direct way, preceded by the clergy and servers who entered with him. When the celebrant genuflects before the altar, all in the sanctuary genuflect with him, except the cross bearer (if any) and his attendant candle bearers.

If the celebrant entered the sanctuary in cope (which does not happen very often at Low Celebration) he removes the chasuble and maniple and puts on the cope while standing in the middle before the lowest altar step, then genuflects, puts on his biretta and returns to the vestry.

It is a pleasing and reverential custom in some churches for the acolyte, who is to extinguish the candles, to enter the sanctuary promptly as soon as the celebrant has reached the vestry, and for the people to remain seated quietly or kneeling until the last candle has been extinguished. This practice is to be recommended.

After the service the tabernacle key is removed to a place of safety.

❊ ❊ ❊ ❊ ❊ ❊ ❊

The Shorter Form when Said by a Priest

The preparations to be made are exactly the same as in the Longer Form. The following differences in performing the Shorter Celebration are, however, to be noted.

At the end of the *Asperges* as described on p. 62, the priest says the Antiphon and Canticle of the Shorter Form in company with the people. The service proceeds as usual until the end of the Absolution. At this point he turns to the altar, joins his hands and says: *With praise and ... be built*, the servers and people responding: *To God alone be the glory*. While the altar may be censed during the saying of the Introit, it is permissible and much to be preferred that it be censed before the Introit is said. The Epistle, Gradual, *Munda Cor Meum* and Gospel may be omitted, but if said, the ritual of the Full Form is followed exactly. There need not be a sermon. The Act of Faith that is printed in the Shorter Form instead of the Nicene Creed may be replaced by any one of the Creeds or Acts of Faith permitted in the Longer Form.

A hymn may be sung and a collection taken immediately after the *Credo*. A rubric in the Liturgy permits the singing of the Offertory Hymn during the second censing of the altar. From every standpoint, except that of saving a minute or two of time, this is the less desirable time for a hymn. If a hymn is sung during the second censing, then the prayers: *As this incense rises before Thee, O Lord...* and *May the Lord...* are said in a moderate tone of voice heard only in the sanctuary. The second censing is exactly the same as in the Longer Form. The *Lavabo* is the same, except that no words are said unless desired by the celebrant, in which case he uses those of the Longer Form.

The *Orate Fratres* is longer than in the Longer Form, but the prayer which follows is shorter. There are only two verses in the hymn, *O come, all ye faithful*.

The hands are extended while saying the prayer: *Wherefore, O Lord and heavenly Father...*, which follows the hymn, but they are joined for a moment at the word: *offer*. When in this prayer the priest reaches the words: *and we pray that Thou...* he bows the head and remains in this position until the words: *eternal Sacrifice*. The ritual actions from this point onwards are exactly the same as in the Longer Form. It should be noted that the Lord's Prayer has been omitted and that the modified Commemoration of the Saints as in the Longer Form should be used instead of that printed in the [original] Shorter Form. The prayer preceding the Salutation of Peace and one Minor Benediction appearing in the Longer Form are omitted in the Shorter Form.

❊ ❊ ❊ ❊ ❊ ❊ ❊

Either Form When Said by a Priest in the Presence of a Bishop

In both the Longer and Shorter Forms for the Celebration of the Holy Eucharist the following points are to be noted whenever there is a Low Celebration by a priest in the presence of a bishop.

In any but a cathedral church (where the bishop will have his throne) a faldstool or suitable seat should be arranged for the bishop on the gospel side of the sanctuary. A praying desk is placed in front of the seat and a cushion on which to kneel. Some device should be arranged at his praying desk to hold the bishop's crozier upright. Other seats may be placed on either side for the bishop's personal attendants, such as the crozier bearer and chaplain. If it can be done without over-crowding, the seats for the other clergy should be arranged on the epistle side of the sanctuary.

In the procession from the vestry to the sanctuary the bishop comes last, unless the celebrant be in chasuble, in which case the celebrant walks last. He is preceded by his crozier bearer. Two candle bearers, if available, walk in front of the celebrant.

Upon reaching the sanctuary all go to their assigned places after genuflecting (or bowing) as usual. The priest gives his biretta to a server to place upon his seat. The bishop retains his mitre or biretta and holds his crozier. (In what follows, it is assumed that the Shorter *Asperges* in being said.) All standing, and making the sign of the cross over themselves, the bishop says aloud the Invocation: *In the Name ... Holy Ghost*. After the invocation he removes the mitre or biretta. He is then seated and the crozier is put in its holder.

A bishop in choir dress always wears his biretta while *seated* at his throne or faldstool. He removes it when he kneels or stands, except when being censed or holding the crozier for the Invocation, Absolution, *Munda Cor Meum* and Blessings.

Upon receiving the aspergill the celebrant crosses himself, and asperses the altar, sanctuary and people in the usual manner.

At the end of the *Confiteor* the celebrant remains kneeling on the lowest altar step before the altar while the bishop gives the Absolution. The bishop rises with mitre (or biretta), takes the crozier and gives the Absolution (Plate 3, Fig. 6), standing at his seat. He makes the sign of the cross four times while so doing: one at the word, *Father*, once at the word, *Son*, once at the words, *Holy Ghost*, and again at the word, *absolve*. At the end of the Absolution the bishop blesses the incense, and resumes his seat. He holds the crozier while blessing the incense. The celebrant continues the Celebration.

Whenever incense is to be blessed, either at the first or second censing, or before the reading of the Gospel, the thurifer (accompanied by the boat bearer if there be one) should go to the bishop and not to the celebrant. The bishop rises, with his mitre (or biretta) on, takes his crozier and blesses the incense with the usual words. (In some churches the arrangements are such that it is much more convenient for the bishop to remain seated while blessing incense. This is permissible.) At the first and second censing the thurifer returns to the epistle end of the footpace and gives the censer to the celebrant, who censes the altar in the usual way. At the end of the second censing the thurifer should cense the bishop immediately after he has censed the celebrant, the bishop standing and wearing the mitre or biretta while being censed.

If the Gospel is to be read by the celebrant, he kneels in the middle on the edge of the footpace and says the *Munda Cor Meum*; the bishop, who stands with mitre or biretta and crozier, gives him the blessing: *May the Lord ... made manifest*. The priest rises, bows to the bishop, goes to stand on the footpace in the middle, turns to the people and says: *The Lord be with you*. He reads the Gospel in the usual way. Meanwhile the bishop stands facing the Book of Gospels, holding the crozier, but not wearing the mitre or biretta. At the end of the Gospel, the celebrant, since he himself read the Gospel, is not censed, but, bowing to the Bishop, returns to the middle of the footpace either to give the notices, deliver the sermon, or continue the service, as the case may be.

The bishop holds the crozier, but does not wear the mitre or biretta, during the recitation of the *Creed* or Act of Faith.

The celebrant, not the bishop, blesses the water at the *offertorium*.

The celebrant, after he himself has communicated, administers Communion first to the bishop and then to the clergy and servers in the sanctuary and finally to the people.

After the Celebrant has said: *Ite missa est*, and the people have responded, he descends from the footpace to the sanctuary floor and kneels on the lowest altar step in the middle. The bishop rises, puts on the mitre (or biretta, if in choir dress), takes the crozier and gives the Benediction. Returning to the vestry the bishop walks in procession in the same position as before.

❀ ❀ ❀ ❀ ❀ ❀ ❀

Either Form When Said by a Bishop

When Low Celebration is said by a bishop either in the Longer or the Shorter Form, the preparations and ceremonial actions are exactly the same as those prescribed for a priest except in the following particulars:

A seventh candle is placed on the tabernacle in front of the altar cross. This must be of such a size as not to obscure the cross. Or this candle may be placed in a socket at the back of the cross.

A bishop wears a mitre in procession to the sanctuary. He may vest in cope, but it is more usual at Low Celebrations to go to the sanctuary by the short way wearing the chasuble. In addition he uses a crozier, ring and pectoral cross. In vesting a bishop does not cross the stole in front as does a priest, but allows each end to hang down straight from the shoulder. The pectoral cross is suspended round the neck by a green and gold cord and is worn over the alb when vested in a cope, but outside the chasuble when vested in a chasuble. This is a departure from the older practice and is done because the cross, as a powerful centre of radiation, should not be covered over by the material of the chasuble. A bishop while walking in procession may either carry the crozier or have it carried before him by a crozier bearer. (The Third General Episcopal Synod ruled that this was optional.) Two candle bearers, if available, walk immediately in front of the bishop if he is carrying the crozier, or in front of the crozier bearer.

At private or semi-private Celebrations a bishop may wear his biretta and dispense with the crozier, or the latter may be stationed permanently at the altar during the service though not moved in the usual way.

The bishop comes last in the procession, except when there is a banner to be carried behind the bishop at the end of the procession. The Presiding Bishop, however, takes the place of honour even over a bishop-celebrant, if vested in cope and mitre.

The bishop blesses the people as he passes among them in procession by making over them at intervals the sign of the cross. The sign should not be too conspicuous or exaggerated, and should be made with a slight motion of the forearm. Care should be taken not to make the sign at such intervals as to give the impression of beating time to the hymn, if one is sung during the procession.

Arriving before the lowest step of the altar the bishop genuflects (or bows). If wearing a cope, the procedure as at *Missa Cantata*, in removing the cope and substituting the chasuble, is followed. The mitre and crozier are used at the Invocation. After the Invocation, he gives the crozier to a server to place in the holder at the gospel end of the altar. The station of the crozier bearer should be at that side of the sanctuary near the crozier. The bishop removes his mitre and gives it to a server to place on the altar at the gospel side. The mitre is usually stood upright, face to the front, the ends of the two fanons hanging down over the edge of the frontal. If little space is available, or if the mitre will not stand alone, it is laid down, point towards the gradine. The biretta is placed in the same position.

The course of the shorter *Asperges* and the Holy Eucharist is now the same as when celebrated by a priest. Upon ascending to the footpace to give the *Absolution* the bishop first puts on the mitre, and then, receiving the crozier from the bearer, turns to the people in the usual way to give the Absolution. A bishop in pronouncing Absolution or in giving a Benediction holds the thumb, forefinger and middle finger extended, the ring finger and little finger being bent so as nearly to touch the palm. (Plate 3, Fig. 6). In giving the Absolution the bishop makes the sign of the cross four times as previously described.

The crozier bearer should present the crozier to the bishop with the curve of the volute reversed from the way it is carried in procession, so that when the bishop takes the crozier it is in exactly the right position for turning to the people. The crozier bearer, in presenting the crozier, ascends, at some point nearest to the bishop's left hand, either to the step below the footpace or to the footpace itself. As soon as he has delivered the crozier he should retire immediately to the sanctuary floor, until such time as the crozier is to be returned to him.

At the end of the Absolution (or of the versicle: *With praise ... built*, in the Shorter Form) the bishop turns to face south. The thurifer (and boat bearer, if any) comes to him with the opened censer. The bishop sprinkles incense upon the charcoal and blesses it in the usual manner. He wears his mitre and holds the crozier. He returns the crozier, removes the mitre and stands it on the altar (an acolyte may receive the mitre and do this for him), takes the censer and censes the altar in the prescribed manner.

Some bishop-celebrants prefer that the mitre as well as the missal stand be removed from the altar while it is being censed, and held by a server (or servers) standing *in plano*. This is optional.

After he has returned the censer to the thurifer, he puts on the mitre, turns back to the thurifer (who stands on the sanctuary floor at the epistle end of the footpace) and is censed with three short triple swings. Immediately he turns back to the altar, places his mitre thereon, and proceeds with the service.

If the Epistle and Gospel are to be read it is best that the bishop wait until the end of the Gradual before blessing the incense, inasmuch as he must put on his mitre and take his crozier before so doing. He returns the crozier and removes the mitre immediately after blessing the incense, if he himself is to read the Gospel, but if the Gospel is to be read by another, the bishop retains the mitre and holds the crozier during the saying of the *Munda cor Meum* by the gospeller and the prayer which comes after. Immediately afterward, if there be a separate gospeller, he gives the crozier to the bearer to hold, takes off the mitre and places it on the altar, and once more takes the crozier to hold during the reading of the Gospel. During the Gospel the bishop stands on the footpace, a little to the epistle side facing the gospeller and holding the crozier with both hands in front of him. The Gospel ended, the bishop gives the crozier to the bearer, puts on the mitre and is censed by the gospeller with three short triple swings. Should the bishop himself read the Gospel he stands as does a priest at Low Celebration on the gospel end of the footpace facing the people. The crozier bearer holds the crozier while standing near the bishop on the sanctuary floor.

It is the general rule that at all services the crozier bearer, while holding the crozier, stands near the bishop, usually to his left, facing in the same direction as the bishop. But at the Gospel, when read by the bishop, the crozier bearer must stand at the bishop's right.

If there be a *sermon* by a priest, the bishop goes to his throne wearing the mitre, which he retains during the sermon. If he himself is to preach, he may do so either from the throne, or while seated on a faldstool placed on the footpace in the middle, or from the pulpit. In the first case the crozier bearer may sit (or stand) beside him to his left, in the second he should stand beside him to his left. If the sermon is to be delivered from a pulpit, the bishop removes his chasuble and maniple and may put on the biretta before going to the pulpit. The crozier bearer does not accompany him.

During the recitation of the *Creed* or Act of Faith the bishop, after he has raised his hands in the opening gesture, takes the crozier and holds it with both hands as he faces the altar. He does not wear the mitre. At the end of the Creed he gives the crozier to the bearer to fix in the holder.

At the second censing he wears the mitre and holds the crozier while blessing the incense, and wears the mitre while being censed. At the end of the service he puts on the mitre, takes the crozier, turns to the people and gives the Benediction as previously described. Should he change from chasuble to cope, the procedure as at *Missa Cantata* is followed.

The following table indicates the occasions the Holy Eucharist a bishop makes use of mitre (or biretta) and crozier.

MITRE or BIRETTA	CROZIER
Invocation	Invocation
Procession	Procession (carried by self or bearer)
Absolution	Absolution
Blessing Incense	Blessing Incense
While being censed	++++++++++
During reading of Epistle	Blessing Incense at Gradual
Blessing Incense at Gradual	*Munda cor Meum* by separate
++++++++++	gospeller
Munda cor Meum by separate	Blessing separate gospeller
gospeller	Held by bearer, if bishop reads Gos-
Blessing separate gospeller	pel
++++++++++	Held by bearer, if sermon at throne
Sermon, unless at pulpit where	or faldstool
Biretta is worn	Creed
Blessing Incense	Blessing Incense
While being censed	++++++++++
Benediction	Benediction
Procession	Procession (carried by self or bearer)

Whenever seated except when Host is exposed.

CHAPTER VI

MISSA CANTATA

The Longer Form When Sung by a Priest or Bishop

Missa Cantata is the same in its ritual actions as Low Celebration, but it differs from the latter in that certain portions are sung instead of being said. Whenever the Full Form is sung by a priest or bishop the following particulars should be noted *in addition* to those mentioned in Chapter V.

Three hymns, if hymns are sung, are usually required: introcessional, offertory and recessional. The first and last are of course sung while the procession is moving to and from the sanctuary, the offertory while the collection is being taken. Processions which take place while a hymn is being sung tend to stimulate the enthusiasm of the congregation and to enable the people to enter more heartily and with greater intensity into the service. The order of such processions may be that of those already described (pp. 41-44) with the exception, of course, that at *Missa Cantata* there is neither deacon nor subdeacon. If, as is usually the case, the number of servers available is small, the work should be distributed as follows: If there is only one server he carries the censer. If two are available, the second has his hands free, since candles are carried in procession in pairs. If there are three servers, the one walking first carries the censer, and the other two may carry processional lights. A fourth server may follow the thurifer carrying the processional cross.

If special music such as an organ voluntary or a vocal solo is desired during the service of the Holy Eucharist, it may come immediately before or after the sermon, or it may take the place of the sermon, or it may take the place of the offertory hymn.

In a large church, more elaborate arrangements may be needed for the collection than outlined in Chapter V. If there are sufficient servers, they may take the collection bags and, genuflecting together before the altar, go out among the congregation, working from the front to the rear of the Church, where they meet and return together to the sanctuary. They present the bags to the M.C. (or a server) who usually receives them upon a plate which he presents to the celebrant. The servers genuflect together and go to their places. If lay ushers are used, they go among the congregation in a similar manner, but generally only two will come forward to the M.C. to present all the offering bags.

The celebrant should vest exactly as for Low Celebration, except that instead of the chasuble he wears a cope, if possible of the colour of the Day. Each church should have at least one white cope which may be used on all occasions by the priest until copes of the other colours are available. Failing such a cope, he may enter in alb. The maniple and chasuble (the latter arranged ready for placing over the head of the celebrant) are placed beforehand on the seat of the celebrant in the sanctuary.

The *Asperges* of the Shorter Form may be used. The celebrant can then enter wearing the chasuble and maniple. In large buildings the cope is usually worn during the procession, more especially on festivals, even though the Short *Asperges* is to be used. The chasuble and maniple must then be put on before the Opening Invocation.

The priest in procession does not make the sign of the cross over the people, this action being reserved to the bishop alone. The priest can greatly help his congregation, however, if he holds in mind the Presence of our Lord and radiates that peace and bless ing as he passes among them. All genuflect (or bow) upon arrival in the sanctuary, and go to their assigned place.

The *Asperges* of the Shorter Form having been described in Chapter V, the *Asperges* of the Full Form will now be taken up in ritualistic detail.

At the conclusion of the hymn, the celebrant (still vested in cope) kneels on the lowest step before the altar. *All others remain standing*, except the server, who may be kneeling at the priest's side. The organist plays over the opening notes of the part to be sung by the celebrant alone, sounds the first note again and immediately the priest sings: *Thou shalt sprinkle me....* At once the singing of the rest of the antiphon is taken up by the choir and people. (These words sung by the celebrant do not indicate that the priest must begin the aspersing at this point. They only indicate the keynote of the entire Psalm.) Again after the organist has played over the opening notes the celebrant sings: *I will lift up mine eyes unto the hills*. The rest of that verse and all the other verses of the Psalm are then sung by the choir and people. As soon as the celebrant has sung the words just mentioned, but *not* before (in order to avoid crowding the ritualistic action of the *Asperges* between the antiphon and the opening words of the Psalm sung by the celebrant), he receives the aspergill from the server and with it makes the sign of the cross over himself. Still kneeling, he sprinkles the altar in the usual manner. Rising, the celebrant turns to the right and asperses first the clergy on the epistle side and then those on the gospel side, next the servers and choir on the epistle side and then those on the gospel side, and finally the people, aspersing them first down the middle of the church, then to the left, then to the right. In doing all this, the celebrant does not move from the middle on the sanctuary floor, but turns in the various directions required for the aspersing. When he turns back to the altar, he gives the aspergill to the server (who places it on the credence) and takes up the singing of the Psalm. Again, after the organist has played the opening notes, the celebrant sings the first part of the antiphon, the choir and people singing the rest.

Immediately after the close of the antiphon, the celebrant sings: *O Lord, open Thou our lips*. (The practice in some churches of making the sign of the cross over the lips while saying or singing this versicle was not approved by the Third General Episcopal Synod.) After the response of the people he sings: *Who shall ascend into the hill of the Lord?* During the singing of the response the celebrant hands the missal to the server. He now turns to the people with hands extended and sings: *The Lord be with you*. At the response the celebrant joins the hands and turns back to the altar.

It may be stated finally that throughout the service all Minor Benedictions are sung by the celebrant and the responses by the choir and people. It should be noted that in short versicles sung to simple tones the organist does not play over the music before they are sung (except in certain cases to be noted hereafter), but merely, *when neces-sary*, sounds the reciting note for the guidance of the celebrant (who sings without ac-companiment) and plays the accompaniment to the response of the people. Those prayers, or portions of the Eucharist, which are not set to music, and are recited by the celebrant alone, may be either said or intoned, *unless otherwise directed*. If the celebrant has a pleasing, well-modulated voice, an intoned service is effective end acceptable, but in the majority of cases, it is better to read the service. The key in which a service is in-toned is a matter to be decided by each celebrant himself, always, however, with the willing cooperation of the congregation. The General Episcopal Synod recommended that whenever possible the key in which the service is printed shall be used by the cele-brant. The sentences announcing the Epistle and Gospel are never intoned.

The celebrant now intones: *Let us pray*. All kneel except the celebrant. He in-tones the *Collect of the Asperges*. (If the celebrant has not a good voice it is permissible to read this Collect.) The Collect ended, all rise. The celebrant, still standing in the mid dle before the lowest altar step, is vested in the chasuble and maniple in the following manner: If there are two servers available, the one unfastens the cope and lifts it from the shoulders of the celebrant. The server then holds up the cope behind the celebrant so that it serves as a screen between the celebrant and the people. The other server, who meantime has brought the chasuble and maniple from the priest's seat, vests the cele-brant in the chasuble. The cope is then taken away to the place where it is to remain dur-ing the service. The celebrant is vested in the maniple. If only one server is available, he will bring the chasuble and maniple to the celebrant and hold the cope while the cele-brant vests.

The celebrant now intones the *Invocation*, crossing himself as he does so. After the antiphon has been sung by all together, the organist plays over the opening notes of the *Canticle* and the celebrant alone sings the words: *I was glad when they said unto me*. The rest of the first verse and all of the other verses of the Canticle as well as the anti-phon are sung by all together. The celebrant sings the three versicles which follow, the choir and people the responses. The *Introit*, *Kyrie*, and *Gloria in Excelsis* are sung by all together, the people, choir and all servers standing during the Introit and Gloria and kneeling during the Kyrie. (The celebrant does not sing alone the opening words of the Gloria, although this may be indicated in the Musical Liturgy.) The celebrant stands throughout. During the singing of the *Gloria in Excelsis* the thurifer stands on the sanc-tuary floor in the middle, facing the altar, and swinging his censer to and fro with long swings.

The celebrant intones: *Let us pray*, before beginning the Collects, and after each Collect the people sing, *Amen*. The *Epistle*, *Gradual* and *Gospel* may be omitted, although this is not usually done at a Sung Eucharist. If not omitted, all stand and sing *Thanks be to God* at the end of the Epistle. The opening words of the Gradual: *He that loveth wisdom loveth life*, are sung by the celebrant alone after the organist has played over the opening notes, the remainder of the Gradual being sung by all. (This same procedure is followed in connection with the Proper Graduals. The celebrant always sings alone the first half of the first verse, the choir and people singing the rest of the Gradual.) The thurifer and boat bearer, the two candle bearers, and any others who may assist at the reading of the Gospel should not stir until just after the celebrant has sung the opening words of the Gradual. They then rise, go to the middle (unless they have been standing at the epistle side of the sanctuary), genuflect and go about preparing for their several duties. (If sufficient servers are available, one should hold the Book of Gospels, while two act as attendant candle bearers. The ritualistic actions of this group, including the thurifer, are similar to those ascribed in Chapter VII.) At a Sung Eucharist, the thurifer goes to the celebrant with the censer during the singing of the Gradual, not afterward as at Low Celebration.

If the Epistle and Gospel are read by other than the celebrant, they conform to the instructions given in Chapter VII for reading by the subdeacon and deacon, page 97, paragraphs 3-5. The persons reading the lessons return to their seats after the gospeller has censed the celebrant at the conclusion of the Gospel reading.

All sing the *Amen* after the *Munda Cor Meum* and after the prayer which follows. As soon as the Gospel is announced all sing: *Glory be to Thee, O Lord*, and after the Gospel has been read they sing: *Praise be to Thee, O Christ*. The Creed or Act of Faith is intoned by all.

The Preface (and the Proper Preface, if any) is sung by the celebrant alone. The *Sanctus* and *Benedictus Qui Venit* are sung by all together. During the Sanctus at each *Holy*, a server rings the sacring bell (or the chimes) once and the thurifer (who will normally be kneeling in the middle on the sanctuary floor) swings the censer with one short swing toward the altar cross. (This is the usual procedure for *Missa Cantata*. In a large church and before a large congregation the usage of High Mass in regard to the ringing of the bell and the number of swings of the censer may be followed here and at the time of the Consecration.) The thurifer continues to kneel and swing the censer to and fro during the rest of the Sanctus and *Benedictus Qui Venit*. If desired there may be candle bearers in the sanctuary as described in Chapter VII.

The hymns: *Thee we adore* and *O come, all ye faithful* are sung, the former while all are kneeling, the latter while all are standing. There should be a short pause for devotion and recollection between the two hymns during which soft music may be played upon the organ while all are kneeling. The second and third verses of the *Adeste* may be provided this is understood by the congregation. If the Lord's Prayer is used, it may be either said or intoned by all.

If there are a number of clergy and servers to receive Communion, they usually come forward and kneel at their assigned places before the altar during the prayer: *O Lord Jesu Christ* preceding the Salutation of Peace.

The *Communio* is sung by all standing. Usually at this time any candle bearers come in from the vestry bearing their lighted candles and arrange themselves on either side of the sanctuary, the two who are to accompany the cross bearer being nearest the sanctuary gates. The next pair nearer the altar should be those who come next in procession, and so on. When this is done, each pair of candle bearers joins the procession without confusion as it leaves the sanctuary.

At the end of the final Benediction the celebrant turns back to the altar. After the *Amen* he descends to the sanctuary floor to stand in the middle before the lowest altar step facing the altar. Custom varies as to whether the celebrant wears the cope for the outgoing procession or not. In large buildings, where there is a choice between long and short ways of entering and going out, the longer way will be taken at festival times. The cope is then worn. The method of changing from chasuble to cope is the same as the reciprocal process described at the beginning of the service.

While the organist is playing over the tune of the recessional hymn, the thurifer goes to the sanctuary gates followed by the cross bearer carrying the processional cross. Upon reaching the gates they turn to face the altar. The clergy should rise and prepare to join the procession. The signal for the procession to start is usually given by the genuflection of the celebrant, all genuflecting with him. (The time to give this signal depends upon the length of the hymn and the distance to be traversed by the procession before reaching the vestry. Sometimes the signal is given at the first verse, sometimes not until near the last verse. Another factor is whether the congregation has been found to continue singing or not once the procession begins.) After genuflecting, all turn by the right to face the sanctuary gates, which have been opened by the thurifer, and pass out in procession. The choir joins the procession at the sanctuary gates.

❀ ❀ ❀ ❀ ❀ ❀ ❀

The Shorter Form When Sung by a Priest or Bishop

Three hymns are usual as in the Longer Form. The *Asperges* may be intoned. After the celebrant has said: *Brethren, let us ... Temple*, all sing the antiphon. The organist plays the opening notes of the Canticle and the celebrant alone sings the words: *We are no more strangers and foreigners*. The remainder of the Canticle and the antiphon are sung by all together. After the Absolution the celebrant, facing the altar, sings: *With praise and with prayer shall our Temple be built*, the people singing the response: *To God alone be the glory*. The remaining sung portions of the service are the same as in the Longer Form.

Either Form When Sung by a Priest in the Presence of a Bishop

When a priest sings the Longer Form in the presence of a bishop, he asperses himself and the altar in the usual manner, rises and gives the aspergill to a server to take to the bishop. The bishop asperses himself and his immediate attendants, and then returns the aspergill to the server. The latter returns to the celebrant and gives him the aspergill. The priest then asperses the clergy, choir and people in the usual way. When celebrating the Shorter Form the aspergill is not taken to the bishop as the celebrant himself asperses all in the sanctuary.

❀ ❀ ❀ ❀ ❀ ❀ ❀

Instructions to the Organist

The following instructions are intended to guide the organist in the playing of incidental music either at a *Missa Cantata* or a High Celebration in the Longer Form, but may with obvious modifications be used in the Shorter Form.

After the *Asperges* Collect:	Soft music until the celebrant is ready.
Confiteor:	The Amen at the end of the Confiteor is said, not sung.
First Censing of Altar:	Soft incidental music during censing of the altar and of the celebrant, unless the Introit be sung during the censing.
Minor Benediction:	Intoning note for celebrant.
After *Introit*:	Modulate between *Introit* and *Kyrie*, unless the Introit has already been sung.
After *Kyrie*:	Modulate between *Kyrie* and *Gloria In Excelsis*.
Gloria In Excelsis:	Sung by all from the beginning. Priest does not sing the opening words alone.
After Epistle:	If Proper Gradual, play *Thanks be to God* in the key of that Proper Gradual.
After *Praise be to Thee, O Christ*	Incidental music until the priest is ready to give the church notices, deliver the sermon, or continue the service, as the case may be.
Credo:	Intoning note for the Creed or Act of Faith, if intoned.
Offertory Hymn:	An organ voluntary may take the place of the hymn, or there may be a solo or a selection by the choir.
Second Censing of Altar:	Incidental music during second censing, censing of celebrant and until *Orate Fratres*. (Play rather softly while celebrant is saying: *As this incense ...Thy blessing* and *May the Lord ... charity*.)

After "Thee we adore"	Play softly for a moment, then modulate to *Adeste Fideles*. Strengthen music just before beginning latter hymn.
Lord's Prayer:	Accompany prayer, if sung or intoned, in G.
Salutation of Peace:	Intoning note (G) for celebrant or singer. Accompany response of people as at a Minor Benediction.
Communion:	Soft incidental music from the time the priest finishes his own Communion until he is ready to begin: *Under the veil of earthly things....*
Benediction:	The Benediction may be followed by by a suitable Amen, such as Stainer's Sevenfold Amen.

✠

CHAPTER VII

HIGH CELEBRATION OF THE HOLY EUCHARIST

The Longer Form When Celebrated by a Priest

High Celebration is the same as Missa Cantata except that the celebrant is assisted by a deacon and subdeacon of the Eucharist, which modifies some of the ceremonies and makes them slightly more elaborate. There may be a Master of Ceremonies (referred to hereafter as the M.C.) and it is useful to have more acolytes. The preparations of the altar and sanctuary are exactly the same as for Low Celebration except that there are often more flowers. The maniples for the deacon and subdeacon, as well as the maniple and chasuble for the celebrant, should be placed on their respective seats in the sanctuary.

When the procession enters the sanctuary, the deacon and subdeacon, when distant about two yards from the lowest altar step, incline to the right and to the left respectively, so that when they reach the step they are in their proper positions before the altar. The celebrant advances along the middle line until he also reaches the lowest altar step. (Plate 4, Fig. 1) When all three are standing before the lowest altar step, they remove their birettas and genuflect together. The M.C., or a server, takes the birettas of the celebrant and his ministers and places them on or near their respective seats. The hymn ended, the celebrant and his ministers kneel before the altar on the lowest altar step, but all others in the sanctuary remain standing. The celebrant now sings: *Thou shalt sprinkle me*, and *I will lift up mine eyes unto the hills,* as in *Missa Cantata*. Meanwhile the M.C., or a server, takes the aspergill and gives it with a slight bow to the deacon, who remains kneeling. As the choir and people continue the singing of the Psalm, the celebrant receives the aspergill from the deacon, asperses himself and the altar, the deacon and subdeacon meanwhile holding up the lower corners of the cope. The celebrant now rises and asperses the deacon and subdeacon by making over each with the aspergill the sign of the cross. As soon as the subdeacon is aspersed, both ministers rise and stand each in his place facing the altar. The celebrant now turns round, by the epistle side, asperses any clergy present, the servers and choir on the epistle side, the servers and choir on the gospel side, finally the people and then turns back to the altar. He does not move from his place while doing all this, although of course he turns from side to side. The Asperges ended, the celebrant hands the aspergill to the deacon, who in turn gives it to the M.C., or an acolyte, to place on the credence.

The celebrant may delegate the aspersing of the clergy, servers, choir and people either to the deacon or the M.C., provided the one assigned is in priest's Orders. In this case the celebrant, after he has aspersed the subdeacon, gives the aspergill to the one who is to complete the aspersing.

The celebrant now joins in the singing of the Psalm which the people have continued to sing during the aspersing. At the end of the *Asperges* Collect the subdeacon removes the cope from the shoulders of the celebrant and gives it to a server to hold up behind the celebrant to serve as a screen. The deacon, assisted by the subdeacon, vests the celebrant in the chasuble, which has been brought to the deacon by a server. The cope is taken to its place. The celebrant and his ministers put on the maniples. All is now ready for the Invocation. (Plate 4, Fig. 2)

The celebrant intones the *Invocation* and the service proceeds as at *Missa Cantata* until the end of the *Confiteor*. (Plate 4, Fig. 3) At this time the celebrant ascends alone to the footpace to pronounce the *Absolution* (Plate 4, Fig. 4), the deacon and subdeacon, still kneeling, remain on the lowest altar step. The Absolution ended, the ministers rise together, ascend to the footpace and stand on either side of the priest.

The thurifer ascends to the epistle end of the footpace, the boat bearer accompanying him; they stand on the upper step. The thurifer holds the opened censer at a convenient height and the boat bearer gives the incense boat to the deacon with a slight bow. As the deacon holds the open boat near the censer the celebrant sprinkles incense on the charcoal and blesses it. (Plate 4, Fig. 5) The deacon returns the boat, takes the censer from the thurifer who has meanwhile closed it, and presents it with a slight bow to the celebrant. The thurifer, accompanied by the boat beater, steps down to his place on the sanctuary floor near the corner of the lowest step and faces north. (If the celebrant prefers to have the missal stand removed from the altar during the censing, this is done by the M.C. or the thurifer.) Meanwhile the M.C. has taken his place on the sanctuary floor near the southern end of the altar, likewise facing north. (Plate 4, Fig. 6)

After the deacon has given the censer to the celebrant, he folds back the edge of the celebrant's chasuble which is on his side and holds it in this position between thumb and forefinger of his left hand. Similarly the subdeacon folds back the edge of the chasuble on his side and holds it in this position between thumb and forefinger of his right hand. As the celebrant genuflects and moves to and fro along the footpace, the ministers genuflect and move with him. (Plate 4, Fig. 6) The more they can move and act in unison as if one body the nearer they approach to the ideal of ceremonial action. Care should be taken while genuflecting that the right foot is not thrust over the edge of the footpace, and that when the altar at either end is being censed the minister at that end does not inadvertently step off the end of the footpace and mar the beauty of the ceremony.

The censing ended the ministers unfold the edges of the chasuble so that they are once more in their normal position. The celebrant turns and gives the censer to the deacon who walks down the steps at the epistle end of the altar to the sanctuary floor until he is in line with the M.C. and the thurifer, whereupon he turns to face the celebrant. The subdeacon meanwhile walks down the front altar steps until he reaches the first or subdeacon's step. He walks south along this step (without genuflecting or bowing in the middle), descends to the sanctuary floor until he is in line with the M.C. and the thurifer, whereupon he turns to face north. (The ministers should so time their descent to the sanctuary floor, that they walk together down the steps at the epistle end, and together turn to face the celebrant.) The celebrant remains at the epistle end of the footpace, and faces south towards the deacon. (Plate 4, Fig. 7) After both ministers have together bowed slightly to the celebrant, the deacon censes the priest with three short double swings, and then gives the censer to the thurifer who retires with the censer.

The celebrant moves to the centre, turns to face the people and sings the Minor Benediction. Turning back to the altar he walks to the epistle end to sing the *Introit*. The position taken up is about midway between the centre and end of the altar. Mean while the deacon has taken his stand upon the deacon's step to the right of the position of the celebrant, the subdeacon upon the lowest step or the sanctuary floor (depending upon the sanctuary arrangements) to the right of the deacon. They either stand in line (Plate 4, Fig. 8-A) as recommended by Bp. Mazel in *The Ceremonies of the Holy Eucharist*, or with the deacon standing a little back of the others (Plate 4, Fig. 8-B), or in a diagonal line (Plate 4, Fig. 8-C) as preferred by Fortescue in the fourth edition of *The Ceremonies of the Roman Rite Described*. Each position has its advantages, depending upon the size of the sanctuary, and each is permissible until the General Episcopal Synod decides in favour of one of them. If there be a M.C. he stands at the epistle end of the altar on the sanctuary floor facing north.

While the people are singing the final *Amen* of the Introit, the deacon and sub-deacon ascend to their places on the footpace on either side of the celebrant. (Plate 4, Fig. 9) In doing so, the subdeacon walks to the gospel side by way of the lowest step. He does not bow or genuflect while passing the middle. When he comes to the gospel side he does not ascend diagonally, but straight up. The ministers should so time their ascent that they take their places beside the celebrant at the same time.

During the singing of the *Gloria In Excelsis* the thurifer stands (facing the altar) in the middle of the sanctuary floor before the altar swinging the censer to and fro with long swings. On the greater Festivals when there may be two thurifers, they should stand in the middle one behind the other (Plate 4, Fig. 10) and so time the swinging of the censers that when one is at the extreme right the other is at the extreme left. At the end of the Gloria the thurifer (or thurifers) goes back to his station, and hangs up the censer, which will not be needed until the Gradual.

Immediately after the Minor Benediction which follows the Gloria, the deacon and subdeacon go to their positions for the *Collects*. The deacon takes his place on the second, or deacon's step, immediately behind the celebrant (who has walked to the epis-tle end for the saying of the Collects), the subdeacon on the first step or on the sanctuary floor (depending upon sanctuary arrangements) immediately behind the deacon. This brings the celebrant and his ministers into line. (Plate 4, Fig. 11) All three face east. The M.C. remains in the position he took during the censing of the altar, kneeling on the lowest altar step at the epistle end. All in the sanctuary, except the celebrant and his ministers kneel during the Collects.

When the celebrant has finished the Peace Collect the M.C. (or an acolyte, if there be no M.C.) rises and gives to the subdeacon the book containing the Epistles, open at the Epistle of the Day. As soon as the response *Amen* to the Peace Collect (which always comes last) has been sung, the subdeacon bows to the altar cross, faces the people and announces the Epistle by reading what is printed in small type at the beginning. At the time the subdeacon turns to face the people, the celebrant and. deacon, without changing position, turn and face north. (Plate 4, Fig, 12) The subdeacon reads the Epistle, taking care always to finish with the statement: "Here endeth the Epistle," which serves as a signal to the organist and to the people that the versicle: "Thanks be to God," should be sung, all standing.

After the reading of the Epistle the subdeacon walks to the middle before the lowest altar step and remains standing there facing the altar. After the celebrant has sung the first line of the *Gradual*, which he does while standing at the epistle end of the footpace facing the altar, the thurifer prepares the charcoal in the censer and the two chief acolytes go to the credence to take each, one of the two lighted candles which were placed on or near the credence at the time when the procession entered the sanctuary. During the Gradual the two acolytes with candles walk to the middle, genuflect, and take their places on either side of the subdeacon, likewise facing the altar. (Plate 4, Fig. 13) The thurifer goes to the celebrant with the opened censer, accompanied by the boat bearer. The celebrant faces south and moves to the end of the footpace, and the deacon steps to the footpace as the thurifer arrives. (Plate 5, Fig. 14) The deacon takes the boat and holds it open conveniently near the censer, while the celebrant sprinkles incense on the charcoal and blesses it in the usual manner. The deacon returns the boat to the bearer and steps back to the highest step.

Meanwhile the M.C. (if there be no M.C., then an acolyte) moves the missal stand from the epistle side to the gospel side, if this is desired, then takes the Book of Gospels, goes to the middle, gives the Book opened at the Gospel of the Day to the subdeacon. If the M.C. is vested in cope, he remains in the middle, standing behind the subdeacon, facing the altar. If not so vested, he returns to his place at the epistle side.

The incense blessed, the thurifer closes the censer and, accompanied by the boat bearer, descends to the sanctuary floor, walks round to the middle, genuflects and stands behind the M.C., or, if there be no M.C., behind the subdeacon. (Plate 5, Fig. 15) This group standing before the lowest altar step should be completely formed about the end of the Gradual. The thurifer swings the censer to and fro with long swings. The Gradual ended, the celebrant returns to the middle and faces south. The deacon kneels at the edge of the footpace, about midway between the middle and the epistle end. (Plate 5, Fig. 16) The deacon intones or says the *Munda Cor Meum* and the celebrant intones or says the blessing which follows. At the end of the blessing the celebrant turns to face the altar. As soon as the deacon has sung the Minor Benediction, the celebrant turns by his left to face the Book of Gospels.

At the end of the blessing, the members of the group standing before the altar step, turn northward together, walk until the subdeacon is opposite the gospel end of the footpace, and then turn and face the altar. Usually the subdeacon stands on the sanctuary floor holding the open Book of Gospels above the level of his head so that it may be conveniently read by the deacon. If, however, local arrangements are such that the subdeacon ought to be at a higher level, he steps up to the first step and stands there during the reading of the Gospel. In this case the two candle bearers step up with him so that they may stand at the same level on either side.

At the end of the blessing the deacon rises, bows to the altar cross, and walks on the deacon's step to the middle, faces the people, extends his hands and sings the Minor Benediction. Joining his hands he turns to face the altar, genuflects, and then walks to a point opposite the subdeacon and faces the latter, still standing on the deacon's step. (Plate 5, Fig. 17) During the reading of the *Gospel* the celebrant stands either in the middle of the footpace, or a little to the epistle side (depending upon the size of the altar), facing the Book of Gospels. (Plate 5, Fig. 17)

The thurifer now leaves his station behind the M.C. (or the subdeacon) and walks round to the right of the deacon. As soon as the latter has announced the Gospel and crossed himself over forehead, lips and breast, the thurifer hands him the censer. The deacon censes the Book with three double swings in the sequence of middle-leftright. (In the Roman Rite the sequence is middle-right-left, but it should be remembered that at High Celebration in that Rite the deacon faces north, not towards the people as in the Liberal Catholic Rite.) After the censing of the Book the deacon returns the censer to the thurifer, who immediately goes back to his place behind the M.C. (or the subdeacon) and resumes swinging the censer.

The Gospel ended, the thurifer again goes to the deacon and gives him the censer. The deacon turns to the celebrant and censes him with three short double swings (Plate 5, Fig. 18) the celebrant facing the deacon, hands joined.

Meanwhile the M.C. (or an acolyte, if there be no M.C.) receives the Book of Gospels and places it on the credence. The two acolytes with candles turn and bow to the subdeacon, go to the middle, genuflect, and return the candles to the credence.

The deacon returns the censer to the thurifer (who puts the censer away), descends to the sanctuary floor and takes his place to the right of the middle, the subdeacon meanwhile moving to his place to the left of the middle. The celebrant descends to stand between them, all three facing the altar. Genuflecting together they go to their seats. If the celebrant is seated while vested in chasuble, it is well, in order to prevent crushing or wrinkling, to place the rear portion of the chasuble over the back of the seat so that it hangs down behind. This is also advisable with the dalmatic and tunicle. If the celebrant preaches from the pulpit, his ministers assist him to remove the chasuble at the seat and to resume it afterward.

The sermon ended, the celebrant (vested in chasuble and maniple) and his ministers go to the altar, the birettas being left at the seats. The three genuflect together when they reach the middle before the lowest altar step and ascend to the footpace. Standing in the middle of the footpace, with his ministers on either side, the *Credo* is intoned. (Plate 5, Fig. 19)

When the collection is brought forward it is received by the M.C. (Plate 5, Fig. 20) or an acolyte, and by him taken to the altar during the singing of the offertory hymn. He hands the plate to the deacon, who in turn gives it to the celebrant. The latter, after offering the collection as usual, returns the plate to the deacon who gives it to the M.C. or acolyte to place on the credence or some other suitable place.

The celebrant gives the veil to fold and place on the altar either to the deacon or to the subdeacon depending upon whether the veil is to be laid on the altar either to the right or to the left of the corporal. (See p.69.)

When the time comes for pouring the wine and water after the prayer: *We adore Thee...* the subdeacon goes round to the epistle end of the footpace by descending to the first step and walking round that step to the epistle end. He takes his place to the right of the deacon and facing the celebrant. (Plate 5, Fig. 21) Meanwhile two acolytes have brought each a cruet from the credence table. The wine cruet is presented to the deacon, the water cruet to the subdeacon. After presenting the cruets the acolytes step down to the sanctuary floor and stand there side by side, facing the ministers (Plate 5, Fig. 21) The celebrant moves to the epistle end, and holds out the chalice, the deacon pours in some wine and the subdeacon a few drops of water, after the celebrant has made the sign of the cross over the cruet of water. The ministers immediately return the cruets to the servers who advance to take them. The acolytes put the cruets on the credence and return to their places. The subdeacon goes directly to his place to the left of the celebrant by way of the first step.

After the prayer *We offer unto Thee...* the thurifer, accompanied by the boat bearer, ascends to the top step as before, the boat is handed to the deacon and incense blessed as usual by the celebrant. (Plate 5, Fig. 22) The altar is then censed. (Plate 4, Fig. 6 and Diagrams 6 and 5)

If there is an additional thurifer, as may be the case on the greater festivals, he brings his censer also at the time the first thurifer ascends. After the incense is blessed, he descends to the sanctuary floor, walks to the middle before the lowest altar step, genuflects, and stands there facing the altar, swinging his censer to and fro with long swings. At the end of the censing of the altar the additional thurifer retires.

It is well for the candle bearers to light their candles about this time, so that they may be ready to enter the sanctuary at the *Orate Fratres*.

At the end of the censing of the altar, the deacon and subdeacon descend to the sanctuary floor at the epistle end and the celebrant is censed exactly as at the first censing. The M.C. and the thurifer also take the same positions as before. (Plate 4, Fig. 7) The deacon turns to the subdeacon and censes him with three short double swings. He now walks round to the middle before the lowest altar step, genuflects (or bows) turns to face any priests who may be present, censing those first on the gospel side and then those on the epistle side. If there are several priests in a group they may be censed collectively. Any deacons present are then censed with three short double swings, and any subdeacons present with three short single swings. The clergy censed, the deacon gives the censer to the thurifer and goes to stand (usually at the corner of the deacon's step) facing the thurifer who takes his place in the middle facing the deacon. The thurifer censes the deacon with three short double swings, censes the groups of servers present collectively with three short single swings and finally censes the people.

Meanwhile the subdeacon, as soon as he has been censed, ascends to the step below the footpace at the epistle end and receives from a server a lavabo towel (which he lays over his left forearm), a bowl (in the left hand) and the cruet of water (in the right). He pours water over the fingers of the celebrant and waits until the latter has replaced the towel on his forearm. (Plate 5, Fig. 23) It is permissible to use a bowl of water into which the celebrant dips his fingers, and not the cruet, although the symbolism of pouring water over the fingers is perhaps more complete. If servers are not available to bring the towel, bowl and cruet, the subdeacon himself may take these from the credence table, and with them walk to the footpace. Returning to the sanctuary floor he assists the deacon to wash his fingers. After this he quickly rinses his own fingers, assisted if need be by an acolyte, and returns to his place on the footpace to the left of the celebrant. The deacon likewise returns to his place to the celebrant's right.

Immediately after the response of the people to the *Orate Fratres*, all the acolytes bearing candles should enter the sanctuary and arrange themselves symmetrically before the altar, either in a semicircle, or in one or more straight lines. (Plate 5, Fig. 24) If there is but one thurifer he takes his place in the middle, the acolytes with candles flanking him on either side. If there are two thurifers, one is stationed at the extreme end of the circle on the gospel side, the other at the extreme end on the epistle side. If more convenient, one may be stationed at the gospel corner of the lowest step, the other at the epistle corner of the lowest step. No fixed rules can be laid down as to the positions of the candle bearers and the thurifer or thurifers, because sanctuaries vary in size and arrangements. Care should be taken beforehand to assign each acolyte to his exact position, so that either the tallest should be in the middle and the smallest at the ends, or the smallest in the middle and the tallest at the ends. The candlesticks need not be of the same size, but it is essential from the standpoint of beauty that those of the same size should be opposite one another and that they be carefully graded as to size, the larger boys having the longer candlesticks and the smaller boys the shorter candlesticks. At a signal from one of the older acolytes, or the M.C., the thurifer and acolytes genuflect together and then kneel in their assigned positions, the latter placing the candlesticks on the floor in front of them. (Plate 5, Fig. 24)

As soon as the celebrant has sung: *Lift up your hearts*, and has turned back to the altar, the deacon and subdeacon face towards the middle and step down behind the celebrant, the deacon to the first step below the footpace, the subdeacon to the second step below the footpace. Both stand in the middle behind the celebrant, facing the altar. (Plate 5, Fig. 25) Here they stand until the end of the Preface, when they ascend to their usual positions on the footpace. (Plate 5, Fig. 24) During the singing of the Sanctus the acolytes elevate their candles by holding them in front of them and above the level of their heads, taking care that the candles are held upright. The stem of the candlestick is grasped by the right hand, the base by the left. Considerable practice is required before the average server can hold the candlestick steadily, vertically, and at the right height so that the line of flame is symmetrical. They are elevated from the first *Holy* to the ending of the Sanctus: *O Lord Most High*. At this point they are lowered slowly and placed on the floor.

At each word: *Holy*, the thurifer (or thurifers) who remains kneeling, swings the censer with three short swings towards the altar cross. At the same time the sacring bell is sounded thrice.

At the beginning of the paragraph: *Wherefore O Holy Lord...* in the long prayer preceding the Consecration, the deacon and subdeacon again descend to stand in line behind the celebrant as they did at the singing of the Preface. This time, however, inasmuch as they have to kneel, the deacon descends to the lowest step, the subdeacon to the sanctuary floor. (Plate 5, Fig. 25) Here they remain standing until the beginning of the paragraph: *Who the day before...* whereupon they kneel. When the celebrant genuflects before and after the Elevation of the Host and Chalice, the deacon should draw the point of the celebrant's chasuble to his breast. When the celebrant rises at each Elevation the deacon should lift the chasuble gently. The subdeacon should hold the dalmatic of the deacon during the same intervals.

At the time the deacon and subdeacon kneel, the acolytes should take up their candlesticks and the thurifer, as noiselessly as possible, should put more incense into the censer. At each genuflection of the celebrant and at each Elevation, the sacring bell is rung thrice, or the chimes are sounded, and the thurifer gives three triple swings in the direction of the Host. At each Elevation the servers raise their candles above their heads, being careful to elevate them and lower them together and in rhythm with the celebrant elevating the Host and Chalice, so that the effect may be pleasing and dignified.

At the end of the hymn: *Thee we adore...* and after the few moments of adoration, the celebrant and ministers rise together. The ministers go to their usual positions on the footpace on either side of the celebrant, to remain without change until the Salutation of Peace. (Plate 5, Fig. 24) The acolytes retire with their candles, put them in the place where they are to stand, and return to their seats in the sanctuary. The thurifer puts the censer away. It will not be needed until the recessional hymn.

For the reception of Communion by the clergy and servers in the sanctuary, it is necessary that they should group themselves before the altar. This should be done if there be adequate space during the prayer: *O Lord Jesu Christ...* preceding the Salutation of Peace, otherwise immediately after the ciborium has been taken from the tabernacle, following the Communion of the deacon and subdeacon. If the former is done, the Salutation of Peace is passed from one to another of the clergy as they kneel before the altar. If the latter is done, the Salutation is passed from one to another as they kneel at their places at the sides of the sanctuary. The essential thing is that there should not be either noise or confusion in the sanctuary during any of the sacred prayers.

When the clergy come forward for Communion they stand in a line on the sanctuary floor before the lowest altar step. If there is a M.C. he takes his position in the middle of the line. The acolytes stand in a row or rows behind the clergy. All kneel together following the lead of the ministers. (Plate 5, Fig. 26)

During the prayer: *O Lord Jesu Christ...* the deacon and subdeacon turn to face one another and as soon as the clergy and servers are grouped before the altar, the ministers kneel on the footpace. (Plate 5, Fig. 26) The celebrant gives the Salutation first to the deacon and then to the subdeacon. (What follows after that depends upon the number of clergy and acolytes present and upon the arrangements of the sanctuary. The various possibilities are discussed in Chapter IV, p. 37.) He immediately turns to the altar and remains silent until the response to the Salutation has been sung by the people.

Should the celebrant himself sing the Salutation of Peace as in the Shorter Form, which is permissible at any service, he first gives the Salutation to the deacon and subdeacon, before turning to the people.

The celebrant now says the prayer: *O Thou Who in this adorable Sacrament...* receives Communion in both kinds and administers the Host to the deacon and subdeacon. If there are consecrated Hosts in the tabernacle, which will be needed during the

Communion of the people, they are taken out at this time either by the celebrant or the deacon, usually the latter. The tabernacle door is opened, all genuflect, the ciborium is taken out, placed on the corporal and the tabernacle door is closed. If the congregation is large there may be two or three ciboria, depending upon whether the celebrant is assisted by one or both ministers in the administration of Communion to servers and people. No one of lower rank than ordained deacon may administer Communion. If the subdeacon of the Eucharist is only an ordained subdeacon and not a deacon or Priest, he may not assist in the distribution of Holy Communion.

The celebrant unassisted may administer Communion to clergy, servers and people. Should this be the case, he administers to clergy, servers and choir in the usual way, while the deacon and subdeacon remain kneeling on the footpace. Before administering to the people the celebrant returns to the footpace and, facing the people, says: *Ye that desire to partake....* All those kneeling in the sanctuary, including the deacon and subdeacon, rise, genuflect and retire to their seats, where they kneel until the celebrant has walked to the communion rail. They are seated while the people receive Communion.

Should the celebrant desire the assistance of the deacon in the administration to the people, he upon his return to the altar after the distribution to clergy, servers and choir, takes the additional ciborium (which he has uncovered) and turns to the deacon, who should be standing. (As soon as the celebrant has returned to the altar after administering Communion to clergy, servers and choir, and has genuflected after placing the ciborium he was carrying on the corporal, the ministers should rise together, still facing the celebrant.) The deacon genuflects, rises, takes the ciborium and turns with the celebrant to face the people as the latter says: *Ye that desire to Partake....* It will have been arranged beforehand at which communion rail each is to administer. If the celebrant wishes the deacon to assist in the Communion of the servers and choir as well as the people, he gives the ciborium to the deacon before administering Communion to the clergy. He himself then administers to the clergy, while the deacon administers to the servers and choir. The subdeacon is seated with the rest of the clergy, during the Communion of the people. If there are two additional ciboria, the subdeacon (if in Major Orders) may also assist. He is given the ciborium by the celebrant immediately after the deacon has received his ciborium. When the celebrant and both his ministers distribute to the people at the Communion rail, one third of the rail area is usually apportioned to each, the celebrant giving Communion to those who kneel at the middle section, the deacon serving at that section on the epistle side, the subdeacon at that section on the gospel side.

The administration of Communion being ended, the celebrant returns to the altar accompanied by whoever assisted him. If one (or both) of the ministers has been seated at the Communion of the people, he joins the celebrant at the foot of the altar steps. All three ascend to the footpace. Upon reaching the altar the celebrant places the ciborium which he has been carrying upon the corporal and genuflects. Turning to the deacon he receives the ciborium from him and holds it before the deacon as the latter genuflects, and then places it on the corporal. Turning to the subdeacon he receives the ciborium from him and holds it before the subdeacon as the latter genuflects and then places it on the corporal. (It must be borne in mind that one never genuflects while carrying the Host, and that ciboria must be handled with conspicuous reverence, held straight at all times and slightly elevated.) All who have assisted in the distribution of the Host rub the thumb and forefinger of the right hand upon the corporal. The ciborium (or ciboria) is now placed in the tabernacle, sometimes by the celebrant, usually by the deacon. Whoever places the ciborium in the tabernacle stands in the middle while so doing. This means that the subdeacon and celebrant must move to the gospel side when the deacon places the Host in the tabernacle. The ciborium is first covered with the lid and with the veil (if any). It is then placed in the tabernacle, all genuflect, the door is then closed and locked. The celebrant and ministers resume their normal positions upon the footpace.

The subdeacon goes to the epistle end of the footpace, by way of the subdeacon's step, to assist in the *ablutions*. (Plate 5, Fig. 27) Two servers have meanwhile come forward from the credence with the wine and water cruets and given them respectively to the deacon and subdeacon. The deacon steps to the middle and pours some wine into the chalice, returns to his place at the epistle end of the footpace, and again, when the celebrant comes to him, pours a little wine over the fingers of the priest. The subdeacon pours rather much water over the fingers of the celebrant, and a moment later, more water directly into the chalice, as described on p. 80. The cruets are then returned to the servers to place on the credence. The ministers return to their regular places on the footpace (Plate 4, Fig. 9), the subdeacon by way of the lower step. The celebrant, standing in the middle, arranges the chalice and paten and folds the corporal, placing the latter in the burse held open by the subdeacon. The celebrant, or deacon, covers the chalice with the veil. The celebrant places the burse on top of the veil.

If, during the Gradual, the missal stand was transferred to the gospel side of the altar, it is at this point brought back to the epistle side by the M.C. or a server.

In the meanwhile those acolytes who are to carry candles in the procession should retire to light them. The thurifer should also blow up the charcoal in the censer. The celebrant now says the prayer: *Under the veil....* This ended the celebrant and ministers take the same position as at the Collects. (Plate 4, Fig. 11) With joined hands the celebrant joins in the singing of the *Communio*. At this point the acolytes with candles enter and take their places in preparation for the procession. During the Communio and until the Benediction the deacon and subdeacon remain in the position as at the Collects. (Plate 4, Fig. 11) The *Communio* ended, the celebrant returns to the middle, turns to face the people and with extended hands sings the Minor Benediction. Turning back to the altar, he again walks to the epistle end of the footpace, faces east, and after the response of the people, intones: *Let us pray*. All kneel except the celebrant and ministers. After the *Postcommunio* is intoned or said, the celebrant returns once more to the middle, turns to the people as before and sings the Minor Benediction. He turns back to the altar as the people respond, momentarily extends his hands and sings: *Ite, missa est*.

During the response, the deacon and subdeacon should descend to the sanctuary floor; one on either side of the middle, facing the altar. As soon as they reach this position they should kneel on the lowest altar step. The celebrant now turns to the people and gives the Benediction. (Plate 5, Fig. 28) This ended, the ministers rise together, the priest turns back to the altar by his right, waits until the *Amen* is sung, and then descends the altar steps to stand in the middle on the sanctuary floor between the deacon and subdeacon, facing the altar. The cope is brought by an acolyte and held behind the celebrant as a screen, while the ministers assist the celebrant to take off the chasuble and maniple. He is then vested in the cope. The ministers lay aside their maniples. All three are given their birettas. After genuflecting, the procession leaves as usual.

❈ ❈ ❈ ❈ ❈ ❈ ❈

The Shorter Form When Celebrated by a Priest

When there is High Celebration of the Holy Eucharist according to the Shorter Form there are very few differences to be noticed.

Upon reaching the sanctuary the deacon and subdeacon assist the celebrant in changing from cope to chasuble before the Invocation is intoned. After the Invocation the M.C., or an acolyte, gives the aspergill to the deacon who in turn hands it to the celebrant. The celebrant makes the sign of the cross over the deacon and subdeacon with the aspergill when he has aspersed the altar. After the Asperges the celebrant returns the aspergill to the deacon who in turn gives it to the M.C., or an acolyte, to place on the credence. During the whole of the Asperges, and the canticle which follows, the ministers stand on either side of the celebrant, facing the altar. They kneel with him for the Confiteor, remain kneeling while he goes to the footpace for the Absolution, and join him on the footpace before the versicle: *With praise and with prayer*.... (Plate 4, Fig. 6)

The shorter way of singing the Salutation of Peace is always followed; but the Salutation is first given to the deacon and subdeacon. The ministers kneel just before the Salutation of Peace and remain kneeling until they receive Communion. The clergy and servers group themselves before the altar preparatory to receiving Communion after the deacon and subdeacon have received Communion.

Either Form When Celebrated by a Priest in the Presence of a Bishop

The following additions to the ceremonial actions described in Chapters V and VI are to be noted whenever a priest, assisted by a deacon and subdeacon, sings the Holy Eucharist in the presence of a Bishop.

In the Longer Form, after the celebrant has aspersed himself, the altar and his ministers, he gives the aspergill to the deacon who gives it to the M.C., or an acolyte. The latter goes immediately to the senior bishop present (if there be more than one) who takes the aspergill, makes the sign of the cross with it over himself and his personal attendants, and returns it to the bearer. (The aspergill is then taken to any other bishop present, who asperses himself and his attendants.) The aspergill is now taken back to the deacon, who gives it to the priest. The latter completes the Asperges ceremony.

In the Shorter Form the aspergill is not taken to the bishop during the Asperges.

At the *Munda Cor Meum* the deacon kneels, facing east, on the edge of the footpace at the *gospel* side so as to be near the bishop. The bishop intones or says the blessing following the *Munda Cor Meum*. At the end of the Gospel the deacon censes the celebrant, not the bishop.

At the second censing of the altar, after the deacon has censed the celebrant and the subdeacon, he goes at once to the bishop and censes him with three short triple swings. (If there be more than one bishop present, each one is censed separately, the senior bishop first.) The deacon then returns to the middle, censes the clergy and is himself censed by the thurifer.

* * * * * * *

Either Form When Celebrated by a Bishop

There are a few special points to be noted whenever a bishop sings the Holy Eucharist assisted by a deacon and subdeacon.

With a few exceptions (noted hereafter) the subdeacon may give the mitre to the bishop and receive it from him. Whoever presents the mitre should hold it upside down, the side with the fanons attached being nearest his own body. When he receives the mitre, he places it right side up on the altar, near the front on the gospel side (or the side opposite to the missal, when the missal is transferred) opened slightly so that it will stand upright. An acolyte may present the mitre to the bishop on three occasions and receive it on one occasion because at these times the subdeacon is otherwise engaged. These occasions are: when the bishop ascends to the footpace to give the Absolution, when he puts on the mitre during the Gradual, when he takes it off just before the Gospel is read, and when he puts it on before the final Benediction. If desired, a server may be designated to handle the mitre at all times.

If the missal stand is transferred from the epistle side to the gospel side during the Gradual, the mitre is placed on the epistle side of the altar after the Gradual, but if the transfer is not made, the mitre, when not in use, is always placed on the gospel side. When on the epistle side, the mitre is handled by the deacon instead of the subdeacon, unless there is a separate mitre bearer.

If the bishop desires that the mitre be removed from the altar during the two censings, an acolyte holds it standing *in plano*, either on the gospel side or the epistle side of the sanctuary, depending upon the side of the altar where the mitre was placed.

After the incense has been blessed, prior to each censing of the altar, the bishop returns to the middle and, facing north, gives the crozier to the crozier bearer and the mitre to the subdeacon or deacon, according to the side on which it will be placed. If the deacon is to receive it, he must not take the censer from the thurifer until he has placed the mitre on the altar. It is much more convenient in this case if there is a special mitre bearer. The Bishop now turns to face the altar. As soon as the deacon turns to him with the censer, he turns to receive it and then back to the altar and proceeds.

When at the sermon the bishop goes to the throne, the deacon and subdeacon accompany him, walking on either side. They are seated on either side of the throne, but at a lower level, or in front of the throne, or even on the epistle side of the sanctuary, depending upon the arrangements in the sanctuary. They remain seated during the sermon whether preached from the throne or pulpit. Should the bishop preach from the faldstool before the altar, the ministers genuflect and go to their seats before the sermon begins. After the sermon they return with the bishop to the altar, or, if he has preached from the faldstool, go to him at the altar.

After the *Ite, missa est*, the ministers kneel on the lowest altar step one on either side of the middle. If the cope is to be worn, they rise after the Benediction and ascend to the footpace. The bishop gives his crozier to the bearer, his mitre to the subdeacon (or bearer) to stand upon the altar. An acolyte brings the cope and holds it up as a screen behind the bishop. The ministers assist in removing the chasuble and vesting the bishop in the cope. The maniples are removed and given to a server. The M.C. or an acolyte brings the birettas for the ministers. The bishop puts on his mitre. The clergy and servers group themselves before the altar and the procession leaves as usual.

CHAPTER VIII

THE NUPTIAL EUCHARIST

The Nuptial Eucharist, or Celebration of the Holy Eucharist on the occasion of a marriage, may not take the place of the chief Eucharist on a Sunday. There is no objection to celebrating a Nuptial Eucharist on the greater Festivals, provided it is not made the principal Celebration. In such a case it would be convenient that another priest celebrate the Feast.

The celebration of the Nuptial Eucharist on the occasion of every marriage is not to be encouraged. The marriage may take place before the ordinary Eucharist of the Day, or else Communion may be administered to the newly married pair (and to those of the bridal party who may desire to partake) immediately after the marriage ceremony. In this case the Form for the Administration of Holy Communion with the Reserved Sacrament should be used.

The colour of the vestments used and the altar frontal is white. The priest vests exactly as at any other Celebration of the Holy Eucharist. There are no changes in the ceremonial actions except the addition of the special Versicles, Responses and Blessing, which come immediately before the Commemoration of the Saints. The celebrant stands at the epistle corner of the altar, facing the newly-married pair. The changes in the wording of the Eucharist are indicated in the Liturgy under *Nuptial Eucharist*.

CHAPTER IX

THE REQUIEM EUCHARIST

The Requiem Eucharist, or Celebration of the Holy Eucharist on the occasion of a funeral, may not normally take the place of the chief Eucharist on a Sunday, but it may do so if a national figure or someone beloved of the whole congregation is to be commemorated. The Requiem Eucharist may, in case of necessity, be held on one of the greater Festivals, provided it does not interfere with the principal Celebration. The Requiem Eucharist need not be celebrated on the same day as the funeral, but may be postponed to a more convenient time, if the burial takes place on a Feast Day.

It is not necessary that there be a Celebration of the Requiem Eucharist on the occasion of all funerals. It is sufficient that mention be made of the deceased at some regular Celebration of the Holy Eucharist following the death or funeral.

The colour of the vestments used and the altar frontal is violet, except in the case of children under the age of seven when white is used. The position of the coffin, if one is present in the church during the Requiem Eucharist, is described under "Burial Service."

Certain changes in wording are noted in the Liturgy under *Requiem Eucharist*. [In addition, the *Gloria in Excelsis* and *Credo* are omitted during the celebration of a Requiem Mass.]

Throughout the service, in the case of children under the age of seven the word *child* is substituted for *servant*.

❊ ❊ ❊ ❊ ❊ ❊ ❊

THE GENERAL REQUIEM EUCHARIST

The directions given above have to do with a Requiem celebrated at the death of some special person. In accordance with Catholic tradition a Requiem may be said at other times for the purpose of helping the departed in general, and at such a service special commemoration will be made of those figuring on the list of the dead being prayed for in the particular church. This ranks with other *votive* Eucharists mentioned on page 403 of our *Liturgy* (Second Edition).

The Requiem Eucharist as printed in the Liturgy will need to be modified in some respects. The Opening Psalm, Gradual and *Communio* are used as printed. The Collect, Epistle and Gospel for All Souls' Day are more suitable for the purpose in view. The *Postcommunio* will be that of the ordinary form of the Eucharist, but will be followed by the versicles and responses and Benediction proper to the Requiem.

APPENDIX

THE SERVER AT MASS

Foreword

It is the traditional usage of the Latin Rite that the missal stand be transferred to the gospel side of the altar at the Gradual, and returned to the epistle side again after the Ablutions, as is described herein, also that while the altar is being censed, the missal stand (and the mitre, if any) be removed from the altar and held *in plano*. The custom has arisen in many Liberal Catholic Churches of dispensing with these actions, leaving the missal stand on the epistle side of the altar throughout the service. The Presiding Bishop thinks it wise to leave this matter optional for the present [1934 Ed.].

If the missal stand is not transferred, there are certain changes from the directions given herein. Obviously those relating to the transfer of the stand will be ignored. In addition, in such cases it is customary for the server to have his station at the epistle side throughout, except when performing his various duties. With two servers, both are stationed at the epistle side, the one as thurifer and the other as server; while with three, one server is stationed at the gospel side, another at the epistle side, the thurifer also being at the epistle side. The exact usage differs, owing to the arrangement in the various sanctuaries.

Where the missal stand is not transferred, at Low Mass or *Missa Cantata*, the Book of Gospels must be held by a server, both while it is being censed and while it is being read. This can be done with only one server, who hooks the ring of the censer over his little finger as he holds the book; but he cannot of course swing the censer to and fro.

Rev. W. H. Pitkin.

Symbols

The following conventional symbols are used in the diagrams accompanying the text:

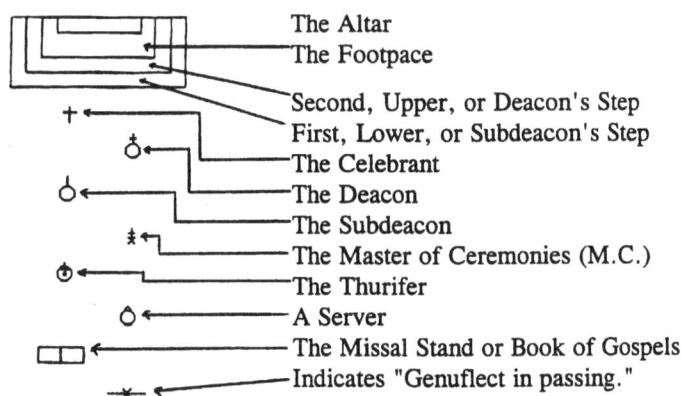

- The Altar
- The Footpace
- Second, Upper, or Deacon's Step
- First, Lower, or Subdeacon's Step
- The Celebrant
- The Deacon
- The Subdeacon
- The Master of Ceremonies (M.C.)
- The Thurifer
- A Server
- The Missal Stand or Book of Gospels
- Indicates "Genuflect in passing."

Note: Arrows show movements, in some diagrams, the points indicating the direction of travel. The arrow tail (>———) indicates the starting point, while the server's symbol shows the final position at the completion of the movement.

DIRECTIONS FOR SERVING LOW MASS AND *MISSA CANTATA*
By the Rev. G. Nevin Drinkwater

Written in consultation with the Rt. Rev. J.I.Wedgwood,
who has kindly supplied many notes and suggestions.

Celebration by a Priest with One Server

Preliminary.
The Censer.   At a private Mass the censer is taken to the sanctuary before the service. At Low Mass with a congregation present, or if the church is large, incense may be blessed beforehand by the priest. At *Missa Cantata*, or Low Mass with an opening hymn, the censer may be taken in procession.

The Missal.   It is convenient if the priest carry this; alternatively place it beforehand on the credence and bring it to the priest with the aspergill. If the priest prefers to recite from memory the earlier portion before he ascends to the altar, the missal may be left on the missal stand, open at the Absolution.

The Server's Position.   The server has two normal positions. The first normal position is before the foot of the lowest altar step, facing east, and little to the gospel side of the centre. This is immediately to the left of the celebrant when the latter enters the sanctuary. This position is adopted until the end of the Collects. (Fig. 2) The second normal position corresponds to the first but is a little to the epistle side of the centre. This position is adopted until the Ablutions, after which the first position is resumed. until the end. (Fig. 1) It will be found in practice that the server is always on the side opposite to the missal. The positions for Epistle, Gradual and Gospel, when included; are described under the appropriate headings. The server leaves these normal positions from time to time to carry out his duties. Unless otherwise stated, he stands, sits or kneels with the people. (see *Liturgy*) If the congregation is small he should lead the responses with a clear voice.

Directions for Server.
Entering the Sanctuary.   Upon entering the sanctuary move to the *right* of the celebrant (Fig. 3), if there is no hymn, genuflecting with him before the altar steps. Take the biretta to the credence or other convenient place and hang up the censer if it has been carried in procession. If there is an introcessional hymn, genuflect on the left of the celebrant (Fig. 4) and hold his biretta there until the close of the hymn, after which retire with the biretta and hymn book, in this way avoiding unnecessary movements in the sanctuary.

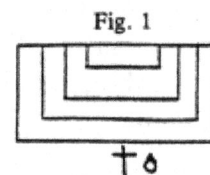

Fig. 1

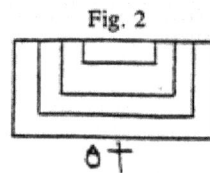

Fig. 2

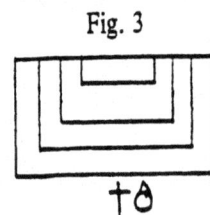

Fig. 3

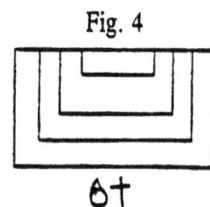

Fig. 4

Fig. 5

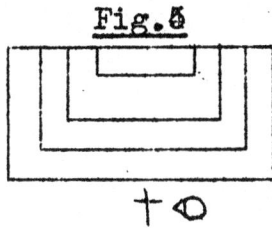

Shorter Form, Invocation and Asperges.   Bring the aspergill and stand on the epistle side a pace or two away from the priest, facing northwards. (Fig.5) The priest should wait for the server to take up this position to avoid movement in the sanctuary during the Invocation. When the priest has said (or sung) the Invocation offer the aspergill to the priest, handle foremost, and step back holding the missal, still facing north, during the *Asperges.* The distance retreated. will be greater in a large sanctuary. Receive the aspergill from the priest and give him the missal for the opening Canticle, with the usual bow.

(Should the priest wish to read the *Asperges* passage, hold the book before him—still facing north—until the aspergill is returned; then face tale congregation with the priest while the latter reads: *Brethren, let us.... Temple.* The priest may prefer to hold the book when aspersing the altar, in that case he will hand it to the server when he turns to the people.)

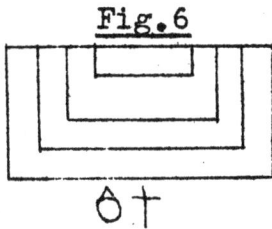

Fig. 6

Replace the aspergill on the credence table and go to the left of the priest *in plano*, facing east, i.e., the first normal position. (Fig. 6)

Long Form, Asperges and Invocation   Except on very rare occasions the Long Form of the *Asperges* will not be used when there is but one server, as the change from cope to the chasuble is not easily made with one assistant. Assuming the Longer Form to be required, bring the aspergill to the left of the priest after disposing of the biretta and kneel simultaneously with him. (Fig. 6) Hand him the aspergill after the opening words of the Psalm: *I will lift up mine eyes unto the hills*, and hold the missal. Rise after aspersion, give the missal to the priest, receive the aspergill, replace it on the credence table, and go once more to the gospel side. (Fig. 6) Hold the book when the priest turns to give the Minor Benediction just before the Collect. Kneel for the Collect and rise after the *Amen.* Present the priest with the chasuble and maniple and hold the cope outstretched behind him while he vests. This is done at the centre, not at the epistle side. Place the cope over a chair or the sedilia and return to the left of. the celebrant for the Invocation. (Fig. 6).

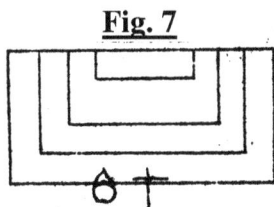

Fig. 7

Canticle, Confiteor and Absolution.   At the *Confiteor* kneel with the celebrant on the first altar step:and remain until after the Absolution. (Fig. 7)

First Censing.   Rise after the Amen following the Absolution and take the boat and censer to the celebrant. In the Short Form, first make the response: *To God alone be the glory*, unless the congregation is familiar with the service or the service is that of *Missa Cantata*. Stand on the step next below the epistle end of the footpace, facing the gospel side. (Fig. 8) Present the boat to the celebrant, hold up the open censer while incense is put into it and blessed as usual, close the censer and hand it to the priest, receiving in exchange the boat which is placed on the credence. Remove the missal stand from the altar, moving down the side steps on the epistle side, face north, and hold it so that the missal faces outwards at a suitable height, and with reverence, while the altar is censed. (Fig. 9) As soon as the priest approaches the south end of the altar for the final swings, replace the missal stand, with the missal facing west so that the priest may conveniently read the Introit. Receive the censer (Fig.8) and cense the priest in the customary manner. (Fig.10) After the censer is hung up return to the normal position on the gospel side. (Fig. l) (It is not necessary to hold the chasuble rolled up on the priest's shoulders during the censing. There is no precedent to guide us here, as neither the Anglican nor Roman Churches use incense at Low Mass, while the latter does not use incense even at *Missa Cantata* unless there are sufficient servers available. The regulation that the chasuble should be held is generally held to have arisen when very heavy and jeweled vestments were widely used. This practice will be discussed when we come to deal with the work of three or more servers at a celebration.)

Fig. 8

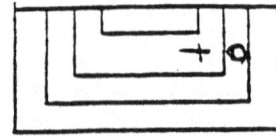

Fig. 9

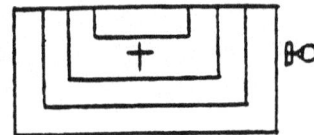

Fig. 10

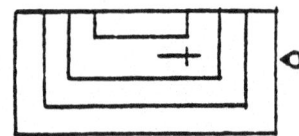

Fig. 11

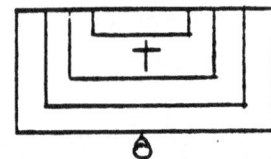

Introit to the Epistle.   At the *Kyrie*, and for the rest of the service whenever kneeling is required, kneel on the first altar step (but not on the footpace if that be the only step). It is not necessary to swing the censer *in piano* for the Gloria at Low Mass. For Missa Cantata swing it as at High Mass, and retire just before the end of the Gloria. (Fig. 11)

Epistle, Gradual and Gospel Omitted.   Immediately after the Collects, go up to the footpace from the epistle end for the missal stand. Take it to the gospel side, walking around *in plano* and genuflecting enroute in the usual manner. (Fig. 12) Ascend by the steps on the gospel side, place the stand on the gospel end of the altar at a convenient angle to the priest. (A server should never use the steps merely to pass from one side of the sanctuary to the other but should always go *in plano*, ascending and

Fig. 12

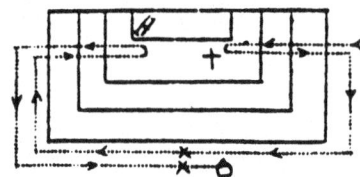

descending the steps at the side if it is necessary to approach the altar.) Return the same way *in plano* to the second normal position which it will be remembered is on the epistle side. (Fig. 2)

Epistle, Gradual and Gospel Included.   If required to read the Epistle, stand *in plano* on the epistle side facing the people. (Fig.13) If someone else is to read it, be seated. The Epistoller should be of mature age and of the grade of Reader or upwards. When the Gradual is begun take the missal stand to the gospel side as previously described. (Fig.12) Alternatively, the priest may move it himself. Bring the, boat and censer to the priest just as at the first censing. (Fig.8) (If because of an insufficient congregation, this would interrupt the Gradual, the incense should be blessed after the Gradual.) After the incense is blessed replace the boat on the credence and, carrying the censer, cross over *in plano* to the gospel side. Ascend the steps on that side as soon as the priest has made the sign of the cross on the book and in the threefold manner on himself. (If there is a special Book of Gospels this will be presented to the priest beforehand.) Present the censer to the priest so that he may cense the Book. (Fig:14) For this the book is left on the stand. It may remain there while the Gospel is read, but if a congregation is present, the priest should turn to face the people for the reading of the Gospel, holding the book in his hands; in either case while the Gospel is read, the server stands facing the priest at a suitable distance from him and with his back to the people (if any) gently swinging the censer at full chain. (Fig.15) If difficulties arise with regard to space in a small chapel, take up a position at the side facing south. (Fig. 16) After the Gospel return *in plano* and hang up the censer. The celebrant is not censed since he read the Gospel himself. Henceforward stand and kneel at the second normal position until the Ablutions. (Fig. 2)

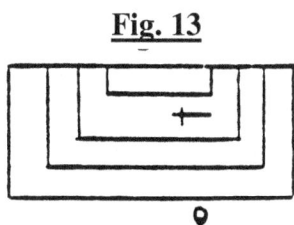

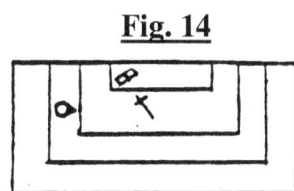

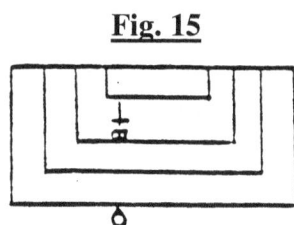

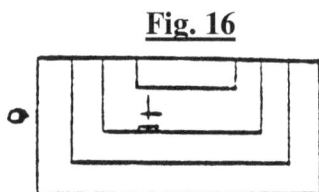

Fig. 13

Fig. 14

Fig. 15

Fig. 16

Sermon to the Second Censing.   For the sermon, if any, give the priest his biretta. If the sermon is delivered from a pulpit help him to remove his chasuble and maniple. Be seated during the sermon.

If there is to be a collection, and there is no offertory hymn, it is best taken by a layman during the offertory sentences. Receive the collection at the sanctuary entrance and present it to the priest (going up the steps from the epistle side) at the first convenient moment, but in any case before the second censing. (Fig. 8)

When the priest begins to uncover the chalice at the Offertory, go to the credence and remain quietly standing there while the priest says: *We adore Thee....* In this way the attention of the people is not distracted while the bread is offered, and the cruets can be brought without delay immediately afterwards—in fact while the priest purifies the chalice with the purificator. Stand in the same position as for the blessing of incense, (Fig. 8) with the lips of the cruets to the right. The priest alone pours the wine and water at the Offertory. Only the water is held up to be blessed.

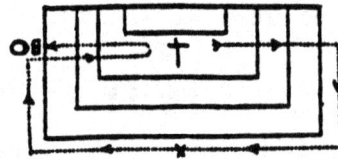

Fig. 17

When the cruets are replaced on the credence, return with the censer and boat for the second tensing. (Fig.8) The procedure is the same as for the first censing except that the missal stand is removed from the gospel side (Fig. 17) and held at that side facing south. Replace it as soon as the priest has commenced the lowermost series of swings from the gospel side. (Fig. 18) Go to the epistle side, receive the censer after the celebrant has said the words of oblation, cense the priest in the same manner as before, (Fig. 10) then go to the middle *in plano* and cense the people with three long (or short) swings: middle, left, right, bowing to the people before and after. (Fig. 19) This ceremony is performed even when there is no congregation. (In the rare event of other clergy being, present, these are censed in the proper order first.) Immediately after tensing the people, hang up the censer and bring the lavabo bowl, carafe, and towel to the celebrant; stand in the same position as for the blessing of incense. (Fig. 8) It will be found helpful to hold the bowl in the left hand, with the towel hanging; over the left forearm and the carafe in the right hand. To give effect to the symbolism the

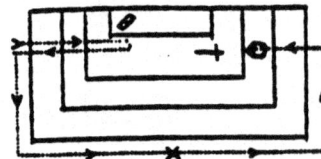

Fig. 18

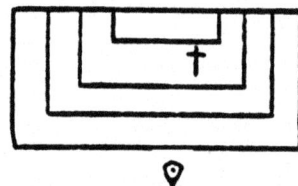

Fig. 19

water should actually be poured over the priest's fingers; hence the priest should wait for the server and not merely dip his fingers in the bowl at the credence while the people are being censed.

The Sanctus to the End of Mass.   Since there is but one server it will not normally be possible to ring the sacring bell and swing the censer simultaneously at the Sanctus and Consecration. However, it is permissible for a member of the congregation to ring the bell from outside the sanctuary, so that the server may he free to swing the censer. Otherwise the bell is rung by the server, and the censer left hanging; at the side. Its use at this point is not necessary at private Masses or if the congregation be small. With a fair sized congregation, and also at festivals, its use adds to the dignity of the rite. On such occasions, the open censer may be placed at the centre of the first step, and fed with incense before the Sanctus and before the Consecration, from the boat which the server should have with him. In any case a copious supply of incense should be placed on the charcoal for this portion of the service, and great care taken that everything shall be done as quietly as possible.

Kneeling at the second normal position (Fig. 2), ring the bell once each time the word Holy is said or sung. If circumstances permit the censer is swung at short chain in unison with the bell, the swings being directed towards the altar from the middle position *in plano*. (Fig. 11) Similarly the censer may accompany the bell at the Consecration.. (In some of our larger churches it is the permitted custom to ring the bell and swing the censer the same number of times at *Missa Cantata* as at High Mass.)

At the Consecration, when the priest kneels on one knee immediately after consecrating the Host, ring the bell three times. Ring it three times when the Host is elevated, and again three times when the priest kneels immediately afterwards. The same procedure is adopted when the consecration of the Wine takes Place, care being taken not to interrupt the priest as he says: *As oft.... remembrance of Me.* It is important that. the bell. be rung carefully and rhythmically. Return the censer, if used, immediately [when] the *Adeste Fideles* is begun. For *Missa Cantata* on a great Feast, the censer may be swung at full chain as at the *Gloria.* (Fig. 11) In this case, retire just before the end of the *Adeste Fideles.*

If, during *Missa Cantata*, the Longer Form of the Salutation of Peace is employed, rise after receiving it from the priest and give it to the people. (See page 38 in the Ceremonial [or the corresponding page in a new version Ed.].)

Fig. 20

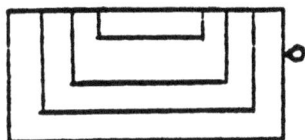

During the Communion of the people, if any, be seated, or kneel, facing north so that the back is not turned to the Host. (Fig. 20) In any case kneel when the priest passes with the Host on his way back to the altar and remain kneeling while any extra Hosts are consumed or placed in the tabernacle.

Fig. 21

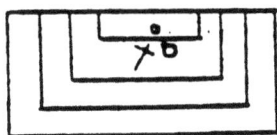

For the Ablutions, bring up the cruets as at the offertorium, (Fig. 8) but this time pour the water and wine yourself. For the first ablution go up on to the footpace and pour wine only, the priest holding the chalice a little to the epistle side but still over the corporal. (Fig. 21) The chalice is not moved from the corporal at this point as it still contains remnants of the Consecrated Wine. Retire to the step below the epistle end of the footpace. (Fig. 8) When the chalice is brought by the priest for the second ablution pour a very little wine over the priest's fingers into the chalice, followed by a much larger quantity of water. When this is consumed, a third ablution with a considerable quantity of water only is taken. (If the proportions of wine and water here indicated are carefully observed, the purificator can be kept unsoiled and. in use over a longer period of time.) If required; assist the priest with the chalice veil. After the Ablutions, move the missal stand to the epistle side, going around *in plano* as before. (Fig. 22) Until the end of Mass take up the normal position on the gospel side, as at the beginning of Mass. (Fig. 1)

Fig. 22

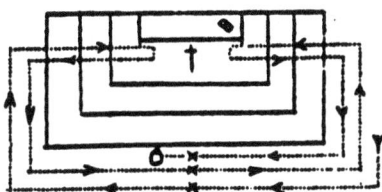

After the final Blessing present the biretta to the priest, genuflect with him *in plano* (Fig. 3) and leave the sanctuary,

Low Mass or *Missa Cantata* by a Bishop with One Server

The ceremonies are much the same as for a priest. The ceremonies with the censer will have to be omitted, but the crozier may be fixed at the gospel side of the altar.

When the Short Form is used, the bishop will normally enter the sanctuary vested in a chasuble. The server would otherwise have to deal almost simultaneously with cope, mitre, chasuble, maniple, crozier, missal and aspergill. Upon entering the sanctuary in the usual manner, stand the mitre or biretta on the gospel end of the altar after the Invocation and then proceed with the *Asperges*. The mitre should face the people and the fanons should hang down over the frontal. (The biretta, if worn, is placed on the altar because, unlike a priest, the bishop will require it when giving blessings.)

Upon entering the sanctuary for the Long Form, stand the mitre on the altar as described above. As soon as the *Asperges* is finished assist the bishop to vest in the chasuble and maniple and present him with the mitre for the Invocation. After the Invocation replace the mitre on the altar.

The remainder of the service proceeds as usual, the bishop serving himself with the mitre or biretta. After each censing of the altar he is censed with three *triple* swings.

Low Mass by a Priest with Two or More Servers

It is not usual to employ two or more servers for a Low celebration on ordinary occasions. On great Feasts two servers may be used. They carry our their duties as described below for *Missa Cantata* with two servers.

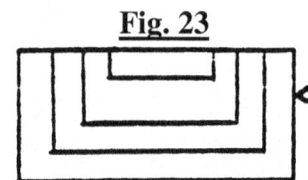

Fig. 23

Missa Cantata by a Priest with Two Servers

Preliminary. The first assistant acts as thurifer, the second as altar server. The thurifer goes first in procession. He may carry the censer since there is a congregation. The server follows without processional cross or candlestick. Arriving in the sanctuary the thurifer goes a little to the right, the server to the left. All genuflect together in line before the first step. (Fig. 24)

Directions for Thurifer. It will be convenient to attend to the biretta, aspergill, books, and collection in addition to the censer. Assistance should also be given with the chasuble and maniple at the vestings in the Longer Form.

The normal position is on the epistle side of the sanctuary facing north. (Fig. 23) For the *Asperges*, stand on the priest's right facing east. (Fig. 24). For the *Asperges*, Longer Form, kneel with the priest and hold the right edge

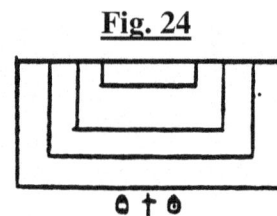

Fig. 24

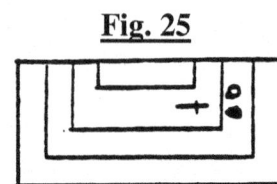

Fig. 25

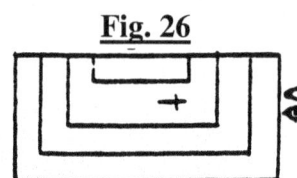

Fig. 26

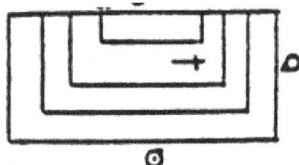

Fig. 27

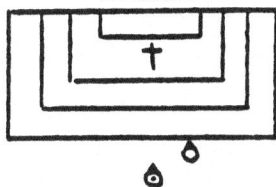

Fig. 28

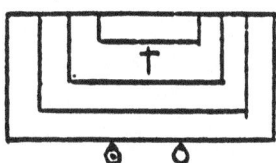

Fig. 29

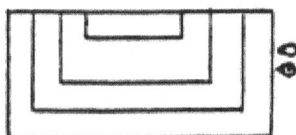

Fig. 30

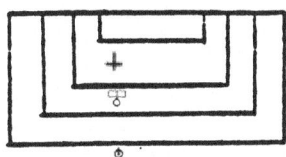

Fig. 31

of the cope (the altar server will do the same for the left) while the priest asperses the altar. Rise when he turns to asperse the people. When the aspergill is handed back, in either form, retire to the side. (Fig. 23)

The ceremonies with the thurible at the First and Second Censings and at the Gloria, Gradual and Gospel are as described above for one server, except that at the Censings and the Gradual, the altar server holds the boat, (Figs. 25, 26) and that at the Second Censing the latter is censed after the priest with one swing from the centre *in plano*. (Fig. 27)

At the Sanctus and Consecration kneel with the censer and boat, preferably in the middle *in plano*. (Fig. 28) If there is a lack of space or if the usage be preferred, kneel on the gospel side in a position corresponding and complementary to that of the altar server. (Fig. 29) Swing the censer in unison with the bell rung by the altar server. Retire when the Adeste Fideles begins, unless it is one of the great Feasts.

At the Salutation of Peace come forward again (without censer) and kneel. (Fig. 29) If the Longer Form of the Salutation of Peace is employed, give it to the people after receiving it from the server. (See page 38 of the Ceremonial.)

After receiving Communion, retire with the server and kneel or be seated facing north. (Fig. 30)

Directions for the Altar Server.   Having arrived in the sanctuary on the left of the celebrant, the positions adopted during the service are the same as when serving unassisted. The censer, aspergill, biretta and books are left to the thurifer. Attention is given to the missal stand, boat, cruets, lavabo, sacring bell and Book of Gospels (if used.)

At the Censings and the Gradual hold the boat open before the celebrant, standing on the right of the thurifer. (Fig. 25) For the Longer Form assist with the cope at the vestings. After replacing the missal stand on the altar at the Second Censing, cross over *in plano* to the epistle side to be censed, (Fig. 27) and then proceed with the Lavabo. (Fig. 8) If the Gospel is read to the people, stand at the gospel end of the step below the footpace, facing east, and hold the Book for the celebrant to read. (Fig. 31)

Missa Cantata by a Priest, Assisted by a Priest or Deacon and a Server

The server carries out his duties as though he were assisting alone, except that he uses the censer from the centre *in plano* at the Sanctus and Consecration, while the assistant priest or deacon rings the bell from his place on the epistle side of the sanctuary.

If the latter reads the Gospel he is handed the censer after it is read in order that he may cense the celebrant. The assistant cleric is censed with three double swings after the celebrant at the Second Censing. (Fig. 27) He may assist at the Lavabo.

Low Mass or *Missa Cantata* by a Bishop with Two Servers

The first server's duties are as described above for a bishop with one server. The second acts as crozier bearer and is seated on the gospel side. The ceremonies with the crozier are the same as with a bishop at High Mass. (See Ceremonial, pages 42, 85-88, 108, 109) On those occasions when the bishop wears a cope, he assists at the vestings.

When the first server is changing the missal stand to the other side, the second, moving simultaneously so that they genuflect one behind the other *en passant*, does the same with the mitre. The mitre and missal are always on opposite ends of the altar. At the Sanctus and Consecration the crozier bearer takes the censer and boat while his partner rings the bell.

Missa Cantata with More than Two Servers

If there are three servers, one may carry incense in procession, since there will be a congregation, and the other two, processional candles. (The Processional Cross and Candles are not used at Low Mass.) The bearing of the Processional Cross is less important. At *Missa Cantata* it may be carried by a fourth server, who will follow after the thurifer when in procession. He may be accompanied by two further candle bearers, one on either side, more especially when there are persons in the procession between the cross and the candle bearers accompanying the celebrant. If there is a fourth server, or an assistant in Major Orders, he may act as Master of Ceremonies.

With three or more servers available it becomes feasible for two of them to assist during the censing of the altar by holding the chasuble, as do the deacon and subdeacon at High Mass. (Fig. 33) The remaining server will in that case hold the missal stand.

The different duties may be divided in various ways between the thurifer and his two assistants, who may conveniently be called the first and second altar servers, respectively. The simplest arrangement, since it is based on the procedure for two servers, is for the thurifer and the first altar server to carry out their duties as described above for two servers. In addition the thurifer and second altar server assist the celebrant to cense the altar and both altar servers act as candle bearers. They make use of the two candles kept one on either side of the credence. The suggested procedure at certain points which require special attention is given below.

Invocation.   Just as at High Mass the candle bearers stand on either side of the celebrant for the Invocation. (Fig. 32)

The Censings of the Altar.   At the first censing, the first server and thurifer stand on

Fig. 32

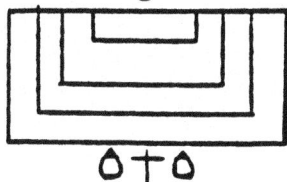

Fig. 33

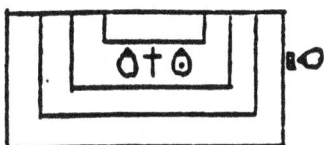

Fig. 34

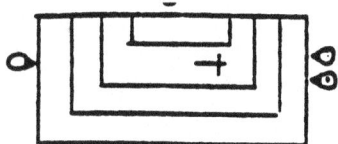

Fig. 35

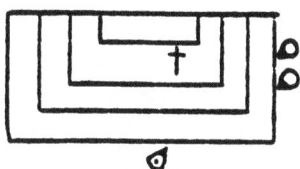

Fig. 36

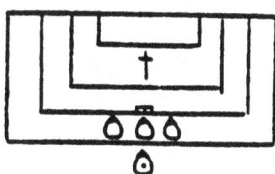

Fig. 37

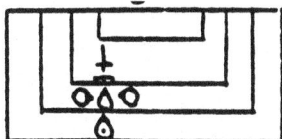

the second step on the epistle side with the boat and censer. (Fig. 25) When the incense is blessed the server takes the missal stand while the thurifer assists the celebrant by holding the chasuble. The second altar server has meanwhile crossed over *in plano* to the gospel side. While the incense is being blessed he stands at the foot of the side steps of the altar on the gospel side facing south. When the incense has been blessed, he ascends to the footpace at the same time as his partner on the other side, and assists the priest by holding the chasuble in the usual manner. (Fig. 33) After the altar is censed he retires the way he came, while his partner censes the priest, standing for this purpose at the base of the altar steps on the epistle side, facing north. (Fig. 26)

At the Second Censing, the preliminary ceremonies are the same. While the priest is censed the second altar server stands at the base of the altar steps on the gospel side, facing south. (Fig. 34) When the priest has been censed, this server and the thurifer proceed simultaneously to the middle, genuflecting in plano one behind the other. The second server then joins the first on the epistle side and they are censed from the middle by the thurifer with a single swing, unless someone of greater dignity be present, who will be censed first. (Fig. 35) They then assist with the Lavabo, after which, carrying candles, they are ready to proceed with the thurifer to the centre for the Sanctus and Consecration.

The Gospel.   Towards the end of the Gradual, a fourth server, if available, will go to the middle of the first, step. He stands there, with the Book of Gospels (or a. *Liturgy*) opened. at the proper place and with two candle bearers, one on either side. The thurifer is *in piano* in the middle, the incense having first been blessed. (Fig. 36) When there are only three servers, the thurifer holds both censer and book. This position is the same as at High Mass, except that the subdeacon has been replaced by a server. When the celebrant has given the Minor Benediction after the *Munda Cor Meum*, all turn and proceed to the gospel end of the steps. The servers then face east and mount up one step. (Fig. 37) (This step is not taken at High Mass, the difference arising from the fact that at High Mass the deacon reads the Gospel from the second step, while at *Missa Cantata* the celebrant reads it himself from the foot pace.) While the Gospel is read the candle bearers may face each other.

Sanctus and Consecration.   At the beginning of the

Canon, the two candle bearers take their places *in plano* one on either side of the thurifer. When there are additional candle bearers they may enter in procession as at High Mass. Just before the Sanctus they kneel. When there are only three servers, one of them will have to ring the bell at the same time as he elevates his candle. This may be managed with practice, or a member of the congregation may ring it. If there is a fourth server or an M.C., he will ring it from the side.

The Crozier Bearer.　　When a bishop celebrates, an extra server is required for the crozier. When there are only three servers available, the ceremonies with the candles at the Invocation and the Gospel will have to be omitted, since candle bearers should work in pairs. It is possible however to have candles for the Sanctus and Consecration, as the crozier bearer is then free.

Boat Boy.　　If there is a special Boat Boy in addition to the other servers, he will accompany the thurifer wherever the latter goes, presenting the boat at the proper time.

HIGH MASS
(by Rev. W. H. Pitkin.)

There are no fixed ritual positions for servers at High Mass as there are at Low Mass and *Missa Cantata*, since the deacon and subdeacon are the ritual altar assistants. The servers remain by their seats except when performing their various duties. The positions and duties of the ministers at High Mass will be found in the Ceremonial. (See plates 4 and 5)

Master of Ceremonies.　　If there be a Master of Ceremonies, he will supervise all actions and in certain instances act as an intermediary between the celebrant or his ministers and the servers. Thus he receives the birettas of the celebrant and his ministers and gives them to a server to place at the sedilia (or does this himself); he receives the aspergill from a server and presents it to the deacon, and after the *Asperges* receives it again and hands it to a server to place on the credence. He supervises the change from cope to chasuble. He removes the missal stand from the altar during the censings, and transfers it from side to side at the Gradual and after the Ablutions. He presents the Book of Epistles, and later the Book of Gospels to the subdeacon, and receives them afterwards. If in cope, he stands behind the subdeacon at the reading of the. Gospel. He receives the collection at the offertory and presents it to the deacon. His normal position when not otherwise engaged is on the epistle side, *in plano*, by the lowest altar step, facing north. (Plate 4, Figs. 2,9, etc.)

If there be no Master of. Ceremonies, the several servers will perform these functions much as they would at *Missa Cantata*.

The Thurifer.　　The thurifer presents the boat to the deacon, when incense is to be blessed, and at the First and Second Censing hands him the censer after it has been closed. The deacon will cense the celebrant at the First and Second Censings, the thurifer standing beside the subdeacon. (Plate 4, Fig. 7) At the Second Censing the deacon will cense the subdeacon and any clergy present, going to the middle *in plano* to do so, accompanied by the thurifer, to whom he then presents the censer. The deacon goes to the epistle end of his own step, and is censed by the thurifer (Fig. 38) who then censes the servers collectively with three short single swings, and finally censes the people.

Fig. 38

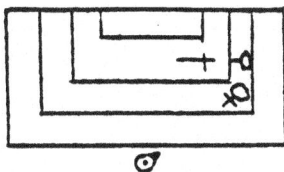

The Servers. The server or servers handling the cruets present the wine cruet to the deacon and the water cruet to the subdeacon, at both the Offertory and the Ablutions. A server presents the bowl, carafe and towel to the subdeacon at the Lavabo, and afterwards receives them again and assists the subdeacon with his ablutions. Servers carry the cope, chasuble and maniples to and from the sedilia at the vestings, and a server holds the cope behind the celebrant while the deacon and subdeacon assist him with the chasuble.

✠

PART III

OTHER SERVICES AND OFFICES

CHAPTER X

VESPERS

General Directions

(In this chapter there has been incorporated, with the permission of the author, the greater part of an article entitled "Ceremonial Directions for Vespers" (The Liberal Catholic, December 1927) by the Rt. Rev. J.I. Wedgwood.)

The ecclesiastical division of the day into canonical hours is based on the Roman civil system of dividing the day into periods of three hours. Vespers is the division of the day, from the liturgical standpoint, corresponding to the time from 3 p.m. to 6 p.m., though the time, strictly speaking, is variable according to the seasons. Vespers is the only one of the Offices of the Hours which has remained in popular use as a public service. Coming, as it does, towards the end of the day, it provides a suitable occasion for gathering people together in church for a second time on a Sunday. Hence in these days [1934 Ed.], though the Roman Church sometimes celebrates it as early as three o'clock, there is a common disposition to use it as a late afternoon or evening service, comparable to the Anglican service of Evensong.

It should not be held earlier than 3 p.m., and it is scarcely fitting to place it later than 8.30 p.m., since already in the early and late hours of this margin of time some license has to be taken in the interpretation of the first verse of the Hymn.

The Office of Vespers is normally intended to be sung, depending much for its effect on the rhythmical and not too slow recitation of the chants. If this is not possible, there is no objection to its being said, though on such occasions the Hymn, and if possible the *Te Deum*, may be sung. If the singing of all the Psalms is beyond the capacity of the congregation, it is permitted to omit either the Psalm of Godly Life or the Psalm of Wisdom or, in rare cases, both; in which case the invitation will run: *Omitting the Psalm of... let us sing etc.*, or intimation may be made before the singing of the Psalms which are to be sung (or omitted).

The three Collects (*Liturgy*, 2nd Ed., p.216) [*Liturgy*, 3rd Ed., p.229, Ed.] at the close are not suitable for afternoon and should not therefore be used at early Vespers. They are for evening use, and are intended to contribute the note of peace at the close of day, which is the especial beauty of Complin and of the Anglican Evensong.

Feasts of major rank (Class A) may be ushered in by Solemn Vespers, sung on the preceding evening. This is called First Vespers, that sung on the day of the Festival being called Second Vespers. Vespers may be sung on any day during the year, except on certain days at the close of Holy Week. On Maundy Thursday it may be sung in the afternoon. On the afternoon and evening of Good Friday Vespers may be replaced by the Office of Complin, which is said. On Holy Saturday Vespers may be sung, whether in the afternoon or evening, and will rank as the First Vespers of Easter.

The colour of the day when Vespers are celebrated may be different from that used at the Holy Eucharist in the morning, because of the rule that the Christian Day begins at sunset. The colour of the vestments used at early Vespers is usually that of the Day on which they are celebrated, but often if Vespers is celebrated after 6 p.m. the colour is that of the Day following. This rule is not always strictly followed, especially on the evening of the Octave of a major Festival.

The celebrant should if possible be in priest's Orders. In the absence of the priest, a deacon may conduct Vespers, by ruling of the Third General Episcopal Synod, but only under the following conditions: (1) he does not go to the altar but officiates from his seat at the side of the sanctuary throughout the service; (2) he does not bless incense or cense the altar, although incense may, of course, be burned in the censer during the service; (3) he always says the Grace and never the Blessing at the end of the service.

Vespers constitute a Choir Office and are therefore celebrated from a seat at the side of the sanctuary, and not before the altar. This seat consists of a suitable chair or *sedilia* on the epistle side. If there be several clergy present it is convenient that the celebrant occupy the stall or chair nearest the people. At Solemn Vespers the two assistants (corresponding to the Deacon and Subdeacon of the Eucharist) are seated one on either side of the celebrant, the first assistant to his right, the second assistant to his left. In front of the seat of the celebrant is placed, if available, a kneeling desk. This may be covered with a silken cloth of the colour of the Day.

Vespers may be either Simple or Solemn. *Simple Vespers* are prescribed on week days which are not major festivals. Only the usual six altar candles are lighted. The celebrant, if a priest, vests in surplice, stole and biretta; if a bishop, in rochet, stole and biretta, wears the ring and pectoral cross and uses the crozier. The wearing of the mozetta is optional. Simple Vespers are also permissible on Sundays of Class B, C or D. *Solemn Vespers* are prescribed on Sundays of Class A and major festivals. Extra candles are lighted on the altar. *If the officiant celebrates without vested assistants* he is vested as follows: if priest, in surplice, stole, cope and biretta; if bishop, in rochet, stole, cope and mitre, wearing the ring and pectoral cross and using the crozier. If *he officiates with two assistants in vestments* certain variations are introduced. By ruling of the Third General Episcopal Synod the assistants at Vespers and at Benediction may vest either in cope or in dalmatic and tunicle. It is on the whole preferable that the dalmatic and tunicle shall be worn only at High Celebration of the Holy Eucharist. It will often happen that three copes of the same colour and style will not be available; in that case dalmatic and tunicle may be worn. It should be noted that the assistants at Solemn Benediction in the Roman Rite may wear dalmatic and tunicle. If copes are used by the assistants at Vespers (and this is much to be preferred if Vespers are *not* followed by Benediction) then the celebrant (if a priest) and his assistants vest in surplice, stole (for those in priest's or deacon's Orders);, cope and biretta. If, however, the assistants are vested in dalmatic and tunicle, and therefore in amice, alb, etc., exactly as at High Celebration of the Holy Eucharist (except that the maniple is never worn) then the celebrant, if a priest, vests in amice, alb, girdle, stole (crossed in front), cope and biretta. In either case, a bishop vests in rochet, stole and cope, wears the mitre, pectoral cross and ring, and uses the crozier.

If there is a choir, the voices may be divided so that an equal number of about the same power may be seated on either side of the chancel or church (depending upon local arrangements). In the same way, with the cooperation of the people, the congregation may be divided. This division of voices is helpful, if not necessary, in order that during the singing of the Psalms, one verse may be sung by those on one side of the church, the next verse by those on the other side, and so on alternately as described hereafter. When this is done the singing is more interesting and spirited. If more convenient, a cantor or group of voices may alternate with the entire congregation led by the remainder of the choir. Whether or not the singing of the Psalms is taken alternately in such fashion will of course depend on the size and resources of the congregation.

If Solemn Benediction follows Vespers and it is thought best to substitute white vestments for those used at Vespers (see Chapter XI) the celebrant and his assistants and any others present vested in copes) may retire to the vestry to change their vestments. Those so retiring should depart from and return to the sanctuary in procession, preferably during the interval between the services when the congregation is singing a hymn. Other priests in the sanctuary who are vested in stoles may quietly change their green or violet stoles (if desired) for white, without leaving their seats. If Vespers are simple, and the officiant is not to be attended during Benediction by two vested assistants, he may, after Vespers, unobtrusively change his stole (if necessary) and assume the cope, while at his seat in the sanctuary.

Few preparations are required for Vespers.

If *Simple Vespers* are to be celebrated the servers required for the celebration of the rite are: thurifer, two candle bearers, and, if possible, a cross bearer and boat bearer. If these are not available, the service can be conducted with the aid of a single server, who will bring the censer at the appointed times. If a bishop is present a crozier bearer will be needed. The altar frontal should be of the same colour as the vestments used, although in small churches white may be used. On the desk or lectern of the officiant is placed a Vesperal (containing both words and music) and a Liturgy marked at the Collect of the Day. A hymnbook (with a list of the hymns to be sung) is also laid thereon, unless it is to be carried in procession to the sanctuary. Similarly the words and music of the Service and a hymnbook should be placed at the seats of non-officiating clergy and of the servers. If Solemn Benediction is to follow Vespers and the officiant is to change to white stole and cope at his seat, these vestments should be placed near at hand. The white stoles (if required for Benediction) of the non-officiating clergy should be laid on their seats. In the vestry the vestments to be worn in procession are laid out, the charcoal is prepared and the processional candles lighted. At Simple Vespers only the six altar candles are lighted, the extra candles for Benediction (if celebrated) not being lighted until just before that service begins. If it is the custom in the church, the candles on the Lady Altar and/or altar of the Patron Saint are lighted.

At *Solemn Vespers*, in addition to the foregoing servers mentioned, there should be two assistants in vestments. They need not be in Major Orders, but should, at least, have been ordained cleric. (If the first assistant has not as yet been ordained deacon he may not wear the stole. If the first and second assistants have not been ordained respectively to the Orders of Deacon and Subdeacon they should wear copes and not the dalmatic and tunicle.) There may be additional candle bearers and, in large churches, an additional thurifer. Additional candles are placed on the altar and are lighted, with the six altar candles, before the service of Vespers begins. There may be a cantor, if desired, especially if the officiant does not possess a sufficiently good singing voice to lead the service. The cantor may vest in cope.

Vespers by a Priest without Vested Assistants

The procession to the sanctuary is like that at the Holy Eucharist. Arriving before the lowest altar step all genuflect (removing their birettas while so doing), and go at once to their seats in the sanctuary, with the exception of the celebrant and his two attendant candle bearers who remain standing before the lowest altar step in the middle. (It is understood, of course, that other servers carrying candles put away and extinguish their candles before going to their seats.)

When all are in their places the officiant removes his biretta (all others in the sanctuary with birettas following his example) and intones the *Invocation*. Again genuflecting, he puts on his biretta and goes to his seat on the epistle side. The two attendant acolytes place their lighted candles on the credence and go to their seats, which may be on either side of the officiant. The officiant removes his biretta, opens the vesperal and is ready to begin the service. (It is understood that all in the sanctuary are standing, faced towards the middle.) In the meantime the organist will have played a few chords.

As soon as the organist has sounded the intoning note, the officiant sings: *Our help... Lord*, all sing the response: *Who hath... earth*. The two following versicles and responses are sung likewise. The officiant then turns to the people, momentarily extends his hands and sings: *The Lord be with you.* As the people respond he turns back to face the middle, the organist immediately gives the opening chord and all sing the Gloria Patri. All turn to the east and slightly bow their heads while singing: *Glory be to the Father, and to the Son, and to the Holy Ghost.* They stand erect for the words which follow, and at the *Amen* turn back to face the middle again. While singing all of the versicles which follow the Invocation, the hands of the officiant are joined before the breast, except of course when he turns to the people at the Minor Benediction.

After the *Amen* all are seated, the celebrant (and any other clergy present putting on his biretta). He now says clearly (he does not intone) so that all may hear: *Let us sing to the praise and glory of God the First Psalm of Praise.* The organist then either sounds the opening chord or plays over the entire antiphon, depending upon the familiarity of the congregation with the music. The antiphon is sung by all. The organist now plays over the opening notes of the Psalm, and then the officiant (or the cantor) sings alone the first half of the first verse, the choir and congregation joining in at the second half. All sing the second verse. If the singing is to be taken alternately, those on the epistle side of the church and sanctuary now sing the third verse while those on the gospel side sing the fourth verse, and so on alternately to the end. (If there be a cantor or small choir to alternate with the congregation, the cantor sings the third verse and every odd-numbered verse thereafter, the congregation the fourth verse and every even-numbered verse.) All sing the Gloria Patri and the antiphon. During the singing of: *Glory be... Holy Ghost*, the officiant and any other clergy present remove the biretta and incline the head slightly, but remain seated. Birettas and the erect seated position are resumed for the second verse of the Gloria Patri: *As it was ... without end. Amen.*

All of the psalms which follow are sung in exactly the same way: the officiant announces the Psalm; the antiphon is sung by all; the officiant (or cantor) sings the first half of the first verse, the choir and people joining in at the second half; those on the epistle side may sing the odd-numbered verses and those on the gospel side the even-numbered verses; all sing the Gloria Patri and the antiphon. A slight pause for rest and recollection may be observed between the various psalms.

During the singing of the last psalm (The Third Psalm of Praise) the thurifer (and boat bearer) takes his place opposite to and facing the officiant, but at a convenient distance so that the view of the congregation is not unduly obstructed. Incense is not blessed at this point, since neither person nor altar is to be censed, but the thurifer may first place incense in the thurible. While the incense is being prepared the two chief acolytes go to the credence, take up their lighted candles, genuflect together in the middle before the lowest altar step and go to the officiant. Bowing slightly to him, they stand on either side of him, a little in front of his lectern and facing one another. (Fig. 1, p.132)

At the *Gloria Patri* the officiant uncovers and bows as usual, and then leaves his biretta on the seat beside him. As the antiphon is being sung, he rises in his place to read the Little Chapter. (Fig. 1) (This is preferably read, not intoned.) All likewise remove their birettas and rise with him. During the reading of the Little Chapter the thurifer swings the censer to and fro. The hands of the celebrant are joined before his breast, unless it is necessary for him to hold the vesperal. The Chapter ended, all sing: *Thanks be to God.* The acolytes and thurifer bow to the officiant, genuflect in the middle before the altar, and go to put away the candles on the credence, the censer in its place.

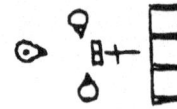

Fig. 1

The *Hymn* is sung, all standing. During the last line of the last verse all incline the head slightly towards the altar. Towards the end of the Hymn the celebrant proceeds to the middle before the lowest altar step, the two chief acolytes, bearing their lighted candles, preceding him and stationing themselves on either side of him, slightly to the rear, facing the altar. Standing *in plano* all three genuflect.

The antiphon of the *Te Deum Laudamus* is sung by all. After the opening notes by the organist, the celebrant (or cantor) now sings the opening words: *We praise Thee O God.* All at this point take up the singing of the Te Deum which should be sung briskly, no pause between verses. The verses are not sung alternately as in the case of the psalms, but by all together.

As soon as the celebrant has sung the opening words, he ascends to the footpace. If he is vested in surplice and stole, the acolytes place their candles on the corners of the lowest altar step, genuflect in the middle together and retire to their seats. If, however, he is vested in cope, they ascend to the footpace with him (first placing the candles on the corners of the lowest altar step) and assist him by raising the corners of the cope during the censing of the altar. They genuflect and move with him in the same manner as the deacon and subdeacon at the Eucharist, keeping the cope spread out like an opened fan, in order that the arms of the celebrant may be free to swing the censer.

When he reaches the footpace, the celebrant moves to the epistle end and the thurifer comes to him as at the Eucharist. The first acolyte may hold the boat while the second acolyte holds up the right corner of the cope. After the incense has been blessed, the thurifer hands the closed censer to the celebrant who censes the altar exactly as it is done at the first censing in the Eucharist. This ended, the acolytes (if they accompanied the officiant to the footpace) bow to him and retire to the sanctuary floor to stand in front of the altar before the corners of the lowest altar step. They take up their candles and hold them. Towards the close of the *Te Deum*, the two acolytes, whether standing before the altar or at their seats, go to the middle, genuflect, and place their candles on the credence. Returning to their places before the lowest altar step during the singing of the antiphon, they genuflect and face the altar. After the censing of the altar the celebrant returns the censer to the thurifer, who thereupon censes first the celebrant, then the clergy and finally the people in the same way as is done at the Eucharist. Meanwhile the officiant returns to the middle of the footpace and stands there facing the altar until the end of the *Te Deum*. After censing the people, the thurifer, if the *Te Deum* is not yet ended, stands in the middle *in plano* facing the altar, swinging the censer to the right and to the left. At the end of the antiphon the thurifer genuflects and returns the censer to its place. The officiant descends to stand *in plano* between the two acolytes, facing the altar. All three genuflect. The acolytes accompany the officiant to his seat, bow slightly to him, and stand before their own seats facing the middle.

Standing at his seat, the officiant turns to the people, extends his hands momentarily and sings: *The Lord be with you.* As the people respond, he turns back to face the middle. Still standing, he intones: *Let us pray.* All kneel except the celebrant. He then intones or reads the Collect of the Day, while holding the book. He then may intone or read the three evening Collects. Lastly follows the Peace Collect, the response, *Amen*, being sung after each Collect. The Collects ended, the officiant sings: *Let us bless the Lord.* After the response he crosses himself and sings: *May the souls ... peace.* All likewise cross themselves. He then sings: *The Lord give us His peace*, and the people respond: *and life everlasting.*

If Benediction of the Most Holy Sacrament is to follow, the celebrant makes the sign of the cross over himself and intones or says the Grace. The sermon, if any, then follows. This ended, an offertory hymn may be sung during which a collection is taken. The celebrant goes to the altar to present the offerings of the people. The service of Benediction then follows.

If no other service follows Vespers, the celebrant omits the Grace and proceeds immediately with the sermon, if any. Then may follow the offertory hymn, the celebrant presenting the offerings at the altar. This ended, the celebrant stands at his seat, turns to the people and blesses them in the usual way as he intones or says: *Unto God's ...evermore.* A recessional hymn may now be sung as the procession returns, usually by the shorter way, to the vestry.

Vespers by a Priest with Vested Assistants

The procession is usually more elaborate, with additional candle bearers and a second thurifer, The thurifers lead the procession, walking side-by-side. In the procession the first and second assistants precede the celebrant as is done by the deacon and subdeacon at the Eucharist. Arriving before the lowest altar step, the first assistant takes his place to the right of the celebrant, the second assistant to the left. All three remove their birettas and genuflect together. As soon as the others in the sanctuary are in their places, the celebrant and his assistants again remove their birettas, and the celebrant intones the *Invocation*. Putting on their birettas, they go to their seats, walking side by side if the sanctuary arrangements permit. Standing in front of their respective seats and removing their birettas, the officiant begins the service.

Just before the *Little Chapter* the same ceremonial grouping takes place as previously described except that the assistants, after they have risen and bowed slightly to the celebrant, go to stand just beyond the two acolytes holding candles (Fig. 2) and turn to face each other. One thurifer only comes forward at this time. He stations himself as described previously and swings the censer to and fro during the reading of the Little Chapter.

Fig.2

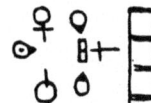

Towards the end of the Hymn the officiant and assistants (without their birettas) go to the altar and genuflect in the middle before the lowest step. As soon as the opening words of the *Te Deum* have been sung by the celebrant, they again genuflect and ascend to the footpace. The celebrant turns towards the epistle end as the thurifer comes forward. The first assistant holds the incense boat, the second assistant lifts up the right corner of the cope, and incense is placed in the censer and blessed as usual by the celebrant. (If there are two thurifers, the second thurifer should come forward first to the footpace, the first thurifer advancing as soon as the second has retired.) The first assistant takes the censer, which has been closed by the thurifer, and hands it to the celebrant. The assistants, on either side of the celebrant, hold out the cope fanwise during the censing of the altar.

Meanwhile the second thurifer stands in the middle *in plano*, facing the altar, swinging his censer to the right and to the left with long swings, starting when the celebrant begins to cense the altar and continuing until the end of the Te Deum. The first thurifer joins him after the censing of the people, provided the Te Deum is not yet ended. He should take his position behind the second thurifer, keeping time with the swing of his censer, but swinging to the left when the second thurifer swings to the right, and so on. At the close of the Te Deum they genuflect together side by side in the middle, go to hang up the censers and return to their seats.

Two acolytes, each holding a candle, may stand *in plano*, one at either end of the lowest altar step facing the altar, during the singing of the *Te Deum*. If additional servers are available, the number of candle bearers may be increased. They should be grouped symmetrically on either side of the sanctuary, care being taken to see that acolytes of much the same height occupy corresponding positions. At the end of the *Te Deum* they genuflect in pairs in the middle, put away their candles, and return to their seats.

At the end of the censing of the altar, the assistants release the ends of the cope, the first assistant takes the censer and descends to the sanctuary floor at the epistle end.

The second assistant also descends, walking down the front steps to the lowest step and thence along to the epistle end. The two assistants, in line with the first thurifer, face north. The first assistant censes the celebrant, the second assistant and the clergy in the usual way. He gives the censer to the thurifer and is himself censed. (The procedure throughout is the same as at High Celebration of the Eucharist.) The thurifer then censes the people, and, if there is time, turns to face the altar and swing the censer to and fro as has been described. As soon as the two assistants have both been censed they return to their places on either side of the celebrant.

At the end of the antiphon the celebrant and assistants genuflect on the footpace and return to their seats. After the Minor Benediction, when the celebrant intones: *Let us pray*, all kneel except the celebrant and his two assistants. If the Grace is said the assistants do not kneel, but only slightly bow their heads. They are seated during the sermon. When the celebrant goes to the altar to receive the offering, the assistants go with him. The first assistant receives the offertory plate from the acolyte and presents it to the celebrant in the same way as is done by the deacon at High Celebration. If no service is to follow and the celebrant therefore intones or says the Blessing, the assistants kneel at their places, facing north.

Priest Officiating in the Presence of a Bishop

When a priest officiates at Vespers in the presence of a bishop, either with or without vested assistants, the only points of difference are:

The priest (and assistants) goes directly to his seat after genuflecting in the middle before the lowest step. The bishop (with mitre or biretta and crozier) intones the Invocation from his throne, and blesses the incense (remaining seated as he does so if the throne is sufficiently raised). He is censed after the officiant (and his assistants). If no service is to follow the bishop intones or says the Blessing, but if a service is to follow, the celebrant, not the bishop, intones or says the Grace.

Simple Vespers by a Bishop

When a bishop, vested in rochet, stole and biretta officiates at Simple Vespers, it is not customary for him to have two vested assistants. The bishop's candle is not placed on the altar, inasmuch as this is lighted only when a bishop celebrates the Eucharist.

The biretta is worn by him during the Psalms, but not during the reading of the Little Chapter; while blessing incense, while being censed, and for the last Blessing, but not for the Grace. In general, he does not wear the biretta when standing or kneeling, but always when sitting. It is of course raised for the first half of the *Gloria Patri*.

Vespers by a Bishop
with Vested Assistants

When a bishop officiates at Solemn Vespers there should whenever possible be two vested assistants. In addition the bishop will need a crozier bearer. Failing a crozier bearer, the second assistant may assist with the crozier. Seats for the assistants should be arranged either in front of the throne, or one on either side of the throne. The first assistant sits to the right of the bishop and therefore nearest the altar rail, the second assistant to the left.

Arriving before the lowest altar step, the assistants take their place to the right and left of the celebrant as previously described. The crozier bearer stands behind the second assistant and therefore to the left of the bishop. While genuflecting the assistants remove their birettas, but the bishop retains his mitre. He wears the mitre and holds the crozier during the Invocation. When the bishop and the two assistants go to their seats, they walk three abreast, if sanctuary arrangements permit. If not, the assistants may precede the bishop and the crozier bearer. During the service the crozier is placed in a holder fastened to the left of the kneeling desk in front of the bishop.

The bishop removes the mitre during the singing of the versicles, but puts it on immediately before the First Psalm of Praise is announced and before he is seated. He bows his head, but does not remove the mitre whenever the first half of the *Gloria Patri* at the end of each Psalm is sung. He wears the mitre during the reading of the Little Chapter. He removes it during the singing of the hymn. He wears the mitre to and from the altar at the *Te Deum*. At the altar the bishop holds the crozier and wears the mitre while blessing the incense; he wears the mitre while being censed; he removes the mitre, but holds the crozier with both hands during the remainder of the *Te Deum*.

The crozier bearer, at the time the bishop goes to the altar to sing the *Te Deum* immediately precedes the bishop. He steps to the left and a little to the rear on arriving before the lowest altar step. Genuflecting with the bishop and assistants, the crozier bearer goes to stand on the sanctuary floor, usually at the epistle end of the altar facing north, or at the gospel end of the altar facing south, whichever is most convenient. When the crozier is desired by the bishop at the blessing of the incense, the bearer ascends to the footpace, gives the crozier to the bishop, retires to the upper step while the incense is being blessed, receives the crozier again and returns to the sanctuary floor. After the bishop has been censed the bearer ascends, gives him the crozier, and returns to his place. At the end of the *Te Deum* he again takes the crozier and precedes the bishop to the throne. The crozier is presented to the bishop if the Blessing is said, but not for the Grace.

Censing of Other Altars

It is the custom in some churches to cense other altars at Solemn Vespers in addition to the altar before which the service is being sung. (For example, if there is a Lady Altar in the church, that altar may be censed on feasts of Our Lady.) This censing of other altars should take place immediately after the censing of the vesperal altar and before the censing of the celebrant. At least two candles should be burning on each altar which is to be censed. A thurifer leads the procession, followed by two candle bearers, the officiant and his assistants, who either walk in front of, or beside, the officiant. Birettas are wom while going from one altar to another, but not during the censing. Incense should be blessed afresh at each altar, and, if necessary, for the procession.

Upon return to the vesperal altar, the celebrant ascends to the footpace. He is then censed, the censing of the assistants, clergy and people following in the usual way. If the *Te Deum* is ended before all this is concluded, the organist extemporizes until the people have been censed.

Vespers Before the Blessed
Sacrament Exposed

It is not recommended that the Blessed Sacrament be exposed simply to give added solemnity to Vespers. But it may happen that a period of Exposition for purposes of special devotion is being observed when Vespers are to be sung. If this period of Exposition is to begin with Vespers, the Host is exposed after the Invocation, exactly as is done at Benediction. If it is already exposed, two lighted candles are placed one on each of the corners of the lowest altar step before Vespers begin, and the two required for the Little Chapter added to them when the procession reaches the sanctuary. Extra reverence is shown at all genuflections. It is permissible to be seated during the psalms, but birettas are not worn. At the censing, the officiant and assistants kneel and cense the Host with three triple swings as at Benediction. They then rise, ascend to the footpace and cense the altar, omitting, however, the censing of the altar cross. Persons are censed as usual but not other altars. No one should turn his back to the altar.

✠

CHAPTER XI

BENEDICTION OF THE MOST HOLY SACRAMENT

General Directions

(In the preparation of this chapter full use has been made of the article by the Rt. Rev. J.I. Wedgwood entitled "Ceremonial Directions for Benediction of the Most Holy Sacrament" which appeared in *The Liberal Catholic* for May 1928.)

In the Liberal Catholic Rite Benediction of the Most Holy Sacrament is a Liturgical Service. It may be celebrated on any day of the year except during the interval between the Eucharist on Maundy Thursday and the First Vespers of Easter on Holy Saturday evening. It is ordinarily an afternoon or evening service. It is highly desirable that Benediction should conclude the service on Sunday evening and the evenings of Festivals. Benediction is frequently preceded by Vespers, but it may be celebrated by itself, independently of any other service. It may even follow Complin, which is a late Office intended to be said at the close of day before retiring to rest, or the Healing Service. Benediction should never precede any other service.

The Liturgy states that "this service may be considerably shortened, the *O Salutaris Hostia*, the *Tantum Ergo*, the Versicles and Responses and the Prayers which follow, and the act of Benediction being the only portions of liturgical obligation." This implies that the Litany may be omitted if it is necessary to curtail the service, but it should also be noted that the service loses considerably by doing this. In some churches, when there is to be no procession with the Blessed Sacrament, verses 12 to 21 of the Litany are omitted. A hymn, duly sanctioned by the Ordinary, may be substituted for the Litany. Such hymn ought to be devotional in character and preferably Eucharistic.

The Third Episcopal Synod ruled that the Collect of the Day and any additional Collects may be said immediately after the *O Salutaris Hostia*, provided the service of Benediction has not been preceded by either Vespers or Complin where these Collects would have already been said. If Benediction is celebrated with the special intent of healing, the Collect for the Sick, taken from the Occasional Prayers in the concluding pages of the Liturgy may be interpolated. When Collects are introduced immediately after the *O Salutaris Hostia* they should always conclude with the Peace Collect, a saying of which is thereupon omitted at the usual place immediately preceding the Ascription. When Collects are said at this point in the service they are introduced as usual by: *Let us pray.*

A rubric in the Liturgy permits a short pause for meditation after the Litany. This should not be overdone. A few moments of contemplative silence, during which the people remain kneeling, may be helpful in certain churches where the people have received special training, but it has been found by experience that the average congregation becomes restless if the pause is at all prolonged. It is advisable that sustained meditation be confined to special days of Exposition, when during the whole day a watch of prayer is kept before the enthroned Host in a monstrance, or that it be only undertaken by groups specially trained in meditation.

In all these changes and variations permitted in the service of Benediction *a conservative attitude is strongly recommended.* Clergy are counseled to avoid distorting the service so that it loses its original meaning. For example, Benediction may be celebrated from time to time with the intent of healing, but it is obviously not desirable that this special intent should gain preponderance over its more usual purpose, that of arousing and directing the devotion of the people to our Lord's Presence in the Blessed Sacrament. The counsel of Bishop Leadbeater in this connection is most wise: "I should be inclined to make such additions occasional rather than customary, for the service *as it is* seems simple, perfect and beautiful."

The Liturgy permits that Benediction may be given with a *veiled ciborium*, following a custom tolerated in the Roman Church. This is much less effective than Benediction with a monstrance and is not recommended. The use was sanctioned for abbreviated services, and to make provision for small or extempore churches which did not own a monstrance. In case the veiled ciborium is used, the procedure is as follows: The priest, wearing surplice and stole, having opened the tabernacle door, advances the ciborium (covered with a white veil) forward in the tabernacle, and leaves the door open. The service proceeds as usual, or in abbreviated form. Assuming the humeral veil, the priest then takes the ciborium, still covered by its veil, in his veiled hands, turns to the people and with the ciborium gives the Benediction. Turning back to the altar, the ciborium is replaced and the tabernacle closed.

The general rule is that when Benediction alone is celebrated the colour of the vestments used is white. Bishop Leadbeater, however, heartily approved and followed the custom of always celebrating Benediction in red when the colour of the Day was red. This has been found to be exceedingly effective. There seems to be no sufficient reason for departing from the Roman sequence of colours at Benediction, when immediately preceded by Vespers. When, however, Benediction is not preceded by Vespers it would be well that white should be the colour, or red on occasions when red is the colour of the Day.

The celebrant at Benediction must be in priest's Orders. He must be assisted by at least one server, who will bring the censer and humeral veil. He will do the censing during the time of Benediction, if someone in the congregation can safely be entrusted with the ringing of the bell, otherwise the censing at this time is omitted, and the server rings the bell. If possible there should also be a thurifer and two candle bearers, among whom the work may be divided. The number of candle bearers may be increased to four, six or eight, depending upon the size of the sanctuary and the solemnity of the occasion. It is preferable that there should be two vested assistants, wearing either copes or dalmatic and tunicle as described in the preceding chapter. On occasions of lesser solemnity the vested assistants may be replaced by two priests, wearing surplice and stole, or by those of lesser rank. As the first assistant places the monstrance on its throne and returns the Host to the tabernacle, he must not be of lesser rank than ordained deacon. If a first assistant of the required rank is not available, the celebrant himself must expose and return the Host.

If there is to be a procession of the Blessed Sacrament during the service, and a canopy is used, there must be sufficient servers to carry the canopy, each vested in cassock and surplice. There may in addition, especially on greater occasions, be another thurifer to carry the second censer, a cross bearer and two attendant candle bearers, a cantor, vested choir, Master of Ceremonies, banner bearer, and so on, as previously described.(p. 47)

The celebrant and assistants vest exactly as for Solemn Vespers. (p. 128) Non-officiating priests wear surplice, stole and biretta. They may on greater occasions wear copes.

The preparations for Benediction are few and simple. The empty monstrance, usually covered with a white silken veil, is placed on the credence, with its edge towards the people to make it inconspicuous. The monstrance, still covered with the veil, will be brought from the credence by a server when the first assistant ascends to the footpace to expose the Host, and placed on the altar to the left of the corporal, with the side containing the little door facing towards the middle of the altar, so as to make convenient the insertion of the lunette. The lunette (which holds the Host), contained in the pyx, should be inside the tabernacle. The key is in the tabernacle door.

During the Exposition of the Host the monstrance is placed on its throne. This may be either the top of the tabernacle, or a special throne behind and above the tabernacle. The tabernacle top can be used to advantage if it is deep enough to hold the altar cross, a vase or two of flowers and the monstrance at the same time. The general rule is. that the altar cross should be removed before the monstrance is placed on its throne. But if the monstrance is placed on top of the tabernacle, so that the cross is concealed, the cross need not be moved. (In some churches the arrangements are such that in order to remove the altar cross and place the monstrance on its throne, a ladder is required. A small, neat, self-supporting ladder for this purpose should be kept either in the vestry or, if it can be hidden, in the sanctuary. A server should be assigned to bring it forward when needed and to take it away when no longer required.) If the cross is so placed that it must be removed, and it is difficult to reach, it is permissible to remove it before the service begins. In such case it is placed on the credence and veiled.

Two linen corporals are needed, one to spread on the altar in front of the tabernacle, the other to be laid wherever the monstrance is to stand for the Exposition. The burse, in which the corporals were brought to the altar, is placed on the gospel side and is laid flat on the altar. A humeral veil, neatly folded, lies on the credence table. The sacring bell (or gong or chimes) should be at hand in the sanctuary near the place where the server kneels who is to sound it. If the steps leading to the altar are without carpet, a cushion for the officiant (and assistants) should be placed in the middle on the lowest altar step. The incense boat should either be put near the place where the second assistant is to kneel or given to him immediately after the Invocation.

At least twelve candles must burn on the altar, six of them being of course the regular altar candles, but there may be as many more as the church can afford, especially on the greater festivals. (If Benediction is being celebrated with a veiled ciborium, the celebrant vested only in surplice and stole, the minimum number of candles may be six.) The bishop's candle is not used when a bishop officiates.

If there is to be a procession with the Blessed Sacrament during the Service of Benediction, the canopy, (if one is used) properly fitted with its poles, should be placed either in the vestry, or inconspicuously to one side of the sanctuary, whichever is most convenient for the server who is to carry the canopy to the sanctuary gates at the time the procession is organized.

If Benediction is celebrated alone without a service or address preceding it, the altar and processional candles are lighted, the censer (or censers) prepared, and the procession goes to the sanctuary as usual.

If, as may be the case, it is preceded by another service or an address, the two services are usually separated by the singing of a hymn. During the hymn any additional unlighted candles on the altar are lit by one or two servers, the collection is taken, the thurifer (or thurifers) retires to the vestry to prepare the censer, the processional candles (if there is to be a procession with the Blessed Sacrament) are lighted. If it is necessary for the officiant (and assistants) to leave the sanctuary in order to change vestments, he and the requisite acolytes leave and reenter the sanctuary in small procession, the other clergy and acolytes remaining in the sanctuary. If it is not necessary for the officiant to leave the sanctuary, the thurifer and candle bearers come in just before the Invocation. When it is time to begin the service, the celebrant (and his assistants) leaving the biretta on his seat, goes to stand before the lowest altar step in the middle.

Benediction by a Priest

In the sanctuary the thurifer (or thurifers) genuflects in the middle and goes to his or her place before the altar somewhat to the epistle side. (If the incense boat is not within reach of the second acolyte, it should be given to him immediately before or after the Invocation.) The additional candle bearers (if any) genuflect in pairs and, if there is to be a procession with the Host, go to their assigned places where they stand holding their candles in front of them. If, however, there is not to be a procession with the Host, they deposit their candles at the credence and return to stand before their seats in the sanctuary. The non-officiating clergy stand at their places at the sides of the sanctuary. The officiant and the two chief acolytes with candles stand in line before the lowest altar step. The celebrant removes his biretta and gives it to the M.C. or a server to place on his seat. The officiant and two acolytes genuflect together. The officiant crosses himself and intones or says the Invocation. The officiant then ascends to the footpace and all in the sanctuary kneel, the two acolytes kneeling *in plano* before the lowest altar step, placing their candles either on the corners of that step or on the step above. The celebrant unfolds the corporal on the altar (if this has not already been done), removes the veil from the monstrance (which is brought from the credence at this time by a server), opens the tabernacle door, genuflects, takes out the pyx and places it on the corporal, closes the tabernacle, opens the pyx, takes out the lunette with the Host and places it in the monstrance. He then enthrones the monstrance on top of the tabernacle, unless there is to be a Procession with the Sacrament and the throne is difficult of access. In that case he places the monstrance facing towards the people and leaves it on the corporal before the tabernacle. Genuflecting he descends the steps to kneel at his place on the lowest altar step. In descending, he should take care not to turn his back directly on the Host. To avoid doing this, it is best to step back a pace or two to the epistle side of the footpace, and descend the steps obliquely. Do not walk backwards down the steps, as this may result in an undignified fall.

As soon as the officiant is kneeling, the thurifer hands the censer to the first acolyte and at the same time the second acolyte should give the open incense boat to the officiant. The first acolyte holds up the open censer and the officiant sprinkles incense on the charcoal, but does not bless it. The celebrant returns the boat to the second acolyte and receives the closed censer from the first acolyte.

Meanwhile the singing of the O Salutaris Hostia begins, usually at the moment when the Host is enthroned. Some celebrants consider it more reverential, however, not to begin the singing of the O Salutaris until the celebrant has the censer ready in his hand. (The latter has the advantage, in small churches, that the priest is free to join with or even lead the singing, which he cannot do very well if he is busy placing incense on the charcoal.) Either arrangement may be followed, depending upon local conditions.

Before beginning the censing, the celebrant and acolytes make a medium bow. The latter then holds up the corners of the cope fanwise while the celebrant censes the Blessed Sacrament with three triple swings. They again bow and the censer is returned via the first acolyte to the thurifer. (If the O Salutaris is said, not sung, the celebrant first censes the Blessed Sacrament and then the hymn is said by all.) In order that much incense may ascend before the Host, some celebrants, after the censing of the Host is ended, continue to swing the censer for a few moments, either to the north and to the south, or seven times in the direction of the altar. This is to be recommended, but is not obligatory.

If Collects are to be interpolated here (this is not obligatory, but is permitted by ruling of the Third General Episcopal Synod), the celebrant rises and intones or says: "Let us pray." He then intones the Collect of the Day and any other Collects desired, ending always with the Collect for Peace. When this is done the Peace Collect is omitted later in the service. After each Collect the response, "Amen," is sung. When the service of Benediction follows Vespers the Collects are said in Vespers and omitted in Benediction.

If there is to be a procession with the Blessed Sacrament during the singing of the Litany (the order of this procession has been described on p. 46) the organist plays softly while it is forming. An acolyte brings the humeral veil and places it on the shoulders of the celebrant. The celebrant rises and ascends to the footpace. Genuflecting, he takes the monstrance from its throne (unless, of course, it is standing on the corporal) and places it on the corporal before the tabernacle. He then turns the monstrance round so that it faces the tabernacle. Covering his hands with the ends of the humeral veil, he takes up the monstrance, grasping the knob on the stem with the right hand and the base with the left. He turns to face the people by the right as soon as the singing of the Litany begins. In the meantime the procession forms. The two chief acolytes take up their candles and go to stand to the west of the thurifer. All taking part in the procession turn to face the altar as they reach their assigned positions. As soon as the singing of the first verse of the Litany begins, all turn and face west and the procession starts. In procession the celebrant holds the monstrance so that the Host contained therein is about the level of his eyes. The thurifer precedes the celebrant, walking backwards and censing the Host, as described on p. 47.

When the procession returns to the sanctuary the non-officiating clergy go to their places at the side of the sanctuary and kneel. (No one genuflects in the middle upon the return of the procession, inasmuch as the Host is behind them.) The acolytes with candles range themselves on either side of the sanctuary and kneel. (The cross bearer and banner bearers do not kneel.) The thurifer (or thurifers) continues to cense the Host until the altar steps are reached, whereupon he kneels at the epistle side; the canopy bearers genuflect after the celebrant has stepped from beneath the canopy, one of them returns the canopy to its place and all go to their places where they kneel. The celebrant ascends to the footpace, places the monstrance on its throne, genuflects, steps back a pace or two to the epistle side and descends obliquely to his place before the lowest altar step on which he kneels.

Meanwhile, as soon as the officiant ascends the altar steps, the acolytes with candles rise and go to their assigned places, the two chief acolytes to their usual places before the lowest altar step on either side of the middle, the additional candle bearers to stand in plano grouped either in an arc or in a semicircle before the altar, or symmetrically on either side of the sanctuary, depending upon local conditions. When in position, they kneel following the lead of the first acolyte, or of the M.C. (if any), placing their candlesticks on the floor in front of them, with the exception of the two chief acolytes who place their candlesticks either on the corners of the lowest altar step, or on the step above that.

If, however, there is not to be a procession with the Blessed Sacrament, all remain kneeling in their places during the singing of the Litany. In this case either the celebrant or a cantor may sing the odd-numbered verses of the Litany, the choir and people the even-numbered verses. This particular arrangement of the singing should not be regarded as an inflexible rule. Any other suitable arrangement of alternate singing may be made, or the verses may be sung by all. This is done, naturally, when a hymn is substituted for the Litany.

It should be kept in mind, that if there is not to be a procession with the Host, the monstrance is always placed on its throne (never left on the corporal before the tabernacle) before the singing of the *O Salutaris Hostia*, and that the humeral veil is placed on the shoulders of the celebrant, not before the Litany, but before the priest ascends to the altar to give the Benediction.

The first verse of the *Tantum Ergo* is now sung. All bow low or prostrate at the second line, but exaggeration of this inclination should be avoided, and care should be taken not to bow too rapidly. During the singing of the first verse the celebrant sprinkles incense on the charcoal in the open censer, but does not bless it, exactly as was done at the *O Salutaris Hostia*. (If the *Tantum Ergo* is said, not sung, the sprinkling of the incense as well as the censing of the Host should take place between the saying of the two verses.) The censing begins at the end of the first verse. The singing of the second verse does not begin until the triple swings are ended and the usual bow at the end of the censing has been made. During the censing there may either be silence, or the organist may extemporize softly. At the end of the censing the thurifer rises, receives the censer from the first acolyte (or the celebrant), and goes to the middle, to kneel either a little behind the celebrant, or in the central point of the semi-circle of candle bearers, depending upon local conditions.

As the thurifer rises to take the censer, the additional candle bearers rise, take their candles and go to their assigned places as previously described (unless there has been a procession and they are already in position.) They kneel, following the lead of the thurifer, and place their candles on the floor in front of them.

At the end of the *Tantum Ergo*, the celebrant rises and sings the Versicles, the people the Responses. He then intones the prayer: *O God, Who in the wonderful Sacrament....* If the Peace Collect has not already been said, either in a preceding service or after the singing of the *O Salutaris*, it is now intoned. He then ascends to the footpace and, facing the Host, says (it is best not to intone) the Ascription. It is a pleasing custom in some churches to lower the lights in the church when the officiant ascends to the altar, so that most, if not all, of the illumination comes from the candles in the sanctuary.

The monstrance is now removed from its throne, placed on the corporal, turned to face the tabernacle, and taken up by the celebrant exactly as previously described. (p. 143) (If the throne is rather difficult of access, it is permissible for the celebrant to be assisted by a priest, vested in surplice and stole, who places the monstrance on the throne earlier in the service and returns it to the altar at this point in the service.) Meanwhile, *as noiselessly as possible*, the thurifer places more incense in the censer, closes it, and takes it up ready for the censing. The acolyte stationed by the bell or gong should make ready. The candle bearers take up their candlesticks and hold them in front of them. As the celebrant takes up the monstrance, the server at the bell rings it once, or sounds a low note on the gong, as a warning to the people that the act of Benediction is about to take place. This also serves as a signal to the candle bearers to raise their candles above their heads, exactly as is done during the Elevations in the Holy Eucharist. During the act of Benediction the bell or gong is sounded. The exact way in which this is done is left to the discretion of the priest in charge of the church. In some churches the bell (or chimes) is sounded continuously during the entire act of Benediction. In other churches this is considered too distracting because of the noise, and the bell or gong is sounded three times three: thrice during the downward movement with the monstrance, thrice at the beginning of the horizontal stroke, and thrice towards the end of that stroke. In other churches it is sounded three times before and after the act of Benediction. (The Roman custom is to ring the bell three times: once as the celebrant turns towards the people, once in the middle of the Benediction, once as the celebrant turns back to the altar.) The kneeling thurifer (or thurifers) censes the Host either continuously or according to the way in which the bell is sounded. The acolytes lower their candles when the celebrant turns back to the altar, but continue to hold them.

For the act of Benediction, the celebrant should turn slowly and with dignity by his right to face the people. With the monstrance he makes the sign of the cross once over the people. No words are uttered. The silence marks the fact that the Benediction is given directly by our Lord Himself through the vehicle of His Presence in the Sacrament, and not as ordinarily through His minister. In making the sign the motions should not be exaggerated, nor the Host raised much above the level of the eyes. The sign of the cross is made somewhat in this fashion. Lifting the monstrance so that the Host contained therein is about a foot above the level of his eyes, the officiant *slowly* traces a vertical line downward until the Host is about a foot below the level of his eyes. Now, raising the monstrance more rapidly until it is eye level, he swings it fairly rapidly to the left in preparation for the horizontal stroke. This stroke is also traced *slowly*. He brings the monstrance back to the centre at the end of the horizontal stroke, moving this time more rapidly, before turning back to the altar by his right, thus completing the circle. The entire act of Benediction should not occupy, at most, more than thirty seconds.

Upon turning back to the altar, the celebrant places the monstrance on the corporal, turns it so that it faces the people, and genuflects. He remains kneeling (on one knee or both, as preferred) while some seconds, perhaps ten or fifteen, of perfect stillness is observed through the church. He then rises and the organist begins to extemporize softly. The celebrant then turns the monstrance edgewise, opens it and takes out the lunette. The latter is placed in the pyx, the monstrance moved to the left, the tabernacle opened and the pyx placed therein. He genuflects, closes and locks the tabernacle door, covers the monstrance with its silken veil, turns it edgewise to the people or hands it to a server to be placed by him on the credence, folds the corporals, places them in the burse which is left on the altar, replaces the altar cross if this has been taken down (unless, because of difficulty, the replacement of the cross does not take place until after the congregation has departed) and returns to his place in the middle before the lowest altar step. (He need not, at this time, walk obliquely down the steps.) He turns to face the altar and the humeral veil is removed. As he descends the altar steps all in the sanctuary rise, and the lights, if previously lowered, are turned on again.

The organist sounds the opening chord and the antiphon is sung by all. The organist plays over the opening notes of the Psalm and the celebrant (or cantor) sings the first half of the first verse, all taking up the singing at this point and continuing until the end of the antiphon. (All as usual face east during the *Gloria Patri*.)

Meanwhile a server takes the celebrant's biretta to him. The humeral veil is placed on the credence, and the cross bearer, banner bearer, thurifer and candle bearers take their usual places preparatory to the procession back to the vestry. All ought to be standing in their places, facing the altar, by the end of the Psalm.

The Closing Hymn may be sung before the procession leaves the sanctuary. Usually, however, the procession starts either at the beginning of the first verse, towards the end of that verse, at the beginning of the second verse, or halfway through the second verse, according to local conditions. When the celebrant desires the procession to start, he gives the signal by genuflecting. All genuflect with him except the cross bearer (and his attendant candle bearers). As soon as they have genuflected, all in the procession turn to face west. The procession usually moves by the short way to the vestry.

Benediction by a Priest
with Vested Assistants

In the procession to the sanctuary the first and second assistants precede the celebrant in the same manner as the deacon and subdeacon at High Celebration. Arriving in the sanctuary the celebrant, assistants, and two chief candle bearers range themselves before the lowest altar step. (Fig. 1) The birettas are removed and given either to the M.C. or to a server to place on the seats. After the Invocation, the celebrant and assistants kneel on the lowest altar step, the two chief acolytes in plano before that step. The acolytes place their candlesticks at either comer of the lowest step. The first assistant (provided he is an ordained deacon or priest, otherwise the celebrant himself) immediately rises, ascends to the footpace and exposes the Host as previously described. (p. 142) Genuflecting, he returns to kneel beside the celebrant, taking care, while doing so, that he does not turn his back directly on the Host.

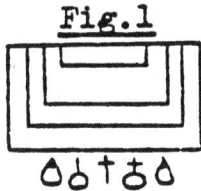

At the time of the censing, the thurifer hands the censer to the first assistant the moment he is again kneeling, and at the same time the second assistant gives the incense boat to the celebrant. The first assistant holds up the open censer while the celebrant sprinkles incense on the charcoal, then closes it and gives it to the celebrant. The celebrant returns the boat to the second assistant, before taking the censer.

The assistants bow with the celebrant and hold out fanwise the corners of his cope during the censing. This ended, the first assistant receives the censer from the celebrant and returns it to the thurifer. The assistants do not rise with the celebrant if Collects are said after the *O Salutaris*.

If there is to be a procession with the Blessed Sacrament, the assistants ascend to the footpace with the celebrant before the singing of the Litany. Either the celebrant or the first assistant (if of required rank) may take down the monstrance from the throne. If this is done by the first assistant, he either places it on the corporal before the tabernacle or hands it, in the correct position for carrying, to the celebrant. The celebrant, first genuflecting before the Host, receives the monstrance while standing. (Fortescue, Fourth Ed., p. 260)

When the celebrant, carrying the monstrance, turns to face the people by the right, the assistants should turn with him, the first assistant by the left, the second assistant by the right, so that neither turn the back upon the Host. As soon as the celebrant has stepped forward, or descended to the sanctuary floor, the assistants change sides behind the celebrant. During the procession they walk on either side of him, a little to the rear, holding upward and outward the corners of the cope. When the procession returns to the sanctuary, the assistants ascend with the celebrant to the footpace. The celebrant places the monstrance on the corporal before the tabernacle and all three genuflect. If the first assistant is qualified to handle the Host, the celebrant and second assistant, each moving back a pace or two to the gospel side, descend the steps obliquely to their places and kneel on the lowest step as the first assistant enthrones the monstrance. The first assistant then descends and kneels beside the celebrant, after genuflecting on the footpace before the Host.

During the singing of the first verse of the *Tantum Ergo* the first assistant holds up the open censer, while the celebrant sprinkles incense on the charcoal, in the same manner as at the *O Salutaris*, The assistants remain kneeling when the celebrant rises to sing the Versicles.

If the monstrance is enthroned on the tabernacle, the celebrant places it on the corporal before the tabernacle, prior to the act of Benediction, or the first assistant (if qualified) may do so. If the monstrance is enthroned elsewhere in a place not easily accessible, the first assistant (if qualified) rises at the end of the Ascription and brings the monstrance to the altar, either placing it on the corporal or giving it to the celebrant, as before. In either case the first assistant genuflects to the Host, after the monstrance has left his hands, and descends to kneel at his place.

After the act of Benediction, the celebrant kneels on the footpace for a few seconds before the Host, while silence is maintained in the church. As he rises the organist begins to extemporize softly. The celebrant steps back a pace or two to the epistle side, descends obliquely to his place and kneels. After a few seconds of music, the first assistant rises and ascends to the footpace. He places the Host in the tabernacle and covers the monstrance, as previously described (p. 146) and returns to his place at the side of the celebrant. Meanwhile, as soon as the first assistant has closed the tabernacle door, the second assistant removes the humeral veil from the shoulders of the celebrant and gives it to a server to put, during the singing of the antiphon, on the credence. As soon as the first assistant turns to descend the steps (this time he need not walk down obliquely) the celebrant and second assistant rise. All in the sanctuary rise with them. (If the first assistant is not qualified to handle the Host It will of course be placed in the tabernacle by the celebrant.)

Benediction by a Priest
in the Presence of a Bishop

When Benediction is celebrated by a priest in the presence of a bishop, the bishop intones the Invocation, while wearing the mitre and holding the crozier. There are no other changes.

Benediction by a Bishop

The ceremony is the same. The bishop retains his mitre while genuflecting, but the assistants remove their birettas. He wears the mitre and holds the crozier at the Invocation. When the first assistant ascends to the footpace to expose the Host, he may take with him the mitre and lay it flat on the altar on the gospel side, with its fanons hanging over the edge; or the second assistant, or best of all, a crozier bearer, may place the mitre on the altar. At the end of the service when the first assistant returns to his place beside the bishop after putting the Host in the tabernacle, he may bring with him the mitre, or the second assistant or crozier bearer may bring it from the altar to the bishop. The crozier is placed in its holder immediately after the Invocation and remains there until the procession forms at the end of the service.

At the act of Benediction the bishop makes the sign of the cross three times with the monstrance, the first towards the people on the left of the church, the second towards the middle of the church, the third towards the people to the right. The bell is sounded either continuously or intermittently as before, but if sounded in groups of three, one group of three is given at each sign of the cross.

During the procession to the vestry the bishop does not bless the people, inasmuch as Christ's blessing has already been given at the Benediction.

Benediction with Special Intention
for the Sick

Benediction of the Most Holy Sacrament may be used as a special service for the sick. When this is desired, the Collect for the Sick, taken from the *Occasional Prayers* at the end of the Liturgy should be interpolated after the *O Salutaris Hostia*. The Litany is sung with special intention for the sick, or it may be replaced by another the words of which refer particularly to the healing of the sick. If there are names of the sick to be specially mentioned, the celebrant rises immediately after the Tantum Ergo and announces: *The prayers of the congregation are desired for...* thereupon reading (usually silently) the names of those to be mentioned.

Notes for the Organist

1. Extemporize softly between the Invocation and the *O Salutaris*. The latter is begun either at the moment the Host is enthroned, or when the celebrant is ready to begin the censing, depending upon the wishes of the priest.

2. Sound the note for *Let us pray*, if the celebrant rises after the *O Salutaris* and wishes to intone the Collects.

3. If there is to be a procession with the Host, extemporize softly until the procession is formed in the sanctuary, before playing over the first line of the Litany, but if there is not to be a procession, proceed at once to the Litany after the *O Salutaris* (or the Collects).

4. If the odd-numbered verses of the Litany are sung solo, the solo part may be taken more slowly than the verses sung by the people. This is quite permissible as a soloist often requires more time for expression and embellishment, whereas the people's

part should be kept reasonably brisk. Later on in the Litany, certain rallentandos may be permitted, especially in the third line of verse 13.

5. Extemporize softly, if desired, between the two verses of the *Tantum Ergo*, while the celebrant censes the Host.

6. Sound the note, if necessary, for the Versicles.

7. After the act of Benediction there is complete silence until the celebrant rises, then extemporize softly until the Host is returned to the tabernacle and the celebrant (or the first assistant) is back in his place before the lowest altar step. Then play the antiphon briskly.

8. In the closing hymn note carefully the time value of the notes, especially at the end of the first line.

CHAPTER XII
PRIME AND COMPLIN

General Directions

Prime and Complin are so much alike structurally and in ceremonial actions that a description of Prime will suffice for Complin. Prime is used in the early morning, Complin in the evening.

The Office of Prime may be said or sung with two sets of conditions:

1. *With the minimum of formality.* In this case it may be of the nature of family prayers in a community, school or home, either without an altar, or with a table serving as an altar, covered with a white linen cloth and bearing a cross and two lighted candles. Or it may be rendered informally in a church, by way of contrast with other services, there being only two candles on the altar, preferably not two of the regular six altar candles. In either case vestments need not be worn, although it is preferable (and in the sanctuary of a church understood) that clergy and acolytes should be in cassocks, No further ceremonial directions, other than those appearing in the Liturgy, are needed under these conditions.

2. *Ceremonially.* In this case the following instructions should be observed: It may be conducted by one in Orders of any rank from cleric to bishop, or even by a layperson. When a layperson, or one in Orders up to the rank of deacon, officiates, he should be vested in cassock and surplice. A subdeacon leader may also wear a biretta. When a deacon officiates he should be vested in surplice, stole worn deacon-fashion and a biretta. When a priest officiates he is vested in surplice, stole and biretta. A Bishop is vested in rochet, stole and biretta. He also wears the ring and pectoral cross, and may use the crozier. He may wear the mozetta (or mantelletta). The cope is not worn. In all cases the stole is of the colour of the Day. The biretta is not worn during any part of the service, except by a bishop, but only to and from the sanctuary, .

Two candles only are lighted on the altar, usually not two of the regular six altar candles, but two placed on the altar for the purpose. Incense may be used if there is a Procession to and from the sanctuary, but the censer will not be needed during the service itself. The officiant may be assisted by two or more acolytes and by a cantor, or he may be alone.

Whenever it is necessary to shorten any of either Prime or Complin, any of those parts in the following table which are enclosed in parentheses may be omitted. Note that the parts which may be omitted are not the same in both services.

PRIME	COMPLIN
Invocation	Invocation
Versicles	Versicles
Confiteor	*Confiteor*
Absolution	Absolution
First Psalm	(First Psalm)
(First Lesson)	(First Lesson)
(Second Psalm)	(Second Psalm)
(Second Lesson)	(Second Lesson)
Act of Faith	Act of Faith
Collects	Collects
(Office Hymn)	(Office Hymn)
(Sermon)	(Sermon)
(Third Psalm)	*Nunc Dimittis*
Prayer	Prayer
Versicles	Versicles
Benediction	Benediction

In Prime the Second or Third Psalm may be substituted for the First.

In order to avoid repetition, where Prime and Complin are said daily, or where Prime is used in conjunction with the Holy Eucharist, other short lections from any part of the Liberal Catholic Liturgy may at the discretion of the ministrant or priest be read as a Lesson instead of the Epistle and Gospel of the Day.

Prime may be used as a separate service, or it may precede the Holy Eucharist. In the latter case the service of Prime ends with the Grace instead of the Benediction. Complin may be used as a separate service, or it may follow an address, or it may precede Benediction of the Most Holy Sacrament. In the latter case, the Grace is said and not the Benediction.

Ministrant Officiating

The ministrant goes to the altar preceded by those who are to assist him. They bow to the altar cross, unless the Host is reserved in the tabernacle, in which case they genuflect. They then go to their seats which may be on either side of the sanctuary. All stand, each at his place, facing the middle.

The ministrant says or intones the Invocation facing east, crossing himself as he does so, He says or sings the Versicles which follow, the congregation saying or singing the Responses. All kneel and say the *Confiteor* in unison. The ministrant, still kneeling, now says the prayer: *May the Lord ... evermore*, the congregation responding: *Thanks be to God*. All cross themselves at the word, *absolve*, in the prayer.

All now stand. The antiphon is said by all together. The Psalm may be similarly said or, alternately, the first verse by the ministrant, the second by the congregation, and so on. If the Psalm is sung, all sing the antiphon, then the ministrant (or cantor appointed for the purpose) sings the first half of the first verse of the Psalm, the people joining in at the second half; and continuing to the end of the antiphon. All say or sing the *Gloria Patri*, regardless of how the other verses were handled. All of the Psalms are said or sung in the same fashion, so there is no necessity in regard to them of further description.

All are seated and the ministrant, or someone appointed by him, reads the Epistle of the Day, or another lection, as the First Lesson. The reader stands at his place, facing the middle, while reading the Lesson. The Lesson ended, all stand and the Second Psalm with its antiphon is said or sung. Again the people are seated and the Gospel of the Day, or other lection, is read as the Second Lesson.

All rise, turn to the east and say or intone the Act of Faith beginning: *We believe that God is Love....* (Any of the Creeds or Acts of Faith appearing in the Liturgy may be substituted for the one mentioned.) All cross themselves at the words: and *Peace for evermore*, or at the appropriate place in the Creed said.

The ministrant then says: *Let us pray.* All kneel, including the ministrant himself. He reads the Collect of the Day and the three Collects which appear in the Office. After each Collect the congregation says or sings: *Amen.* The Collects ended, all rise and the Office hymn is sung. If Prime is to be the only service and there is to be a collection, it is taken during the singing of the hymn. If there is to be a sermon, it follows the Hymn.

The Third Psalm is now said or sung. The ministrant then says: *Let us pray.* All kneel, including the ministrant. The ministrant says the prayer: *Be with us ... ever and ever*, the people respond: *Amen.* The Versicles and Responses are then said or sung alternately by ministrant and people, all still kneeling. The ministrant now says the Grace, all crossing themselves, and the people respond: *Amen.*

All rise. Those in the sanctuary group themselves before the altar and bow (or genuflect) to the cross. They return to the vestry in procession, the ministrant walking last.

Priest Officiating

When a priest conducts Prime or Complin the following changes are to be noted. After the *Confiteor*, the priest rises in his place turns towards people and says the Absolution: *God the Father ... holy Spirit.* He makes the sign of the cross twice over the people, once at the words: *God the Son*, and once at the word: *absolve.* The people cross themselves at the word: *absolve*, and at the end of the Absolution respond: *Amen.* The priest stands during the saying of the Collects and during the prayer, versicles and Benediction following the Third Psalm. At the Benediction: *Unto God's ...evermore*, he turns to face the people and with raised hand makes the sign of the cross over them in the usual way at the words: *Lord bless.*

Priest Officiating in the Presence of a Bishop

When Prime is conducted by a priest in the presence of a bishop, the bishop intones or says the Invocation, pronounces the Absolution (making the sign of the cross four times) and gives the Benediction (making the sign of the cross once). The bishop may wear the mozetta (or mantelletta). He wears the biretta and may use the crozier in the foregoing.

Bishop Officiating

There are no points to be noted in addition to those mentioned in the preceding paragraph.

Communion at Prime

The Third General Episcopal Synod ruled that if it is desired to administer Communion to the people at a time when Prime has been said, the Communion shall take place after the service of Prime is ended, the Form for the Administration of Holy Communion with the Reserved Sacrament being used. In such cases, provided of course that a priest officiated at Prime, the Confiteor and Absolution need not be repeated, as those which have already been said at Prime shall suffice. The service of Prime will under these conditions end with the grace and not with the Benediction.

CHAPTER XIII

HOLY BAPTISM

General Directions

The baptismal font should be placed if possible near the entrance of the church. It may stand either in a separate chapel, or in a part of the nave railed off from the rest of the church.

The font itself is a large basin-like receptacle, supported on a pedestal. Its shape and ornamentation are not prescribed. The font may be made of wood, terra-cotta, metal or stone, but if any other material except marble is used, the interior of the cavities in which the baptismal water rests should be plated or lined with some noncorroding substance. An excellent style of font is one in which there are two cavities of sufficient size to receive two glass bowls; one small bowl to hold fresh baptismal water and another considerably larger bowl to catch the water after it has been used. The flat surface of the font between the bowls serves to hold the oil stock, shell and other things needed during the ceremony. The font ought to be supplied with a cover to keep out dust and other impurities.

In the usage of the Liberal Catholic Church the baptismal water is not kept in the font, but is freshly prepared on each occasion when the baptismal service is to take place. It should be noted that the preparation of baptismal water differs from the blessing of holy water only in that an additional prayer is said. This prayer is given in the section of this book describing the blessing of holy water.

It is convenient if a small cupboard, equipped with a lock, is fastened to, or built into, the wall of the baptistry. In this cupboard are kept: (1) a stock of towels for wiping the candidate after baptism and to protect the clothes from being made wet; (2) a vessel or shell for dipping the water out of the font and pouring it over the head of the candidate; (3) a white silk cloth or handkerchief or other vesture to be used in the baptism of infants and children when the parents or sponsors do not themselves provide this white vesture; (4) a small candlestick with candle, preferably a special baptismal candle; (5) an oil-stock containing the oils needed for the ceremony; (6) a stock of cotton wool or absorbent cotton to wipe the brow of the candidate and the thumb of the priest after the application of the oils (the cotton wool used should be burned afterward); and (7) a few application blanks.

If the top of the font is not suitable for the purpose, a small table covered with a white cloth should stand near it on which the articles needed during the ceremony may be placed.

The Liturgy provides that for each child baptized there should be a godfather and godmother. The Anglican custom is also permitted, according to which for a male child there are two godfathers and one godmother, and *vice versa* for a female child. The godparents should preferably be adult Liberal Catholics who have received the Sacrament of Confirmation. The godmother holds the infant during the ceremony; the godfather standing by her side. If the child is a girl the godmother says the words of presentation, but if a boy the words are said by the godfather. If, as sometimes happens, there be only one godparent, he or she holds the infant and says the words of presentation. Parents are not supposed to act as sponsors.

The head of the child should not be covered. The parents should be instructed to open the dress in front at the neck so that the Oil of Catechumens may be applied without difficulty to the throat in front and the nape of the neck behind. The parents or godparents ought to be instructed beforehand to bring with them a white silk handkerchief or other item to serve as the white vesture. If this vesture is not brought one kept in the church for the purpose should be used.

Baptism may take place at any hour and wherever it is most convenient, but it is best that it should be administered publicly in the church. If the ceremony is to take place in a house, a small temporary altar should be provided (a table covered with a white cloth will serve) and two glass bowls (one small, one large), some salt (not the free-running variety which is contaminated with other ingredients, but ordinary salad salt), and some water should be supplied. The priest brings with him an altar cross and two candlesticks, as well as the holy oils, vestments and other things required.

Baptism of Infants

Before the ceremony of baptism begins the following preparations are made in the baptistry, either by a server or by the officiant.

The table (if any) in the baptistry is covered with a white cloth. On this table, or on the font, are laid: (1) the baptismal shell, (2) an oil stock containing the oil of catechumens and chrism, (3) a white stole, unless the priest is wearing a reversible stole, white on one side, violet on the other, (4) a small towel to be used in wiping off the baptismal water, (5) some cotton wool to be used by the priest to remove oil from his thumb after each anointing, (6) the baptismal candlestick, (7) the white vesture, (8) the officiant's book containing the ceremony, and (9) an "Application for Membership" form duly filled out giving the full name of the infant, the place and date of birth, whether previously baptized or not and if so in what Church, and lastly the names and addresses of the parents. Flowers may also be placed on the table. Two candles are lighted, either on the main altar or on some side altar which may be near the font.

The priest vests in surplice, violet stole and biretta. His server (or servers) should be vested in cotta or surplice.

The priest should prepare the baptismal water and see that it is placed in the font or bowl to be used.

The priest goes to the baptistry preceded by the server. (If desired, there may be a thurifer swinging a censer. In this case the thurifer walks first in the small procession to the baptistry.) Removing his biretta the priest crosses himself and says the Invocation. His biretta is placed on the table or other convenient place. He turns now towards the people who have brought the infant and are standing somewhere near the font. Prompted by him, if necessary, one of the godparents says the words of presentation. If there be more than one infant, they are presented at the same time, the words of presentation being changed from *this child* to *these children* and from *him* or *her* to *them*.

The priest, still facing the people, says: *Brethren, our fair....* At the end of the reading of the Gospel of St. Mark he places his right hand in blessing on the head of the child. If there be more than one infant, he blesses each in turn before saying: *Let us pray*. In the prayer which follows he should be careful to say *he* or *she*, *him* or *her*, according to the sex of the child. (Some priests find it convenient to underscore in red ink in their ritual such words which have to be changed.) If there are several children *they* and *them* should of course be used. This prayer is in a sense a preparation for the Exorcism, indicating as it does the ideal to be obtained by the purification which immediately follows. The priest should utter the words of the Exorcism and make the three signs of the cross with definite intent to free the child from any inward tendency towards evil. If there be more than one child, the priest says the Exorcism over each separately and places his right hand on each before proceeding with the ceremony. At the words: *For He Who is the Lord...* he again places his right hand on the head of the infant.

From this point onwards to the final Charge, each infant receives individual attention. Therefore, if there be several children, all parents and sponsors, except those who are with the first infant to be baptized, are seated somewhere near at hand. The sponsor or sponsors and the parents stand with the child a few feet from the font. If the infant becomes noisy or struggles, it is sufficient that the priest at the point indicated in the service touch momentarily the head of the child.

The priest changes from violet to white stole. Going to stand before the person holding the infant, he raises his right hand, palm towards the child, and says slowly and with purpose: *Ephphatha: that is be thou opened*, meanwhile making the sign of the cross four times, once over the brow, once over the throat, once over the heart, and once over the navel of the child. He does not touch the body of the child, but has clearly in mind the opening up of the child to the divine grace. He now lowers his hand and proceeds to read the prayer: *Let thy mind ... living God*, The thought to hold in mind is that the child should be prepared to receive to the full the spiritual power which is shortly to be called down for his helping. The next prayer: *Do Thou... Christ our Lord*, is for the purpose of protecting the child, whose body has been made abnormally sensitive, from undesirable influences. The priest then lays the end of his stole (the left end according to

Fortescue) on the child's right shoulder as he says the words welcoming the child: *Come into ... life eternal.*

The server should now present the oil stock containing the Oil of Catechumens so that the priest can moisten his right thumb. Standing before the child the priest begins the words which accompany the first anointing: *In the Name....* The first cross is made by anointing the bare skin of the infant at the throat with the oil on the thumb of the priest. He should trace an even-armed cross on the skin about an inch and a half in size. Without moving from where he is standing he should then reach round and trace a similar cross at the nape of the neck. The person holding the child can assist by moving the infant and raising its head. The third cross is made in the air before the child and should reach the entire length of the body. This time the priest uses his entire hand, the palm being opened towards the child. The cross is made about eighteen inches from the body. The fourth cross is made in a similar manner, but this time behind the child, the priest changing his position in order properly to make the sign of the cross. The priest walks round to the front of the child while saying: *may He be with... thy ways.* If more convenient, the person holding the infant may turn it round for the making of the cross behind the child.

The baptism with the sanctified water now takes place. The priest steps to the font, the person holding the infant going with him. It is recommended that the infant be held with its face sidewise over the font or basin, so that when the water is poured over the head and forehead, it will not flow into the eyes and nostrils. The priest fills the shell with the baptismal water. He says: *N. ...* (mentioning the several Christian names selected by the parents) *I baptize thee in the Name of the ✝ Father, and of the ✝ Son, and of the Holy ✝ Ghost. Amen.* At the mention of each Person of the Holy Trinity water is poured in the form of a cross over the forehead. It is at this time that spiritual power is imparted to the child through the agency of the sanctified water, and inasmuch as the flowing of the water on the bare skin of the child is a technical condition for the validity of the baptismal rite, care should be taken to see that some of the water at least touches the bare skin. To insure this, especially if the child has struggled, the priest may pass his fingers over the moistened skin. During the baptism it is convenient if the server holds the *Application for Membership* form so that the priest can read the Christian names of the child. The priest wipes the head of the infant with the small towel after the baptism.

Immediately the baptism is ended, the person holding the infant steps back and the priest, having moistened his right thumb with Oil of Chrism, anoints the infant on the crown of the head in the form of a cross, saying: *With Christ's Holy Chrism...everlasting.* The priest should be exceedingly careful not to press too strongly on the crown of the head, because in an infant the suture there is not as yet closed by bone. He now proceeds to anoint the brow of the infant with Chrism by making upon it the sign of the cross with the thumb, saying: *I receive....* He lifts his hand after making the sign of the cross at the place indicated in the Liturgy, but again places it on the head of the child at the words: *and that he ... ages of ages.*

At this point he makes the sign of the cross in the air over the brow, over the throat, over the heart and over the navel of the child, saying *silently* with intent: *Be thou closed.* This, of course, refers to the centres.

The server now brings the white vesture to the priest, who blesses it in the usual manner while saying silently: *In the Name of the Father, and of the ✠ Son, and of the Holy Ghost.* Placing the vesture round the neck and over the shoulders of the child, he says: *Receive from Holy Church ... His peace.* If the white vesture is the property of the church, it is removed by the priest at this point and given to the server to replace on the table.

The server brings the lighted baptismal candle to the priest who hands it to either of the godparents to hold near the infant. If possible, the infant's hand should be placed on the candle. The priest now says: *Take this burning light ... fellowmen.* Care should be taken that a sudden movement on the part of the infant does not cause melted wax to fall upon it. The priest takes the baptismal candle and gives it to the server to place on the altar.

The priest lays his right hand on the head of the child, saying: *N...* (repeating the Christian names) *go in peace and may the Lord be with thee.*

The parents and godparents now return to their seats if there are other children to be baptized. (If it is impracticable for them to wait, the priest of course finishes the ceremony.) For each child to be baptized, the priest turns back in his ritual to the exorcism and proceeds with the ceremony from that point. When all have received baptism, the priest stands before those who have brought the children and says: *Ye who have... confirmed by him.* Care should be taken to change the wording of this Charge according to the sex of the child and if there be more than one.

Baptism by a Bishop

If a bishop administers baptism there are no changes to be noted except that he blesses the white vesture by making the sign of the cross over it three times. The bishop is vested in rochet, stole, and biretta and wears the pectoral cross and ring. The crozier is held near him during the ceremony.

Baptism of Children

The foregoing ceremony is intended for infants in arms. When the child is old enough to walk, but is not old enough to understand, it is well to use the form of Baptism of Children, but to say the Charge to sponsors found in the Baptism of Infants. When the child is able in some measure to understand the service, then the Charge appearing in the Baptism of Children should be used.

When the form of Baptism of Children is used there are some differences to be noted. The prayer: *O God, Omnipotent... Christ our Lord*, may be omitted at the discretion of the priest. The priest changes from violet to white stole immediately after the Exorcism. The child is seated or held for the early part of the service, but stands or is held upright for the first anointing. For the baptism the child is usually held sidewise with head over the font by one of the godparents. Care should be taken to see that some of the water flows over the forehead of the child. The second anointing is made either while the child stands or is held.

Should the child have been previously baptized in any Church, the rite of baptism of which is less complete than our own, the formula to be used at the baptism itself is: *N...*, *if thou art not baptized ... Holy Ghost. Amen*. When this formula is used the baptism is said to be *conditional* or *subconditione*. If conditional baptism is administered, it should be noted that the words: *receive you into the fellowship of Christ's holy Church and do*, in the Reception, and the word, *to-day* in the bestowal of the white vesture, are omitted.

Baptism of Adults

The priest changes from violet to white stole immediately after the Exorcism. During the Exorcism and the prayer which follows the candidate kneels on a hassock placed for the purpose near the font. He stands for the first anointing and should step to the font or basin and bend over it for the baptism. In many cases the priest will experience less difficulty if it is suggested *beforehand* to any ladies to be baptized that they arrange their hair so that the crown of the head can be anointed. The two long crosses made in the air before and behind the candidate should reach as nearly as possible the entire length of the body, but the priest should not bend over in an undignified manner in order to achieve this end. The candidate kneels for the second anointing. The giving of the white vesture and of the lighted candle is optional, but these form a picturesque conclusion to the ceremony and are of some symbolical value. For these the candidate may stand.

Baptism by Other Than Priest or Bishop

The First General Episcopal Synod ruled that a deacon, in the absence of a priest, may administer baptism using the full service as printed in the Liturgy. It will not be possible for a deacon, of course, to prepare baptismal water, but it is permissible for him to use any holy water found in the church, or, in emergency, even plain water. He will also not be able to bless the various object presented to the candidate. Whenever possible, however, the priest should administer baptism and not the deacon.

The Synod also ruled that if, as may sometimes occur, one of lesser rank than a deacon, or a layman, administers baptism, he must use only the words: *N..., I baptize thee in the Name of the ✠ Father, and of the ✠ Son, and of the ✠ Holy Ghost. Amen,* pouring water thrice in the form of a cross on the head of the candidate, and taking care that some of the water touches the forehead. In such a baptism plain water will suffice, but holy water is to be preferred. Later, a priest may re-baptize the candidate condition-ally, using the sacred oils and baptismal water.

CHAPTER XIV

HOLY MATRIMONY

General Directions

Inasmuch as the marriage laws of the various countries, and even of the states within them, differ, it is impossible here to give any instructions regarding the legal requirements. Each priest should acquaint himself with the requirements of the marriage law in his own country and state. He should satisfy himself, when people come before him for marriage, that there is no illegality or impediment, especially if either of the contracting parties is of foreign birth, or under age, or has been divorced.

No banns of marriage need to be proclaimed unless required by the law of the land. In the Liberal Catholic Church there is no restriction in regard to marriages between Liberal Catholics and non-Catholics. The Liberal Catholic Church does not in all cases view with disfavour the remarriage of divorced persons, the matter being left to the discretion of the priest, who in a difficult case may consult the bishop. It holds that where the contracting parties are earnest and sincere, the Divine Blessing may rightly be asked. There will be difference of opinion as to whether such a remarriage has full sacramental status.

The marriage ought if possible to take place in a church, but it may be celebrated in a private chapel or house, if preferred. Two witnesses should be present.

The preparations are simple. In the sanctuary, either on the usual credence table, or on a small table placed conveniently near the sanctuary gates, are placed an aspergill containing holy water, and a tray or salver on which the ring is laid. Cushions are placed where the bride and groom are to kneel. The six altar candles are always lighted, and there may be additional candles on the altar if desired.

The priest is vested in surplice, stole and biretta. It is recommended that he also wear a cope, inasmuch as marriage is a great event in the lives of those concerned. The server is vested in cotta or surplice. The colour of the vestments used is white.

The Marriage Service

The priest enters the sanctuary preceded by the server. He bows (or genuflects) before the altar and goes to stand at the closed sanctuary gates with his back to the altar. The man and the woman to be married stand before him, in front of the sanctuary gates, the woman at the man's left. The attendants group themselves round the bridegroom and the bride. (The marriage procession through the church before the ceremony does not form part of the Sacrament, and whether there shall be a procession or not is a matter left entirely to the people concerned. If there be a procession, the bridegroom and best man usually await, at the sanctuary gates, the arrival of the bride. Acolytes, processional cross, thurifer with censer, may go down to meet the bride and her party on arrival, and conduct them to the sanctuary gates.) The priest now turns by his left to the altar, removes his biretta and says the Invocation. He gives the biretta to the server to place on his seat or some convenient place. Turning back by his right, he addresses the people as follows: *Dearly beloved ... peace.* Any impediment alleged, except stupid irrelevancies, should be inquired into before proceeding with the ceremony. If no impediment is alleged, he first questions the man: *Wilt thou, N...* (he mentions the first Christian name only) *take N...* (first Christian name) *here ... Church*? The man answers: *I will.* In a similar way the priest questions the woman. Now receiving the ring (usually from the best man), the priest places it on the salver, which is held before him by the server. Taking the aspergill, also presented by the server, he sprinkles the ring with holy water in the form of a cross, with the intent that it be freed from all undesirable influences, and returns the aspergill. Holding his right hand palm down over the ring, he makes the sign of the cross twice as he says the blessing: *Bless ... Christ our Lord. Amen.* If the woman is also giving a ring to the man, it is then blessed using the same form, but altering the words appropriately.

The priest again turns towards the couple, saying: *Who giveth this woman to be married to this man*? The father, if present, or a friend or even the bride herself, if no friend is available, places her right hand in that of the priest, who in turn places it in the right hand of the bridegroom, saying: *Receive the precious gift of God.* (Because of widespread misunderstanding, the Third Episcopal Synod ruled that the saying of these two passages was optional with the people to be married. At the same time the Synod desired to make clear that the passages did not imply the bestowal of the bride as a chattel, but symbolically indicated the giving of the bride into the divine care, the priest receiving her on behalf of the Master, and then, in God's Name, giving her to the bridegroom.) Thus clasping hands, the bridegroom plights her his troth, repeating the words after the priest. The bridegroom uses one or more of his Christian names and addresses his bride by one or more of hers. This ended, the priest instructs them to loose hands, the bride thereupon taking the right hand of the bridegroom in her own. She then plights her troth, repeating the words after the priest.

The server presents the salver to the priest, who takes the ring and gives it to the bridegroom. The bridegroom takes the bride's left hand in his left and, instructed by the priest, puts the ring on the thumb of the bride's left hand, saying: *In the Name of the Father*; then on the forefinger, saying: *and of the Son*; then on the ring finger, saying *and of the holy Ghost*; finally he slips the ring on the ring finger and says: *Amen.* He drops his left hand and with his right holds her left hand and the ring as he repeats after the priest: *With this ring ...thee shield. Amen.* The groom's ring, if any, may then be placed on his left ring finger by his new wife, no words accompanying the act.

The priest joins their right hands, the woman's within that of the man. He receives the aspergill from the server and touches the forehead, first that of the man and then that of the woman, and returns the aspergill to the server. Facing the couple he says: *I join ... Holy Ghost. Amen*, making the sign of the cross over the newly married pair. Covering their joined hands for a moment with the right end of his stole, the priest says: *Those whom... asunder.*

The priest now addresses the people: *Forasmuch as ... Holy Ghost.* The people respond: *Amen.* At this point the priest should instruct the bridal pair (but not their attendants) to follow him to the first altar step, where they should kneel for the remainder of the service. If the Nuptial Eucharist is to follow the Marriage Service, the portion of the service in brackets is omitted. If there is to be no Nuptial Eucharist, as is usually the case, the versicles are said alternately by priest and congregation, the priest standing on the footpace with his back to the altar, facing the newly-married pair who are kneeling on the first step. The server should be ready to lead the responses of the congregation. At the end of the prayer: *O eternal God... Christ our Lord*, the people respond, *Amen.*

If there be an organist the wedding hymn is sung, the people standing. The hymn may be omitted, if desired. It is always omitted if there is no organist. Alternately special music may be substituted for the wedding hymn. The priest now pronounces the *Blessing: Almighty God ... your lives end*, making the sign of the cross once as indicated.

Is there is to be a Nuptial Eucharist following the Marriage Service, or an ordinary Eucharist at which the newly-married pair are to be present, they kneel either before the sanctuary gates, or at two kneeling desks placed in the middle near the sanctuary gates, or are seated in the front pew.

Care should be taken to see that the marriage is duly recorded, that any legal documents required are signed by the two witnesses present, and that all other legal requirements are met. Record must also be made in the Parish Marriage Register, or in the Record of Services, or both. If the bride is a Church member, her name on the Membership Record may be changed and her new address noted. This information should be sent to the Diocesan and Provincial Headquarters to be recorded there.

Marriage by a Bishop

When a bishop performs the marriage ceremony there are no changes to be noted except that he makes the sign of the cross thrice over the newly-married pair after he joins them in marriage: *I join you ... Holy Ghost. Amen.* He is vested in rochet and stole, and wears the pectoral cross and ring. It is recommended that he vest in cope and mitre, otherwise he may wear the mozetta (or mantelletta) and will wear his biretta. The colour of the vestments is white. The bishop uses the crozier at the opening Invocation, when giving blessings, and when joining the pair in marriage. During the other portions of the ceremony the crozier bearer stands near him.

CHAPTER XV

BURIAL OF THE DEAD

General Directions

Inasmuch as the funeral ceremony may take place in a church, in a private house, in a funeral parlour, in a cemetery chapel, or out-of-doors in a cemetery, it is impossible to give instructions which will fit all occasions. The ceremony will be described, therefore, as it would take place in a church. Afterward, suggestions will be made indicating how the ceremony may be modified according to circumstances.

The colour of the altar frontal and of the vestments used is purple if the funeral is that of an adult, but if of a child under seven years of age, the colour is white, Inasmuch as the Liberal Catholic Church does not make of death a great tragedy, it is a pleasing custom to place flowers on the altar. Coloured flowers are preferable to white.

The coffin should be placed on a bier or trestles in the middle of the church outside the sanctuary gates, The body of a layman, acolyte, subdeacon or deacon is set with feet towards the altar, but that of a priest or bishop with head towards the altar. In the case of clergy the following symbols of office or rank may be placed upon the coffin: if a bishop, a mitre and crozier; if a priest or deacon, a purple stole and biretta; if a subdeacon or cleric in Minor Orders, a biretta; if a peer of the realm, a coronet; any civil orders or decorations he may have received, or the insignia of his university degree. It is fitting that the body of one in Orders should be clothed in a cassock.

At equal distances around the coffin there should be six large candlesticks (the standard height is 4' 6") with candles, three on each side. Flowers may be placed on or around the coffin, but space should be left so that the officiant can walk around the bier. It may be necessary to move some of the front benches in the church to enable this to be done.

The officiant is vested in surplice, violet stole and biretta. If the Requiem Eucharist is to follow the funeral service, he may vest in amice, alb and girdle instead of in a surplice. He may on solemn occasions wear a purple cope. The aspergill with holy water should be placed in the sanctuary, unless there are sufficient servers so that it may be carried in procession. Also if the burial service as well as the funeral service takes place in the church, a bowl containing some earth should be placed near the coffin.

The priest should have at least one server to assist him. Additional servers are desirable, There may with advantage be a thurifer, a cross bearer with two attendant candle bearers, a server to carry the aspergill and holy water, and a server to hold the ritual.

The censer is prepared, and the six altar candles and the six candles round the bier (if not already burning) are lighted. (The latter are preferably lighted when the coffin is placed in position.) The procession forms in the usual order. If there be only one server, he should carry the censer and precede the priest.

The Funeral Service

As the procession moves through the church, the priest at intervals should read one of the passages given in the Liturgy. He should so time these readings that he is saying the *Gloria Patri* as he nears the sanctuary gates. During the procession the church bell may be tolled and there may be soft music on the organ. When the procession enters the sanctuary all bow (or genuflect) before the altar and go to stand in their appointed places: the thurifer and the server with the aspergill to the epistle side facing the middle, the cross bearer and attendant candle bearers to the gospel side facing the middle, the priest in the middle before the lowest altar step facing the altar, the ritual bearer to his right. Before the priest bows (or genuflects) he gives his biretta to the ritual bearer to put in some convenient place.

The priest now says or intones the *Invocation*, He then turns to the people by his right and reads the *First Charge*, which begins: *Brethren, we are met....* This ended he turns back to the altar and either reads the *Te Deum Laudamus* or part of the 23rd Psalm, or one of them is sung. (Naturally the matter of singing depends upon several factors: the presence of an organist, the wishes of the people concerned, the availability of singers familiar with the music.)

This ended, those in the sanctuary take their places before the altar preparatory to leaving the sanctuary: The thurifer and the acolyte with the aspergill stand side by side behind the priest facing the altar; the cross bearer and two candle bearers in turn stand behind the thurifer and acolyte, also facing the altar. Following the lead of the priest, all make the usual reverence to the altar, turn by the right and walk out of the sanctuary, the ritual bearer immediately preceding the officiant. Outside the chancel (or the sanctuary gates, if there be no chancel), the cross bearer and attendant candle bearers take their place at the head of the coffin, but at a sufficient distance from it to permit the priest to pass when he encompasses the coffin. When the deceased is not a priest or bishop the cross bearer and candle bearers stand at the end of the coffin farthest from the altar, facing the sanctuary. If the funeral is that of a priest or bishop the position is reversed, and they stand nearest the altar, facing the people. The thurifer and acolyte with aspergill separate and go to stand near the foot of the coffin, facing the people (unless the funeral be of a bishop or priest, when they are facing the altar.) The officiant, with ritual bearer to his right, stands between these two servers.

Taking the aspergill from the server and accompanied by the ritual bearer, the priest goes to the epistle side of the coffin and stands facing it. He sprinkles the coffin thrice with holy water, first in the middle, then the foot, then the head. Reading from the ritual held open by the server, the priest says or intones: *Rest in the eternal grant unto him, O Lord.* (Note that here and in the versicles which follow, him or her is used according to the sex of the deceased.) After the response of the people, the officiant continues round the coffin to the other side and sprinkles it thrice in the same way, He now says: *Come forth to meet him, Ye angels of the Lord.* As the people respond, the priest completes the journey round the bier so as to stand once more at the foot of the coffin. He returns the aspergill to the server, and, turning to the thurifer, puts incense on the charcoal and blesses it in the usual way. Censer in hand, and again accompanied by the ritual bearer, he once more encompasses the coffin. Stopping at the epistle side and facing the bier, he censes the coffin thrice, first the middle, then the foot, and lastly the head. He now says: *May the choirs of Angels receive him.* As the people respond he walks round to the other side of the bier, and, after the same triple censing, says: *Rest in the eternal grant unto him, O Lord.* With the response he returns to his place at the foot of the coffin, and returns the censer to the thurifer, (In the case of a bishop or priest, the gospel side of the coffin will of course be aspersed first, then the epistle side, and similarly with the censing.)

With upraised right hand he pronounces the Absolution: *O God ... Christ our Lord*, making the sign of the cross once as indicated. In the case of very young children the Absolution is omitted.

The priest, preceded by the servers, reënters the sanctuary. After the usual reverence to the altar the servers put away the things they are carrying and go to their seats. If there is to be a Requiem Eucharist, the priest vests in chasuble and maniple and the service begins. If there is not to be a Eucharist, but the priest wishes to speak a few words of consolation or spiritual instruction to those present, he may do so at this point in the service, either from the sanctuary, or from the pulpit, or while standing near the coffin. A hymn or reading from some suitable source may also be introduced now. This part of the service ended, the priest ascends to the footpace, and, turning by the right to face the people, either says or sings: *The Lord be with you.* As the people respond he turns back to the altar and either says or intones: *Let us pray.* The two Collects follow. While saying them, he extends his hands in the usual way. (It is to be noted that in the case of children the words *this Thy child* are to be used instead of *this Thy servant.*) After the Collects there may be a hymn, if desired. The service ended, the procession returns to the vestry by the shortest way.

Depending upon circumstances, the funeral service as described will have to be modified, when it takes place outside the church. It is permissible to omit those passages read at the beginning of the service, which are prefixed by an asterisk. Not infrequently a procession is impossible. In this case the officiant will simply stand beside the coffin while reading the passages. The funeral may take place in a house or cemetery chapel where there is not an altar. Under these circumstances, there is nothing to do but face towards the coffin while saying the Invocation, the *Te Deum* or *23rd Psalm*, and the Collects. Sometimes, because of family prejudice, it is not advisable to use either holy water or incense. The aspersing and censing of the coffin are therefore omitted, but the versicles and responses and the Absolution are said, while the priest stands at the foot of the coffin. Again, the service of burial may follow immediately after the funeral service, while the coffin still remains in the church, chapel or house. When this happens in the church, the procession does not leave the sanctuary until after the burial service is read. Naturally, under these circumstances, the prayer in which the grave is blessed is omitted.

The Burial

The procession bearing the coffin having reached the grave, the priest takes the aspergill and sprinkles the grave with holy water. It is not necessary that he should walk round the grave. Returning the aspergill, he sprinkles incense on the charcoal in the censer and censes the grave, making three swings over it and lowering the censer for a moment within it. Returning the censer he now says the prayer of blessing: *O God, Who ... Christ our Lord.* The two signs of the cross are made over the grave with the right hand, palm down.

The coffin is now lowered and the Second Charge is read. The priest, or someone appointed for the purpose, should scatter some earth upon the coffin in the form of a cross, at the words, *earth to earth.* (When the Burial Service is read in a church, the priest himself takes a few grains of sand from the bowl placed nearby and scatters them in the form of a cross upon the coffin.) Following the Charge, he may add at his discretion the prayer: *Almighty... Christ our Lord.* The closing prayer and Grace are now said, all crossing themselves.

When the body is to be cremated, the Burial Service usually takes place at the church, or at the house, or in the chapel connected with the crematory. A bowl containing earth should be placed near the coffin. At the end of the service the body is taken to the crematory itself, and several hours transpire before it is reduced to ashes. The receptacle containing the ashes is usually placed without any ceremony in the niche where it is to remain. If it is to be placed in a grave, the ceremonies already described may be carried out.

Funeral Conducted by a Bishop

If a bishop conducts an ordinary funeral service he is vested in rochet, purple stole and biretta, and wears the pectoral cross and ring. The crozier is held near him. He may wear the mozetta, and on more solemn occasions a purple cope and mitre. He uses the mitre and crozier when saying the opening Invocation, when blessing incense and when pronouncing the Absolution.

✠

CHAPTER XVI

SERVICE OF HEALING

General Directions

The Service of Healing may take place at any convenient hour, either in the morning, afternoon, or evening. The morning is the most suitable time as the bodies have not by then been subjected to the stress of the day's life and work. In some churches, however, one evening a week or a month is devoted to the work of healing, it having been found that more people in need of help can attend at that time. It is a public service, non-members as well as members being free to come forward for anointing and Communion.

The matter of receiving Communion in the afternoon or evening involves a delicate situation. In the Roman Catholic Church the rule governing the reception of Communion out of Mass is: "But no priest may make any difficulty against giving people Communion at other times, if their request is reasonable...and if they satisfy the law, being in a state of grace and fasting from the midnight." (Fortesque, 4th Edit., p.430) Because of the law in the Roman Church that Communion must be received fasting, it rarely happens, except in the case of approaching death, that the Host is partaken in other than the morning hours. Inasmuch as in the Liberal Catholic Church it is not required that the people should receive Communion while fasting, we are theoretically free to administer Communion at any hour in the afternoon or evening. The practice of administering Communion out of the morning hours often alienates those accustomed to the older traditions, however, and as a matter of expediency, it is perhaps best to omit the administration of Communion when the Service of Healing is conducted in the late afternoon or evening and substitute instead a shortened form of Benediction. Unless and until this matter is decided by the General Episcopal Synod, it is left to the discretion of the priest.

It has been found helpful in some churches to place in the pews before the service pads of paper and pencils for the use of the people. The people are instructed beforehand that those who come forward for the anointing may carry with them a slip of paper on which has been written the nature of the affliction of which they desire to be healed. The paper is shown to the officiant before he begins the anointing. It should be emphasized to those present that this is not obligatory, because the general intention of healing is sufficient in ordinary cases.

Red vestments are used at the Service of Healing. The officiant, if a priest, is vested in surplice, stole and biretta. The biretta is worn to and from the sanctuary, but not during the service itself. A bishop is vested in rochet, stole and biretta. He wears the pectoral cross and ring, and uses the crozier. He may wear the mozetta (or mantelletta). He wears the biretta for the Invocation, the Absolution and the final Benediction.

If Communion is to be administered, there should be in the tabernacle, preferably contained in a ciborium, consecrated Hosts sufficient for the needs of the people. A corporal is spread upon the altar in front of the tabernacle and a burse placed nearby to the gospel side. A small bowl of water, usually with a cover, and a purificator are placed to the right of the tabernacle door to the rear of the altar. In this bowl of water the officiant dips his fingers and dries them on the purificator after the administration of Communion to the people. This arrangement is recommended by Fortescue (4th Ed., p. 431) and has much to commend it. (The contents of the bowl may then be drunk or later poured, as is our custom, upon clean grass or upon soil in a garden.) A missal stand may be placed on the altar to the epistle side, although it will be used only during the saying of two or three prayers. The six regular altar candles are lighted. Incense is not required during the service, but the censer, if desired, may be carried in the procession to and from the sanctuary. On the credence may be placed a large bowl, lemon, bread crumb, water and a towel, to be used for the cleansing of the fingers of the officiant after the anointing is over. This is especially necessary if he is to administer Communion.

There are two possible arrangements in connection with the coming forward of the people for anointing. If there are many people to anoint, and therefore as little time as possible should be lost between the individual anointings, a number of people may come forward at once to the altar rail when summoned by the priest. In this case the ome forward at once to the altar rail when summoned by the priest. In this case the officiant passes from person to person, new people coming forward to take the place of those returning to their seats. The other arrangement is for the people to come forward one by one, each kneeling on a cushion or hassock at the altar at the place where the officiant stands during the entire anointing.

Two servers are desirable and three can be used: one to hold the service book, one to present the oil stock to the officiant and to offer the cotton wool whenever the officiant wishes to cleanse his fingers after an anointing, a third who remains outside the sanctuary to marshall and assist the people who come forward and to wipe off the excess oil from the brow and neck of the person anointed before assisting him to rise. If only one server is available he carries the oil stock and takes the service book from the officiant when the latter lays on both hands. He fetches the cotton wool when needed, placing the book and oil on a table for the time being.

It should be impressed upon the people that those with contagious diseases should not come forward at a general service.

The officiant must not be of lesser rank than priest. In a church where there are several priests it is advisable to assign to one priest alone (that priest who by experience has been found to be the best natural channel for the forces of healing) the duty of conducting all Services of Healing. A Service of Healing at which several priests officiate conjointly often does more harm than good to those anointed. A priest should not attempt to officiate unless he himself is in good health. If he becomes ill, or his health is impaired, and there is no other priest available to take his place in the service, it is better that the service be postponed for the time being than that he should officiate and possibly convey something of the condition of his body to those who come forward for anointing. Priests should not introduce other healing methods into this service. These methods may be effective and valuable in their own place, but it is not well to mix two types of healing, and to do so has not the necessary authorization of the Church.

Priest Officiating

The officiant goes usually by the short way to the sanctuary preceded by the servers. All genuflect upon reaching the lowest step before the altar (unless the Host is not reserved in the tabernacle, in which case they bow), the priest first removing his biretta and giving it to a server to place in a convenient place. Standing in the middle before the lowest altar step, the officiant intones or says the Invocation, asperses himself, the altar and the people with the same words and in the same way as in the Shorter Form or Brief Form Asperges. It should be noted, however, that the prayer at the end of the Asperges is different from that in the Eucharistic Service. All kneel and say the Confiteor. This ended, the officiant rises, ascends to the footpace, turns to the people by his right and pronounces the Absolution in the usual way. He turns back to the altar and the people are seated. (If the service follows immediately after the Holy Eucharist, the aspersing, Confiteor and Absolution may be omitted, but the prayer at the end of the Asperges, invoking the Angel of healing, should be said.)

(The Service of Healing, as printed in the *Liturgy,* is a revision by Bishop Leadbeater of a Form for this service which I submitted to him for approval in 1922. Later, about 1926 or 1927, he further revised this service by deleting the hymn: *Great Master, Whose Name is the* Healer, and transferring the hymn: *Immortal Love, for ever full*, to that part of the service immediately following anointing, but preceding the Communion. This gives opportunity to the priest to cleanse his hands of oil, and at the same time marks the division between the two parts of the service. In the description which follows I shall follow this later revision.—I.S.C.) [The 3rd Edition of *The Liturgy* moves the hymn to directly after the Absolution and makes it optional. Ed.]

Taking his service book the priest walks to the epistle end of the footpace and turns by his right to face the people. He announces and reads the words of the Apostle James. Turning back to the altar and going to the middle, he kneels on the footpace and joins in the singing or saying of the *Veni Creator*. Rising and standing *in plano* in the middle, the priest turns to the people and says: *Let us pray*. Raising his right hand in blessing he continues: *O Lord ... Christ our Lord*, making the sign of the cross once over the people where indicated.

Now descending to the sanctuary floor, the priest goes to the place where he is to anoint the people. He is accompanied by the servers who are to assist him, namely, one to carry the oil-stock containing oil for the sick and a supply of cotton wool (which may be laid on a tray or in a shallow bowl), the other the service book. Arriving before the altar rail, the officiant gives the invitation, using the words: *Let those who desire to be anointed come forward.* [In the Third Edition of the *Liturgy* these words do not appear. Ed.] Those desiring to be anointed either come forward one by one to kneel before the priest, or a number of them come forward at once and kneel at the altar rail, while the priest passes from person to person, as previously described.

As each person kneels before him, the officiant, with right hand raised, palm towards the person as at Absolution, says the words of the Exorcism. He uses a low or moderate tone of voice during the exorcism and the anointing. The server on his left holds the book from which he is to read. Music may be played on the organ during the entire time that the people are being anointed. This music should be quiet, devotional, uplifting, inspiring, free from sorrow or lamentation.

After the Exorcism the officiant moistens his right thumb with oil for the sick, presented to him by a server on his right, and proceeds to anoint the person in the form of a cross upon the forehead, saying: *In the Name ... soul and body.* Immediately afterward he anoints in the same manner as before, but in silence, the centre at the crown of the head, the front of the throat, the nape of the neck. The last-mentioned cross is made without moving from his place in front of the person. It may not always be possible to contact the skin when making the sign of the cross on top of the head, but at the last two crosses the skin ought always to be touched.

Now placing both hands upon the head of the person (*be careful not to bear down too heavily upon the head*) and thinking intently of the Christ with the will to heal, the officiant says slowly: *Christ the Son of God ... Light of His Love.* If he has been informed of the nature of the affliction of the person, he may direct the healing power to that part of the body which is affected. The officiant should refrain from trying to use his own personal power of healing, but rather think of offering himself as a channel for the healing power of Christ and His holy Angels. A server, stationed outside the altar rail, may assist after the anointing by wiping off any excess of oil with a fragment of cotton wool and helping the person to arise. The officiant cleanses his fingers on cotton wool, held out to him by a server.

When all have been anointed, and the priest has cleansed his hands after the last patient, he faces the congregation and reads the prayer: *As with this visible oil ... Christ our Lord.*

The Hymn: *Immortal Love for ever* full, is now usually sung. It is helpful, but not an essential part of the service. It may be omitted if its singing is difficult. While it is being sung and priest goes to the credence and cleanses his hands with lemon, crumb and water. In the meanwhile a collection may be taken. [The hymn has been deleted from the Third Edition of *TheLiturgy*. Ed.] Returning to the middle before the altar; the priest ascends to the footpace. He presents the offerings of the people (if any) in the usual manner. The officiant, facing the altar, says: *O God, Who ... ages of ages*, if Communion is to be administered.

Communion is given in the usual way, after inviting the people to come forward as is done at the Holy Eucharist. After he returns the ciborium to the tabernacle and closes the door, he wipes the thumb and forefinger of the right hand on the corporal and then, if necessary, dips them in the bowl of water standing on the altar, drys them on the purificator, folds the corporal and places it in the burse.

Standing on the footpace in the middle, facing the altar, he says: *Let us pray*. Extending his hands, he continues: *We who have ... Christ our Lord*. After the response he turns to the people by the right and says the Benediction in the usual way. Turning back to the altar, he genuflects, all in the sanctuary genuflecting with him, puts on his biretta and returns to the vestry preceded by the servers.

If the service is to be followed by the Holy Eucharist the administration of Communion should be deferred till the appropriate place at that service; the Grace in that case will be used instead of the Benediction at the Healing Service; similarly if the service is followed immediately by Benediction of the Most Holy Sacrament the Grace takes the place of the Benediction of the Healing Service.

Bishop Officiating

A server to hold the crozier will be required. The bishop holds the crozier at the Invocation, Absolution and final Benediction. The ceremony otherwise is exactly the same except that at each anointing, after the laying on of hands, the bishop having cleansed his hand of oil with cotton wool, takes his crozier and lays the central part of the spiral on top of the head of the person. Holding it there a moment, he returns the crozier to the bearer and proceeds with the anointing of another person.

☩

CHAPTER XVII

OCCASIONAL CEREMONIES

Administration of Holy Communion with the Reserved Sacrament

The normal time for the administration of Holy Communion is during the Celebration of the Holy Eucharist. Occasionally, however, people have satisfactory reasons for asking for Communion at other times and, when this is the case, the priest should use the Form for the Administration of Holy Communion with the Reserved Sacrament. This form has been found useful the case of sick people and for those too weak to attend an entire Eucharistic service.

For this administration the priest vests in surplice, stole of the colour of the day and a biretta. It is helpful, but not essential, that there should be a server to assist him. Two candles on the altar are lighted, preferably not two of the regular six altar candles. On the altar before the tabernacle door a corporal is spread and to one side the burse is placed. Near the tabernacle, to the rear of the altar is placed a small bowl with water and a lavabo towel, as recommended by Fortescue. (4th Ed., p. 431) No incense is needed.

The priest goes to the sanctuary by the shortest way. Standing in the middle before the lowest altar step, he removes his biretta, gives it to a server to put in some convenient place, genuflects and says the Invocation. He kneels on the lowest altar step and all say the Confiteor. This ended he ascends to the footpace, turns to the people and with outstretched right hand pronounces the Absolution. Joining his hands before the breast for an instant, he extends them as usual and says: *The Lord be with you.* As the people respond, he turns back to altar and says: *Let is pray.* The hands are extended while saying the prayer which follows. At the end of the prayer, he opens the tabernacle door, genuflects, takes out the ciborium, closes the door, uncovers the ciborium, and taking up the ciborium and a Host in the usual way, turns to the people and invites them with the customary words and sign to come forward to Communion. He administers Communion as at the Eucharist.

Returning to the footpace, he puts away the ciborium, genuflects, closes the tabernacle, wipes the thumb and forefinger of the right hand on the corporal and then dips them in the bowl of water, dries them on the purificator, folds the corporal and places it in the burse. (After the service the bowl of water is poured on clean grass or on earth in a garden, or the officiant may drink the water.)

Facing the altar and standing in the middle on the footpace, he says: *Under the veil ... Father's glory.* The hands are joined before the breast during this prayer. At his discretion he may at this point say the *Communio* and *Postcommunio* of the Eucharistic Service, or any other prayers which are suitable. Now, turning to the people and with right hand extended in blessing, he says the Benediction. Turning back to the altar by his right, thus completing the circle, he genuflects, puts on his biretta and returns to the vestry.

If a bishop administers Communion, he is vested in rochet, stole and biretta. He may wear the mozetta (or mantelletta). He wears the pectoral cross and ring. He wears the biretta and uses the crozier at the Invocation, Absolution and Benediction. The ceremony is the same.

❋ ❋ ❋ ❋ ❋ ❋ ❋

The Third General Episcopal Synod ruled that in the absence of the priest a deacon may administer Communion using the prescribed form, but subject to two conditions:

1. That instead of ascending the footpace and pronouncing the Absolution as is done by a priest, he shall remain kneeling on the lowest altar step and say as he crosses himself: *May the Lord bless us, and ✠ absolve us from all our sins, and may His Peace rest upon as this day and evermore.* The people also cross themselves at the word *absolve*.

2. That instead of the final Benediction, the deacon, kneeling in the middle on the footpace, shall say: ✠ *The grace of our Lord Jesus Christ, and the love of God, and the fellowship of the Holy Ghost, be with us all evermore.* All cross themselves at the beginning of the Grace, and respond, *Amen*, at its end.

❋ ❋ ❋ ❋ ❋ ❋ ❋

Holy Unction and Communion of the Sick

Whenever a priest is called upon to administer Holy Unction and Communion to one who is ill, he will require, in addition to the cassock, the following vestments: surplice, a reversible purple-white stole, or a purple stole and a white stole. He will also require a small altar cross, two small candlesticks with candles, a corporal in a burse, a purificator or lavabo towel, some cotton wool, holy water and an aspergill. (Instead of holy water, salt alone may be taken and the holy water prepared at the house before the ceremony.) These things may either be sent to the house beforehand or carried there by the priest. The people at the house should be asked to supply a small bowl with water, a slice of lemon and some bread crumb, which are used to cleanse the fingers of the priest after the anointing with oil. The priest should carry with him an oil-stock containing oil for the sick, and, *never intrusted to anyone else*, a small pyx, resembling a watchcase, in which has been placed one or more consecrated Wafers. The family may wish to take Communion with the sick person, and so more than one Wafer is usually carried. The pyx is carried concealed beneath the coat, sometimes in a small burse or bag which hangs by a string round the neck, sometimes in an upper waistcoat pocket. The important matter is to safeguard the Host from any injury or loss.

At the house, by the bedside of the sick person, a table is placed and covered with a white cloth. On the table are arranged the small altar cross and the two candlesticks, the corporal, the holy water and the aspergill. There may be vases with flowers. Nearby are placed the bowl of water, lemon, crumb and lavabo towel.

Upon his arrival the priest puts on his vestments, blesses the holy water, if none was brought with him, sees that the table is properly prepared and the candles lighted, and then lays the oil stock on the altar and the pyx on the corporal. Wearing the purple stole, he takes his place by the bedside facing the altar cross. The Invocation is said in the usual way. Taking now the aspergill, which either contains, or has been dipped in, holy water, he touches with it the forehead of the sick person and sprinkles the surroundings. At his discretion the priest may read the words of the Apostle James. The sick person should now recite the Confiteor, prompted if need be by the priest. If the patient is very weak, either the priest or someone else, may say the Confiteor on behalf of the sick person. Even a mental act of aspiration suffices. If the sick person is troubled by some matter and desires to make a special confession to the priest, the latter should ask any other people present to leave the room for the time being. The sick person should be encouraged to open his heart to the priest, because in this way great relief is often given. No set form of confession need be followed, but the form in the Liturgy, under "Confession and Absolution," is recommended. After the confession the friends of the sick person may be asked to return.

If the illness is likely to prove fatal the priest proceeds at once to the Unction. Taking the oil stock, he moistens his right thumb with oil for the sick. If the oil in the stock is not retained in cotton-wool, but is contained merely in a bottle, so much oil will adhere to the thumb of the priest, that it will be necessary after each anointing to wipe the skin of the sick person with a fragment of cotton wool. (These bits of cotton should afterward be gathered together and burned.) Using his thumb he anoints the patient with oil in the form of a cross, first on the closed eyelids, then on the ears, the nostrils, the closed lips and the palms of the hands, saying in each case the words prescribed. (If it is a priest who is ill, the backs of the hands and not the palms are anointed.) He may at his discretion anoint the small of the back and the feet, but this is rarely done. In each case he first anoints the organ on the right side of the body, and then that on the left. If an organ or limb is wanting or is mutilated, that part of the body nearest to it is anointed. In cases of extremity, or at the discretion of the priest, the forehead only need be anointed, and the one accompanying prayer said. It is recommended that in case of severe illness or great urgency the forehead alone be anointed. The priest now pronounces the Absolution: *Our Lord Christ ... Holy Ghost. Amen*, while standing beside the sick man and extending the right hand over him. He then says the prayer which follows: *The King of Love ... glorious Image.*

In cases where the illness is not likely to prove fatal, the priest omits the foregoing Unction and proceeds directly to the Absolution. Following this, he uses the alternative Unction prefaced by: *Let us pray*. In the prayer which follows: *O Lord ... Christ our Lord*, the sign of the cross is made over the sick person, the priest holding in mind the bestowal of health and strength. The priest anoints the sick person with the oil for the sick upon the forehead, using his thumb and making the sign of the cross, while saying: *In the Name ... soul and body.*

Regardless of the form of Unction which has been used, the priest now proceeds to anoint in the same manner as before, but in silence, all or some of the remaining centres of the body. The anointing of the first three centres may be done, but is usually omitted. These three centres are: the centre at the base of the spine, the centre in the neighborhood of the spleen, and the centre at the solar plexus. It is customary to anoint the other centres which are: the centre over the heart, the centre at the front of the throat, the centre on the forehead between the eyebrows (unless this has already been done), and the centre at the top or crown of the head. In the case of contagious diseases the priest should not use his thumb, but apply the oil by means of a cotton tipped applicator or pencil of wood or a piece of cotton wool. Naturally anything that has once touched the patient must not again touch the oil in the stock, so there must be a separate applicator or piece of cotton for each anointing.

At the end of the anointing the priest says: *As with this visible ... Christ our Lord*, taking care to omit the portion in brackets if the illness is not likely to prove fatal. If, for any reason, Communion is not to be given, the Blessing: *Unto God's... evermore*, is now said by the priest.

Care should be taken during the foregoing ceremony not to turn the back directly on the Host contained in the pyx.

The priest should now cleanse his hands with lemon, crumb and water. If Communion is to be administered, he changes from purple to white stole. He then administers Communion using the Form for Administration of Holy Communion with the Reserved Sacrament, but omitting the Confiteor, the Absolution and the Minor Benediction. The abbreviated form is therefore as follows: Facing the altar cross the priest crosses himself and says the Invocation. He then says: *Let us pray*, and proceeds with the prayer: *O God, Who ... ages of ages*. If others in the sick room in addition to the sick person are to receive Communion, the priest, opening the pyx and making the sign of the cross with a Host, says: *Ye that desire ... holy Sacrament*. If, however, only the sick person is to receive Communion, he does not say the words of invitation, but goes at once to the sick person and administers Communion with the usual words. Replacing the pyx on the corporal, he joins his hands before the breast and says: *Under the veil ... Father's glory*. Turning to the sick person, the priest blesses him saying the words of the Benediction: *The peace of God ... you always*.

If the patient is very weak, Communion may be administered at once using only the customary words: *The Body of our Lord Christ keep thee unto life eternal*. The final Benediction, however is said. In cases where the sick person is unable to swallow the Host, it is sufficient to place the smallest imaginable Fragment, or even a single Crumb, on the tongue.

Procedure "In Extremis"

The Procedure *In Extremis* is a shortened form of Holy Unction and Communion used when the sick person is in imminent danger of death. The priest wears a purple stole during the Absolution and Unction, but changes to white for the Communion, if the condition of the dying person permits.

At the beginning of the ceremony the priest exhorts the dying person to turn his thoughts with love and trust to his Master. He then pronounces the Absolution, either the form found in Holy Unction, or, if the person is near death, the shorter form appearing in the Procedure *In Extremis*.

If time permits he may administer Holy Unction, anointing the forehead of the dying and saying: *By this holy ... of thy body*. If time is short the fingers should be hastily wiped on a bit of cotton wool and the Sacrament given to the patient, unless there is danger of the person rejecting or being unable to swallow. A small Particle may be placed in a spoon and given with a little wine or water. (See also p. 177.) As this Communion is the last the man will receive it is given as viaticum, the words of administration being those found in the Liturgy: *Brother ... go with thee*. The ceremony closes with the Benediction.

The Third General Episcopal Synod ruled that in the absence of the priest, a deacon may use the form *In Extremis*, provided the following changes are made:

1. Instead of the Absolution he says: *May the Lord bless us and ✠ absolve us from all our sins; and may His peace rest upon us this day and evermore*. The deacon makes the sign of the cross over himself, not the sick person, inasmuch as ordination to the diaconate does not bestow upon him the power to grant absolution.

2. The Unction must be omitted.

3. Instead of the Benediction, he shall say: *✠ The grace of our Lord Jesus Christ, and the love of Gad, and the fellowship of the Holy Ghost, be with us all evermore*. Again he makes the sign of the cross over himself, not the sick person.

Holy Unction may be given to those who are unconscious or delirious, provided there is no danger of profaning the Sacrament. It is not given more than once during the illness in which the man is in danger of death. It may be given again, however, if the man partly recovers, and then again becomes dangerously ill. (The Service of Healing may be given at intervals during a protracted illness.) If the sick person dies during the rite, the priest must stop at once, and proceed to the Absolution set forth in the Burial of the Dead.

In emergency, or in a hospital or other place where vestments are impracticable, the Procedure *In Extremis* may be given without vestments. This, however, is not recommended.

If a bishop administer Holy Unction and Communion he is vested in rochet, purple and white stole, wears the pectoral cross and ring. The ceremony is exactly the same except that at the Absolution the bishop makes the sign of the cross four times as usual.

Admission to the Liberal Catholic Church

When those who desire to become members of the Liberal Catholic Church have been validly and fully baptized and confirmed according to the rite of some other Church, the "Form of Admission to the Liberal Catholic Church" is used when admitting them. If the rites of baptism and confirmation previously administered, however, were less complete than our own it is customary to rebaptize conditionally and then to confirm. The essentials of the complete baptismal rite are: "The proper use of water (by process of ablution at least) and the usual Trinitarian formula, together with the application of the Oil of Catechumens and Chrism." Those of the complete Confirmation rite are: "The imposition of the bishop's hand with proper formula, and use of Chrism." As a matter of practice, those who have been baptized and confirmed according to the Roman Catholic, Old Catholic and Eastern Rites are usually the only ones admitted to membership by using the Form of Admission.

The admission may take place at any hour and the ceremony may be performed by either priest or bishop. The priest is vested in surplice, stole of the colour of the day and biretta. On more important occasions he may wear a cope. He enters the sanctuary and goes to stand in the middle before the lowest altar step. He faces the altar, removes his biretta, genuflects (or bows, if the Host is not reserved in the tabernacle), says the Invocation, and goes to the sanctuary gates, which are closed. (The biretta is not worn during the ceremony.) The candidate stands just outside the gates, facing the priest.

The candidate now says, prompted if need be by the priest: *Reverend Father... Liberal Catholic Church*. The priest then questions the candidate as indicated in the Liturgy. After the response to the last question the priest says: *The Lord keep ... goodness*, and immediately continues *Let us pray*. The candidate kneels on the cushion before the sanctuary gates. Extending his right hand in blessing, the priest says: *O Lord Christ ... for evermore*. He makes the sign of the cross, where indicated in the text, over the candidate. Placing now his right hand on the head of the candidate, and lifting it only long enough to make the sign of the cross, the priest ends the service by giving the blessing: *The blessing ...thy life*. Returning to the middle before the lowest altar step, he genuflects, puts on his biretta and returns to the vestry.

If a bishop admits a member he is vested in rochet, stole of the colour of the day and biretta. He may wear the mozetta (or mantelletta). He wears the pectoral cross and ring, and the crozier is borne at his side. On more important occasions he may wear a cope and mitre. At the beginning of the service the candidate should be prompted to say: *Right [or Most Ed] Reverend Father*, instead of *Reverend Father*. No other changes are made.

In cases where fully baptized children, who are too young to be confirmed, are to be admitted to membership in the Church, the Third General Episcopal Synod ruled that the Form of Admission shall be used with the following changes:

(1) The child shall be accompanied by one or both parents, or a member of the Church, who shall say: *Reverend Father, we ask that this child be received into the fellowship of the Liberal Catholic Church.*

(2) The questions and answers are omitted.

(3). The prayer is changed as follows: *O Lord Christ, look down, we pray Thee, upon this child whom we now admit to our fellowship ... adoration for evermore.* ℞. *Amen.*

The blessing follows as usual.

❀ ❀ ❀ ❀ ❀ ❀ ❀

Admission of a Singer and of a Server

The structure of these three services is identical although the wording is different. The rubrics in the Liturgy are complete and additional amplification is unnecessary. The priest is vested in surplice, stole of the colour of the Day and biretta. Should a bishop conduct the service he is vested in rochet, stole of the colour of the Day and biretta. He may wear the mozetta. He wears the pectoral cross and ring and uses the crozier.

❀ ❀ ❀ ❀ ❀ ❀ ❀

Confession and Absolution

The introductory note in the Liturgy under the heading: "Confession and Absolution" should be read with care. The Third General Episcopal Synod authorized the insertion of a new paragraph 2 to that note, which reads as follows: "At his ordination a priest is given authority to withhold Absolution, and this passage sometimes causes much soul-searching to people unfamiliar with the whole subject. It is a duty to be used with the greatest moderation and discretion. But it is the priest's duty, in the first place, to be satisfied that the candidate is sincere before giving him Absolution; secondly, he may be justified in reserving Absolution to a person until the person in question has made some act of restitution to the one he has wronged." [The text is not included in the Third Edition of *The Liturgy.* Ed.]

The systematic practice of auricular confession is not encouraged in the Liberal Catholic Church, because for the vast majority of people the Confiteor and Absolution in the Holy Eucharist suffices. When a member, however, is in serious personal difficulty, or has made a grave mistake, the priest can often be of real service to him by listening to his confession and administering Absolution. It should be made clear to the supplicant, however, that Absolution does not relieve him of the responsibility for any wrong doing. Sins cannot be "forgiven" in the old sense of the word, by taking away the consequences. Absolution is intended only to restore the penitent to a condition of grace, not to relieve him of responsibility. The priest does not impose any penance, but strives only to assist the supplicant to rectify his mistakes and to relieve his mind.

For the purpose of this Sacrament, a kneeling desk or prie dieu should be placed in some convenient spot in the church and beside it a chair placed for the priest. The confessional box is not used in the Liberal Catholic Church, although the place where the kneeling desk stands may be screened off so that the supplicant is not exposed to the curious gaze of casual visitors to the Church. In case of necessity, confession may be heard in some other place, but whenever possible it is best to hear it in the Church.

The priest vests in surplice and purple stole. He may omit the surplice, although this is not ordinarily done. In case of urgent necessity he may hear confession in any dress. He administers the Sacrament sitting.

The supplicant kneels at the *prie dieu*, crossing himself as he says: *In the Name ... have sinned.* The priest holds his right hand towards the supplicant while saying: *The Lord be ... offenses*, making the sign of the cross where indicated. The supplicant then makes his confession, using the words in the Liturgy and adding in his own language any matters which are troubling him. The priest should hear the confession without interruption, unless it is necessary to elucidate some point or obtain additional information. He must be very careful never to ask for the names of those implicated in any wrong doing which may be confessed. He should not adopt the attitude of a stern judge, but should strive earnestly to help the supplicant by sympathy, lovingkindness and sound advice. In the Liberal Catholic Church formal penances are not imposed, but the priest may suggest any way which occurs to him by which the supplicant may right a wrong which has been done. The service is ended when the priest pronounces the Absolution and gives the Grace.

The Priest must never forget that he is obligated to maintain inviolable secrecy concerning anything told him in confession.

Should a bishop administer the Sacrament he vests in rochet and purple stole, and wears the pectoral cross and ring. He does not use the crozier. In case of emergency he may hear confession in any dress. During the Absolution he makes the sign of the cross four times as is customary.

❀ ❀ ❀ ❀ ❀ ❀ ❀

The Blessing of Holy Water

The blessing of holy water may take place at any hour. Inasmuch as both the salt and the water are exorcised, the general rule is followed and a purple stole is worn, but in emergency a stole of any colour will suffice. The priest is vested in surplice (or amice, alb and girdle) and stole. If the water is needed for use in a house, and vesting is inconvenient, he may do the blessing in ordinary clothes.

Before him should be placed a vessel of water and some salt. It is best to avoid boiled or distilled water and to use freshly drawn water. Care should be taken to see that the salt is pure kitchen salt and not that specially prepared for the table—called free-running salt—by mixing it with starch or other substances to prevent the caking or hardening of the salt. It is a good plan to keep in the church a covered, wide-mouthed glass or porcelain jar or bowl in which a supply of salt may be stored.

The priest, duly vested, holds his right hand, palm down, over the salt and exorcises it saying: *I exorcize thee...and glory*, making the sign of the cross where indicated then blesses the salt with the words: *We pray Thee...Christ our Lord*, making the sign of the cross twice. In exactly the same way the water is exorcised and blessed. Now taking up some of the salt in his right hand he casts it thrice into the water in the form of a cross, saying: *Let salt and water ... Ghost*. More salt may be taken up, if required, before making the second and third sign, but the water must not be turned into brine, although it should be made distinctly salty.

The Minor Benediction and the *Amen* which follows each prayer are omitted, if the service is not public.

Again extending his right hand over the vessel of holy water, the priest says: *O God the Giver ... ages of ages.*

Whenever the holy water is to be used in the rite of Baptism, the following additional prayer should be said over it, the priest making the sign of the cross as usual with the right hand:

O Lord Christ, who in the mystery of Thy boundless love didst take upon Thyself the limitations of human form, and in Thy gracious compassion didst gather little children into Thine arms; stretch forth, we pray Thee, the right hand of Thy power over this Holy Water and fill it with Thy heavenly ✚ grace and ✚ blessing, that those to be baptized therewith may receive the fullness of Thy love and ever remain in the number of Thy faithful children.

It should be remembered that whenever holy water falls upon the silk of a vestment it causes the fabric to crumble away leaving a hole in the material. Actual drops of water need not fall on the object sprinkled, when there is danger of causing damage. The influence of the holy water, directed by the intention of the priest, will suffice.

When a bishop prepares holy water he vests in rochet and purple stole, wears the cross and ring, and may use the crozier.

❀ ❀ ❀ ❀ ❀ ❀

The Blessing of a House

When he is called upon to bless a house the priest should take with him the following vestments: cassock, surplice and stole. As there is no exorcism in this form of blessing, the priest may wear a stole of the colour of the Day or a white stole. He should also take with him holy water, an aspergill, censer, charcoal and incense. Two servers are required, one to carry the vessel of holy water and aspergill, the other the censer. (Catholic furnishing stores usually have for sale quite small silver aspergills capable of containing sufficient holy water for such purposes as this or for funerals.)

When he has reached the house and vested, he goes outside the chief entrance of the house, preceded by the servers, and formally enters it, saying: *Peace be to this house and to all that dwell therein.* Taking now the aspergill, which has been dipped in holy water, he draws a line with holy water before the door and says: *We pray Thee, O Lord, so to bless this doorway by Thy mighty Power that those who enter through it may leave behind them all unworthy thought and feeling, that this house may ever serve Thee in peace and holiness of life, through Christ our Lord.* He then goes to all the other entrances to the house, and draws a line of holy water before each, repeating the same prayer. (The foregoing prayer and rubrics regarding the drawing of the line of holy water appeared in a supplementary sheet headed: "Additions," which was prepared by Bishop Leadbeater and sent out with the Second edition of the Liturgy. For some reason it is not included in all bound copies of the Liturgy. [It appears in the Third Edition. Ed.]

Sprinkling incense on the charcoal and blessing it in the usual way, the priest, preceded by the thurifer and accompanied by the server carrying the vessel of holy water, walks through all the rooms of the house sprinkling them with holy water and censing them. He should hold in mind constantly the thought of purification and blessing. Returning to the central hall or chief room of the house, he says: *O God Who... Christ our Lord*, making the sign of the cross twice during the prayer. This ends the ceremony.

If a bishop blesses a house he vests in rochet and stole. He may wear the mozetta (or mantelletta). He wears the ring and pectoral cross, and may use the crozier.

✦ ✦ ✦ ✦ ✦ ✦

Blessing of a Church by a Priest

There are occasions when an oratory is used temporarily for the services of the Church, or when a church must be used before it can be consecrated by a bishop. Under these circumstances, it is permissible for a priest to hold a simple service of blessing. This service ought to precede the first Eucharistic service celebrated in the oratory or church.

The priest is vested in surplice (or amice, alb and girdle), white stole, biretta, and, if desired, in white cope. For this ceremony it will be helpful to have several servers, although two will suffice. There should be a server to carry the processional cross, two candle bearers to accompany him, a thurifer, other candle bearers and a server to carry the vessel of holy water.

The altar should be bare except for the linen cloths, the six altar candlesticks and the altar cross. (The altar stone should have been consecrated by a bishop, but in emergency it may be blessed by the priest.) Other candlesticks and vases of flowers, later to be placed on the altar, may stand on the sanctuary floor or on a table to one side. The chalice and paten are placed on the credence. The frontal, if any, should stand to one side or remain in the vestry until needed.

The priest may go to the sanctuary, either the short way, or in procession round the church. A hymn may be sung. He is preceded by the servers in the usual order. Upon reaching the sanctuary he takes his place in the middle before the lowest altar step, removes his biretta and gives it to a server to place upon his seat, bows to the altar cross, and then intones the Invocation. After the response, *Amen*, he continues: *Let us pray*. The people kneel. He then says or intones the Collect of Purification found at the beginning of the Service of the Consecration of a Church which reads: *O God, omnipotent and omnipresent... ages of ages*. After the response, *Amen*, all rise and the people are seated.

Taking the aspergill, which has been dipped in holy water, the priest sprinkles the altar thrice, once towards the middle, once towards the gospel end, once towards the epistle end. If possible he goes once round the altar (moving in a clockwise direction) sprinkling it meanwhile. He then asperses the sanctuary, turning to either side as he stands in the middle before the lowest altar step. Now, turning to the people, he asperses them thrice in the same way as at the Holy Eucharist. He turns back to the altar, gives the aspergill to the server and says: *Let us pray*. He then says or intones: *Guide us, O Almighty Father... Christ our Lord*, thereby calling the Angel of the Eucharist. At the end of the prayer the people are seated.

The procession forms and leaves the sanctuary by the central gates. Incense should meanwhile have been prepared, and the censer is swung at the front of the procession. The procession encircles the church, moving in a clockwise direction, the priest meanwhile sprinkling the walls with holy water. A hymn may be sung or music played on the organ. When the procession has again returned to the sanctuary, the priest, having relinquished the aspergill, stands before the lowest altar step and faces the altar. He then says: *Let us pray*. The people kneel. He then says or intones the Collect of Consecration appearing in the Service of the Consecration of a Church, which reads: *God the Father ... gate of heaven*, but making the sign of the cross once instead of thrice. After the response the people are seated. The altar is now dressed with the frontal, if any, and with the flowers and extra candles. The chalice and paten are arranged thereon and the candles lighted. The Holy Eucharist begins and is said or sung as usual, except that the Asperges and the Collect calling the Angel of the Eucharist are omitted.

❀ ❀ ❀ ❀ ❀ ❀

The Blessing of Objects in General

When objects are blessed, the general rule is that the priest wears a surplice and purple stole, provided there is a form of exorcism. If there be no exorcism the colour of the stole is white. Where less formality is involved the priest may wear his ordinary clothes. While saying the exorcism, he holds his right hand palm down over the object. He mentions the name of the object in the exorcism and in the blessing as indicated in the Liturgy. After the exorcism he may sprinkle the object thrice with holy water. This is always omitted if the object is made of silk or other material which the salt water would injure. He may also cense the object thrice with the censer with the usual sequence of swings: middle, left, right. In the blessing he makes the sign of the cross twice over the object.

❁ ❁ ❁ ❁ ❁ ❁ ❁

PART IV

THE LITURGICAL YEAR

CHAPTER XVIII

SERVICES OF THE LITURGICAL YEAR
REQUIRING SPECIAL PREPARATIONS

Presentation of our Lord in the Temple, or Candlemas

The Feast of Candlemas, which is celebrated on February 2nd, is logically divided into three parts: first, the Blessing of the Candles; second, the Procession; third, the Celebration of the Holy Eucharist before the Exposed Sacrament. Special preparations are required for the first two parts, and special liturgical directions for the third part.

The preparations are as follows: The altar is bare except for the linen cloths, the six altar candlesticks and the altar cross. A corporal is laid on top of the tabernacle, or the throne, wherever the monstrance is to stand during the Exposition. The bringing in of the Host in procession as part of the symbolism of this Feast is peculiar to this Church. Usage differs as to whether the ciborium containing Hosts for the Communion of the people is left in the tabernacle or not. Some have thought that the symbolism is more complete if the tabernacle is empty, but this involves a certain element of difficulty in regard to the Reserved Sacrament. One way out of this difficulty is to consecrate enough fresh Hosts during the Eucharist at the High Altar to take care of the needs of the people. The sanctuary lamp will then not be lighted. Others think that the symbolism is adequately carried out by the procession of the Host and that there is no need to go to the length of emptying the tabernacle as at the close of Holy Week, and so depriving the church of the blessing of the Reserved Sacrament during the earlier part of the rite. The lamp will then be kept burning. As an alternative use, the ciborium can be placed veiled on the credence table (divested for the time being of its other objects) or on a neighboring side altar, and be brought up ceremonially after the main procession. If altar frontals are used, two should be attached to the altar, a violet frontal over a white frontal, the former so fastened that it may be quickly removed at the time the altar is dressed. Any additional altar candlesticks and candelabra, the vases with flowers and the missal stand are placed either on the steps at each end of the altar, or on a special credence table.

On the usual credence table, in addition to the things regularly required during a celebration of the Holy Eucharist, there should be placed the sacred vessels arranged exactly as when they are carried to the altar before any Eucharist, and the candles to be blessed. If candles are provided only for the clergy, servers and choir, one tray on which the candles are laid may suffice. If, however, there are candles also for the congregation, several trays may be required and an additional table supplied, on which all the trays with candles are placed. The tray (or trays) is covered with a purple or white veil.

The white chasuble and maniple of the celebrant, and (if there is to be High Celebration) the white maniples of the deacon and subdeacon, are laid in their usual places in the sanctuary.

In the vestibule of the church the following should be placed: white cope and stole for the celebrant and (if there is to be High Celebration) white stole and dalmatic for the deacon, white tunicle for the subdeacon. White copes (if available) and white stoles are laid out for those entitled to wear them, There will also be required the canopy (if the canopy and the necessary servers to carry it are available), processional banners (if available), the humeral veil, matches and tapers for lighting the candles. A small table, screened from the view of the people entering the church, should be at hand in one corner of the vestibule. On this table a corporal is laid.

Before the people have arrived at the church, the celebrant, or some priest, should place the lunette with the large reserved Host in the monstrance and cover the monstrance with its veil. Then, vested in surplice, stole and cope and wearing the humeral veil, and preceded by three servers, two carrying candles and one sounding the bell as a warning, the priest carries the monstrance to the vestibule and places it on the corporal on the table. Before the monstrance are placed the two lighted candles. A cleric should guard the sacred Host from this point onward until the Host is carried back to the sanctuary.

Two servers should be instructed to remain behind in the sanctuary, when, after the blessing of the candles, the procession moves to the vestibule of the church. If candles are to be distributed to the people, other servers will be required to assist the people in lighting their candles during the time the procession is in the vestibule.

In order to simplify the description of the ceremony which follows, it is assumed that the celebrant is assisted by a deacon and subdeacon. Should this not be the case, the place of the ministers is taken by the first and second acolytes, who aid the celebrant in all ways lawful to those not ordained to the subdiaconate and Major Orders. In the description it is also assumed that the Hosts for the people have been removed from the tabernacle on the main Altar to a side altar. If this has not been done and the Hosts for the people are still reserved on the main Altar, then instead of bowing to the altar cross, wherever this is prescribed, a genuflection should be made.

The celebrant and ministers vest as for a Eucharist, wearing violet cope, dalmatic and tunicle. Other clergy present vest in surplice and violet stole, and, if available, in violet copes. The procession is arranged in the usual order, but processional candlesticks are not carried to the sanctuary. (All banners are, of course, in the vestibule.) The six altar candles are lighted. (Fortescue, 4th Ed. p. 276) The procession moves to the sanctuary by the shorter way, singing a hymn. All, upon entering the sanctuary, bow to the altar cross and take their customary places. The cope of the celebrant is not removed.

The ceremony of the Asperges now takes place, preferably that of the Shorter Form. This ended, the celebrant and his ministers bow to the altar cross, and go to the credence table on which the candles are laid. The candles are uncovered either by the Master of Ceremonies or an acolyte. Receiving the aspergill from the deacon (or the first acolyte), the celebrant sprinkles the candles thrice in silence, first towards the middle, then the left, then the right. Extending his right hand over them palm down, he says the Exorcism: *Let these candles ... be burned*, making the sign of the cross twice where indicated. Now, sprinkling incense on the charcoal in the censer held open before him by the thurifer, the celebrant blesses it in the usual way, takes the censer and censes the candles in silence with three double swings: middle, left, right. During the sprinkling, exorcism and censing of the candles, the deacon (or the first acolyte) raises the right side of the cope at such times as the right arm of the celebrant is extended. The organ is not played during the foregoing ceremony.

The distribution of the candles now takes place. The priest highest in rank receives a candle from the M.C. and in turn presents it to the celebrant. If no other priest is present the M.C lays the candle for the celebrant unlighted on the altar. In no case may the deacon or subdeacon give the celebrant this candle. (Fortescue, 4th. Ed. p. 277) The celebrant, if given his candle by a priest, in turn gives it to the subdeacon to place unlighted on the altar. The celebrant himself gives a candle to the deacon, subdeacon, Master of Ceremonies, and to any other clergy present, in the order of seniority. Lastly he gives candles to the acolytes and choir, or he may delegate this duty to the ministers, the deacon presenting candles to the acolytes, the subdeacon to the choir. Each one while receiving a candle bows slightly. If candles are to be distributed to the people, two or more acolytes should give them out, either as the people come forward to the altar rail, which is the best way if the congregation is small, or while passing among the people, which is preferable if the congregation is large.

After those in the sanctuary have received their candles the celebrant and his ministers return to the middle before the lowest altar step facing the altar. The clergy and acolytes group themselves symmetrically before the altar. As soon as the distribution is finished and all in the sanctuary are in their places, the celebrant says or intones: *Blessed Lord... our hearts*. After the response he turns to the people and says or sings: *Let as go forth in peace*. As the people respond: *In the Name of the Lord*, he turns back to the altar.

The procession now forms in the sanctuary. All bow to the altar cross, following the lead of the celebrant, put on their birettas, turn by the right and leave the sanctuary, singing a hymn. The procession moves to the vestibule of the church, all carrying unlighted candles with the exception of course of the thurifer, cross bearer, banner bearers and celebrant. The candle of the celebrant is left on the altar, because he must carry the monstrance on his return to the sanctuary.

As soon as the procession nears the vestibule, or has entered the vestibule, those delegated to remain in the sanctuary remove the violet frontal leaving the white frontal exposed, and place on the altar the additional candlesticks and candelabra, the vases with flowers, the missal stand and missal. The sacred vessels are left on the credence. They will be moved later. The additional candles are then lighted. If not too inconvenient the sanctuary lamp is also lighted. In the meantime other servers have been moving along the aisles, provided candles were distributed to the people, lighting the candles of those who are at the ends of the pews. The people should be instructed to pass the light from one to another until all the candles are burning.

In the vestibule the clergy first remove their birettas. The birettas of the celebrant and his ministers are taken at once to the sanctuary by a server and put on their seats. The birettas of the other clergy may also be taken to the sanctuary at the same time, or each may carry his own biretta in procession. All purple vestments are replaced by white. The humeral veil is laid on the shoulders of the officiant. All candles are lit, everyone carrying a candle who can do so conveniently. (The candle is carried in the outside hand, that is, when two people walk side by side, the one on the right carries the candle in the right hand, the one on the left in the left hand.) When the procession is ready all kneel facing the veiled monstrance. The celebrant solemnly unveils the monstrance and, lifting it in his veil-covered hands, takes his place under the canopy. Everyone now rises and faces in the direction the procession is to move. The thurifers walk backwards (as described on p. 47) as they cense the Blessed Sacrament. (If the censers need replenishing in the vestibule before the procession starts, the incense is not blessed.) When all in the vestibule are ready, the candles of the people in the church are lighted, the altar is dressed and the additional altar candles lighted, the organist is signaled, usually by the M.C. As the procession moves back to the sanctuary a hymn is sung. Only a bow is made to the altar cross upon entering the sanctuary by those walking ahead of the celebrant. The clergy go to their usual places, but the candle bearers group themselves on either side of the sanctuary as is done at Solemn Benediction. When the celebrant enters the sanctuary with the monstrance, the canopy bearers retire and all others kneel, except, of course, the celebrant and his ministers. The celebrant places the monstrance on the altar and genuflects with his ministers. The deacon takes down the altar cross if this is necessary (see p. 140) and enthrones the monstrance. (This is done by the celebrant himself if assisted by acolytes only.) The candle bearers rise and go to their customary places in the sanctuary. All in the sanctuary, choir and church now extinguish the candles they have been holding. Before the celebrant leaves the footpace the sacred vessels on the credence are brought to him by the deacon (or the first acolyte). The deacon (or the celebrant) spreads the corporal on the altar before the tabernacle and arranges the vessels in the usual way. Genuflecting again, the celebrant and his ministers step back a pace or two, the celebrant and deacon towards the epistle end of the footpace, the subdeacon towards the gospel end, and descend obliquely to their places before the lowest altar step. Here the celebrant changes from cope to chasuble, and, with his ministers, puts on the maniple.

In small churches where there is a limited number of servers, and in churches where there may not be a suitable vestibule, the second part of the ceremony of Candlemas which has just been described may be simplified. Nothing is prepared in the vestibule of the church. Instead, the lunette with its Host is left in the tabernacle, and the monstrance covered with its veil is placed on the credence. The white stole and cope which will be worn by the celebrant during the procession with the Host are either left in the vestry adjoining the sanctuary, or placed conveniently in the sanctuary itself. The humeral veil is laid on the credence. One server is delegated to remain in the sanctuary after the procession with the Host leaves, in order to dress the altar and light the additional candles while the procession moves round the church. The candles are lighted as soon as they are distributed. Then the celebrant changes to white stole and cope, and now says or intones the prayer: *Blessed Lord ... our hearts*, which is followed by the versicle. After the humeral veil is placed on his shoulders, he ascends to the footpace, places the Host in the monstrance which is brought to him by a server, and takes up the monstrance. Now preceded by the crucifer, two candle bearers carrying the candles given them, and by the thurifer walking backwards, the celebrant goes round the church in procession with the Host, while a hymn is sung. Upon the return of the procession, as soon as the Host is enthroned, the people extinguish their candles.

The celebration of the Holy Eucharist is now resumed. If the Asperges of the Lnger Form was used, the celebrant begins with the Invocation, but if that of the Shorter Form was said, he begins with the words: *Brethren, let us ... our Temple* or the Canticle, respectively.

During the course of the Eucharist those in the sanctuary and choir, and if possible the congregation, should hold lighted candles in their hands while singing the *Adeste Fideles* and while listening to the Gospel. The celebrant will probably be able to hold his candle only during the Gospel and the Recessional Hymn. Servers may be delegated to light the candles at these times, both in the sanctuary and in the church.

If the Hosts reserved at another altar are to be used at the Communion of the people, the deacon, or the celebrant, after his own Communion, should vest in the humeral veil and, preceded by the cross bearer and two candle bearers, go to that altar and return with the ciborium.

When a bishop is celebrant, the mitre, at the time the procession is in the vestibule, may be returned to the sanctuary with the birettas of his ministers, or in the procession back to the sanctuary a bearer, walking beside the crozier bearer, may carry the mitre back to the sanctuary. The subdeacon cannot very well carry the mitre during this procession, because he should hold the cope of the celebrant in his right hand and a lighted candle in his left.

Certain ceremonial points must be carefully observed whenever the Holy Eucharist is celebrated before the Exposed Sacrament. At all times during the course of the Eucharist, the celebrant before turning to face the people while standing in the middle must genuflect, move a little to the gospel side, and then turn to the people by his right. This is done so that he may not turn his back upon the Host. When he turns back to the altar he must again genuflect in the middle. [Note that this second genuflection is omitted from the instructions given on page 78 for celebrating the Holy Eucharist. Ed.] Again, at the *Orate Fratres* after facing the people, he does not turn back to the altar by his right, thus completing the circle, but by his left. (This change in ceremonial direction does not apply to the Benediction at the end, because at that time the Host is again in the tabernacle.) Incense is not blessed in the Presence of the Exposed Sacrament. Birettas, zucchettos and mitres are not worn, nor are bows exchanged as is customary when various ceremonial actions take place. At the censing of the altar, the celebrant and ministers descend obliquely to kneel on the lowest altar step as at Solemn Benediction. After the Host is censed with three triple swings, they rise, ascend to the footpace and cense the altar, omitting, however, the censing of the altar cross. After the Communion of the people, the monstrance is taken down from its throne, and the Host placed in the tabernacle. The monstrance is then veiled and returned to the credence, the altar cross (if removed) restored to its place.

❀ ❀ ❀ ❀ ❀ ❀ ❀

Palm Sunday

There are some preparations to be made on Palm Sunday, in addition to the usual arrangements. The crosses on every altar in the church and the processional cross should be covered with violet veiling or gauze. The usual way is to drape a section of veiling loosely over the cross and tie it at the bottom with a piece of purple ribbon. Palm branches may be placed gracefully between the six altar candlesticks and arranged in other parts of the sanctuary and church. A length of purple ribbon with which to tie a branch of palm to the processional cross, is laid on the credence table. On a special credence table placed on the epistle side of the sanctuary palm branches of various lengths are laid. The longer ones are given to the clergy, the shorter to the acolytes and choir. For the people little branches six to eight inches In length, or little crosses made of folded strips of palm leaves, are prepared and heaped on trays also placed on the special credence table. If there is difficulty in obtaining palms of intermediate size, the clergy and servers are given palms like those of the congregation. The palms can be bought at church shops. The branches on the table are covered with a violet cloth. Only the six altar candles are lighted.

The celebrant and ministers vest as for the Eucharist, the celebrant wearing a purple cope, the deacon and subdeacon (if any) purple dalmatic and tunicle.

The procession forms in the usual order and moves to the sanctuary by the shorter way while a hymn is sung or soft music is played. As they enter the sanctuary the servers and clergy either arrange themselves symmetrically before the altar, or they go to their places. When the celebrant and his ministers reach the lowest altar step, they remove their birettas and genuflect together. The birettas are given to a server to put in some convenient place. The celebrant, flanked by his ministers, goes at once to the special credence table. The M.C. or a server, removes the violet cloth and so uncovers the palm branches. The celebrant sings or says: *Hosanna ... Name of the Lord* and the people respond: *O King ... highest.* Receiving the aspergill from the deacon or M.C. the celebrant sprinkles the palms thrice, once towards the middle, once towards his left, once towards his right. He then says or intones: *Let us pray,* still facing the table of palms. All kneel except the celebrant and his ministers. He says: *O God ... Christ our Lord,* making the sign of the cross over the palms twice as indicated in the Liturgy. After the response the people are seated. The celebrant now blesses incense in the usual manner and, still standing before the table of palms, censes the branches with three double swings; two towards the middle, two towards his left, two towards his right. Returning the censer, the celebrant proceeds to the distribution of the palms to the clergy. The celebrant reserves a palm branch for himself by giving one to the M.C., or a server, to place on the altar. He then gives a branch to the deacon, to the subdeacon, to any bishops present, to the M.C. and to the clergy. Finally the acolytes and choir each receive a branch. In this distribution the ministers may assist the celebrant, so that the service be not unduly delayed. When everyone in the sanctuary and choir has received a branch of palm the celebrant turns to the people and says: *Receive a ... joy and gladness.* Immediately those appointed for the purpose are given trays of small palm branches or crosses and depart to distribute them quickly to the people. In small churches the people may come forward to the altar rail for their branches or crosses, to receive them from the celebrant. Meanwhile the cross bearer fastens a branch of palm to the processional cross, using some violet ribbon.

As soon as all have received branches, the celebrant, facing the altar and holding his palm branch in the right hand, says or sings: *Let us go forth in peace.* The people respond: *In the Name of Christ.* The procession forms as usual, (all putting on their birettas after genuflecting) leaves the sanctuary and moves through the church and out of the vestibule door singing an appropriate hymn. Or, with a view to shortening the service, the hymn may be omitted and the organ play during the outgoing procession. Or verses 1 and 2 of hymn 132 (St. Alban Hymnal) may be sung as the procession moves to the vestibule and verses 3 and 4 as it returns to the sanctuary; hymn 131 being sung whilst the clergy and servers are in the vestibule. When the procession has entirely left the church, those in the vestibule group themselves round the closed door. Following the instructions of the M.C., or someone appointed for the purpose, the people within the church turn round and face the vestibule door. The people and those who have taken part in the procession now sing the hymn: *All glory, laud and honour* in the alternate manner described in the Liturgy. (It may be necessary for the vestibule door to be opened slightly to permit the organist and those outside the vestibule door to keep in time. Usually the organist must follow the singers, and not the singers the organist, simply because the organ cannot be heard by those outside while they are singing.) When the hymn is ended and all is silent in the church, the cross bearer knocks on the vestibule door three times with the lower end of the processional cross. The door is immediately opened, the organist begins the hymn, and the procession returns to the sanctuary. As before, music on the organ may take the place of the third hymn, or verses 3 and 4 of hymn 132 may be sung. As soon as the knock is heard, the people turn back to face the altar.

The palm branches are held by all present during the singing of the *Adeste Fideles*, and the Recessional Hymn, and during the reading of the Gospel. It is intended that the people should take their branches or crosses home after the service and keep them during the ensuing year. In countries where palms do not grow naturally, branches may usually be purchased at Church Stores.

In small churches where there are few clergy and servers the procedure may be altered. The knocks are given on the door before the hymn: *All glory, laud and honour*; that hymn is then sung by all together, the first verse being repeated, and the procession enters during the singing of this hymn.

❀ ❀ ❀ ❀ ❀ ❀

Maundy Thursday

Maundy Thursday is celebrated with festal splendour, the only suggestion of the lenten season being that the altar cross and the processional cross are covered with white veiling or gauze. Many candles are lighted on the altar, there may be two censers, banners may be carried in the procession and there is a procession with the Blessed Sacrament round the church following the singing of the *Adeste Fideles*. During this procession a Litany or some Eucharistic Hymn is sung. In small churches the procession may take place during the singing of the *Adeste Fideles*, no Litany or other hymn being used. If the Eucharist is celebrated in a cathedral church the Blessing of Holy Oils, to be described hereafter, takes place after the procession.

The celebrant should remember to consecrate two large Hosts. One serves for this Celebration, the other is placed in the tabernacle of the High Altar before the First Celebration on Easter Day, or on Saturday evening, if the First Vespers of Easter and Benediction of the Most Holy Sacrament be celebrated.

In the evening of Maundy Thursday the ciborium containing the large Host and the Hosts consecrated for the people, are carried from the tabernacle of the High Altar to the vestry to be placed in a locked tabernacle or other safe place. A light should be kept burning before this place of reservation. If there be an evening service the ciborium may be carried out at the end of the service. First there should be an acolyte carrying the processional cross; then two candle bearers; then the thurifer walking backwards, censing the ciborium; lastly the priest, vested in cope and carrying the ciborium with the use of the humeral veil.

The altar should be stripped of flowers, linen cloths and frontal, leaving only the altar cross and six altar candlesticks. The altar cross is covered with violet veiling and the door of the tabernacle left open. The sanctuary lamp is extinguished.

Good Friday

The Third General Episcopal Synod deleted the Eucharist of the Presanctified from the Services of Good Friday and Holy Saturday. This implies that the only service permissible on the morning of Good Friday is that of Prime. The altar is covered with a plain linen cloth. If a frontal is used the colour should be violet. No candles are lighted on the altar or carried in procession; there are no flowers on the altar; the altar cross and processional cross are covered with violet veiling; the tabernacle door is left open; incense is not used. The hymn: *Take up thy cross, our Master said,* (Liturgy, Second Edition, p. 74)[Liturgy, Third Edition, p. 80-81. Ed.] may be sung.

❀ ❀ ❀ ❀ ❀ ❀ ❀

Holy Saturday

At a convenient time before the service on Holy Saturday, the priest, or one delegated by him, should, with the aid of a lens, kindle fire by means of the rays of the sun. If this is impossible, the fire may be struck from flint and steel. Implements of this sort, for lighting gas fires, can be bought. The fire is placed in a suitable vessel and maintained by laying on it small pieces of wood, A server should be assigned the duty of looking after the fire until the ceremony of the Blessing of the Fire takes place in the vestibule of the church. This server should also see that some pieces of charcoal are prepared for the censer just before the ceremony begins. The best way to do this is to place the charcoal in a coarse wire basket with a long handle over the fire. (Such baskets are sold in some Church Stores for the purpose of lighting incense charcoal.)

The altar is prepared as for Prime on Good Friday. The missal stand will not be required. On its support in the sanctuary the empty censer is hung. On the credence is placed the incense boat, holy water and the aspergill, and a tray on which are laid five grains of incense (preferably olibanum) each contained in a nail-shaped case of wood or metal, or pressed into a nail-shaped piece of wax. (The cases are obtained in Catholic Shops where the paschal candle and triple candle are sold. They fit into five holes in the paschal candle.) On the gospel side of the sanctuary near the altar the unlighted paschal candle in its massive candlestick is placed. Near it should be a stand or holder in which to put the triple candle. To the west of the paschal candle may stand a lectern on which is laid the book containing the Gospel to be read. This lectern should so stand that the reader of the Gospel faces *north*. (Instead of a lectern it is permissible for the Book of Gospels to be held by a server, in the usual way.)

In the vestibule there should be placed before the service the vessel containing the fire, some incense charcoal and tongs. Near at hand is a table covered with a white cloth on which is laid a white stole and either a white cope or a white dalmatic, depending upon circumstances mentioned in the next paragraph. On the table or in a special holder is placed the triple candle. If there is to be a baptism, the font should be prepared in the customary manner for this ceremony, except that plain water and not baptismal water is placed in the font. Near it should stand a bowl of salt and a copy of the ritual containing the Form for the Blessing of Baptismal Water. In a small church, in order to dispense with the procession from the sanctuary to the font, the font may be placed before the sanctuary rail, provided there is to be a baptism.

The vestments worn during the saying of Prim are as prescribed in Chapter XII. If the Mass of the Presanctified be not sung, the vestments worn for the Blessing of the Fire are as follows: for the priest a surplice, purple stole and purple cope; for the deacon a surplice, purple stole worn after the manner of a deacon, and a purple cope; for the subdeacon a surplice and purple cope. If these vestments are worn, or if the priest is officiating alone without the assistance of a deacon and subdeacon, then in the vestibule are placed a white stole and a white cope. But in those churches where three purple copes are not available, then the priest and his ministers vest in amice, alb and girdle, and in addition the priest wears a purple stole crossed in front and a purple cope; the deacon a purple stole worn after the manner of a deacon and a purple dalmatic; the subdeacon a purple tunicle. The maniple is not worn. All three wear birettas, except when otherwise directed. When these vestments just mentioned are used, then in the vestibule are placed a white stole and white dalmatic.

In the following description of the ceremony of the Blessing of the Fire it is assumed that the officiant is assisted by a deacon and subdeacon, and that there is a M.C., a thurifer and two acolytes. At the end of this description, however, will be indicated those changes required in the ceremony when the officiant is not assisted by a deacon and subdeacon.

The clergy process to the sanctuary and Prime is said, not sung, as on Good Friday, except of course the lections read are those of Holy Saturday. At the end of the service the hymn: *Take up thy cross, the Master said*, may be sung, During the hymn the priest and the two who are to assist him as ministers retire to the vestry and vest for the ceremony of the Blessing of the Fire.

The Blessing of the Fire

Returning to the sanctuary the officiant and his ministers go to stand before the lowest altar step. Removing their birettas they bow to the altar cross and give the birettas to the M.C. or to a server. The officiant now says the Invocation, receives the aspergill and asperses himself, the altar and the people using the Shorter Form of the Asperges. At the end of the Asperges, the officiant and deacon (and of course other nonofficiating clergy) put on their birettas, but the biretta of the subdeacon is left behind in the sanctuary inasmuch as he is to carry the processional cross. The subdeacon goes to get the processional cross, the thurifer the empty censer, the first acolyte the aspergill which has been dipped in holy water, the second acolyte the tray with the five grains of incense. The procession now forms in the sanctuary as follows: The three servers walk in front, the first acolyte in the middle carrying the officiant's missal and the aspergill, the thurifer to his right carrying the empty censer and the boat with incense, the second acolyte to his left carrying the tray with incense grains. Behind them walking alone is the subdeacon with the processional cross. Then the choir (if any) and nonofficiating clergy. Lastly comes the officiant, with the deacon to his right and the M.C. to his left. (Fig. 1) Following the lead of the officiant all bow to the altar cross, turn by the right and move in procession from the sanctuary to the vestibule. The procession is without processional candles, banners or incense.

Fig. 1

Upon reaching the vestibule, the clergy and choir group themselves to the north and to the south of the vessel with the fire (which may stand upon a table) the clergy of higher rank being nearest the officiant. The subdeacon with the processional cross takes his position in the east (with his back towards the High Altar) facing west; the officiant stands opposite him facing east; between the two is the vessel with the fire. To the left of the officiant stands the first acolyte holding the officiant's missal and the aspergill; to the right of the officiant is the deacon and beyond him the M.C. Behind the M.C. the thurifer with the empty censer and the second acolyte holding the tray with the incense grains take their places. (Fig. 2)

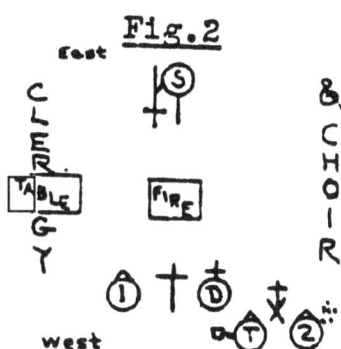

Fig. 2

The officiant and deacon take off their birettas and give them to the M.C. The officiant now blesses the fire, saying: *Let this fire ... kindled*, making the sign of the cross over it twice as indicated, the first acolyte meanwhile holding up the book so that the officiant may read. The deacon (or the M.C. when the deacon is not available) holds up the end of the cope whenever in blessing, sprinkling or incensing during the ceremony in the vestibule the officiant must raise his right hand. The thurifer now goes to the vessel of fire and with the tongs puts some of the glowing incense charcoal into the censer. While he is doing this the second acolyte holds before the officiant the tray with the five grains of incense. The officiant blesses the incense, making the sign of the cross twice, while saying: *Let this incense ... dedicated.* The thurifer then goes to the officiant with the opened censer and the incense boat. The officiant sprinkles incense on the charcoal and blesses it with the usual formula, the deacon assisting by holding the boat. The thurifer steps back and the deacon gives the aspergill (which he receives from the first acolyte) to the officiant, who sprinkles first the fire and then the grains of incense. Returning the aspergill to the deacon (who gives it to the first acolyte) he receives the censer from the deacon and censes first the fire and then the grains of incense with three single swings in the usual sequence: middle, left, right. He returns the censer to the deacon, who gives it to the thurifer.

The deacon, bowing to the officiant, now goes to the table and (assisted if need be by the first acolyte) takes off the violet vestments and puts on the white ones. Taking the triple candle, he lights it at the fire (using a taper, if need be, to prevent the wax of the triple candle from melting) and goes to stand in front of the officiant. The latter blesses the candle, saying: *Let this candle ... world.* The procession now forms in this order: First the thurifer with the second acolyte at his right carrying the tray with the. incense grains; then the subdeacon with the cross walking alone; the choir and nonofficiating clergy; the deacon holding the lighted triple candle; lastly the officiant with the M.C. to his left and the first acolyte to his right. (Fig. 3) The officiant wears his biretta, but the deacon does not. (Sometime, during or immediately after the procession, the server who has tended the fire carries the aspergill and the deacon's biretta back to the sanctuary.)

Fig. 3

Upon signal from the M.C. (or officiant) the procession starts back to the sanctuary. As soon as the officiant is inside the church, the procession halts at a signal, usually from the thurifer, all genuflect, except the subdeacon with the cross. While genuflecting the clergy remove their birettas. Before anyone rises, the deacon sings: *Christ is our Light*, the people responding: *May His Light shine in our hearts*. All now rise and the procession moves to the point where the deacon is about midway between the vestibule door and the sanctuary gates. Again it halts on signal and the versicle is sung exactly as before. This is repeated for the third time as the deacon approaches the sanctuary gates, and for the fourth time when he stands before the lowest altar step.

As they approach the altar the various members of the procession group themselves before the lowest altar step as follows: The thurifer stands at the gospel side; the second acolyte with the incense grains at the epistle side; the subdeacon with cross to the right of the thurifer, the first acolyte to the left of the second acolyte; the officiant in the middle with the deacon to his right and the M.C. to his left. (Fig. 4)

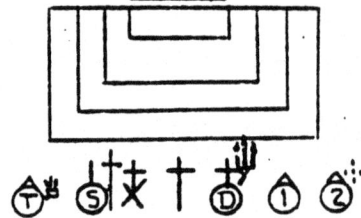

Fig. 4

After the last versicle has been sung by the deacon, he gives the triple candle to the first acolyte to hold. The officiant, giving his biretta to the M.C., ascends to the footpace to stand in the middle facing south. The deacon likewise ascends to kneel on the edge of the footpace to the epistle side. (The position of the two is the same as at the *Munda cor Meum* in the Holy Eucharist.) The deacon now says or intones the *Munda cor Meum* and the officiant the blessing which follows. The deacon thereupon rises, walks to the middle on the deacon's step; faces the people and says or sings: *The Lord be with you*, the usual response being made by all. The deacon now descends the steps to go to the paschal candle. As he does so the officiant walks to the epistle end of the footpace and turns to face the paschal candle. Upon reaching the sanctuary floor the deacon turns to face the altar and bows to the altar cross. All standing before the lowest altar step bow with him and go directly to their places near the paschal candle as follows,

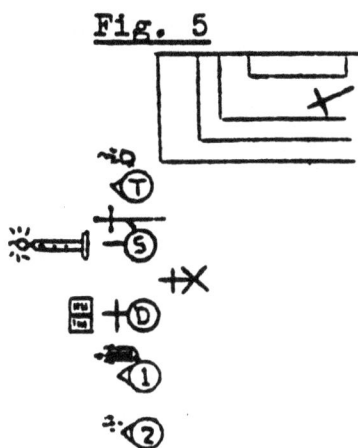

Fig. 5

all facing north. The deacon stands before the lectern, at his left being the first acolyte with the triple candle and to the west of him the second acolyte with the incense grains. At the right of the deacon stands the subdeacon before the paschal candle still holding the cross, then the thurifer with the censer, The M.C. stands to the right of the deacon, a little to the rear. (Fig. 5)

Receiving the censer from the thurifer, the deacon censes the Book of Gospels on the lectern with three double swings in the usual way. Returning the censer and joining his hands, he reads the Gospel: *In the beginning... grace and truth.* All genuflect and remain kneeling on one knee while the deacon is saying: *And the Word was made Flesh.* The Gospel ended, the deacon goes to the paschal candle, the second acolyte with the incense grains on the tray accompanying him. The deacon now places the nail-shaped holders or cases of metal or wax containing the incense grains in the holes in the paschal candle in the order shown in Fig. 6.

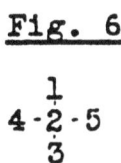

Fig. 6

```
    1
    +
4 - 2 - 5
    +
    3
```

The celebrant, remaining in his place at the epistle end of the footpace, lifts his right hand palm towards the candle and blesses it, saying: *Let this candle... burned.*

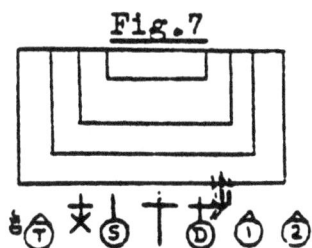

Taking the triple candle, the deacon lights the paschal candle, usually with the aid of a taper. The subdeacon then hands the processional cross to the first acolyte to fix in its holder. The deacon, carrying the triple candle and accompanied by the subdeacon, walks to the middle to stand before the lowest altar step. The ministers are joined by the celebrant, who descends the steps to stand between them. The M.C. and acolytes take their places to the right of the deacon and to the left of the subdeacon (Fig. 7) the M.C. standing where previously the subdeacon stood. The deacon alone then ascends to the footpace and with the triple candle lights the six altar candlesticks. He may also light any other lamps of the church, save that which burns

Fig. 7

before the Blessed Sacrament. Descending to his place beside the officiant, he gives the triple candle to the first acolyte to place in its holder. The officiant and his ministers now ascend to the footpace. Facing the altar, the officiant says or intones: *Let us pray*, and with hands extended says the prayer: *Blessed Lord ... righteousness*. If there is not to be a baptism, the procession forms in the usual way (one of the acolytes carrying the processional cross) and returns to the vestry.

But if there is to be a baptism, a procession forms (unless the font has been placed before the altar rail) in the following order: Thurifer, first acolyte carrying the triple candle, second acolyte with the processional cross, choir, nonofficiating clergy, the M.C., lastly the officiant walking between his ministers. All wear their birettas. Arriving at the font they uncover. The officiant and his ministers stand facing the font, the first acolyte with the triple candle standing to the right of the deacon, the M.C. to the left of the subdeacon. The crucifer and thurifer stand on the opposite side of the font facing the officiant. The others group themselves round the font. (Fig. 8)

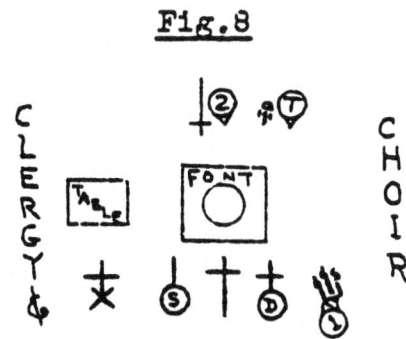

Fig. 8

The officiant first blesses the baptismal water, using the Form for the Blessing of Holy Water, but adding the prayer which is said whenever holy water is to be used for the purpose of baptism. Then the deacon, receiving the triple candle from the first acolyte, hands it to the officiant, who lowers the base of the triple candle into the baptismal water and traces with it in the water the sign of the cross thrice while saying: *In the Name ... Holy Ghost*. He now returns the triple candle to the deacon (who in turn gives it to the first acolyte) and proceeds in the usual way with the baptism. Throughout the ceremony the subdeacon holds the book for the priest, while the M.C. brings what is needed from the nearby table. The baptism ended, the procession forms and returns to the vestry .

The Ceremony in a Small Church

When the priest in charge of a small church performs the ceremony of the Blessing of the Fire without the assistance of a deacon and subdeacon and with only a few acolytes to help, the following changes in the ceremony, and in the preparations therefore, are necessary.

In the vestibule, *in addition* to the preparations previously mentioned, there is placed on the table a missal stand, the tray with the five grains of incense in their cases, and the incense boat. The empty censer is also placed nearby. (It is helpful if, instead of the priest carrying the missal from the sanctuary to the vestibule, a book containing the words to be said in the vestibule is laid, open at the proper place, on the missal stand.) The fire is kindled as previously described and is put in a suitable vessel, which may stand upon the table. The acolyte prepares the charcoal for the censer. The aspergill will be needed in the sanctuary during the Asperges and is therefore not taken to the vestibule beforehand.

Four servers vested in cotta or surplice are desirable, three to serve in the sanctuary from the beginning and one to guard the fire in the vestibule and return in procession to the sanctuary after the Blessing of the Fire. If need be, the processional cross can be dispensed with, also the guarding of the fire.

The Shorter Form of the Asperges may be said, the first and second acolytes standing on either side of the priest as at the Eucharist. The order of the procession to the vestibule is as follows: Thurifer walking with joined hands, second acolyte carrying the processional cross, first acolyte carrying the aspergill (possibly the book), the officiant wearing his biretta. (If there are any nonofficiating clergy, they should walk behind the processional cross.)

Fig.9

In the vestibule the cross bearer stands to the east of the fire facing west, the officiant opposite him facing east; to the right of the officiant stands the thurifer and to his left the first acolyte with the aspergill. (The third acolyte, who has guarded the fire, stands somewhere near the table where he may assist at the fire and in the change of vestments.) (Fig. 9)

The officiant removes his biretta, and blesses the fire as previously described. The thurifer then prepares the censer (with the assistance of the third acolyte) and presents it to the officiant for the blessing of the incense. This done, the thurifer steps back and the officiant, receiving the aspergill from the first acolyte, asperses the fire and the grains of incense which lie on the tray on the table before him. Then, taking the censer, he censes the fire and the grains of incense. Returning the censer, he goes to the table upon which the vestments lie and changes from purple to white cope. Taking up the triple candle, he lights it at the fire. Giving the candle to the first acolyte to hold (the latter will have placed the aspergill on the table) the officiant blesses the candle and then takes it into his own hands.

Fig.10

The procession to the sanctuary now forms as follows: First the thurifer, walking side by side with the third acolyte carrying the tray with the incense grains, then the second acolyte with the processional cross, then the nonofficiating clergy (if any), last the officiant carrying the lighted triple candle and with the first acolyte walking by his side, to the right and slightly to the rear, carrying the biretta of the officiant and assisting the latter to rise, if need be, after each genuflection. (Fig. 10)

During the procession to the altar the officiant genuflects and sings the versicle: *Christ is our Light*, exactly as described previously. As they approach the altar the various members of the procession arrange themselves before the lowest altar step as follows: The thurifer to the gospel side, the third acolyte with the incense grains to the epistle side, the officiant in the middle, with the first acolyte to his right and the second acolyte to his left. (Fig. 11)

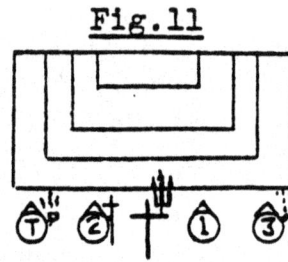

After the last versicle is sung the officiant gives the triple candle to the first acolyte to hold. He then ascends to the footpace and, standing in the middle, says the Munda cor Meum and the prayer which follows exactly in the same way as at the Eucharist. This ended, he says or sings the Minor Benediction and descends to the middle before the lowest altar step, all bow to the altar cross and go to the gospel side, standing in the following order, all facing north: The officiant takes his place in front of the lectern, the cross bearer is to his right in front of the paschal candle, beyond him is the thurifer. To the left of the officiant stands the first acolyte with the lighted triple candle, and beyond him the third acolyte with the incense grains. (Fig. 12)

After the Book of Gospels has been censed and the Gospel read, the incense grains in their cases are placed in the holes of the paschal candle, and the officiant, standing before the candle, blesses it saying: *Let this candle ... burned.*

Taking the triple candle the officiant now lights the paschal candle. The processional cross is now put away and all go to stand before the lowest altar step, occupying the same positions as indicated in Fig. 11. The officiant alone ascends to the footpace and with the triple candle or taper lights the six altar candles. This ended, he gives the triple candle to the first acolyte to place in its holder, and proceeds with the prayer: *Blessed Lord ... righteousness*, after saying or intoning: *Let us Pray.*

If there is to be a baptism, and the font is at a distance from the altar rail, a procession is formed as follows: Thurifer, first acolyte carrying the lighted triple candle, second acolyte with the processional cross, lastly the officiant with the third acolyte walking beside him to the left and slightly to the rear. The latter may carry, if desired, the book containing the wording of the ceremonies for the Blessing of Holy Water and Holy Baptism. The officiant wears his biretta. At the font the officiant and the second acolyte with the processional cross stand facing each other, one on either side of the font (Fig. 13); the first acolyte with the triple candle stands to the right of the officiant, the third acolyte to the left of the officiant. The thurifer stands to the left of the second acolyte, facing the first acolyte.

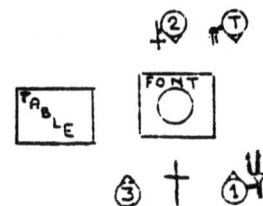

Should there be a priest or deacon to assist the officiant, that priest or deacon will vest in dalmatic and carry the triple candle in procession, preceding the officiant. In the evening, the First Vespers of Easter and Benediction of the Most Holy Sacrament may be celebrated. The altar cross and processional cross are unveiled, the colour is white, and the altar and sanctuary may be adorned with flowers. Many candles should blaze on the altar and the service is celebrated with festal splendour.

In the Roman Rite, inasmuch as Benediction is not a Liturgical service, the paschal candle in the Easter season is not lighted at Benediction of the Most Holy Sacrament, unless it is preceded by a liturgical service at which the paschal candle is lit. (Fortescue, 4th Ed., p. 365) In the Liberal Catholic Rite the paschal candle is lighted during the Easter season at Celebrations of the Eucharist at the High Altar, at Vespers and at Benediction. If the Holy Eucharist is celebrated during the week at a side altar, it is permitted to move the paschal candle to that altar, and it will be returned to its place before the High Altar for the Sunday services.

❀ ❀ ❀ ❀ ❀ ❀ ❀

Easter Sunday

Easter is the greatest Festival of the Christian Year and every effort should be made to adorn the altar, sanctuary and church as sumptuously as possible. Every available candlestick and candelabra should be used so that the altar is a blaze of light. There should, if possible, be two thurifers, many processional candles and banners. There may be a procession round the church with the Sacred Host after the singing of the *Adeste Fideles*, during which a Litany or Eucharistic Hymn is sung. In small churches this procession may take place during the singing of the *Adeste Fideles*. The order of such a procession is the same as that during Solemn Benediction and the same preparations should be made. As in all cases where a procession with the Host takes place at this part of the Eucharistic Service, a cleric in vestments must remain in the sanctuary to guard the Blessed Sacrament which remains upon the altar. He may stand at the south end of the altar steps, or kneel on the lowest step.

❀ ❀ ❀ ❀ ❀ ❀ ❀

Ascension Day

Ascension Day is celebrated with festal splendour, an abundance of candles and flowers, if available, being placed on the altar. After the reading of the Gospel and the deacon has censed the celebrant, the latter is given an extinguisher. He reverently extinguishes the paschal candle while saying: *The great forty days ... continually dwell.* The putting out of the flame should be made to coincide with the saying of the word: *extinguish*.

The unlighted paschal candle remains in the sanctuary until after the service when it is taken to the vestry. If available for a further period of use, it will not be required until Holy Saturday of the year following.

❋ ❋ ❋ ❋ ❋ ❋ ❋

Corpus Christi

Corpus Christi falls on the Thursday following Trinity Sunday. The celebration of the Holy Eucharist on this Festival should be marked by a procession round the Church with the Sacred Host after the singing of the *Adeste Fideles*. In small churches this procession may take place during the singing of the *Adeste Fideles*. The order of the procession is the same as that in Benediction of the Most Holy Sacrament and the same preparations should be made. On the Sunday following Corpus Christi, in addition to the procession with the Host, it is permissible to celebrate the Holy Eucharist before the Blessed Sacrament Exposed. As always when such a procession takes place, a cleric in vestments remains in the sanctuary, at the south end of the altar steps, to guard the Blessed Sacrament remaining on the altar.

❋ ❋ ❋ ❋ ❋ ❋ ❋

All Souls' Day

In preparation for All Souls' Day the members of the congregation should be asked to send in the names of those in whom they are personally interested, who have died during the preceding year. It is well to give notice to this effect at least two weeks before All Souls' Day. The people should be asked to write the names carefully and in full, it being explained that in the Church of Christ, Christian names have a value and significance. A list of these names is laid on the altar before the service and they are read aloud by the celebrant (except when the request is made that they be read silently) at the usual place in the Consecration Prayer. In some churches the names are read immediately before the *Orate Fratres*, the reading being preceded by the statement: *The prayers of the Church are asked for....* This arrangement is preferable if there are many names.

Though the colour is violet, there should be no trace of mourning in the Celebration. The altar is adorned with flowers, many candles are lighted, there may be two thurifers, and banners may be carried in the procession. Note that All Souls' Day ends at sunset, so that if Vespers be celebrated they should be of All Saints' Day and the colour is white. If he so desires, a priest may celebrate three times on All Souls' Day.

Christmas

One of the most popular services of the Church, attended oftentimes by large numbers of people who apparently rarely come on other occasions, is that of the Midnight Eucharist on Christmas Eve. The Eucharist, if sung, should not start earlier than 11.30 p.m. so that the actual consecration will take place at or after midnight. If the Eucharist is said it should start later. The service may be preceded by a half-hour of music, especially if there is a good pipe organ in the church. The violin, harp and human voice may heighten the effect of this occasion. There should be many candles and the altar, sanctuary and church ought to be sumptuously adorned. A procession of the Blessed Sacrament may follow the *Adeste Fideles*. In small churches this procession may take place during the singing of the *Adeste Fideles*. The order of the procession is the same as at Solemn Benediction, and a cleric will be left in the sanctuary to guard the Blessed Sacrament remaining upon the altar. If possible, the Midnight Eucharist should be a High Celebration with deacon and subdeacon.

On Christmas it is permissible for each priest, should he so desire, to celebrate the Holy Eucharist three times: at the Midnight Eucharist, at dawn, and on Christmas Day.

❀ ❀ ❀ ❀ ❀ ❀ ❀

Dedication Festival

The anniversary of the Consecration of a Church by a bishop should always be observed as a Dedication Festival. This Festival takes precedence of all but the greatest Festivals and has an octave. If the Dedication Festival does not fall on a Sunday, the special ceremonies may be repeated on, or reserved for, the Sunday within the octave, but not on the octave itself. If the Dedication Festival intrude on another Class A Festival, or if it fall in Lent or Advent, it should be transferred to the nearest convenient date.

The Holy Eucharist is celebrated with festal splendour and, if possible, it should be High Celebration with deacon and subdeacon. As there will be a procession with the Blessed Sacrament, the same preparations as at Solemn Benediction should be made.

The procession in the usual order enters the sanctuary by the shorter way. There may be a short hymn. After the Asperges, the priest repeats the Collects in the Form for the Consecration of a Church (pp. 387-391 in the *Liturgy*, 2nd Edition) [pp. 404-410 in the *Liturgy*, 3rd Edition. Ed.] as follows: Standing in the middle before the lowest altar step the priest says or intones: *O God, Whose wisdom ...Thy holy truth, through Christ our Lord*. The procession reforms and leaves the sanctuary by the central gates. As it moves along the walls of the church towards the Ray Cross in the southeast corner, the first two verses of the hymn: *Blessed City, heavenly Salem*, are sung. The procession halts opposite the cross. The celebrant bows to the Ray Cross, turns to face the congregation, and either says or intones: *O Thou Whose beauty... indwelling Presence; through Christ our Lord*. The third verse of the hymn is sung as the procession moves to the Ray

Cross in the southwest corner. Here the priest says: *O Thou great ...Thy sight; through Christ our Lord*, having first bowed to the cross and turned to the congregation, as is done in each case. The fourth verse is sung as the procession moves to the cross in the west. The priest then says: *O God, the King ... glorious service; through Christ our Lord*. The fifth verse of the hymn is sung as the procession moves to the cross in the northwest corner, where the priest says: *O Christ the Lord ... infinite Light; through Christ our Lord*. The sixth verse is sung as the procession moves towards the cross in the northeast comer, where the priest says: *O God, Who meetest...earthly life; through Christ our Lord*. As the procession moves to the Ray Cross in the centre of the church the seventh verse of the hymn is sung. Here the priest says: *O God, the Rock of Ages ... holy service; through Christ our Lord*. Lastly the eighth verse is sung as the procession enters the sanctuary.

The Celebration of the Holy Eucharist begins as usual, the Collect, Epistle and Gospel of the Service of the Consecration of a Church being used. During the hymn, *Adeste Fideles*, the Host is placed in the monstrance and when the hymn is ended the procession, in the order of that at Solemn Benediction, moves out through the sanctuary gates and round the church while a litany is sung. In small churches this procession may take place during the singing of the Adeste Fideles. A cleric in vestments (preferably a priest or deacon) should remain in the sanctuary near the altar to guard the Host thereon, Upon the return of the procession to the sanctuary the Eucharist is continued to its close.

❀ ❀ ❀ ❀ ❀ ❀ ❀

Festival of a Patron Saint

On the Day assigned in the Christian Calendar to the Saint who is the Patron Saint of a Church, there should be a sung Celebration of the Holy Eucharist. If possible there should be a High Celebration, with deacon and subdeacon, and with the use of many altar candles, banners, and two thurifers. Such a Festival in honour of a Patron Saint has, for that Church, the rank of Class A with an Octave. If the Festival of a Patron Saint does not fall on a Sunday, the Festival should be repeated on, or reserved for, the Sunday within the Octave. If it conflicts with another Class A Festival, or if it fall in Lent or Advent, it should be transferred to the nearest convenient date. The colour of the vestments is either red or white depending upon whether the Saint was a Martyr or not. This is determined by the calendar.

The Collect of the Day is as follows: *We praise Thee O Lord, for the example and assistance given to us by Thy holy [martyr] St. N, the Patron of our church, and we pray Thee that under* his *protection this Church may continually serve Thee in all good works. Through Christ our Lord.* ℞*./ Amen.* The Epistle and Gospel shall be the same as those appointed for the Feast of St. George. [In the Third Edition of *The Liturgy* the appointed Epistle and Gospel are those for the Patron Saint of a Country. Ed.] There may be a procession with the Blessed Sacrament after or during the singing of the *Adeste Fideles*, the order of procession being as at Solemn Benediction and the usual guard remaining in the sanctuary to safeguard the Host remaining on the altar. In the evening Vespers and Solemn Benediction may be sung.

Anniversary of the Consecration of a Bishop

The anniversary of the consecration of a bishop in charge of a Province, or of a bishop in charge of a Diocese, may be celebrated in that Province or Diocese with festal honour. The colour is white and many candles are lighted on the altar. The Collect is that entitled "For a Bishop," appearing in the Liturgy under the heading "Occasional Prayers" (p. 416) [Third Edition of *The* Liturgy, Pg. 415. Ed.] and the Epistle and Gospel are those appointed for Whitsunday.

❊ ❊ ❊ ❊ ❊ ❊ ❊

Solemn *Te Deum*

On national holidays and other days of rejoicing a Solemn *Te Deum* may be sung. This takes place before the Holy Eucharist. The procession moves to the sanctuary in the usual way, but the clergy and servers, instead of going to their seats, arrange themselves symmetrically before the altar, the celebrant and his ministers standing in the middle before the lowest altar step. Behind the celebrant should be stationed one or two thurifers, swinging a censer to and fro. After the usual genuflection before the altar, the national anthem may be sung by all, provided the day is a national holiday or one of national rejoicing. The *Te Deum* from Vespers is now sung, preceded and followed by the usual antiphon. The celebrant alone sings the opening words: *We praise Thee, O God.* At the close of the *Te Deum* the clergy go to their places, the servers retire with the processional candles, the thurifers put away the censers, and the Eucharist begins as usual.

✠

✠ ✠ ✠

✠

PART V[1]

EPISCOPAL FUNCTIONS

CHAPTER XIX

CONFIRMATION

Confirmation may take place in the morning, afternoon or evening. If there are a large number of candidates, it is best to arrange the Confirmation as a separate service, but if there are only a few persons to confirm the sacrament may be administered in the morning during the celebration of the Holy Eucharist, or in the evening preceding Benediction of the Most Holy Sacrament. If the ceremony takes place during the Eucharist, it is customary to omit the sermon and to confirm after the reading of the Gospel. It is preferable that Confirmation take place in the morning.

The Candidates should at least be old enough to understand something of the significance of the ceremony in which they are to participate. The age differs between the sexes and varies in individuals. Usually it is between ten and fourteen years, but there may be exceptions at either end of this age limit, as applied to adolescents. Older people who have not been previously confirmed may of course receive this sacrament at any age.

Candidates do not require sponsors for this Sacrament, but if the baptismal sponsors are still alive and able to attend, it is a pleasing custom to ask them to be seated near the candidates. In the Liberal Catholic Rite a name is not usually taken at Confirmation (although this may be done, if desired) so there is generally no need to supply each candidate with a card bearing his Confirmation name. The candidates need not wear any special dress, nor are girls and women asked to cover their heads; in fact their heads should be uncovered so that the bishop may experience no difficulty in placing his hand on the head during the Confirmation. All the candidates should be seated either on special seats placed before the sanctuary gates, or in the front pews of the church. Provision should be made so that they may kneel in comfort during the service, and on each seat a book containing the service should be laid. Children to be confirmed should be so placed that they may come up first.

On the credence table are placed a vessel with water and a lavabo towel, a bowl containing bread crumbs and a slice of lemon, a gremial to place on the bishop's lap, an oilstock containing Chrism, and some cotton wool.

Only the six altar candles need be lighted, but it is customary to light a number of additional candles so as to give the occasion a touch of festal beauty. The altar may be adorned with flowers. If Confirmation is arranged as a separate service a white altar frontal is used, but if it takes place in connection with some other service, a frontal of the colour used at that service will suffice. A book stand will not be needed for the service of Confirmation itself. Before the altar in the middle on the footpace a faldstool or suitable chair will be placed during the Confirmation ceremony. If Confirmation takes place in connection with some other service, this faldstool may stand at some convenient spot in the sanctuary (usually on the gospel side) until it is needed. If Confirmation alone is to take place, the faldstool may be put on the footpace before the ceremony begins. The faldstool may be covered with a white silken cover. Near at hand should be a white cushion or kneeling pad, which will be needed at the time the candidates kneel before the bishop.

The bishop wears the rochet, white stole, white cope, mitre, pectoral cross and ring. He uses the crozier. If required by the needs of another service, he may vest in amice, alb and girdle instead of the rochet. Those assisting in the ceremony wear the surplice, and a white stole and a biretta, if their rank entitles them to do so.

The bishop will need at least two assistants, who may be priests or of lesser rank. One of them, who stands at his left as he is seated in the faldstool, will hold the crozier and service book; the other on his right will hold the oil stock (and cotton wool if desired). Other servers, if available, are useful. There may be a thurifer, a cross bearer, and two or more candle bearers. These servers are also helpful in the sanctuary in handling the faldstool, cushion and gremial, and assisting with the lemon and crumb, water and towel when the bishop cleanses his hands. There should be a member of the clergy, preferably the priest of the parish, to present the candidates.[2]

The Ceremony

If the Confirmation ceremony has been arranged as a separate service, a procession is formed which goes, either by the short way, or round the church, to the sanctuary. A processional hymn may be sung.

If, however, the ceremony is to take place during a Celebration of the Holy Eucharist, the clergy who are to take part in it are already in the sanctuary. After the reading of the Gospel and while any announcements are being made, the bishop (if he is also the celebrant) changes from chasuble and stole of the colour of the Day to white stole and cope. Meanwhile the a server places the faldstool or chair upon the footpace in the middle facing the people.

The bishop, wearing the mitre and holding the crozier, and accompanied by his assistants, goes to his place in the middle before the lowest altar step facing the altar. The bishop and his assistants genuflect together. The bishop intones or says the Invocation (unless Confirmation is given during the Eucharist). Ascending to the footpace with his assistants, the bishop turns to face the people, gives the crozier to the assistant at his left and is seated in the faldstool. He retains the mitre, but his assistants should be without birettas.

If desired, a short address may be delivered at this time to the candidates, explaining to them the nature of the sacrament and the responsibilities which fall to those who receive it. Generally, however, this is unnecessary, because the candidates will have already received the necessary instruction in a confirmation class.

If there are children to be confirmed, the bishop begins the Charge with the words: *My beloved children, on your....* If the candidates are all, or practically all, adults he begins: *Since you are members....* At the end of the Charge all the candidates rise and the bishop proceeds to the Interrogations, to each of which the candidates answer: *I Will.* The candidates now kneel and the bishop, rising, blesses them saying: "May the blessing ... your ways." During the blessing the bishop holds the crozier in his left hand and extends his right in the usual manner towards the candidates.

The bishop and his assistants now turn to face the altar. Still retaining his mitre and holding the crozier in both hands, he kneels with his assistants on the edge of the footpace during the singing of the *Veni Creator.* At the end of the hymn all rise and the people and candidates are seated. The bishop with mitre is seated in the faldstool. The assistants face the people, the one on the left of the bishop holding the crozier. A server brings the gremial, cotton wool and oil stock with the Chrism. The gremial is spread upon the knees of the bishop, the oil stock and cotton wool given to the assistant at his right. The cushion is placed on the step below the bishop. The crozier bearer holds the service book at such an angle that it may easily be read, if necessary, by the bishop.

At a signal from the bishop, the parish priest (or one appointed for the purpose) goes to the epistle end of the line of candidates and leads the first one forward to the bishop. Thereafter, with well-instructed candidates, it is only necessary for the parish priest to beckon each candidate when his turn comes to go forward, the priest meeting him at the sanctuary gates. On reaching the sanctuary the candidate genuflects, and then is instructed to kneel on the cushion and to place his hands together, palm to palm, on the lap of the bishop. The latter places his hands together one on either side of those of the candidate. Prompted, if need be, the candidate says: *Right (Most) Reverend Father, I offer ... service.* Lightly pressing the candidate's hands, the bishop replies: *In Christ's ... accept thee.*

Turning to the assistant at his right, the bishop moistens his right thumb with Chrism. Taking the crozier in his left hand and laying his right hand on the head of the candidate, he says: *Receive the Holy ... godly life.* (If a Confirmation Name is to be taken by the candidate, the bishop addresses the candidate by this name before saying the words of Confirmation.) Without pause he continues: *whereunto ... the cross,* with these words making the sign of the cross with his thumb on the forehead of the neophyte. After the words: *and I confirm ... salvation,* which follow immediately, and during which the hand is laid on the head of the candidate, he lifts his right hand to make the sign of the cross thrice over the neophyte as he calls upon the Holy Trinity. While the people are singing the response, *Amen,* he again lays his hand on the head of the neophyte. He then says: *Therefore go ... all things*. Whenever a girl or woman is confirmed he of course says sister instead of brother. Turning the back of his right hand to the neophyte, the bishop touches lightly the neophyte's cheek with the end of the fore and middle fingers, and says: *Peace be with thee*. This is intended to show symbolically that the neophyte must be prepared to meet the blows of life, but that our Lord's peace will always overshadow him.[4] The neophyte does not reply, but is assisted to rise by the priest. The neophyte bows to the bishop (he does not genuflect) and returns to his seat. Another candidate is immediately conducted to the bishop to kneel on the cushion. Meanwhile the bishop returns the crozier to the assistant and, if he so desires, wipes his thumb on the cotton wool while he awaits the candidate.

When all have been confirmed the people and neophytes rise and the hymn: *O Master I have promised....* is sung. This hymn may be omitted when for good reason the service must be shortened or an organ is not available.

Meanwhile two servers go to the bishop, one bearing the lemon and crumb, the other the vessel of water and lavabo towel. (One server will suffice if these things are carried on a tray.) After the bishop has cleansed and dried his hands the gremial is removed and placed on the credence table.

At the end of the hymn the bishop is seated in the faldstool facing the people and wearing the mitre. He then says: *My brothers ... greater glory*. He rises, the faldstool is removed, and he turns to the altar, placing the mitre thereon, and singing or saying the versicles alternately with the people. The crozier bearer takes his place at the gospel end of the footpace, and any other assistants return to their seats. The bishop turns by his right to the people for the Minor Benediction, the crozier bearer then facing south. After the response of the people, he intones or says: *Let us pray*. The people and neophytes kneel. Extending both hands, palms towards the neophytes, he continues: *O Lord Christ ... Angel host*. He now puts on the mitre (which may be handed to him by a server who comes up at the gospel end), takes the crozier and gives the Benediction: *God the Father... evermore*.

If the ceremony has taken place in the midst of a Celebration of the Holy Eucharist and the bishop is the celebrant, he now changes back to chasuble and stole of the colour of the Day and resumes the maniple. The faldstool is put away and the assistants go to their usual places in the sanctuary.

If the ceremony has preceded Benediction of the Most Holy Sacrament, the faldstool is taken away and the bishop proceeds with that service without change of vestments.

If Confirmation formed a service by itself, the bishop returns in procession to the vestry.

CHAPTER XX

CONFERRING OF HOLY ORDERS

Preliminary Notes

The General Episcopal Synod has ruled that the ages of candidates for ordination shall be as follows:

Minor Orders: No fixed age, but usually not before	14
Subdiaconate:	22
Diaconate:	23
Priesthood:	24
Episcopate:	30

These ages may be altered at the discretion of the Ordinary.

The Second General Episcopal Synod ruled that the Papers of Ordination should preferably be in the language of the country, but may be in English or Latin.

Minor Orders

General Directions

Ordination to the Office of Cleric may take place at any hour, but the four remaining Orders may be conferred only in the morning. The giving of one or more of the Minor Orders may constitute a service by itself, but if the Ordinations take place during a Celebration of the Holy Eucharist, the Office of Cleric is conferred after the Introit and the other four Offices after the *Kyrie*.

The ordinands may be given as many of the Minor Orders at one time as may seem wise or necessary to the Bishop. Sometimes all five Orders are conferred on a candidate at the same service, but it is better if an interval separate them in which the especial work of each Order can be studied and practised. It is sometimes convenient to give Orders up to and including that of Reader at one service, and up to Acolyte later. Or, the grade of Cleric at one service (which may be in the evening) and the rest on another occasion is a natural division.

The preparations are simple. On the usual credence table (or on a special table, if necessary) are laid the following: For the grade of *Cleric*, a linen surplice for each ordinand; for that of *Doorkeeper*, the key of one of the outside doors of the church or oratory in which the service takes place, and a small bell (not the sanctuary sacring bell or chimes); for that of *Reader*, a copy of the Bible; for that of *Exorcist*, a small sword and a copy of the Liturgy; for that of *Acolyte*, an empty cruet and a candlestick containing a candle. A small candle extinguisher and a tray sufficiently large to hold all the candles carried in procession by the candidates should also be on the credence. Unless lighted processional candles are to be placed there, a lighted candle should stand on the credence table from which the candles of the ordinands can be lighted when needed.

In the sanctuary there should be enough extra chairs or stools so that each ordinand may be seated during the ordination. These are usually placed in some convenient position before the service begins and then, after the procession has entered the sanctuary, placed in a row within the sanctuary gates facing the altar. A hassock or kneeling cushion should be provided for each candidate so that he or she may kneel in comfort during certain parts of the ordination. An alternative method which may be followed in any of the ordinations up to and including that of the priesthood, is that the candidates shall come forward at the appointed time for the ordination, and chairs then be placed for them. This has the advantage in small sanctuaries that it leaves room *in plano* for the clergy and various servers at the opening part of the Eucharist. Similarly, the newly-ordained may be seated at the side when the ordination is over. There must be a faldstool, or suitable chair, for the bishop. If the ordinations are given apart from the Eucharist, the faldstool may be placed in the middle of the footpace facing the people before the service begins. If, however, they are to be conferred during the Eucharist, then the faldstool should stand to one side (usually the gospel side) of the sanctuary until needed. A cushion should be at hand to place on the step below the bishop at the time the candidates come forward for ordination and for investiture with the symbols of office.

In the vestry enough candles, whether with or without candlesticks, are laid out so that each ordinand may carry a lighted candle in his or her right hand during the procession to the sanctuary and when summoned by the priest before each ordination.

The ordinands are vested in red or dark purple cassocks, according to their age. Younger candidates are usually in red, those of maturer age in purple. If already ordained Cleric, the candidate wears a surplice.

If the ordinations are to be given apart from the Eucharist, the bishop vests in rochet, stole, cope and mitre. He wears the pectoral cross and ring, and uses the crozier. The colour of the vestments used may be either white or the colour of the day. If the Orders are to be given during a celebration of the Eucharist, he wears the Eucharistic vestments of the colour of the day.

Only the six altar candles need be lighted for an ordination service, but more are permissible. If the ordination takes place during the Eucharist and the bishop is the celebrant, the bishop's candle is also lighted. The candle on the special credence table (which is used to light the candles of the ordinands before each ordination) should also be lighted.

The bishop, during the service of ordination, will need an assistant to hold the crozier. That same assistant may also hold the book, or there may be a second assistant to hold the book, if the bishop so prefers. The crozier bearer, during the ordinations, stand on the epistle side of the faldstool, facing the people.

During the procession to the sanctuary the ordinands, each carrying a lighted candle in the right hand, should walk behind the clergy and immediately in front of the personal attendants of the bishop. In leaving the sanctuary after the ordination service, they take their normal positions in the procession according to their rank. They do not carry candles in the return procession inasmuch as they are no longer candidates.

The structure of all five of the Minor Orders is the same, although the wording in parts is different. A detailed description of the conferring of the Order of Cleric will therefore suffice as a description of them all, and only a few supplementary notes under the heading of each Ordination will be needed.

Ordination of Clerics

As soon as the procession from the vestry has entered the sanctuary, and all in turn have made the customary reverence to the altar, servers close the sanctuary gates and may now place near them, side by side, the chairs for the ordinands facing the altar.

If the ordination service is being conducted as a separate service, the ordinands take their places in front of their respective chairs, retaining their lighted candles.

If, however, there is to be a Celebration of the Eucharist, the candidates go to their seats on the epistle side of the sanctuary, and a server collects the candles and places them on the credence table. They are usually extinguished until the ordination begins. The service of the Eucharist takes its usual course. At the end of the Introit the candidates who are to be ordained to the Order of Cleric go to their seats before the sanctuary rail where they are handed lighted candles. In the meantime the bishop, wearing his mitre, is seated on the faldstool which has been placed on the footpace in the middle. He does not change to cope, but retains the chasuble, although the maniple is removed and placed on the altar. As he faces the ordinands, the crozier bearer stands to his left. If there is a second assistant to hold the book, he should stand to the bishop's right.

If the ordinations form a service apart from the Eucharist, the bishop, before ascending to the footpace and seating himself on the faldstool, stands in the middle before the lowest step, wearing the mitre and holding the crozier. He genuflects and intones the Invocation. The assistants, who stand at either side of him, if there are two, ascend with him to the footpace and turn to face the people when the bishop turns.

As soon as the bishop is seated and the ordinands are ready, a priest designated for the purpose, at a signal from the bishop, announces: *Let those (or him) who ... come forward.* The ordinands advance one step together, bow slightly to the bishop, and give their candles to a server or the M.C. to be extinguished and placed on the credence. This done, the ordinands step back to their chairs and are seated. In this and in all subsequent ordinations described, it is understood that the ordinands rise together, move together, bow together, and so on, so far as is reasonably possible. Such concerted movement adds to the beauty of the service. It should also be remembered that at *each* ordination, before the ordinands are summoned by the priest, they should each be given a lighted candle to hold in the right hand. This means that a server must go to the ordinands with the candles before they are summoned, and take them away after the ordinands have been presented. If all five Minor Orders are to be conferred at the one service this distribution and collection of lighted candles takes place five times.

The bishop, still seated and wearing the mitre, reads the Charge. The ordinands should listen attentively and not read the service from their Liturgies while he is speaking. When there is need to shorten the service, especially on those occasions when all five Minor Orders are being conferred, the Third General Episcopal Synod ruled that the portion of the Charge, beginning with words: *as in the next stage...* and ending with words: *with regard to the body,* may be omitted. [This in indicated with brackets in the Third Edition of *The Liturgy.* Ed.] The Charge ended, the ordinands rise, walk forward and kneel either on or below the lowest step, as the arrangement of the sanctuary and the number of candidates may determine. Meanwhile the bishop rises and says: *Let us pray.* Holding both hands extended, palms towards the kneeling candidates, and still wearing the mitre, he continues with the prayer: *O Lord Christ... for ever and ever.* He takes the crozier in the left hand when the sign of the cross is to be made.

If there is but one candidate he now kneels before the bishop on a cushion or kneeling pad placed for the purpose. The bishop, still standing, wearing the mitre and holding the crozier in his left hand, places his right hand on the head of the candidate and says: *In the Name... Order of Cleric.* The crozier is returned to the bearer. A surplice is brought to the bishop who, assisted if need be by a server or the M.C., vests the new cleric. Taking his crozier in the left hand and touching for a moment the surplice with the right hand, the bishop says: *I clothe thee... good effect.* The new cleric rises, bows to the bishop and returns to his seat. If there are several candidates, they are seated and come forward one after the other, or they may come forward in their turn two by two. The others will be seated in the meantime. The bishop first ordains the two, the one after the other, then invests both with the surplice, then says the words of investiture. Where there are many candidates he may, at his discretion, say to each the opening words: *I clothe thee with the vesture of holiness,* as he touches him wi the right hand, and remainderof the sentence to both. This somewhat expedites this part of the ceremony.

If any of those just ordained are not to receive another Order at this time, they now come forward and kneel on or before the lowest step. The bishop rises with mitre and crozier and blesses them in the usual way while saying: *The blessing ... have undertaken.* They thereupon rise, bow to the bishop and retire to their seats at the side of the sanctuary. Those who are to receive another Order remain in their seats before the altar rail.

Ordination of Doorkeepers

If there are clerics to be ordained to the Office of Doorkeeper, and the ceremony is not taking place within the Eucharist, each ordinand is now given a lighted candle to hold in the right hand while being summoned by the priest. The ceremony of Ordination then follows.

If, however, the Ordinations are taking place during the Eucharist, the faldstool is moved temporarily to the side, the bishop gives the crozier to the bearer and turns with his assistants to face the altar. He places the mitre on the altar and the *Kyrie* is said or sung. The bishop then resumes his mitre, the faldstool is replaced on the footpace, and the bishop is seated. The assistants turn to face the people with the bishop. Candles are given to the ordinands.

The portion of the charges, beginning with words: *It will be thus...* and ending: *...mark the work of our earlier brethren,* may be omitted.

The symbols of office given to each new doorkeeper are first a key and then a bell. The key used is that of an outside door of the church. Inasmuch as it was the church tower bell that the doorkeeper in ancient times rang, the sacring bell is not used as a symbol of office. Any other small bell, however, will suffice. After each new door-keeper has had these symbols of office laid in his right hand for a moment during the words of investiture, they all rise, bow to the bishop and, under the leadership of the priest or another of the clergy appointed for the purpose, go to the door to which the key belongs. The last doorkeeper to be ordained carries the symbols of office. (Servers should be assigned the duty of moving the seats and opening the sanctuary gates so that the little procession may pass out without delay.) They go outside the church door, which is then closed. Each new doorkeeper in turn locks and unlocks the door and rings the bell thrice. When this has been done by all, the priest leads them back to the sanctu-ary, and the symbols of office are deposited on the credence.

If there are candidates who are to receive additional Orders, they go to their seats near the entrance to the sanctuary and are given lighted candles preparatory to being summoned by the priest. Those of the newly ordained doorkeepers who are not to re-ceive any further Order at this time go to kneel on or before the lowest altar step to re-ceive the Blessing from the bishop.

Ordination of Readers

That portion of the Charge, beginning with the words: *you have learned...* and ending with the words: *...that study to others,* may be omitted.

The symbol of office is a copy of the Bible.

Ordination of Exorcists

Those portions of the Charge beginning with the words: *The candidate was admonished...* and ending with: *...within himself;* beginning with the words: *Moreover, our conception...* and ending with the words: *days of ignorance,* may be omitted.

A sword and a book are the symbols of office. The style of sword generally used is a small ceremonial sword, but a miniature sword will suffice. The book used is *The Liturgy.*

Ordination of Acolytes

Those portions of the Charge beginning with the words: *You will have noticed...* and ending with: *sacrifice to God;* beginning with the words: *In may forms...* and ending: *children of light,* may be omitted.

The symbols of office are a lighted candle in a candlestick and an empty cruet.

General Directions

The ordination to the Order of Subdeacon may take place only during a Celebration of the Holy Eucharist. It follows immediately after the saying of the Collects.

The preparations are as follows: On the usual credence table (or on a special credence table, if necessary, because of the space required) are laid one tunicle (this may be hung over a chair, if preferred) for each ordinand, one maniple for each ordinand, an empty chalice and paten, the cruets filled with wine and water, the lavabo basin with finger towel, the Book of Epistles (or a copy of *The Liturgy*), a salver or metal tray, a candle extinguisher, and a candle in a candlestick, if needed for lighting the candles of the candidates before the presentation. The tunicle and maniple should be white, but if several are required, those of other colours may be used. The paten is laid on top of the chalice without any purificator between.

The seats for the candidates are arranged as in the Minor Orders. There must be a faldstool for the bishop, which is placed at the side of the sanctuary (usually the gospel side) until needed.

In the vestry enough candles, either with or without candlesticks, are provided so that each ordinand may carry a lighted candle in his or her right hand during the procession to the sanctuary and at the time when summoned by the priest.

The ordinands are vested in deep purple cassock, amice, alb, girdle and biretta. The bishop is in Eucharistic vestments, the colour used being that of the Day. He will need an assistant to carry the crozier. (If desired by the bishop there may be two assistants, one to hold the crozier, the other the Ordinal.)

Only the six altar candles need be lighted, although additional candles are permissible. Inasmuch as the bishop will celebrate the Eucharist, the bishop's candle is lighted. (The candle on the credence table may need to be lighted before the service begins.)

In the middle of the sanctuary floor, before the lowest altar step, a rug should be spread, unless the floor is already carpeted. This rug should be wide enough and long enough so that all the ordinands may lie down upon it side by side, face down, head towards the altar. It may be rolled or folded and kept at one side until the time it is needed. There should also be a cushion for each ordinand to be used at the time of the prostration.

It is advisable for a rehearsal of the ordination ceremony to be held before the actual service in order that all who take part may know exactly what to do.

In the procession from the vestry to the sanctuary the ordinands should be placed in the position of honour, that is, immediately in front of the personal attendants of the ordaining bishop.

Service of Ordination

The procession moves to the sanctuary and the Celebration of the Holy Eucharist proceeds as usual until the end of the Collects, the ordinands taking their places before their respective chairs that stand in line within the sanctuary rail. The second Collect said (in the Shorter Form it will be the first Collect said) is that found in the Ordination of Subdeacons. (If the ordination to the Diaconate is to follow immediately after that of the Subdiaconate, the Collect of the former service is substituted for the latter.) The other Collects follow as usual. At the end of the Collects the faldstool is placed in the middle of the footpace by a server, and the bishop is seated thereon, wearing the mitre, the crozier bearer to his left. If a second server is desired to hold the Ordinal, he should stand to the right of the bishop. A server lays cushions, one for each ordinand, on the rug on the sanctuary floor, about one foot from the lowest altar step. The candles of the ordinands are now lighted. If the regular credence table is used to hold the things required at the ordination, the ordinands' candles are lighted at one of the processional candles standing thereon. But if a special credence table is used, then the ordinands' candles are lighted at the lighted candle which was placed there before the service began.

At a signal from the bishop, the priest summons the candidates, saying: *Let those who are to be ordained to the Order of Subdeacon come forward.* (Note that here and hereafter throughout the service, in the Charges, Litany, Questions, Prayer and final Blessing, the wording must be changed to the singular when there is only one candidate. This is true of all Ordinations.) The ordinands advance a pace or two, bow to the bishop, wait until the candles have been taken from them, retire to their chairs and are seated. The bishop addresses them, saying: *Dearly beloved sons ... crown of our Master.* He thereupon rises and, still wearing the mitre, addresses the congregation: *Let us pray ... the Subdiaconate.*

The bishop turns to face the altar, the assistant (or assistants) turning with him, kneels on the edge of the footpace, removes the mitre and lays it on the faldstool in front of him. The assistant (or assistants) kneels with him. In the meantime the ordinands prostrate themselves on the rug as in the following manner: They rise, advance until they are about five feet from their respective cushions, kneel on both knees, bend forward, put their right hands on the floor and lower themselves until they are flat on the floor and lower themselves until they are flat on the rug breast down, with the forehead resting on their crossed arms, which in turn rest on the cushion. It is not easy to prostrate gracefully, and in the rehearsal it is well to repeat this part of the ceremony until it can be done together without undue or awkward movement.

The Litany is sung, all kneeling. (If it should happen that all candidates are to receive the Diaconate immediately after this Order, the Litany given in the service for the Ordination of Deacons is substituted for the one in this Ordination. The Litany is not sung alternately as at Solemn Benediction, but by all together. Three verses towards the end of the Litany are sung by the bishop alone. When the verse is reached which begins: *Holy, loving as Thou art...* the bishop rises and puts on the mitre. He then faces the candidates, the assistant holding the book so that the verses may easily be read by the bishop. Taking now the crozier in his left hand, the bishop sings the three verses, making as indicated the signs of the cross over the candidates. As the last verse of the Litany is sung by all the bishop and his assistants turn back to the altar, he resigns the crozier, removes the mitre, and they kneel once more.

The Litany ended, all are seated, the bishop upon the faldstool wearing the mitre, the ordinands upon their chairs. The bishop then proceeds with the Charge: *Dearly beloved sons ... creation.* The Charge ended, the ordinands rise, prompted if need be by the priest. The questions and reply follow. The bishop, still seated, rejoins: *The Lord keep you ... all goodness.*

The candidates now come forward and kneel, either on or below the lowest altar step, depending on the arrangement of the sanctuary. They should be at some distance from the bishop. The bishop, wearing the mitre and holding both hands extended, palms towards the candidates, and says: *O Lord Christ ... Angel host.* He takes the crozier in his left hand when the sign of the cross is to be made.

The ordinands are again seated. They come forward in sequence, one by one, beginning with the candidate on the epistle side, to kneel before the bishop and receive Ordination. Each returns to his seat after Ordination. When ordaining, the bishop holds the crozier in his left hand, lays his right hand on the head of the candidate, and says: *In the Name of our Lord Christ... Subdeacon.* Each returns to his place after ordination, bowing to the bishop when he has risen. When all have received the imposition of the bishop's hand, the bishop is seated and the one first ordained advances to kneel once more on the cushion before the bishop. The various symbols and vestments of office are brought to the bishop as needed from the credence table by a server or one of the clergy.

The bishop first hands the empty chalice, surmounted by the paten, to the new subdeacon, who touches them with the right hand as the bishop says: *Take heed to that... sight of God.* The bishop then returns the chalice and paten to the server. In the same way, but in silence, he presents to the new subdeacon the cruets, the lavabo dish and towel. Taking the crozier and touching for a moment with his right hand the amice of the subdeacon, he says: *Take the amice...Holy Ghost.* He hands the crozier to the bearer for a moment, receiving the maniple from a server, places it on the left fore-arm of the subdeacon. Again taking the crozier, and touching the maniple for a moment with his right hand, he says: *Take the maniple ... Holy Ghost*. The crozier is again given to the bearer. The tunicle is brought forward and, with the aid of a server or the M.C., the subdeacon is vested therewith. (It is helpful to roll the maniple round the arm of the subdeacon before it is thrust through the sleeve of the tunicle). The bishop, taking the crozier again and touching the tunicle for a moment with his right hand, says: *May the Lord ... Holy Ghost*. The crozier is now given back. He now hands with both hands the Book of the Epistles (i.e., *The Liturgy*) to the subdeacon, takes his crozier, and says: *Take the Book ... Holy Ghost*. Returning the crozier, the bishop hands the Book of Epistles back to the server. The new subdeacon rises, bows to the bishop and returns to his seat. (When seated, the rear portion of the tunicle should be lifted for him and placed over the back of the chair or so disposed that it will not become creased or soiled.) (If sufficient tunicles are not available for all ordinands, the tunicle will be removed and returned to the credence for use with the next ordinand. It will be left on the last one to be invested, for the reading of the Epistle.) The next ordinand now comes forward and is invested with the symbols and vestments of office. When all the ordinands have thus been invested, they come forward together and kneel on the lowest altar step. The bishop rises and with mitre and crozier blesses them as follows: *The blessing ... undertaken*.

If the candidates are numerous, they may come forward in pairs, first for the act of Ordination and subsequently for the investiture and delivery of instruments.

If Ordination to the Diaconate is not to follow immediately, the new subdeacons after the Blessing take the seats prepared for them at the side of the sanctuary and the chairs they occupied during the ordination service are removed.

One of the new subdeacons, vested in tunicle, now reads the Epistle of the Day.

If any of the newly ordained subdeacons are to receive forthwith the Diaconate, they go to take their places once more at the seats facing the altar. Those vested in tunicles retain them until after the reading of the Epistle. In such case the Epistle read is that found in the Ordination of Deacons and not the Epistle of the Day.

In the Prayer of Consecration the bishop should remember to insert the words: *Especially for these (or him) whom... Order of Subdeacon*.

✠   ✠   ✠

Ordination of Deacons

General Directions

If the Ordination of Deacons is not preceded or followed by another Ordination there is no need for a special credence table. Over the back of a chair is laid a white stole and a white dalmatic for each ordinand. On the credence is laid a copy of *The Liturgy* or a Book of Gospels. Other than the foregoing, exactly the same general directions given in the preceding ordination apply to the Ordination of Deacons. In addition to the vestments previously mentioned, each candidate wears a white maniple.

In regard to the colour of vestments worn by the bishop when ordaining to Major Orders, the general rule is white, except that when the colour of the Day is red, Major Orders may be given in that colour.

Before the ordination takes place, the bishop asks each candidate to sign a Declaration of Canonical Obedience. No further written promise is required should the deacon be advanced to the Priesthood.

Service of Ordination

After the procession reaches the sanctuary the Celebration of the Holy Eucharist proceeds as usual until the end of the Epistle, which is always that of the Ordination Service. From the beginning of the service the ordinands take their places before their respective chairs which were placed in line before the rail as soon as the procession entered the sanctuary. At the end of the Epistle, the faldstool is brought to the footpace and the bishop is seated thereon wearing his mitre. To his left stands the crozier bearer. If there is an additional server to hold the Ordinal, he stands to the right of the bishop

Lighted candles are given to the ordinands as previously described. The priest who is to present the ordinands stands to the right of the first candidate, facing the bishop. (It adds to the solemnity of the occasion if each candidate can be presented by the priest of the parish where he is to work.) At a signal from the bishop, they all (priest and ordinands) step forward a pace and bow to the bishop. Taking for a moment the right hand of the first ordinand in his own right hand, the sponsor addresses the bishop, saying: *Right Reverend Father the ...diaconate.* hand of the one whom they present). The bishop questions: *Knowest thou them to be worthy?* After the priest's reply: *As far as ... office*, the bishop replies: *Thanks be to God.* The candles are now given to a server, extinguished, and placed on the credence. The ordinands are seated, and presenting sponsors retire to their places. The bishop, still seated, and wearing the mitre, charges the clergy and people: *Dearly beloved brethren ... own estate.* He pauses for a due space of time to determine whether anyone has anything to say. The resumption of the service should not be hurried so as to give any semblance of mere outer formality to this demand. There being silence, he continues, charging the ordinands: *Dearly beloved sons ... peace.* At a signal from the sponsor, the ordinands rise and are questioned by the bishop as in the preceding ordination. After the bishop has said: *The Lord keep... all goodness,* he rises and, still wearing the mitre, addresses the people: *Let us pray ...Diaconate*. The bishop turns round to face the altar, kneels on the edge of the footpace and places his mitre on the faldstool in front of him. The assistant (or assistants) kneel with him. Meanwhile the ordinands prostrate themselves on the rug before the altar as previously described. The Litany is now sung.

If, however, this Litany has already been sung in an immediately preceding Ordination to the Subdiaconate (See Page 220) it is here omitted. In this case the ordinands do not prostrate. It should be noted that in four of the verses sung by the people, changes will have to be made in the wording if there is only one ordinand. It would be well before the service to draw the attention of the people to the changes which are necessary. During the three verses of the Litany sung by the bishop alone, he wears the mitre and holds the crozier.

At the end of the Litany the ordinands rise, come forward and kneel either on or below the lowest altar step, according to the arrangement of the sanctuary. They should be at some distance from the bishop. The people are seated. The bishop puts on his mitre, rises, turns towards the ordinands (the assistant or assistants rising and turning with him), extends both hands towards the ordinands, palms down, and says: *O Lord Christ ... Angel host*. He makes the sign of the cross twice over them collectively as indicated in the Liturgy, taking his crozier in his left hand while doing so.

Turning back to the altar, the bishop kneels on the edge of the footpace, retaining his mitre and holding the crozier in both hands. The assistant (or assistants) turns and kneels with him. The *Veni Creator* is now sung by all. The ordinands are then seated. They come forward in sequence, one by one, beginning with the candidate on the epistle side, to kneel before the bishop, as described in the previous ordination to the subdiaconate. The bishop takes the crozier in his left hand, places his right hand on the head of each ordinand, and says slowly: *Receive the Holy Ghost ... God*. After a short pause, the newly ordained deacon, bows with reverence to the bishop and is led to his seat. The next candidate advances, meanwhile, and kneels before the bishop. After the last candidate has been ordained, the bishop hands the crozier to the bearer, faces west and extends both hands, palms towards the new deacons, who are again kneeling as before, saying: *O God the Holy Ghost ... ages of ages*.

When this prayer is ended, the bishop is again seated on the faldstool. The new deacons rise, bow to the bishop and return to their seats. The deacon first ordained advances to kneel in front of the bishop.

The bishop now takes the white stole, which is brought to him, and places it over the left shoulder and fastens it, with ends crossed, right over left, under the right arm of the new deacon. Taking now his crozier he says: *Take thou...and glory*. He makes the sign of the cross over the heart of the new deacon at the point indicated in the Liturgy. The dalmatic, which may be of any colour, but preferably white, is now brought and, assisted if need be, the new deacon is vested by the bishop. The bishop, touching the dalmatic for a moment with his right hand and holding the crozier in his left, says: *The Lord clothe ... Holy Ghost.* He returns the crozier. Taking the Book of Gospels (usually a copy of the *Liturgy*) with both hands, he delivers it to the new deacon. Taking the crozier he says: *Take thou authority ... Holy Ghost.* (If the candidates are numerous, they may come up two by two for this investiture.)

The new deacon now rises, bows to the bishop and returns to his seat. (When taking his seat the rear portion of the dalmatic should be placed over the back of the chair.) The next new deacon comes forward to the bishop, kneels and is invested. When all the new deacons have been invested, they come forward together and kneel as before, either on or below the lowest altar step. The bishop rises, and, with mitre and crozier, blesses them, saying: *O Christ the lord ... ever and ever.*

The new deacons rise and take the seats prepared for them at the side of the sanctuary. The chairs they occupied at the ordination are removed, the faldstool and cushion are removed. The rug may be removed. The faldstool is removed from the footpace.

After the Gradual, one of the new deacons, kneeling at the epistle side of the footpace and says the Munda cor Meum, is blessed by the celebrant, and then reads the Gospel in the usual way after singing the Minor Benediction. When he has censed the celebrant he returns to his assigned seat in the sanctuary.

In the Prayer of Consecration the bishop should be careful to say: *Especially for these (or him) whom... diaconate.*

✠   ✠   ✠

Ordination of Priests

General Directions

Ordination to the Priesthood may take place only in the morning during a celebration of the Holy Eucharist, On account of the importance of this Ordination it is customary for the service to be held on a Sunday so that as many of the congregation as possible may be present. The Ordination follows immediately after the Gradual.

The following preparations are made: On the usual or a special credence table in the sanctuary are placed one chasuble for each ordinand (chasubles may be hung over the back of a chair); a chalice, containing some grape juice and a few drops of water, on the top of which is laid a paten holding a large priest's wafer; a linen strip for each ordinand; oil of catechumens in an oil stock; a gremial; a salver or metal tray on which the candles of the ordinands are placed after they are extinguished, provided, that is, they are not carried in candlesticks; a candle in a candlestick from which to relight the candles of the ordinands, unless they can be lighted from processional candles; and a small candle extinguisher. If possible, the chasubles with which the new priests, are to be invested should be white, but, in emergency, those of another colour may be used. Each chasuble should be so folded that it may quickly and easily be put over the head of the new priest. The linen strips are about two and a half inches wide and from two to three feet long. In emergency a linen handkerchief may be used.

On the usual credence table, in addition to the things needed at a service of the Holy Eucharist, should be placed bowls of water and lavabo towels, the number of which depends upon the number of ordinands. There should also be two or more bowls containing some crumbs from the moist interior of a loaf and slices of lemon.

In the sanctuary there should be a chair and a cushion for each ordinand. These chairs are placed in line within the gates facing the altar as soon as the procession has entered the, sanctuary. The ordinands take their places in front of their respective chairs as soon as the service begins. In this Ordination they are not seated at all at the sides of the sanctuary. A faldstool, or suitable chair, for the bishop should be provided. It stands to one side of the sanctuary (usually the gospel side) until it is needed at the end of the Gradual.

The altar is arranged as usual for the Holy Eucharist. It should be adorned with flowers and there may be extra candles.

It is assumed in these general directions and in the description of the ordination which follows that there are not more than two candidates. If there be only one ordinand the ceremony is somewhat simplified. If, on the other hand, there be more than two candidates; the bishop must determine what arrangements are to be made. For example, if there be only one candidate, a missal stand is put on the altar at the epistle end, so that the new priest may stand at that end of the altar at the time he says the Eucharistic service concurrently with the bishop. If there be two candidates, another missal stand is put on the altar at the gospel end. If there be more than two ordinands, it is usually so difficult to accommodate them all at the altar, that the best arrangement is to have them grouped at the sides of the altar step during the time they repeat the service. In such case the extra missal stands will not be required.

A rug is spread in the middle of the sanctuary floor before the lowest altar step, unless the sanctuary is already carpeted, on which the ordinands may lie prostrate during the singing of the Litany. The rug ought to be large enough to accommodate all of the candidates.

Enough candles, either without or with candlesticks, should be on hand in the vestry so that each ordinand may carry a lighted candle in his right hand during the procession to the sanctuary, when presented by the priest to the bishop, and when making his offering at the time the offertory hymn is sung. Each candidate is vested in dark purple cassock and biretta, amice, alb, girdle, white maniple, and white stole worn after the manner of a deacon. The ordaining bishop is vested as for the holy Eucharist, the vestments being white, unless the colour of the Day is red, when they may be of that colour.

It is the custom of the Catholic Church for some of the priests present, not more than twelve in number, to vest in chasubles as for the Eucharist (although maniples are not worn) and take part in the laying on of hands. They may, under these circumstances, be so vested during the procession from and to the vestry.

The bishop will need a crozier bearer and there may be an additional server to hold the ordinal.

A rehearsal of the Ordination should by all means take place some time before the ceremony so that all may be familiar with the course of the service.

In the procession to the sanctuary the ordinands should be placed in the position of honour immediately in front of the personal attendants of the bishop, that is, the crozier bearer, acolytes with candles, deacon and subdeacon.

Service of Ordination

The procession, singing a hymn, goes to the sanctuary. As soon as it has entered, the chairs for the ordinands are put in front of the altar rail and the ordinands take their places before the chairs. The candles carried by the ordinands are extinguished and placed on the credence, the tray being used if they were carried without candlesticks. The celebration of the Eucharist proceeds as usual until the end of the Gradual. The first Collect of the Day and the Epistle are those found in the Ordination of Priests.

The Gradual ended, the faldstool is brought to the footpace and the bishop is seated, wearing his mitre. The crozier is held at his left. If there is an additional assistant to hold the Ordinal, he stands at the bishop's right. The ordinands rise and lighted candles are given to them. The priest who is to present them stands to the right of the first candidate, also facing the bishop. (As in the case of the Diaconate, candidates or groups of candidates may be presented severally by the priest from the parish where they are to work or have worked.) At a signal from the priest, they all, both priest and ordinands, step forward a pace or two and bow to the bishop. Taking for a moment the right hand of the first ordinand into his own right hand, the priest addresses the bishop: *Right Reverend Father ... Priesthood.* The bishop questions: *Knowest ... worthy?* The priest replies: *As far as ... this office.* If different priests are presenting candidates, the presentation just described will be done in succession, but may be done together if the candidates are numerous. The bishop finally responds: *Thanks be to God.* The candles are taken from the ordinands and extinguished, and the ordinands are seated, The bishop charges the clergy and people, saying: *Dearly beloved brethren .... own estate.* After a sufficient pause, so as to give opportunity to any to speak; he continues, addressing the ordinands: *Dearly beloved sons ... deign to grant.* As in the case of the Diaconate, the resumption of the charge should not be hurried so as to the demand any semblance of outer formality. At a signal from the priest the ordinands rise together. The bishop questions them: *Will you ... to you?* and they answer in unison: *I will.* He continues: *The Lord keep ... goodness.* The bishop then rises and, still wearing the mitre, addresses the people: *Let us ... Priesthood.* He turns to the altar, the assistants turning with him, and they kneel on the edge of the footpace. He removes the mitre and places it on the faldstool. In the meantime the ordinands prostrate themselves on the rug as described in the Ordination of Subdeacons. The Litany is sung by all kneeling. The wording of four verses should be changed, if there be only one candidate. (It is perhaps wise to draw the attention of the people to this before the service begins.) The bishop rises with his assistants, and with mitre and crozier, sings three of the verses alone exactly as previously described. He then turns back to the altar with his assistants, yields his crozier, removes his mitre, and kneels while the last verse is sung by all.

At the end of the Litany the people are seated. The ordinands rise and kneel on or below the lowest altar step, whichever is most convenient for the laying on of hands. The bishop puts on his mitre, rises arid turns towards the ordinands. Extending both hands towards them he says: *O Lord Christ ... Angel host.* Now, in silence, the bishop lays both hands on the head of each ordinand in turn, beginning with the one at the epistle end of the line. He does this with the intention to ordain and without any hurry. The crozier is held at his left. When all have been ordained the bishop steps up to the side of his faldstool out of the way. Any other bishops present, together with the priests (or a selected number of the priests as previously indicated) form into a row. They enter before the ordinands at the epistle end of the line and lay their hands on the head of each ordinand in succession. The priests need only apply their hands for a moment to the heads of the ordinands, inasmuch as they do not ordain and the special contribution they are to make is given instantaneously. (The priests should have been instructed about this beforehand and have had it explained to them that it conveys a wrong impression if they keep their hands on the head for the same length of time as the ordaining bishop.) After each bishop and priest present has laid on hands, they proceed to group themselves symmetrically behind the line of kneeling ordinands, each with the right hand extended towards them. The bishop, holding his right hand towards them, says: *O Lord Christ ... Thy Name.* He continues: *Let us ... Priesthood.* All lower their hands, the clergy return to their seats, and the bishop faces the altar. All kneel while the *Veni Creator* is sung. The bishop retains his mitre and holds his crozier in both hands. The *Veni Creator* need not be sung in the Ordination to the Priesthood if all the candidates have just been ordained to the Diaconate.

When the hymn is ended, the bishop rises and stands before his faldstool. The candidates kneel, one by one, before him in succession. If there are many, two may kneel at a time before him. Still wearing the mitre, the bishop again lays both hands on the head, this time saying slowly: *Receive the Holy Ghost ... retained.* The crozier bearer stands at his left. The newly ordained priest rises, bows reverently to the bishop, and returns to his place. When all have received this imposition, the newly ordained priests come forward and kneel, as before, either on or below the lowest step. The bishop, still wearing his mitre, extends both hands towards the new priests and says: *O God, the Source ... God.* He makes the sign of the cross over the new priests collectively at the place indicated in the Liturgy, taking the crozier in his left hand at the time. When the prayer is finished, the priests rise, bow to the bishop and return to their seats.

The bishop, still wearing the mitre, is seated on the faldstool. If there be several candidates, they may come up two by two for the investiture, anointing and delivery of instruments, the others meanwhile being seated. It is preferable that they come forward singly.

On account of the anointing of the hands of the new priests with oil, it is most convenient, especially if there be a large number of ordinands, first to invest each one in turn with the stole and chasuble, and then to anoint each in turn and present the chalice.

When the new priest kneels before the bishop on the second step, the bishop changes the arrangement of the stole of the new priest so that it crosses over his breast after the manner of a priest. Either the M.C. or a server assists him in doing this. Holding the crozier in his left hand, the bishop touches the stole of the new priest for a moment with his right hand and says: *Take thou ... Christ's love.* The chasuble is brought to the bishop and, with the assistance of the M.C. or a server, the new priest is invested therewith. Again taking the crozier and touching the chasuble for a moment with his right hand, the bishop says: *Take thou ... and Blood.*

The gremial is brought to the bishop who spreads it on his lap. At the same time the oil stock containing the Oil of Catechumens is presented to the bishop by a server standing on his right whenever he wishes to moisten, his thumb. The ordinand lays his hands side by side, palms upwards, on the gremial. Moistening his thumb with the Oil of Catechumens, the bishop anoints the hands of the new priest in the following manner. First he traces a line with the oil from the tip of the right thumb of the newly ordained priest across the palms to the tip of the left forefinger. He then traces another line with oil from the tip of the left thumb across the palms to the tip of the right forefinger. Next a cross is traced with oil on the palm of the right hand and on the palm of the left. Finally, with a circular motion, he anoints the entire palm and fingers of each hand. Taking the crozier in his left hand, he consecrates the hands of the new priest; saying: *Be pleased ... Lord Christ*. He makes the sign of the cross twice during this prayer over both hands collectively. The new priest is now instructed to join his hands, palm to palm. The bishop takes the linen strip, which is brought to him, and wraps it loosely round the joined hands, allowing the free ends to hang down. The ends of the fingers of the new priest should be left uncovered. The chalice and paten with their contents are now brought to the bishop. He instructs the new priest to take the paten between the index and middle finger of each hand (so that the index fingers touch the wafer), while at the same time he touches the cup of the chalice with the tips of the middle and lower fingers. With the fingers of the new priest in this position the bishop says: *Take thou authority ... of the Lord*. It is a pleasing custom if the new priest can be presented at this solemn moment with his own chalice and paten.

When all of the priests have thus had their hands anointed and have been presented with the chalice and paten, they rise, bow to the bishop and go to the credence table. The linen strips are removed and they cleanse their hands with lemon, bread crumb and water. In the meantime two servers go to the bishop, one carrying a bowl with lemon and crumb, the other a bowl with water and a lavabo towel. After the bishop has cleansed and dried his hands, the gremial is taken away. The bishop rises and the faldstool is removed from the footpace.

The celebration of the Holy Eucharist now continues, all of the new priests, except the one appointed to read the Gospel, going to their seats before the altar rail. The new priest who is to read the Gospel kneels on the edge of the footpace at the epistle side, says the Munda Cor Meum, is blessed by the bishop, rises and sings the Minor Benediction, and then in the usual way reads the Gospel appearing in the Ordination of Priests. After censing the celebrant, the new priest goes to his seat before the altar rail.

After the offertory hymn, if sung, the faldstool is again brought to the footpace, and the bishop is seated thereon wearing his mitre,. the., crozier bearer standing at his left. Lighted candles meanwhile are given to the new priests. When the bishop is seated, each newly ordained priest in turn goes to the bishop, kneels on the altar step in front of him, and, with a slight bow, presents the lighted candle. The bishop receives the candle with a slight bow and gives it to a server, who retires and extinguishes the candle. If numerous, the new priests may all kneel together before the bishop and present one candle collectively.

The newly ordained priests bow to the bishop and go to stand: one at either end of the altar. (Their chairs are removed from before the altar rail and put in some convenient place. They will be needed towards the end of the Eucharist.) They face towards the middle of the altar during the service and not towards the east. From this point forward, each new priest acts as a co-celebrant with the bishop, reciting the service word for word with the celebrant. They also make the signs of the cross in blessing whenever he does, either over the oblations on the altar, over themselves, or over the people, as the case may be. They should be particularly careful, when saying the words of consecration of the Bread and of the Wine that they do so with intention to consecrate.

In the Prayer of Consecration the bishop alone says: *Especially for these (or him) whom ... Priesthood.*

During the prayer which precedes the Salutation of Peace the new priests should go round to the middle and kneel on the altar step (or the edge of the footpace, if the latter is wide enough so that kneeling there does not interfere with the celebrant) behind the celebrant. They should carry their missals with them so as to continue the repetition of the service, word for word. The bishop gives the Salutation to each of the new priests before giving it to the deacon and subdeacon. They continue to kneel on the altar step until after receiving Communion. After the bishop has received the Sacred Host he turns to the new priests and administers to them. Again, after he has received the chalice he administers to them from his own chalice, the last new priest draining the chalice. (If preferred, the bishop may administer to the new priests by process of intinction. When this is done, he receives the Host and Wine but is careful not to consume all of the Sacred Blood. He then goes to each new priest, dips a portion of the Host into the Wine and, being exceedingly careful that no drops adhere to the Host, administers to the new priest. In this case he uses the words: *The Body and Blood ... eternal* at the time of administration. When all the newly ordained priests have been communicated in this manner, the bishop himself consumes the remainder of the Sacred Blood.) When all the new priests have received Communion they rise and return to their places at the ends of the altar. After the celebrant has administered Communion to the deacon and subdeacon and the clergy, he may call upon the new priests to assist him in administering to the servers, choir and people. During the Ablutions the new priests are seated in their chairs, which have been returned to their places before the altar rail.

When the sentence: *Under the veil of earthly things...* (which should be repeated word for word by the new priests is ended, the faldstool is brought once more to the footpace and the bishop is seated thereon, wearing his mitre. (The organist must be on the alert not to begin the music of the Communio until after the part of the Ordination which follows is over.) The crozier is held on his left. The new priests come forward one by one, beginning with the first priest on the epistle side, kneel on the altar step before the bishop and place their hands palm to palm between those of the bishop. In this position each one takes the Oath of Canonical Obedience, (If the bishop be not the Ordinary, he substitutes the name of the latter for *myself* and *his* for *my*.) After his promise and response, the new priest rises, bows to the bishop, and returns to his seat as the next priest goes forward to kneel and take his vow of canonical obedience.

When all have taken the oath and are seated the bishop charges the new priests, saying: *Dearly beloved sons ... detail.* As he now rises and takes his crozier the new priests kneel together in front of their seats. The bishop blesses them, saying: *The blessing ... ages of ages.* Again all are seated and the bishop, wearing the mitre and holding the crozier, charges them as follows: *Dearly beloved sons ... freely give.* The bishop rises, relinquishes his crozier, turns towards the altar, takes off his mitre and stands it on the altar, or it is done for him by the mitre bearer. The faldstool is taken from the foot-pace by a server. The new priests meanwhile return to their places at either end of the altar, and the chairs on which they were seated before the altar rail are removed.

The service of the Eucharist is resumed by the singing of the Communio. The new priests at the benediction face the people and make over them only one sign of the cross (the bishop of coarse makes the sign three times) saying the words concurrently with the bishop.

During the procession to the vestry the new priests walk in the position of honour in front of the personal attendants of the bishop. The lighted candle is not carried, it having been presented to the bishop at the offertorium.

General Directions

Consecration to the Episcopate may take place only in the morning during a Celebration of the Holy Eucharist, which, except in an emergency, should be High. The Consecration is usually held on a Sunday, and one of the best Days in the Christian Year for this magnificent ceremony is Whitsunday, but there is more likelihood of being able to secure the attendance of the priests of the Diocese if the Consecration is held on a weekday.

It is presumed that the proper vestments, instruments and symbols of office for the Bishop-Elect have been provided, as set forth in *The Liturgy*. It should be noted that the seven Ray jewels set in the crozier and the seven Ray jewels in the pectoral cross must have been consecrated previously by a bishop in the manner prescribed for altar jewels. If any of the instruments of office have been previously blessed for and used by another bishop their blessing is not repeated prior to bestowing them upon the new bishop.

The High Altar is prepared as usual for the Celebration of the Holy Eucharist. It should be adorned with many flowers and candles. On the High Altar are placed the following: an extra missal stand at the epistle end; the crozier of the bishop-elect; a silver salver on which are laid the ring and pectoral cross of the bishop-elect; and (if there is room and no danger of falling candle grease) the mitre and gloves of the bishop-elect. (If this is inadvisable the mitre and gloves should be placed on an extra credence table.)

If there is not already a second altar in the church, a side altar is prepared at the side of the sanctuary. It is usually more convenient to arrange this on the gospel side, and it may face east or not. The frontal should be white. On this side altar are an altar cross, six altar candlesticks, the customary linen cloths, vases of flowers, a missal stand, and a salver on which have been placed two small loaves of bread, two candles in candlesticks, and two miniature barrels containing either wine or grape juice. One of the loaves and one of the barrels should bear the Arms of the Consecrator emblazoned on a golden shield; the other two should bear the Arms of the new bishop upon a silver shield. (These can be painted in water colour on gold and silver paper.)

On the credence table are arranged those things always required at a Celebration of the Holy Eucharist. Extra ciboria with fresh wafers may be required if the congregation is large. In addition there, should be a bowl with soft bread crumb and a slice; of lemon; a bowl with water and an extra lavabo towel, which will be used by the Consecrator. Bread crumb, lemon, water, towel, comb and mirror should similarly be provided. in the vestry whither the new bishop can retire and cleanse himself after his anointing. If this is not convenient, these extra things may be placed on the usual credence.

On an extra credence table, which is placed most conveniently· on the epistle side of the sanctuary, are laid the following: a large white silk handkerchief to be used in binding the head of the new bishop just before the anointing; a safety pin, provided the handkerchief is not large enough to permit it being tied round the. head; an oil stock containing Chrism; a linen strip with ends fastened together forming a loop, large enough so that, when, placed round the neck, it may form a sling to hold the freshly anointed hands of the new bishop; a copy of the Gospels or the Bible in the language of the country or in Greek; a gremial and an extra salver.

The colour of the vestments used by the bishop-elect is always white. Those used by the consecrator and all other clergy in the sanctuary are white, unless the colour of the Day is red, when red vestments may be worn. If there are not enough white copes for the clergy, red may be worn.

In the sanctuary there are several special arrangements to make. The chasuble and maniple of the celebrant and the chasuble and maniple of the bishop-elect are placed conveniently at hand. In the sanctuary should also be placed the maniples for the deacon and subdeacon, the mantellettas (or a mantelletta and a mozetta, if one: happens to be the Ordinary) and birettas for the Senior and Junior Assistant Bishops, a faldstool for the Consecrator, a cushion on which the Consecrator will kneel during the ceremony, three chairs and three cushions for the bishop-elect and two assistant bishops, stools for the crozier bearers of the assistant bishops, and sufficient chairs so that all the clergy and servers may be seated. A copy of the Liturgy or service book and of the hymnbook should be laid on each chair. In the middle of the sanctuary floor before the lower altar step is spread a rug, unless the sanctuary floor is already carpeted.

The Consecrator and the deacon and subdeacon of the Eucharist are vested as for a Celebration of the Holy Eucharist, the former therefore in cope for the Asperges. The assistant bishops are vested in rocket, stole, cope and mitre. They wear the ring and pectoral cross and use the crozier. The bishop-elect wears a cassock and biretta of the bishop's purple and is vested in amice, alb, girdle, white stole hanging crossed in front after the manner of a priest, and white cope. Other clergy present are vested in surplice, stole and. cope, and of course wear birettas.

In addition to the usual candle bearers and other servers required during High Celebration of the Holy Eucharist, each bishop and the bishop-elect will need the services of a crozier bearer, who in addition to carrying the crozier may also act as book bearer. The Consecrator may find it more convenient to have an assistant who serves only as book bearer. If the bishop-elect wears a cassock with a train, he may require the services of one or two small acolytes to hold up the train during the procession round the church while the Te Deum is sung. There should also be an extra thurifer as' two censers will be used. There must be a Master of Ceremonies (two M.C. are preferable) who is thoroughly conversant with the details of the ceremony. He need not be in priest's Orders, but it is preferable that he be at least an ordained subdeacon. In addition to the crozier bearers, all of whom of course wear vimpas, the one who is to hold the Book of Gospels over the bishop-elect should also wear a vimpa.

It is imperative that two or more rehearsals of the ceremony take place on the days immediately preceding the consecration so that all who take part in the service, including the organist, know exactly what to do. The consecration is long and complicated and only with practice can it be conducted smoothly.

The Protocol of Election is usually given to one of the clergy, preferably a priest, to read. The protocol is either placed on his seat in the sanctuary before the service, or he carries it with him in procession to the sanctuary. He should be prepared to read the protocol without hesitation and in a clear voice so that all may hear. During the reading a candle bearer stands on either side of the priest. It may suitably be read by the Chancellor of the Diocese or the Vicar General.

The order of the procession from the vestry to the sanctuary is as follows:

Thurifer and boat bearer
Cross bearer and candle bearers
Vested choir
(Banner bearer)
Master of Ceremonies
(Candle bearers)
Clergy
(Banner bearer)
Second thurifer
Candle bearers
Crozier bearer
Junior Assistant Bishop
Candle bearers
Crozier bearer
Senior Assistant Bishop
Candle bearers
Bishop-Elect
(Banner bearer)
Subdeacon
Deacon
Candle bearers
Crozier bearer
Consecrator
Banner bearer

If the passage is sufficiently wide, the bishop-elect is escorted by the S.A.B. on his right and the J.A.B. on his left, the crozier bearers of the two bishops preceding them.

Service of Consecration

The procession forms and moves through the church while a hymn is sung. Upon entering the sanctuary the processional candles are extinguished and put away. As soon as the consecrator has entered the sanctuary the three chairs for the assistant bishops and the B-E and the two stools for the crozier bearers of the assistant bishops are placed before the altar rail, and those to be seated thereon take their places before their respective chairs. The grouping is as follows: The B-E is in the middle, the S.A.B. to his right, and the J.A. B. to his left. Behind each assistant bishop, but a little farther from the middle, is his crozier bearer. The attendant of the B-E, who will later carry the crozier, is at this time seated at the side of the sanctuary. The crozier bearers are stationed near their respective bishops so that they may be in a position quickly to step forward to present or take the crozier, give or receive the mitre, hold the book, as the case may be. They must be constantly on the alert to assist in any way required. If there is not room enough in the sanctuary for this grouping during the Asperges, the B-E group may go to the side of the sanctuary for the Asperges, following which their chairs are placed for them before the altar rail.

The B-E removes his biretta. The assistant bishops likewise remove their mitres and give them to the crozier bearers to hold. At the Asperges, after the deacon and subdeacon have been aspersed, the M.C. takes the aspergill to the B-E group and the assistant bishops and the B-E asperse themselves and their crozier bearers.

At the conclusion of the Asperges, the faldstool is brought to the footpace and placed in the middle. The consecrator, wearing his mitre, is seated thereon. The deacon and subdeacon go to their places at the sedilia until the Eucharist is resumed, the crozier bearer and book bearer ascending to the footpace to stand as usual at either side of the consecrator.

Without mitres or birettas, the assistant bishops and B-E rise. Taking the right hand of. the B-E in his own, the S. A.B. addresses the consecrator: *Most reverend Father ... Episcopate.* After the questions and answers and the consecrator has ordered that the protocol be read, all are seated. The assistant bishops put on their mitres, the B-E his biretta. Two candle bearers, taking the lighted candles from the credence, go to stand on either side of the one who is to read the protocol. He is usually seated on the gospel side. Rising in his place and facing south he reads the protocol so that all may hear.

The protocol ended, the candle bearers return the candles to the credence and a cushion is placed on the altar step before the consecrator. Without biretta, the B-E rises, goes to the consecrator and kneels on the cushion before him. The attendant of the B-E goes forward and kneels beside the B-E so as to hold the book while the latter reads aloud the Oath of Canonical Obedience. (The attendant should step to one side as soon as the promise is read.) The consecrator presses lightly the hands of the B-E, which lie palm to palm between his own, and. says: *The peace of the Lord be always with thee,* to which the B-E responds: *Amen.* The B-E now rises, bows reverently to the consecrator and returns to his seat. The attendant returns the book to the B-E and goes to his seat at the, side of the sanctuary. The B-E resumes his biretta.

Henceforward in all parts of the ceremony additional to the usual course of the Eucharist, the assistant bishops in a very, low tone of voice repeat all that is said by the consecrator, making also the various signs of the cross over the B-E with him. (This rubric, appearing in the first edition of the Liturgy, but omitted at this place in the second edition, was restored by the Third General Episcopal Synod.)

Whenever, during the questions and answers which follow, the B-E answers a question, he raises his biretta with the right hand and bows slightly to the consecrator. At the end of the questions the consecrator says: *The Lord increase ... Divine Wisdom.* All mitres are now removed.

The consecrator, assisted by his ministers, and the B-E, assisted by the assistant bishops, assume the Eucharistic vestments. At this vesting the B-E changes his stole so that it hangs straight down. The consecrator faces the altar and begins the Holy Eucharist. The bishops wear the mitre and hold the crozier for the Invocation. The B-E and assistant bishops remain in their places before the altar rail until after the Absolution, which is pronounced by the consecrator. At this point in the service, the B-E, escorted by the assistant bishops who walk on either side of him, genuflects with them in the middle and goes to the side altar. The crozier bearers walk side by side immediately in front of their respective bishops. The assistant bishops wear their mitres in this procession, but remove them at the side altar. If there is sufficient room, the second thurifer, the cross bearer and two candle bearers may precede the B-E to the side altar.

From this point forward up to the end of the Gradual the consecrator and B-E both say concurrently (with the exception of the Collect of the Consecration of a Bishop) the Eucharist in the usual way. The B-E, however, should speak in a low tone of voice so that only the voice of the consecrator may be heard by the congregation. At the side altar, the assistant bishops do not take the various positions assumed by the deacon and subdeacon at high Celebration, but remain standing at either side of the B-E, slightly to the rear. The Epistle at the High Altar may be read by the J.A.B. If this is done, his position at the side altar should be taken by the subdeacon for the time being. The side altar is censed in the usual way.

At the end of the Gradual, the deacon and subdeacon of the Eucharist go to the sedilia. The faldstool is brought to the footpace and the consecrator is seated thereon, wearing his mitre. To his left stands the crozier bearer, to his right the book bearer (if any). In the meantime the B-E is escorted by the assistant bishops to his seat before the altar. The assistant bishops are preceded by their crozier bearers, and in the little procession they wear their mitres and he the biretta. All three genuflect together, bow to the consecrator and are seated. The B-E removes his biretta for the genuflection, but wears it when seated. The assistant bishops retain their mitres.

The consecrator addresses the B-E, saying: *It appertains to ... to judge.* Rising, he continues, addressing the congregation: *Let us pray, dearest ... ministry.* The consecrator gives the crozier to the bearer, turns to face the altar, kneels and places his mitre on the faldstool. Meanwhile the B-E removes his biretta, and prostrates himself on the rug breast down, with his forehead resting on his crossed arms, which in turn rest on a cushion placed there by a server. The Litany is now sung by all.

During the singing of the verse: *May he stand before Thy Face*, the consecrator rises, puts on his mitre, faces the candidate and takes the crozier. (Inasmuch as he has just been kneeling on the edge of the footpace, he is now standing on the second step in the middle.) At the same time the assistant bishops rise, put on their mitres, and take their croziers. Accompanied by their crozier bearers who now hold the books, they go to stand on the lowest altar step, on either side of the consecrator, facing the prostrate B-E. The consecrator and assistant bishops sing together the three verses of the Litany which follow, making the signs of the cross where indicated over the prostrate candidate. Beside each bishop, on the left of the consecrator and the S.A.B. but to the right of the J.A.B. (so that the server is not in the way of the consecrator) is the crozier bearer, who holds the book so that it may be easily read by the bishop he is serving. At the end of these verses each bishop returns his crozier to the bearer, and all kneel facing the altar during the singing of the last verse of the Litany.

At the conclusion of the Litany the clergy and people are seated. The B-E rises, comes forward and kneels on the lowest altar step in the middle. The three bishops stand, wearing mitres, the consecrator in the middle on the second step, the assistant bishops on the lowest altar step, one on either side of the B-E. Beside each bishop on the left is the crozier bearer, who also holds the book so that the bishop he is serving may read.

The consecrator now takes a copy of the Bible or the New Testament, in the language of the country or in Greek, opens it to some portion of one of the Gospels and, aided by the assistant bishops, places it printed side down upon the neck and shoulders of the B-E, so that the printed page touches the neck. One of the clergy appointed for the purpose, vested with vimpa, kneels behind the B-E and holds the Book in place, through the vimpa. The consecrator, with both hands extended over the B-E now says the following prayer, the assistant bishops likewise extending their hands and accompanying him in a low voice: *O Lord Christ ... Angel host.* The mitre is worn during the saying of this prayer.

At the end of the prayer the consecrator and assistant bishops turn to face the altar holding the croziers and, retaining their mitres, kneel. The crozier bearers kneel beside their respective bishops. The *Veni Creator* is now sung by all. At its end, the people remain kneeling, but the three bishops rise and turn to face the B-E. All three of them simultaneously and solemnly lay both hands on the head of the B-E and together say slowly and distinctly the words of consecration: *Receive the Holy Ghost ... Church of God.* While this is said each crozier bearer stands beside his respective bishop, holding both crozier and book. The Book, which during the words of consecration, has been held over the neck and shoulders of the candidate, is now placed on the altar by the one who has held it, still through the vimpa.

After a moment of silence, the consecrator, still with hands extended towards the new bishop, continues with the following prayer: *O God ... from above*, the assistant bishops likewise extending their hands and accompanying him in a low voice. During this.prayer the mitres are retained. The sign of the cross is made simultaneously by the three bishops over the new bishop where indicated in the Liturgy. The people may now be seated.

The consecrator, still retaining his mitre, takes his seat upon the faldstool. The new bishop rises and kneels on the second step before the consecrator. The assistant bishops stand on either side of him, wearing their mitres. The gremial is brought to the consecrator who spreads it on his lap. A server stands near holding the ampulla or vessel of Chrism. The Master of Ceremonies, or a priest, with the silk handkerchief (and safety pin, if needed) approaches the kneeling new bishop from behind and binds his head with the handkerchief. It is knotted or fastened behind, and so arranged as to leave uncovered the top of the head. Its purpose is to prevent the Chrism from flowing down onto the face or neck. The consecrator dips his thumb into the Chrism and anoints the head of the new bishop, first in the form of a cross over the entire top of the head, and. then in a series of extending circles till all is covered with the sacred oil. A *very* thin stream of oil may actually be poured onto the head before the thumb is used. The consecrator returns the Chrism and, accompanied by the assistant bishops, says: *May thy head ... Holy Ghost*. The sign of the cross is made three times over the head of the new bishop. After this anointing, the gremial is put aside, the consecrator rises and; again extending his hands, says: *Thou Who ... all ages of ages*. The assistant bishops, still wearing their mitres, likewise extend their hands and repeat the words in a low voice.

The consecrator is again seated and the gremial is once more spread on his lap. The new bishop lays his hands on the gremial, side by side, palms uppermost. The consecrator anoints his hands with Chrism in the following manner. First he traces a line with the oil from the tip of the right thumb of the new bishop across the palms to the tip of the left forefinger. He then traces another line with Chrism from the tip of the left thumb across the palms to the tip of the right forefinger. Next a cross is traced with Chrism on the palm of the right hand and on the palm of the left hand. Finally, with a circular motion, he anoints the entire palm and fingers of each hand. Holding his right hand over the hands of the new bishop the consecrator says, accompanied by the assistants: *May these hands ... Holy Ghost*, the sign of the cross being made thrice over the hands during the invocation of the Holy Trinity. In the prayer which follows: *Mayest thou ... our Lord Christ*, the sign of the cross is made over the heart of the newly consecrated bishop, and then over his hands.

The linen strip is brought to the consecrator who places it over the head of the new bishop so that it hangs like a sling. Joining the consecrated hands palm to palm; the right resting on the left, he places them within the sling. Lemon and crumb, water and towel are brought to the consecrator and he cleanses his hands.

The consecrator rises, his faldstool is moved to one side, and he turns his attention to the instruments and symbols of office which have lain on the altar. The assistant bishops stand at either side of him, facing the altar, The Master of Ceremonies first gives him the crozier. Taking this in his hands, he anoints it with Chrism and blesses it, saying: *Eternal Triune God ... Christ our Lord.* The crozier is handed to an attendant vested with a vimpa (the one who held the Book of Gospels) to hold until it is needed. The Master of Ceremonies now presents the silver salver on which are the pectoral cross and ring of the new bishop. Holding the cross between his hands the consecrator anoints it with Chrism and blesses it, saying: *Almighty God, Who ... cross forever.* Replacing the cross upon salver, he takes the ring, anoints it with Chrism, and holds it between his joined hands as he blesses it, saying: *Christ, pure Lord ...healing grace.* The salver is replaced on the altar. The new bishop is now assisted to rise. He bows to the consecrator and retires to the place where he is to cleanse his head and hands. The assistant bishops do not go with him on this occasion. His hands are unbound and cleansed with lemon, crumb and water. The handkerchief is removed from his head, any excess of oil wiped away, and his hair combed. During this time soft organ music should be played. Having completed his ablutions, the new bishop returns to the middle, genuflects, and kneels a-gain before the consecrator.

The latter, with the assistant bishops standing near, presents the pastoral staff to the new bishop, who holds it with his left hand. The consecrator says: *Receive this staff ... power of love.* The new bishop, without rising, gives the staff to his crozier bearer, who comes forward to receive it. The bearer then takes his position behind and a little to the left of the new bishop. The silver salver with cross and ring is presented by the M.C. to the consecrator. Taking the cross, the consecrator suspends it round the neck of the new bishop, saying: *Receive this cross ... sacrifice.* He places the ring on the ring-finger of the right hand of the new bishop, saying: *Receive this ring ...His love.* Lastly he delivers to the new bishop the Book of Gospels, which is taken from the altar by the one who previously held it (again using the vimpa) and handed to the consecrator. The consecrator says: *Receive the Book ... to thee.* The new bishop hands the Book to the M.C. to place upon the credence table.

The consecrator gives the Salutation of Peace to the new bishop by touching his left shoulder and right elbow, while the new bishop touches the left shoulder and right elbow of the consecrator, the latter meanwhile saying: *Peace be unto thee,* while the new bishop responds: *And with thy spirit.* The consecrator rises and steps to one side while the senior assistant bishop and the Junior assistant bishop in turn give the saluta-tion to the new bishop. The new bishop, accompanied by the assistant bishops and pre-ceded by their several attendants, withdraws to the side altar. The faldstool is removed and the consecrator resumes the Celebration of the Holy Eucharist, assisted by the dea-con and subdeacon who return to the altar.

Incense is first blessed by the consecrator at the high altar and by the new bishop at the side altar. The Gospel is read at the high altar as usual, while at the side altar it is read by the new bishop, in a low tone of voice. He places the Gospel book upon the mis-sal stand on the gospel side of the altar for the censing and the reading, as at Low Mass. (See p. 66)

The S.A.B. may read the Gospel at the high altar, in which case he and the J.A.B. will exchange places with the deacon and subdeacon for this ceremony, the two latter going to attend the new bishop at the side altar. The two crozier bearers of the assistant bishops, may stand at the gospel side, facing south. The S.A.B. kneels for the Munda cor Meum, and the reading of the Gospel proceeds in the usual way. After the S.A.B. has read the Gospel and censed the consecrator, he and the J.A.B. genuflect in the middle before the lowest altar step, resume their mitres and return to the side altar to join the new bishop. The deacon and subdeacon return to the footpace to assist the consecrator.

The Creed or Act of Faith (preferably the Creed on such an occasion) is now intoned by all. The assistant bishops and their attendants, together with the attendants of the new bishop, face in the direction of the side altar. After the singing of the Offertory Hymn which follows, the newly consecrated bishop and the assistant bishops, wearing biretta and mitres respectively, go to the middle to stand before the lowest altar step, the new bishop bearing upon a salver his symbolic offerings. Meanwhile the faldstool is placed on the footpace and the consecrator is seated thereon. The new bishop hands the salver to the M.C. to hold, removes his biretta, kneels before the consecrator and, taking in succession the various offerings, presents them to the consecrator. First he offers the two candles (which must be lighted), then the two small loaves of bread, and lastly the two miniature barrels of wine. After receiving each of the offerings the consecrator gives them to a server who stands near holding an extra salver, to be replaced on the special credence. This ended, the faldstool is removed, and the new bishop, resuming his biretta and accompanied by the assistant bishops and the several attendants, proceeds to the epistle end of the high altar and, having laid aside the biretta, says in a low tone of voice the remainder of the Holy Eucharist word for word and sign for sign with the consecrator. The only part not said by the new bishop is the special clause inserted in the Prayer of Consecration after the words: *for all our bishops, clergy and faithful*, the words of which are: *Especially for him whom in Christ's holy Name we have admitted to the Order of the Episcopate.* If there is room, the mitres of the assistant bishops are placed upon the high altar when not in use; otherwise they may be placed upon a credence table.

The consecrator gives the Salutation of Peace first to the new bishop who passes it to the S.A.B. and to the J.A.B. The consecrator, then gives the Salutation to the deacon and subdeacon of the Eucharist who pass it on to the rest of the clergy in the usual manner.

At the Communion the consecrator consumes one half of the Host and of the Wine, and then moves to the gospel side. The new bishop advances to the centre of the altar and communicates himself. The two assistant bishops receive Communion before the deacon and subdeacon of the Eucharist.

At the end of the Benediction the deacon and subdeacon go to the sedilia as they will not be needed until the procession from the sanctuary to the vestry.

After the benediction the consecrator and the new bishop assume the cope. The faldstool is placed on the footpace and the consecrator is seated thereon, wearing his mitre. Meanwhile the new bishop wearing his biretta and. the assistant bishops wearing mitres, go to the middle to stand before the lowest altar step. The new bishop removes his biretta and kneels before the consecrator. The Master of Ceremonies, having placed the mitre and gloves of the new bishop on a silver salver, holds them before the consecrator, who blesses them silently. Then the three bishops place the mitre on the head of the new bishop, the consecrator saying, accompanied as usual by the assistant bishops in a low voice: *Receive this mitre ... of love.*

With the aid of the assistant bishops, the consecrator puts the gloves on the hands of the new bishop. It should be noted that his ring must be taken off and put on again outside the glove. This accomplished, the consecrator rises and says: *Do Thou, we pray Thee ... and actions.* The new bishop rises and is solemnly enthroned in the faldstool. In doing this the consecrator takes his right hand and, as he turns round to face the people, the S.A.B. takes his left hand. He is seated upon the faldstool facing the people. His crozier bearer now brings his crozier to the consecrator who places it in his left hand. The consecrator and assistant bishops stand on the altar step in front of the new bishop and bow to him in respect. If the consecration takes place in the cathedral church of the new bishop, the enthronement will take place in his own throne instead of in the faldstool.

The assistant bishops descend to the sanctuary floor, genuflect together in the middle before the lowest altar step and go to the side where they remove mitre and cope and are vested in mantelletta and biretta. Meanwhile two thurifers come with their censers, two candle bearers with processional candles, and two small acolytes, if required, to hold the train of the new bishop. A Solemn *Te Deum* is now sung, as the new bishop, attended by the assistant bishops, proceeds round the Church and gives his blessing to the people. The order of procession is as follows:

Two thurifers
Two candle bearers
New bishop, bearing crozier
(Acolytes holding train)
Assistant bishops
Two crozier bearers (unless assistant bishops also carry crozier)

It should be noted that the assistant bishops do not walk beside the newly consecrated bishop but behind him, and that in turn their crozier bearers walk behind them. The consecrator intones the Te Deum and remains at the altar holding his crozier.

Upon the return of the procession the new bishop is again enthroned on the faldstool (or throne if in his own diocese) the consecrator standing to his right, facing him.

The assistant bishops retire to the side, remove the mantelletta and biretta and are vested in cope and mitre. They return to the middle, genuflect and go to stand to the left of the new bishop, facing him. The consecrator, turning to the people, sings: *The Lord be with you.* The: people respond: *And with thy spirit.* The consecrator turns now to face the new bishop and intones: *Let us pray.* The new bishop remains seated, the assistant bishops standing. The consecrator prays: *O God, the Shepherd ... Christ our Lord.*

After the response: *Amen,* the new bishop rises, and as soon as the faldstool is removed, ascends to the footpace. In the meantime the consecrator and assistant bishops descend to the sanctuary floor, genuflect together in the middle and go to stand at the gospel side of the sanctuary (or if in the cathedral of the new bishop, they remain on the gospel side.) The consecrator stands in the middle of the three, the S.A.B. to his right, the J.A.B. to his left. They face towards the middle. Behind them, and to the left of each, stand their respective crozier bearers. (If the footpace is large enough to accommodate the following ceremony, it takes place thereon, the consecrator and his assistants standing at the gospel end.)

The new bishop, wearing the mitre and holding the crozier, intones while facing the altar: *Blessed be the Name of the Lord,* and the people respond: *From this time for evermore.* He then intones: *Our help is in the Name of the Lord,* while the people respond: *Who hath made heaven and earth.* The new bishop now turns to face the people and with upraised right hand in episcopal manner, gives them his blessing: *The peace of God ... you always.* The crozier bearer is at hand to hold the book, if necessary, for the new bishop while he pronounces the blessing. At its end he descends to the sanctuary floor and, wearing the mitre and carrying the crozier, goes to stand toward the epistle side facing the consecrator, his crozier bearer meanwhile crossing over to the gospel side. Genuflecting, the new bishop sings: *Ad multos annos.* Rising he walks half way to the consecrator, again genuflects, and sings in a somewhat higher tone: *Ad multos annos.* Rising, he walks to the consecrator and genuflecting before him, sings for the third time and in a still higher tone: *Ad multos annos.* Rising, he gives his crozier to the bearer, and receives from the consecrator the Salutation of Peace. The assistant bishops in turn give him the Salutation.

The procession is then formed and proceeds to the vestry. In this procession the new bishop takes the same place as when entering, unless he be the Ordinary, in which case he walks behind the Assistant Consecrators.

In the event that a consecration must take place without the aid of one or both assistant bishops, one or two priests may assist, performing all the actions prescribed for the assistant bishops except those which pertain to the exercise of episcopal power. Such priest assistants shall not take part in the laying on of hands, the various blessings of the B-E and his instruments, the Salutation of Peace to the new bishop, the placing of the mitre on his head, or the reception of his homage in the ceremony *Ad multos annos,* nor shall they accompany the consecrator in saying the consecration rite.

Consecration of Two Bishops

When two bishops are to be consecrated at the same service, certain modifications must be made in the ceremonial directions. Two side altars are prepared (one may be at the epistle side) and additional vestments, seating arrangements etc. are provided for the additional bishop-elect and attendant. The croziers, rings, crosses, mitres and gloves of both bishops-elect are placed on the high altar, and a missal stand is placed at each end for the two new bishops to use after the offerings (or they may be brought from the side altars at the time of the offerings). Two Books of Gospels will be required, and two clergy vested in cope and vimpa to hold them. There may be two Protocols to be read. Silk handkerchiefs, pins, linen strips and empty offering trays for both B-Es are placed on the credence table. Two faldstools will be required for the second enthronement of the new bishops after the Te Deum. (They should be as alike as possible; if need be, two low-backed chairs may be used at this time.) Three thurifers and two assistant Masters of Ceremony are needed.

The Bishop-Elect who is to be the senior is always placed to the epistle side of the junior B-E, and in all ritual actions the senior is dealt with before the junior B-E except where both are dealt with together. The Presentation is repeated for each B-E in succession, from *Right or Most Reverend Father* to *Thanks be to God.*[47] The two B-E come forward in succession to take the vow of canonical obedience.

The consecrator interrogates both B-Es together. Here, and in all parts of the service where the consecrator addresses both candidates together, you or your is used for thee, thou, thine, changing the wording as necessary (such as *will you* for *wilt thou*, etc.), but each B-E in succession replies *I will* or *I do* in answer to the questions.

After the Absolution the S.A.B. escorts the senior B-E to the first side altar and the J.A.B. escorts the junior B-E to the other. Thereafter whenever the assistant bishops are to escort or to attend the B-E, they divide in this manner, each escorting one of the bishops-elect.

In the Litany, and whenever both B-Es are addressed or mentioned together, the proper plural form is used instead of the singular, and when both are addressed together, the signs of the cross are made over both collectively as in the ordination of priests.

The two B-Es will kneel a few feet apart for the consecration itself, so that the consecrator and assistant bishops may have room to move and to group themselves around each B-E in succession. If there is insufficient space on the altar steps, this part of the ceremony may take place *in plano*. The imposition of the Book of Gospels will be made on the two B-Es in succession, but the prayer accompanying the imposition will be said over them collectively. The imposition of hands with the words of consecration, and the prayer immediately following, *O God ... above*, are given for the first B-E, then the consecrator and assistants move to the second B-E and repeat the entire formula of consecration. The second new bishop now is seated while the first N-B kneels before the consecrator for the anointing and the blessing of the instruments of office. After the blessing of the ring, the first N-B retires to cleanse head and hands, returns, he kneels before the consecrator to receive the personal instruments of office and continuing through the Salutation of Peace, and is then seated while the second N-B is similarly invested and saluted.

At the Offertory, the first N-B, escorted by the S.A.B., makes the offering and then moves to the epistle end of the high altar, the S.A.B. standing in plano behind him; then the second N-B escorted by the J.A.B. similarly makes the symbolic offering and goes to the gospel end.

The ceremony of investiture with mitre and gloves, enthronement, and bowing to the N-B is repeated for each in succession, the other meanwhile being seated.

At the procession during the *Te Deum* the junior N-B with attendants precede the senior N-B with attendants in two processions round the church, an interval of a few paces separating the two processions. Each procession will be headed by one thurifer and two candle bearers. Meanwhile two faldstools (or chairs) are placed side by side on the footpace, and on their return to the sanctuary the two new bishops are enthroned therein. The prayer which follows is said over both together; both together chant the versicles and pronounce the Benediction, and both advance side by side and chant the *Ad multos annos* together. They receive the Salutation of Peace in succession from the consecrator and the assistant bishops.while the second NB kneels for the anointing and blessing of the instruments of office. When the first N-B

INDEX

247

✠✠ ✠✠ ✠✠ ✠✠✠✠✠✠ ✠✠ ✠✠ ✠✠
✠✠✠✠
✠✠✠
✠

NOTE ON THE INDEX: In the foregoing INDEX no attempt has been made to be comprehensive. Service details are listed only in regard to the Eucharist [and the pages that preceded it in the book Ed.]. For details of other services it will be necessary to look through the services themselves.

The first part of the text was printed before it was decided to include the plates from The Science of the Sacraments, so references are by plate and figure number in that book, and not by the page on which it appears in this reprint. All the plates and figures mentioned in the text will, however, be found on Pages K, L and M.

APPRECIATION: The publisher [Bp. Cooper Ed.] wishes to express his deep thanks to Mrs. Irving S. Cooper, Bishops Wedgwood, Pigott and Hampton, and Rev. G. Nevin Drinkwater, for their most helpful cooperation in the work of completing this Book after Bishop Cooper's passing. He also wishes to thank Mrs. Ruby J. Pitkin for the arduous work of proof-reading the mimeograph stencils.

- W.H. Pitkin.

NOTE ON THE USE OF THE BINDING COVER: [Included for historical purposes. Ed.] When removing or inserting pages from the binder, the following procedure should be followed. Lay book, face down, on a table, binding edge to the left. Open back cover, exposing the brass binder ribbons, their brass locks, and the guide strip. Push locks towards centre, freeing ribbons. Bend ribbons straight up. Half way to the top of each ribbon, bend it towards the other ribbon in an easy curve. Twist these bent portions of the ribbons to the left. The binding strip will now slide off the ends of the ribbons readily. Bend the ribbon ends back to face each other, and straighten them up. The pages can then be removed and shifted. In replacing, reverse the process, i.e., with pages in. place, kink the ribbon ends and twist to the left, slide the binder strip over their ends, twist back and straighten the ribbons, press down firmly on one end of the binder strip, bend down sharply the corresponding ribbon and lock in place, do the same with the other ribbon. If you wish the free edge of the book smooth, tap the pages on the table before replacing them, and have someone hold them tightly while the binder is being clamped on. Clamping the ribbons tightly will keep the pages in alignment.